# A Quite Remarkable Man

# A Quite Remarkable Man

## The Life of Patrick Brydone and His Family
## (1736-1818)

BY

JOHN EVANS

AMBERLEY

First published 2014

Amberley Publishing
The Hill, Stroud
Gloucestershire, GL5 4EP

www.amberley-books.com

British Library Cataloguing in Publication Data.
A catalogue record for this book is available from the British Library.

ISBN 978 1 4456 3890 4

Typeset in 10pt on 12pt Sabon.
Typesetting and Origination by Amberley Publishing.
Printed in the UK.

*To the memory of all those Scots who lived on
the continent of Europe during the Eighteenth Century*

# Contents

# Illustrations

(Acknowledgements are shown with the illustrations, as appropriate)

1. Coldingham Priory, Berwickshire.
2. Cottages in Coldingham, Brydone's birthplace.
3. Francis Hauksbee's frictional electricity machine.
4. Portrait of Sir John Pringle (1707–1782) by Sir Joshua Reynolds in 1774.
5. Detail of a mezzotint portrait of an elderly Patrick Brydone by William Ward.
6. Engraving of Thomas Cadell, the elder (1742–1802), by Henry Hoppner Meyer.
7. Portrait of William Strahan (1715–1792) by Sir Joshua Reynolds.
8. Charles Turner's mezzotint of Frances d'Arblay (1752–1840), 'Fanny Burney'.
9. A pastel of William Cowper (1731–1800), painted in 1792 by George Romney.
10. Engraving of Ralph Griffiths (c.1720–1803).
11. Frontispiece of Volume 1 of Brydone's *Tour,* published in 1773.
12. Lausanne on Lake Geneva where Brydone lived when he became a tutor.
13. The elderly William Morton Pitt (1754–1836), one of Brydone's charges in 1776.

14. Robert Bertie (1756–1779), the young Lord Lindsey who died aged 23 years.
15. An engraving of Alleyne Fitzherbert (1753–1839) who visited Brydone in 1775.
16. Portrait of Empress Maria Theresa (1717–1780) by Jean-Étienne Liotard.
17. Georg Decker's drawing of Kaiser Joseph II (1741–1790).
18. Franz Josef I, Prince of Liechtenstein. A portrait by Alexander Roslin.
19. Liotard's portrait of Prince von Kaunitz, the Austrian Chancellor.
20. Engraving of King Frederick II (the Great).
21. Frederic Reclam's portrait of Elisabeth, Frederick the Great's consort.
22. Portrait of Duke Karl II of Mecklenburg-Strelitz by Johann Georg Ziesenis.
23. Portrait of Sophia, Duke Karl's daughter who became Queen of the United Kingdom.
24. Thomas Gainsborough's portrait of Francis North (1704–1790).
25. Nathaniel Dance's portrait of Frederick North (1732–1792), prime minister.
26. Portrait of George Augustus North (1757–1802) by George Romney.
27. Francis North (1761–1817) painted by Charles Turner, who went into the army.
28. Engraving of Frederick North (1766–1827), the prime minister's youngest son.
29. Portrait of Prince Nikolaus Esterházy, patron of Franz Joseph Haydn.
30. Prince Albert of Saxony's portrait, painted two years before Brydone's visit.
31. Detail of Sir Henry Raeburn's portrait of John Campbell (1762–1834).
32. Portrait of the third Earl of Breadalbane (1696–1782) by John Wootton.
33. Oelenhainz's portrait of Johann Kaspar Lavater, a Swiss pastor.

brother-in-law.
57. The memorial tablet in Westminster Abbey to the first Earl Minto.
58. Dr Samuel Spiker (1786–1858), Berlin journalist.
59. Francis Rawdon Hastings (1754–1826) who replaced Lord Minto in India.
60. Detail of Sir Thomas Lawrence's painting of Queen Caroline of Brunswick.
61. The Höhenweg, near the village of Interlaken in 1830.
62. The mezzotint portrait of an elderly Patrick Brydone by William Ward.

# Maps and Plans

# Acknowledgements

Before acknowledging the enormous amount of assistance received from those who not only supplied photocopies of relevant manuscripts and other material in their care, and who took the trouble to research questions put to them, the author owes a special debt to Dr Katherine Turner, Associate Professor of English at Mary Baldwin College, Virginia, USA. With no biography on the market, the author of the essay about Brydone in the Oxford Dictionary of National Biography not only agreed that a book about Brydone 'would be an exciting subject for a biographer', but in effect became its progenitor.

It naturally gives me great pleasure to thank all those who helped throw light on Brydone's life. British Library's curator of Historical Papers (Christopher Beckett), and Rare Books and Manuscripts Reference Services (Christian Algar and Zoe Stansell respectively), together with the National Library of Scotland (Olive Geddes and her staff) were especially important and helpful contributors. Archivists and researchers employed by other national sources, such as the National Archive at Kew and the National Records of Scotland (Dr Alison Rosie and Jane Jamieson) also played their part. The Archives Officer of Bristol Record Office (Alison Brown), Guildhall Library London (Rosie Eddisford), the Mitchell Library in Glasgow (Jamie Flett) and the curator of the Royal Library at Windsor Castle (Emma Stuart) also gave valuable assistance together with the National Library of the Netherlands (Margreet

Vos), the German National Library in Leipzig (Dr Stephanie Jacobs and Bettina Rutiger) and Zentral Bibliotek Zürich (Peter Tschuck).

Among bodies supplying illustrations were the National Portrait Gallery, London, who are to be congratulated on their innovative scheme which enables fees to be waived for the non-academic use of images; the Scottish National Portrait Gallery, Edinburgh; the British Museum; the Science Museum London; the Witt Library and the Courtauld Institute of Art; Grimsthorpe and Drummond Castle Trust Ltd; Coutts & Co.; the Holburne Museum, Bath; the Royal Society; the Dean and Chapter of Westminster; the UK Government Art Collection; Victoria Art Gallery, Bath; the Bridgeman Art Gallery and the Universal Images Group. Others outside the UK included the Biltagentur für Kunst, Berlin, the Museum of Art & History in Geneva, the Albertina Museum and the Art History Museum in Vienna, along with the Stiftung Preussische Schlösser und Gärten in Berlin-Brandenburg and the Swiss National Museum in Zürich.

Among County libraries, often those with local studies staff and whose special contribution is acknowledged, were Hampshire Record Office (Steve Hynard), Devon County Council (Ian Maxted), Northumberland Council (Linda Bankier); Scottish Borders Council (Helen Darling, Sheila Brodie and Stuart Young), and Suffolk County Council (Kerry Meal). The coordinating service provided by 'Ask Scotland', managed by the Scottish Library and Information Council (Gillian Hanlon), was particularly valuable, as was help from the Coldstream History Society (Gerald Tait).

Given the extraordinarily broad range of Brydone's interests it is not surprising that there were so many academic institutions and professorial or other teaching staff with an interest in him and whose assistance it is pleasing to acknowledge. These include St Andrew's University Library (Moira Mackenzie); the Lonsdale Curator at Balliol College Oxford (Anna Sander); University of Edinburgh's archivist (Arnott Wilson); the Centre for Research Collections (Tricia Boyd) and the Rare Books Librarian (Dr Joseph Marshall); the Fitzwilliam Museum, Cambridge (Nicholas Robinson); University College London (Dr Nicholas Cambridge); University of East Anglia (Dr John Charmley); University of Exeter (Chantal Stebbings); University of Derby (Dr Paul Elliott); Oxford's

Bodleian Library (Eva Oledzka); University of Glasgow (Clare Paterson) and University College, London, School of Slavonic and East European Studies (Dr Richard Butterwick-Pawlikowski). Among institutions in the USA whose valuable muniments proved useful were Yale University's Beinecke Rare Book and Manuscripts Library (Graham Sherriff and Cynthia Ostroff); the University of Michigan (Bob Ahronheim) and Utah State University (Professor Jeffrey Smitten).

Before turning to those quasi-governmental institutions holding material relevant to the Brydone story, I would like to acknowledge the help given by the Historians Group at the Foreign and Commonwealth Office (Tara Finn), along with the Slovak and Polish Embassies in London. Among 'quangos' was the Royal Commission on the Ancient and Historical Monuments of Scotland (Caroline Torres); the Royal Botanic Gardens (Lizbeth Gale); the Royal Society (Rupert Baker, Emma Davidson, Joanna Hopkins and Joanna Corden); the Society for the Protection of Ancient Buildings (Elaine Byrne and Gillian Darley); the Institution of Engineering and Technology (Sarah Hale); the Royal Humane Society (Wendy Hawke); the Science Museum in London and Swindon (John Underwood}.

Three researchers whose services deserve particular acknowledgement were Mr R W O'Hara (military records), Janet Bishop (Scottish genealogy), and Dr Jenny Macleod who undertook the no mean task of transcribing for me many of Brydone's letters and journals held in the Blairadam Muniments, a private archive owned by Keith Adam, whose ancestor married into the family. A special medal must be reserved for Andrina Gammie of Highland Library Service in Inverness. Without her continual invocation on my behalf for books and reference material through the Inter-Library Loan Scheme a work like Brydone's biography could not have been undertaken 600 miles from London, or even 250 miles from Edinburgh.

Every attempt has been made to obtain copyright and licence holders' permission in respect of the publication both of manuscripts and illustrations, and if, for any reason I have failed to obtain or record my appreciation, I can only offer my most sincere apologies.

Finally, I would like to thank my publisher on this occasion for the expert team they put together. Special thanks go to Jonathan Jackson and Alex Bennett. A *Croix de Guerre* goes to my wife who was in the trenches with me throughout the time it has taken to bring this book to press, and whose perspicacity and patience has been of enormous value.

# Preface

Sir Walter Scott described Patrick Brydone Esq. as 'My venerable friend ... so well known in the literary world'. The father of Lord North heard from all quarters about 'the improvement, good conduct and proper behaviour' of Brydone's charges, the prime minister's sons, and 'was sensible of the share' the tutor had had in it. For Dugald Stewart, the Scottish philosopher, Brydone was 'the well-known author of one of our most elegant and popular books of travels', whilst Robert Burns diary recorded that Brydone had 'a most excellent heart, kind, joyous and benevolent'.

This, the first-ever biography of Patrick Brydone is long overdue, and whilst many others in his profession as a tutor to the sons of the aristocracy and the gentry wrote of their travels, few matched his style or so helped their readers understand what travellers endured. He provided a lens through which many aspects of 18th century life in Britain and across a large swathe of Europe were refracted. Brydone was a *cicerone,* or learned guide, who explained matters of historical and artistic interest to those in his charge, becoming a scientist, polymath, explorer, un-paid diplomat and writer. However, as the *'Annual Biography and Obituary for the year 1820'* said 'It is greatly to be lamented that the materials for a life of this ingenious gentleman are scanty and incomplete. We know little of him indeed, but from his travels; and even in respect to these he does not appear to have communicated to the public an account of all his peregrinations'.[1] Fortunately, this is no longer true.

The present biography is not a piece of non-fiction whose climax is finally reached at its end, rather a steady climb of a mountain, and a closely woven story with constantly fascinating highs and lows. In his youth, and before serving in the army, there was evidence of his microscopic and limitless fascination with design, creation and invention, and a curiosity which never diminished.

What the public knew of Brydone derived from the book he wrote in 1773 based on letters written to a friend under the title *A Tour through Sicily and Malta*. It proved a great success and a best-seller, being subsequently published in France, Germany and the USA, and marked a major turning point in Brydone's career. His reputation grew hugely, and attracting the attention of a higher rank of clients, he began to be received as a serious enquirer and someone who put the pursuit of knowledge high in his philosophy. His life criss-crossed with many other significant and interesting eighteenth century individuals, both British and European. Bishops, abbots and princes, dukes, landgraves and margraves would dine and entertain him at courts and palaces from the Baltic States, Russia and St Petersburg in the north to Palermo and Malta in the south.

The opposites and contrariety he so much enjoyed using in his thinking and written work make Brydone a challenging subject for the biographer. They are, however, playful in character, not evidence of a confused self, but of a determination to catch the imagination or understanding of others. A kind and generous man who showed little if any real prejudice, Brydone could be cantankerous, but it was a crotchety device he often used to draw out the opinion of others who might otherwise remain silent. In approach, Brydone combined the detecting characteristics of a Sherlock Holmes with the forensic reporting skills of Watson, exercising a personal and individualistic concern for the welfare of rich as well as poor people. One result is that such adjectives as unusual, exceptional, eccentric, impressive, miraculous, odd, outstanding, peculiar, uncommon, unique and unconventional, hardly begin to describe this *Quite Remarkable Man*. Although there are weaknesses in his armoury, particularly in matters of religion when he is trapped by a repeated impulse to ridicule some of the traditional practices of the Catholic

Church. Nevertheless, Brydone worked constantly to explain to his listeners and readers what the world about him looked like when seen through the eyes of a geographer, astronomer, engineer, banker, economist, doctor or farmer. Welcome as visiting foreigners could be, to question a manager underground in the gold and silver mines of Slovakia, and achieve empathy to the extent he obviously did on numerous occasions was one thing but to recall and remember much of the background and heredity of the many hundreds of eminent people he met was another and called for consummate skill. As Dr Katherine Turner, the author of the essay about Brydone in the Oxford Dictionary of National Biography, said 'his style was conversational, rather than elegant' and when providing a scientific explanation it was accompanied by 'a sense of awe'. In his own words, Brydone's professional aim was to 'make ourselves masters of the reader's imagination, to carry it along with us through every scene'.[2]

Having successfully tutored Lord North's two eldest sons and been awarded the sinecure post of comptroller at the Stamp Office in London, Brydone married the daughter of the principal of Edinburgh University in 1785. Such events may have put an end to the travels that had taken him some 10,000 miles across Europe but for the reader they opened a door into a new phase of his life. His surviving three children grow up in a rural idyll south of Edinburgh and, like the twenty-five-year-old Jane Austen, we see him, his wife and daughters experiencing the vanity, snobbery and dissipation of the age in Bath, the Mecca of society. To his own lively account is added that of his eldest daughter Mary whose meticulous and colourful correspondence demonstrates the care and warmth so apparent in the family. Subsequently, the reader is able to hear the voice of the Elliot family when Mary marries Gilbert Elliot who is soon to become the second Earl Minto in Roxburghshire.

Overlying the period between 1807 and 1814 when the groom's father is in India, a number of inevitabilities add to the Brydone/Elliot families' trials. The dispatch of a letter to or from the subcontinent, the only method of communication available, would usually be followed by a three or four month silence. Those with family members could well write four or five letters a week, sometimes using friends to carry those that had missed being put aboard the lightly armed and faster Post Office packet boat. Even the governor-general had few methods of emergency communication open to him and the family at home inevitably feared the worst in their ignorance. Numerous misplaced rumours about his future and the length of his appointment only increased the pain of separation, and his unexpected death once back in England in 1814 was to alter all expectations.

The eventual defeat of Napoleon at Waterloo in 1815, however, set the scene for the wider Elliot family to follow in Brydone's footsteps and undertake a grand tour to Italy themselves. All went to plan until they reached Interlaken on their return from Naples. Halfway through September 1817 there was increasing concern about the deterioration of young Gilbert's health, then ten years old and his father's heir. The late arrival of a doctor from Geneva who had thought his patient to be the father not the child, and a diagnosis that 'a bowel fever' would work itself out, seriously misled the parents and he died a day or so later.

After some dithering, the family decided to go 'straight home' but by the time they were back in Paris it was realised how much cheaper it would be for Mary and the children to remain there for the winter. Her husband would ensure that Minto House, where much new construction work was in progress, was readied in all respects for occupation in the late Spring of 1818. The couple's separation would have to be endured and if Gilbert was 'sure of being settled there by the beginning of June, she would leave by the first of May'. Meanwhile, with Brydone's blindness accelerating, an effort had been made to have Brydone seen by a London physician. Mary and Gilbert feared he might catch cold during the journey south. His wife, on the other hand, had originally approved of the plan but when a house was offered them, and it looked as if the whole of Brydone's household would also have to move to London, the project was abandoned.

With 'the agony of the last day' upon her, and her seven-month sojourn in Paris without Gilbert over, it was the middle of May when Mary's party sailed from Calais and lodged at a hotel in London which Gilbert had arranged before leaving for the north.

Some of the household were to travel by the Carlisle coach, with a newly recruited cook and a kitchen maid who were to be sent to Minto by post coach to Carlisle and Hawick. Sadly, the eighty-two-year-old Brydone died quietly at Lennel House on 19 June 1818, probably before his daughter and son-in-law arrived back in Scotland. The handful of obituaries all followed the lead given in the *Gentleman's Magazine, the Scots Magazine* and the *Annual Obituary of 1820* report, making reference to 'his justly celebrated performance'.[3] Later, more considered biographical references were still recalling the *Tour,* where 'it may be fairly doubted ... whether there be any publication of a similar kind so deserving of notice'.

The melding of hitherto unused archives, particularly those in a private collection at Blairadam in Fife, with English and Scottish manuscripts in national collections produces a rounded picture of Brydone's life. Inconsequential in appearance, the twenty or so journals and letters in the Blairadam muniments are often scribbled in pencil on small scraps of paper sewn together with a single piece of string, and suggestive of having been written soon after he had dismounted from his horse or carriage. They come to a close as the North family record at the British Library begins, whilst the National Library and the National Records of Scotland take the story to its conclusion. Mary (née Brydone) Elliot's correspondence and journals from the Minto Papers, interject a blast of warm family detail involving three or four generations of the family.

Readers who find themselves wanting to know more about the Elliot family may like to explore the author's earlier book entitled *The Victorian Elliots in peace and war – Lord and Lady Minto, their family and household between 1816 and 1901.*

CHAPTER I

# Early Years and
# the Context of History
# (1736–1758)

Patrick Brydone was born on 5 January 1736 at Coldingham in Berwickshire, Scotland. His parents, Revd Robert Brydone (1686–1761) and Elizabeth Dysart, were married in Coldingham on 10 June 1727. His father had left Edinburgh University with a Master of Arts degree in April 1709 and was licensed to preach by the Presbytery of Edinburgh in June 1719. He was then elected by Edinburgh City Council to be the conjunct preacher at Skinner's Hall (a chapel-of-ease) and called to the parish of Coldingham in September 1724. Mention is made of the couple possibly having nine children but the four known for certain were John (1730–1755), Matthew (1731–1800) a merchant in Berwick, Patrick who was born in 1736 and died in 1818, and Robert born in 1740.[1] Local historians suggest that Robert and Elizabeth lived at Abbey Park, just outside Coldingham but by the time Patrick was born they were probably living in the old manse (or vicarage) which stood to the south of the priory.

Elizabeth, their mother, was the second child of the first marriage of the Rev John Dysart (1660–1732). He married Elizabeth Bishop in 1699 and, when she died in 1702, he married Mary Sandilands of Couston who bore him another son. He started his ministry at Dalton in Northumberland before moving to Langton and Coldingham. He was a fiery character whose appointment on one occasion caused such dispute that the military had to be called out to suppress a riot and who for a time thereafter always carried two pistols with him when he went into the pulpit. He was, nevertheless, a man of bold and determined character, ever ready to defend the Presbyterian cause and zealous in maintaining what he considered the interests of the Church. During his ministry he held 1,169 meetings of his kirk-session and most of the men in his parish were at one time or another brought before it.

Our 'pilgrim', as Sir Walter Scott later described Patrick Brydone, was born into a world characterised by war and the building of empires. Britain had stood by during the War of the Polish Succession (1733–38), leaving France, Spain and Turkey to defeat Austria. Supported by Charles Emmanuel III of Sardinia, the Bourbons moved against isolated Hapsburg territories, and France seized the Duchy of Lorraine fearing that as a Hapsburg possession, it would bring Austrian power too close to France. At home, Robert Walpole, the prime minister, took the view that the country's best interest was served by avoiding wars in which she had no direct interest, in spite of the desire of many of his colleagues to revive the old Whig feud against the Bourbons. Nevertheless, the alliance of France and Spain boded ill for England, especially when Philip V and Louis XV determined to work together in their efforts to end her naval superiority.

In February 1736, a month after Patrick Brydone's birth, Francis I, the Holy Roman Emperor, married Maria Theresa of Austria, the ruler of the Hapsburg Empire, in Vienna. The Treaty of Vienna in November 1738, which ended hostilities, saw the Kingdom of Naples and Sicily ceded by Austria to Duke Charles of Parma, the younger son of King Philip V of Spain. Charles in turn was forced to cede Parma to Austria and give up his claim to the throne of Tuscany. Within a year, however, Britain was at war with Spain, when public feeling about the way the Spanish had treated Robert Jenkins, the captain of a British merchant ship, at last boiled over, forcing Walpole, Britain's prime minister, to declare war in October 1739.

The Balkans and Eastern Europe were also in turmoil. The Russo-Turkish War broke out a year before Patrick Brydone's birth. It had been caused by a series of raids into the Ukraine by Muslim Tartars speaking a Turkish dialect from the Crimea. The Russian

Dnieper Army of 62,000 men took the Turkish fortifications at
Perekop towards the end of May 1736 and occupied the old city
of Bakhchisaray the following month but disease forced a retreat
to the Ukraine. In June, however, the Russian River Don army and
navy successfully seized Azov. The war represented part of Russia's
continuing struggle for access to the Black Sea and in 1737 Austria
entered the war, only to be defeated at the Battle of Banja Luka.
Two years later, the Dnieper Army went on to defeat the Turks at
Stavuchany but another defeat of Austria by the Turks at Grocka,
coupled with the threat of an invasion by Sweden, forced Russia to
sign a peace treaty with Turkey in September 1739.

*The London Gazette* described events on the days following
Brydone's birth. On 8 January, His Majesty, who had returned to
Hanover when another conflict on the continent threatened, was
reported to be on the Dutch coast at Helvoetsluys, some 20 miles
south of The Hague, unable to return to England on account of
unfavourable winds. Other naval vessels trying to reach the Downs
had suffered badly. The day before, the Court of Directors of the
South Sea Company, meeting in Threadneedle Street, had given
notice of a meeting later in January to declare a dividend. In addition,
the directors of the lottery appointed under an Act of Parliament
in the previous session, for the building of the new Westminster
Bridge (to be designed by the Swiss architect Charles Labelye)
announced an improved deal for those purchasing tickets. Among
other notices in the *Gazette* were more than twenty in respect of
bankruptcy proceedings. February saw another first performance
of a work by Handel when 'Alexander's Feast' was given at Covent
Garden Theatre. Written to celebrate Saint Cecilia's Day, it was a
great success, so encouraging Handel to move away from Italian
opera to a variety of English choral works.

Meanwhile, back in Scotland, the Porteous Riots broke out in
Edinburgh during April 1736 after the city guard, Captain John
Porteous, ordered his men to fire into a crowd which had attended
the execution in the Grassmarket of a smuggler by the name of
Andrew Wilson, causing six deaths. In London, an increase in the
tax on gin inspired another set of riots, and in July cheap Irish
immigrant labour was greatly resented. Although the last witch had

been hanged in Scotland eight years before, 1736 saw the passing of the Witchcraft Act in May, a piece of anti-fraud legislation intended to protect the gullible from cheats and tricksters. People 'found practising or claiming they practiced witchcraft' faced hefty fines and imprisonment. Less punitive was the opening in November that year of Scotland's first public theatre in Carruber's Close, Edinburgh, whilst the publishing trade launched a collection of maps of Great Britain by John Owen and Emanuel Bowen in the fourth edition of *Britannia Depicta,* designed for use by travellers.

The Matriculation Roll at St Andrews University for the year 1750–51 shows the name of Patrick Brydone. He was taught Greek there by Walter Wilson of United College, a professor who seems to have endowed him with a lifelong enthusiasm for the classics. As a 20th century critic has observed, Brydone 'was later delighted to have had the classics poured into him', they being apparent on almost every page of the *Tour,* 'where names like Diodorus Siculus and Apollonius Rhodius drop like rain'.[2] He seems also to have learned some science, as he later recalled, when writing to his friend William Beckford, that 'I remember when I was at college to have seen a heretic to their rigid Newtonian doctrine of gravity very suddenly converted by being tossed in a blanket; and another who denied the law of centripetal and centrifugal forces, soon brought to assent, from having the demonstration made upon his shoulders, by a stone whirled at the end of a string'.[3]

The heretical youth that came out of his teens soon left classics behind and moved his interest towards scientific experimentation. By the time he was twenty, Patrick was already someone aspiring to follow in the steps of some of the great scientific names of the age. One such exemplar might well have been the French mathematician and philosopher, Pierre-Louis Moreau de Maupertuis, who had made an expedition to Lapland to determine the shape of the earth and measure the length of a degree along the meridian, a Brydonian challenge if ever there was one. Admitted to the Académie des Sciences in 1723, he extended the work of Isaac Newton which was not widely accepted outside England and argued against the waning Cartesian mechanics. Maupertuis predicted that the earth would probably be found to be the shape of a flattened sphere, while Jacques Cassini, his rival, measuring it astronomically, took the view it was prolate or extended in the direction of its longer axis. Louis XV and the Académie decided to send two expeditions to determine an answer. One, led by several French astronomers, went to Ecuador on the equator, where it arrived in May 1735. The second, under the Swedish scientist Anders Celsius and Maupertuis, left Dunkirk in May 1736 and set up a base camp at Tornio in north Finland. They managed to spend a summer and winter close to the North Pole, making their measurements despite insects in the former and the cold weather in the latter. Despite being shipwrecked on their way home their measurements were not lost.

News of the experiments and discoveries being conducted in America by the hugely versatile Benjamin Franklin (1706–1790) would have certainly aroused Brydone's curiosity. Franklin believed inventions and scientific enquiry could be used to improve productivity and influence human improvement. Never patenting any of his inventions, he held that since man enjoyed great advantages from the work of others, all should have access to inventions, 'freely and generously'. After satisfactorily extracting sparks from a cloud, he turned his attention to the concept of electrical earthing, or the path to ground, inventing the lightning rod and installing such equipment on the roof of his own home. Four years later, Franklin and John Hadley (1731–1764), soon to be the fourth professor of chemistry at Cambridge, England, collaborated to develop the theory of refrigeration by continually wetting the bottom of a mercury thermometer with ether and evaporating it. Their work led to the conclusion that one might see 'the possibility of freezing a man to death on a warm summer's day'.

Franklin was awarded the Copley Medal of the Royal Society in London at the end of November 1753, then the most distinguished prize in the world for scientific achievement, after receiving honorary degrees from Harvard and Yale. He was elected a fellow in April 1756 and formally admitted to the Royal Society in London on 24 November 1757, where he had been sent by the Pennsylvania Assembly as a protest against the influence being exerted by the Penn family. He was to remain in Britain for five years (becoming a member of the Society's council in 1760), staying at his main

London residence of No.7 Craven Street, near Covent Garden.[4] He was soon in the habit of attending the 'Club of Honest Whigs' which met on alternate Thursdays at the London Coffee House, which was originally in St Paul's churchyard and later moved to Ludgate Hill. Boswell and Joseph Priestley were among its members. Franklin was also a fellow of the 'Society of Arts', made up of scientists, philanthropists and explorers which occupied a building in John Adam Street, south of the Strand. He was still busy, inventing in 1758 alone, a clock with only three wheels, a damper for ovens and chimneys, and an early form of air-conditioning. The following year Franklin visited Edinburgh with his son and after giving him an honorary degree from the University of St Andrew's, the town made him a freeman of the Borough. Three years later, it was Oxford University's turn to award him an honorary doctorate of civil law.

In an age when electricity was the fashionable wonder, a development in European philosophy which excited everybody, although none knew how it worked, Francis Hauksbee had been admitted as a member of the Royal Society in 1703. Becoming Isaac Newton's laboratory assistant, he first demonstrated a new air-pump and the phenomenon of 'mercurial phosphorus', or electrostatic discharge. When the society's president, Newton, restarted an earlier practice of weekly lectures, Hauksbee found himself their useful demonstrator and some three years or so later his own research produced his friction machine for generating static electricity.[5] Then, in 1742, a Scot born in Banffshire, Andreas Gordon, replaced Hauksbee's glass globe with a cylinder and produced the most powerful electrical discharges up to that time. However, this was before the invention of the Leyden jar in 1745 where electrical discharges from these machines could be stored, and therefore larger shocks administered. He went on to publish eight textbooks about natural philosophy and the usefulness of electricity. In 1751, Robert Mowbray was successfully treated at The Royal Infirmary of Edinburgh for palsy of the tongue, and Richard Lovett, a lay clerk at Worcester Cathedral who had witnessed lectures given by John Theophilus Desangliers, an eminent French member of the Royal Society, was able to claim in 1756 that he was treating many conditions including mental disease by electric sparks and current. Although severely criticised by the *Monthly Review* when it appeared, Lovett's *The Subtil Medium Prov'd* greatly impressed John Wesley with his treatments. The Methodist leader advocated electrical therapy for some 49 conditions, including angina, gout, poor circulation, gravel in the kidneys, and numerous aches and pains.

Brydone seems likely to have been aware of many of the forces at work popularising electricity, but unlike Lovett who read many of the works of Franklin, he probably did not have a friction machine in his room. With electricity being looked to for all manner of therapeutic benefit, the young Brydone may have applied himself to helping those sick parishioners with painful long-term medical conditions whom he met at the manse in Coldingham. The mezzotint portrait made of him towards the end of his life shows what appears to be a variation of Hauksbee's globe, a belt-driven glass globe machine with a lead from the prime conductor going to a Leyden jar on the desk, which would have stored the charge from the electrostatic machine, and perhaps a spark coming off. From his descriptions, measurement for Brydone depended on his counting the number of shocks, although he may have regulated his machine in other ways.

Certainly by the spring of 1757, both Patrick and his father were in contact with some members of the Royal Society in London.[6] Dr Robert Whytt had studied in Edinburgh, Paris and Leyden and was a professor of medicine at the University of Edinburgh, specialising in unconscious reflexes, tubercular meningitis and the treatment of urinary bladder stones. Very much a product of the Scottish Enlightenment, he had been elected to a fellowship of the Royal Society in 1752, publishing an essay on *The Vital and other Involuntary Motions of Animals,* and another on *The Virtue of Lime-Water in the cure of the Stone.* Much of his work concerned reflex action; he suggested that persistent dilation of the pupil could be produced by compression of the optic thalamus, and that the spinal cord, rather than the brain, could be the source of involuntary action. Brydone's second contact was Dr John Pringle who had become a Council Member of the Royal Society in 1752, having been a military physician. He now lived in London where he had become physician-in-ordinary to the Duke of Cumberland and published a number of important works on the theory of medicine.[7]

Someone to whom Pringle wrote about Brydone was Dr John Birch, a London surgeon, who was extremely enthusiastic about the use of electricity and believed it offered an alternative to surgery. At his clinic his therapy, built on the discovery of the electrical nature of the nerve impulse, involved transmitting shocks from a Leyden jar to patients seated in an insulated chair. By stimulating weak nerves, muscles and other vessels in the body, he hoped to improve the circulation.

Interest in his experiments was evidently serious enough for Brydone to consider writing a paper on the subject which he did at the beginning of November 1757. By the first day of December, it was clear that the project had the support of Dr Whytt who wrote to Dr Pringle at Pall Mall Court in London, including a copy of Brydone's account of 'the success of the electrical shocks in a paralytic patient, attested by the patient herself and by Mr Brydone's father'. At the same time, Whytt also heard from the Rev James Allan, the minister at Eyemouth and author of *Moderation Explained and Recommended* (1749), who 'had examined the patient particularly, and found Mr Brydone's account to be perfectly true', that he had 'never observed the electric shock so strong from any machines as from Mr Brydone's', adding 'that gentleman has not only applied himself to the study of natural philosophy but also medicine'.[8]

With his mentor having corrected one or two expressions by the second week of December, Brydone's paper was read to the Royal Society on Friday 15 December. Entitled: *An Instance of the Electrical Virtues in the care of a Palsy*, it told the story of Elizabeth Foster, aged 33, who in poor circumstances and unmarried, had been seized 15 years before by a violent nervous fever, and 'accompanied with an asthma'. She had lived in 'a weakly uncertain state' till July 1755 when she became troubled with more nervous symptoms, ending in 'a paralytic disorder which sometimes affected the arm, sometimes the leg of the left side'. In the spring of the following year, she unexpectedly grew better but not so far as to be rid of her paralytic complaints and she continued to be 'apprehensive of a more violent attack'. This soon happened, and in a very short time she lost all motion and sensation in her left side. During the winter of 1756 her symptoms worsened: her head now shook constantly, and her tongue 'faltered' so much when she attempted to speak that she could not articulate a word. Her left eye grew so dim that she could not distinguish colours with it, and she was often seized with such a universal coldness and insensibility that those who saw her at such times scarce knew whether she was dead or alive.

Seeing that the woman was in this miserable condition, and observing that she had some periods during which she could converse and use her right leg and arm, Brydone proposed trying to relieve her during one of these intervals by the power of electricity. He arranged for her to be supported in such a manner as to receive the electric shocks standing, holding the phial in her right hand whilst the left was made to touch a gun barrel. After receiving

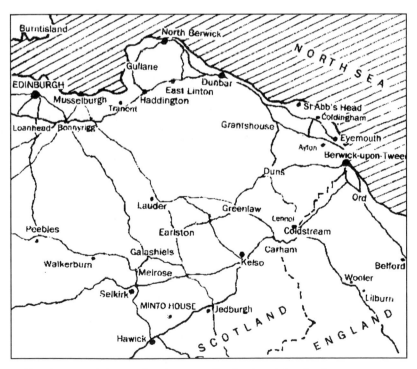

Sketch map of the Borders between England and Scotland.

several very severe shocks, she 'found herself in better spirits than usual and said she felt a heat and a prickling pain in her left thigh and leg, which gradually spread over all that side'. After undergoing the operation for a few minutes longer, Brydone told of her crying out with great joy. She had felt her foot on the ground.

With the electrical machine producing such extraordinary effects, the action was continued, and that day the woman patiently submitted to receive above 200 shocks from it. The consequence was that the shaking of the head gradually decreased, till it entirely ceased. She was able at last to stand without any support, and on leaving the room quite forgot one of her crutches, and walked to the kitchen with very little assistance from those around her. That night the patient continued well and slept better than she had done for several months. About midnight, however, she was seized with a faintness and noticed a strong sulphurous taste in her mouth but both disappeared after a drink of water. Next day, 'being electrised as before, her strength sensibly increased during the operation, and when that was over, she walked easily with a stick and could lift several pounds weight with her left hand which had been so long paralytic before'.

The experiment was repeated on a third day, by which time the woman had received in all upwards of 600 severe shocks. Then, having told Brydone and his helpers that she had 'as much power in the side that had been affected as in the other', it was decided unnecessary to proceed further as, to all appearances, the 'electricity hiding' had already produced a complete cure. Indeed, the patient continued to be well till the Sunday following, when she caught a cold going to Church, and the next day complained of a numbness in her left hand and foot. Nevertheless, she was again 'electrised' and Brydone was able to close his paper by reporting that she had been 'perfectly well ever since'. Thereupon, Elizabeth Foster attached her signature, attesting that the above was a true and exact account of her case, and 'the late wonderful cure' wrought on her. Brydone's father, the minister at Coldingham, followed, declaring that he had been 'an eye witness to the electrical experiments made by my son on Elizabeth Foster, and saw with pleasure their happy effects. By the blessing of God accompanying them, from a weak, miserable, and at sometimes almost insensible state, she was in a very short time restored to health and strength; of which the above is in every respect a true account'.[9]

It would have taken barely ten minutes of Dr Pringle's time on that Friday in 1757 to read the twenty-one-year-old's paper to the men of the Royal Society, meeting together much as the founding members had gathered to witness experiments and discuss scientific topics in 1660. Their reaction to an item about the medical uses of electricity is not recorded, but not all those present would have properly understood it. Many still attributed almost magical powers to electricity.

On 9 January 1758, Pringle asked Whytt to find out from Brydone the name of the parish where the woman lived, and the time when she was cured. The paper had also not been properly dated and Brydone was clearly irritated by such exactitude but he furnished Whytt with the following reply: 'The woman on whom the cure was performed,' he wrote, 'had lived all her life in the parish of Coldingham, and for the last twelve years in that town.' He explained that her father had died of the palsy seven years previously, after having been subject to that distemper for several years. The cure, he said, was performed in his father's house at Coldingham on the 4th, 5th, 6th, and 11th days of April 1757; a circumstance he had noted down. As to the date of his paper, he only recollected that it was written some day at the beginning of November 1757, and 'as the woman still continued well, he hoped the precise day of the month was no material omission?'[10]

Brydone wrote a second letter to Dr Whytt that day with more examples of cures effected by electricity, describing himself as 'something like a fellow at the gallows, who often takes leave but is very unwilling to dispatch the audience'. Plaguing him with more postscripts, he begged leave to mention 'one observation which obtruded itself'.

Having said that 'electric powers were adhesive to all matter', he thought it might be asked 'why not then to the particles of air?'. Leaning on his many experiments and observations, Brydone went on to say he thought it highly probable that they were. Given the many uses of air in nature, he considered it highly necessary that electric powers should be joined with them, saying that 'many effects of the air show that they are so'. He did, however, foresee a ready objection to what he called 'the ascent of vapour and exhalations', namely, that 'if electric powers are added to the particles of air in proportion to their specific gravity, how can the affixing of them to particles of vapour in the same proportion, render them specifically lighter than air?'. His answer was that 'the extent of the atmosphere affixed to each particle must be in proportion to the mixture of the electric powers adhering to the … [indecipherable] and consequently the particles of vapour may have much more … atmospheres than the particles of air. Concluding his first postscript, Brydone wrote that, 'whole surfaces may be electrified (as we call it) and therefore the particles detached from them may bring off the electric powers affixed to each particle, in very different quantities … thus, my system of the ascent of vapours and exhalation, thunder, rain etc may be better explained than before. But this would require a paper by itself'.[11]

Turning to his electricity machine, Brydone wanted to describe the cylinder he used for Dr Whytt so that his experiments might be better understood, and 'to show another circumstance in the easy fitting up of globes or cylinders'. His was 'a clear glass bottle four inches and half diameter and seven inches long in the sides, with an iron passed through the middle'. The latter did not prevent the working of the bottle, 'for the ends of the bottle, the iron axis and the spikes of the lath, upon which it is turned, are all electrified with the resinous power while the wheel is turning which shows that the vitreous power does not fly off that way. A communication from the spike to the coating of the bottle will make the bottle charge sooner and higher than a communication with any other non-electric because the resinous power is there prepared to fly off to the bottle'.

Although the young scientist felt he could now tell how heat excited and friction separated the electric powers, he admitted to Whytt that 'this would require a recital of experiments too prolix to insert'. Instead, he ended by enclosing copies of two attestations witnessed by those cured, Brydone and his father. The first was in respect of Robert Haig in Coldingham, a labouring man who,

Brydone said, 'after having been for ten days subject to a regular tertian ague, at my desire, underwent the electrical shocks in the common way. After having received about thirty or forty very severe ones he grew pale, and staggering several paces, would have fallen down, had he not been supported. He fell into a fit which continued near half an hour. I desired him to come back the next day, immediately before the fit, which he said came on about ten o'clock. He accordingly came and told me he had not the usual symptoms preceding the fit. He was that day strongly electrised again and he had no aguish tendency since, viz. for the space of four months'. The second testimony concerned Ann Torry in Coldingham, a young woman of about 20, who although she had a regular tertian ague suffered from the ague for near a fortnight for the first time ever. The fit came on early in the morning. She was 'electrised on her well day in the afternoon and the next morning, having had only a slight shivering ... (then) again about ten o'clock and has had no symptom of the ague since ... these two months'.[12]

As the new year came in, the manse at Coldingham must have given the impression of being a homeopathic casualty clearing station, and on 11 May 1758, another paper entitled *A further account of the effects of electricity in ... some of his cases* was read at the Royal Society. Part of a letter from Brydone originally sent in January that year to Dr Whytt concerned a young woman of Ayton, a village a few miles from the Brydone home, who had not been able to put her foot to the ground for near a twelvemonth. The advice of some surgeons in the country and several remedies proved of no avail, and, hearing of Brydone's cure of the paralytic woman, she insisted on being brought to Coldingham. There she underwent a course of electrical shocks for nearly two months, receiving fifty or sixty every day in the following manner. She sat close by the machine, and grasping the vial in her hand, presented the wire to the barrel or conductor, and drew the sparks from it for about a half a minute.

Other studies mentioned a soldier's wife, a genteel-looking woman of about 30 who had been seized with a slight palsy while travelling from Newcastle to Coldingham. She lost all feeling in her left side and was brought to the Brydones in a cart. After receiving 'six hundred shocks from the electrical machine, in the usual way, and in the space of two days', she was able to resume her journey carrying a recommendatory letter with her from Brydone to a surgeon in Haddington who also had 'an electrical apparatus'. There was also the case of a young woman from Home, a village 12 miles to the west of Coldingham who complained of insensibility in her left wrist of two years standing. She was required to be wired up for about a half an hour with her hand in a piece of flannel, so enabling her to again put on her clothes without assistance. Additionally, there were several people whose rheumatic pains were relieved by 'electrising the parts affected'.[13]

Little publicity resulted from these events. Volume 50 of the Royal Society's *Philosophical Transactions* for 1757–58 was, however, duly published and its index appeared in the semi-annual, *London Chronicle*. It included over 115 papers on subjects as far apart as *Rare Species of Barnacles, Observations of the Comet* and *A Discourse on the usefulness of inoculation of horned cattle*. Brydone's first paper was preceded by one entitled *Some Observations on ... Carlsbad Waters, Lime-water and Soap*, in the form of a letter from Dr Whytt.

It was to be 15 years before Brydone became a fellow of the Royal Society and his own and other records revealed more of the happenings during these early years, despite the glimmer of limelight that had fallen upon him.

CHAPTER 2

# Brydone goes to War
# (1759–1763)

The Seven Years' War was in its third year. In the spring of 1758, Britain had been forced to send some 10,000 troops to re-enforce Ferdinand of Brunswick's Hanoverian army but the French were to be beaten at Krefeld later and held on the Rhine.[1] Meanwhile, Prussia and Frederick II had become increasingly concerned about Russia, fighting their superior army to a standstill at the Battle of Zorndorf in August. In October, Austrian forces successfully surprised the main Prussian army in Saxony but after failing to take Dresden, they returned home for the winter. 1759 started with a new French minister in charge. The Duc de Choiseul was determined to end the war with strong attacks on both Britain and Hanover, and even planned to invade England. However, two defeats in August and November, one in the Mediterranean, the other off Quiberon Bay on the western coast of France, prevented the assembly of troops near the mouth of the river Loire and the unification of their fleets at Brest and Toulon.

The Army List shows that a twenty-three-year-old Patrick Brydone was commissioned 2nd Lieutenant in the 85th Regiment of Craufurd's Royal Volunteers on 14 October 1759.[2] That day Brydone wrote to his parents informing them that he was in Durham, a 'very costly, though otherwise pleasant' place and nothing could 'exceed the politeness and affability of its inhabitants'. There were only three officers with two companies spending seven or eight hours 'daily on field exercises'. A Lieutenant Dawson was 'very agreeable', as was his first lieutenant, and Brydone thought 'it might not be impossible ... to get a first Lieutenancy ... if proper application were made'.[3]

It was 23 February 1760 when Brydone wrote to his mother from Newcastle about army life and his prospects. The editor of the *Newcastle Magazine* reported in the following month that a regiment had marched to Killingworth Moor, north of Newcastle-Upon-Tyne, where it had camped and set about various exercises. Preparations were being made for an expedition against the French. By the beginning of August, Brydone was bemoaning his inability to buy a commission, and seeking the advice of James Allan, the minister at Eyemouth who had vouched for the efficacy of his electric shock treatment three years before. When in the pump room at Bath on his way to Devon he had apparently met a Mr Home quite by chance. Whether this was John Home, one of Brydone's classmates at Dalkeith Grammar School is not known. The soldier went on to tell his mother how he had played the second fiddle in a small music group, only playing ripieno passages with the full orchestra, and gave a long account of life with the French prisoners they were called upon to guard, as well as how they too became involved in both music-making and dancing. Brydone had heard also from a friend, Harry Trotter, who although then suffering from the ague was about to be made a first lieutenant. Generally speaking, he was happy with his life, but worried about his seventy-four-year-old father's health.[4]

By the beginning of October, Brydone and his regiment were in the docks at Plymouth from where he again wrote to his mother, telling her that General Geoffrey Amherst had not only taken Montreal but the French governor, Pierre François de Rigaud, had surrendered the whole of Canada to him. Three weeks later, Brydone explained that he had still not embarked, and during one off-duty excursion it seems he had 'a series of mishaps with a mare and a fowling piece'. In the years till her death in 1764, there was an almost daily flow of letters from Patrick to his mother.[5]

From the beginning of 1761, two British admirals had kept a continuous watch on the movements of French ships in the Vilaine and the Charente, and as the year progressed it was decided that

Commodore Keppel, in command of the naval force, and Major-General Studholm Hodgson, with a land force, should 'reduce' the island of Belle-Isle off the Brittany coast rather than Mauritius. At Plymouth on Sunday 22 March, Captain Adam Duncan went on board HMS *Valiant*, Commodore Keppel's flagship, bringing word that the expedition was to embark over the next two days, and that 'the marines were to succeed Brydone's regiment', at Devonport. Unknown to Brydone, his father had died five days before. The Amity Succession, the transport vessel in which Brydone's company had 'a small, dirty and very disagreeable' cabin, was generally 'in very bad repair'.[6] The signal indicating whether or not it was convenient to pay a visit to a particular ship was determined by 'a towel hung out at the wardroom window'. Monday saw companies' accounts being made up, the embarkation of Stewart's and Colvil's Regiments, and twenty-four hours later, Brydone wrote in his journal: 'Alone on board; wrote letters'.

The staff officers for the expedition were Captain Pearse, aide-de-camp to Major-General Hodgson, and Mr Pink Esq., his secretary, together with Major-General Crauford and Captain Preston, his aide-de-camp. Listing the security measures for carrying arms and for sufficient paper to be taken aboard for the making of ball cartridges, and noting the importance of keeping the ship ventilated at all times, Brydone said that the roll would be called on deck three times a day. Officers were to see that men's hair was combed, and that they were kept as clean as possible, with bedding put on deck as often as possible. There was to be no smoking between decks, or lights of any kind except in lanthorns. All fires and lights were to be put out at six o'clock. Freshwater was not to be used for washing, and during the voyage a sentry would be posted on the jars or vessels it was stowed in.

At Portsmouth, early on the morning of Wednesday 25 March, Brydone was joined for breakfast on HMS *Hampton Court* by two of his fellow officers, Dawson and Bruce, who had joined the ship the previous night. Captain Carr Scrope and his officers had used them 'most genteelly', and deserved to be 'gratefully remembered by them all'. With reconnaissances going on, diversionary action to confuse the French about the target, and Keppel being inclined to leave many transports behind, Scrope would have been especially pleased to be part of the expeditionary force. However, after inspecting other transport vessels Brydone found his company was 'much worse accommodated that any other'. While seamen were busy the following day laying in stores, Brydone bought a telescope and charts, and despite 'the hurry and confusion of the last two days', two regiments were embarked from Southsea beach on 27 March. With the arrival of General Craufurd and Lord Warkworth's company, the fleet sailed with a fair wind at 5.30 a.m two days later, not before, as Brydone said, 'there had been a push to change our ship, but in vain', and the arrival of the sheep. The *Hampton Court* and the *Téméraire* both ran aground, 'but got off again with difficulty'. The fleet anchored overnight off Yarmouth on the Isle of Wight, with the coast looking 'remarkably beautiful'.

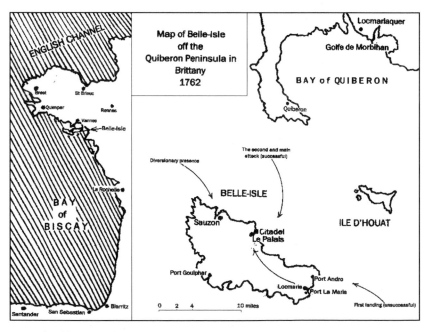

Map of Belle-Isle off the Quiberon Peninsula in Brittany 1762.

On Tuesday 31 March, having been 'excessively seasick' the previous day, Brydone was well enough to report that 'by our steering … we begin to suspect that our destination is for Belle-Isle instead of Mauritius'. When the helmsman continued to steer for the French coast, and orders were received from the *Valiant* with respect to 'the order of landing, instructions on the contents of a soldier's knapsack, and safeguarding of the ship', there was no doubt. The sixth of April was a beautiful day with a west wind, and 'six frigates were sent off to deprive the enemy of any communication with the continent'. At eleven o'clock the next day, Brydone said:

> we were within shot of the coast, and several guns were fired at us. Flags of defiance were hoisted on every part of the island. The whole fleet anchored about twelve in the Great Road. The coast appeared strongly fortified both by nature and by art. The rocks (cliffs) are entirely inaccessible, and two little bays that we passed are flanked by cannon, and defended in front by strong entrenchments. We received orders to embark in the flat-bottomed boats tomorrow at four o'clock. Two boats came alongside us late this evening for that purpose.

That night and the following morning it rained very hard but Brydone and his brother soldiers went into the boats as scheduled. They then assembled around HMS *Superb*, a newly constructed seventy-four-gun ship commanded by Captain Joshua Rowley while the marines were sent to make a feint at Sauzon, the north part of the island. About nine o'clock, Brydone's party left *Superb*, but with the wind against them they failed to make their landing on the south-east coast at Port Andro, till near one o'clock. A four-gun battery at the entrance of the bay was silenced, and the signal given for all boats to push on shore, but few of them had reached the bay by that time. The rest formed a line of 2 miles length. They had advanced about 30 yards when the enemy started up from behind an entrenchment. They bravely returned their fire and attacked them with bayonets. All the officers were killed or wounded and the men were overpowered by numbers and obliged to retreat in great confusion. 'Attempting to creep on all fours to the rocks, several fell two or three times … about 17 reached the rock, and Captain Rowley very bravely went in his barge and took them up'. With perhaps a thousand French defenders observed behind the hill overlooking the beach, Lieutenant Anderson from the *Superb* ordered his men to stop, and return to their respective transports. About the same time, Major Purcell ran in with five or six boats full of troops, immediately below the battery on the left of the bay, only to see the heads of the French. 'Our people fired', Brydone wrote, but could do them little hurt.

> They kept an incessant fire on us and almost every shot took effect. Numbers of the soldiers threw down their arms and called out for quarter, but our bombardier very foolishly continued throwing shells, and it was at first denied. At last an officer fixed a white handkerchief on his bayonet, and immediately they stopped firing. Our people laid down their arms and went over the parapet, and were that moment marched off prisoners to the Citadel. Purcell was killed.

Five hundred men were lost in a day, along with fifty boats. Ten days or so passed during which very little happened on either side, apart from a few shells being fired at the Citadel above Le Palais, and an order of the day aboard Brydone's ship gave the layout of the guard, passwords and 'instructions on returning the numbers of dead and wounded with names and rank'. It was midnight on 21 April 'when we were all abed that Captain Maxwell came on board with orders to be in readiness to land the next morning'. They were ordered to rendezvous and follow HMS *Swiftsure*, commanded by Captain Sir Thomas Stanhope. A three-pronged attack was planned, the first and most important at the bay of La Maria, the second at Sauzon, and the third, to make a feint at a small gully to the east of La Maria. The gun attack by the ships started about 10 o'clock.

The French fired 'both mortars and cannon all the way along the coast. Some shells came pretty near us. We were ordered to pull in for the land about two o'clock. The men-of-war covered us and made a most infernal noise. Every shot must pass within a few yards of our heads, and it is almost inconceivable the noise the balls made in the air. I am sure the nobleness and grandeur of the scene tended very much to inspire with courage and resolution, and must inevitably had the contrary effect on our enemies'. Although Brydone reckoned that some 20,000 cannon balls were thrown at the island that day, he estimated that 'not one in ten did execution'. Nevertheless, after the first boats landed, he saw that 'our people had gained the rocks, regardless of the fire from the shipping ... there was a little bank that defended our people from the enemy's fire, but the place was so narrow that only nine or ten could fire over it at once'. Brydone thought that they might have kept the enemy at bay, but a lieutenant, bravely but foolishly leapt over the bank and with his sword in his hand dared them to advance. 'One of their officers' he wrote, 'ordered his men not to fire at him, as he was certainly mad'. Whereupon, the servant of a captain shouted that 'he would shoot him if he did not instantly return', a command he obeyed. Describing what followed as 'a strange infatuation', Brydone said that a few moments later, the lieutenant was tempted to repeat the incident. Two or three men followed him, and he was immediately shot. With their bayonets fixed, the French then advanced up to the bank, taking prisoner all those who did not escape into the sea.

At this juncture, Major William Skinner, observing a cliff where he thought it was possible to climb without an order, made his boat pull in about 150 yards to the left of the gully. According to Brydone, this happened at the same moment that the other party was withdrawing to its transports. From the top of the cliff, Skinner was able to observe the enemy position, whilst Brydone described what happened:

The remainder of our five companies, some of Beauclerc's and some marines, were pulling in for the same rock. He waved for us to make haste, and likewise made a signal to some boats with the marines and Loudoun's (regiment) to incline to the left, that they may take the enemy's flank. We climbed up the rock which was so steep that only one could get up at a time, and that with such difficulty that we were obliged to hand up our arms that we might have the free use of our hands ... As soon as a few had reached the top (the Grenadier company and a part of ours), the French began to fire. The Grenadiers of Nice, flushed with their former conquest, inclined to the right, down the rock. We were obliged to incline to the left, and at last got a more advantageous spot. The battalion of Nice was advancing on our front, and kept a perpetual fire. They had the advantage of being formed in order of battle, and we in the utmost confusion. No word of command was given, but everyone fired when and where he thought proper. Skinner was all the time in the hottest of it. He fell and his hat flew off. I did not doubt of his being shot, but he immediately got up and encouraged the men to advance ... The fire continued for a half an hour, very brisk on both sides, but the enemy seeing us reinforced from all sides, and receiving a smart fire from the marines and Loudoun's on the left, began to give way. We advanced to a little wall that served us as a parapet. They continued to retreat, and we leaped over the wall. The grenadier's march was beat. The men seemed inspired with fresh courage, and I believe at that time would have despised the most eminent dangers. The enemy retreated to a village 200 yards distance.

Leaving behind three field pieces, the French 'set off with great expedition' for the Citadel, and one of Brydone's sergeants set fire to some tents as a signal to the boats in the main landing that they were safely on shore. Fired with victory, the men were congratulated very warmly for their behaviour. Craufurd was at a loss for words to express his joy, and called out to his men: 'My brave fellows, you have now shown yourselves worthy of the name'.

Brydone and his detachment marched towards the Citadel till it was dark, when they lay down till daylight. 'We were all wet to the skin' he wrote, remarking that 'this always happens after a great firing of cannon. The air is so rarefied by the fire that the vapour can no longer be supported but must condense and fall down'. The rain continue the whole of the following day. About 11 o'clock they were sent off the line to act as light infantry, and after taking possession of a village that had been abandoned and killing some fowls, sheep and hogs, and cooking them on a fire made of barn doors, parties were sent out every hour 'but nothing material happened', Every fort along the coast, the soldier reported, was 'deserted, and all the cannon and mortars nail'd up, We continued here all night – and a strange night we had of it'.

On Friday 24 April, Burgoyne's Horse landed, and Brydone was sent off with a small party to protect the village of La Maria, the inhabitants of which had not, like the rest of the island, deserted their houses. Although finding a bar with 'plenty of excellent wine', there was little meat to be had for the soldiers. Whereupon, Brydone went to the priest to 'desire him to order every inhabitant to furnish their proportion'. So terrified was he that he fell on his knees when Brydone went to his room, and it took some time before he relaxed and begged the intruder to stay in his house. Visiting the field of battle, Brydone attempted to reckon the number of dead there had been, but bodies were scattered everywhere, and he saw 'several thrown in by the sea three miles west of the landing area'.[7] The next day, he found a marine robbing the church. He had the richly decorated communion cloths wrapped about him, and his pockets were full of the oblation money. 'To the great joy of my friend, the priest', wrote Brydone, 'I immediately stripped him of his fine robes, and emptying his pockets, sent him off a prisoner'.[8]

The French were driven from Le Palais into the Citadel which dominated the area on 13 May. Three days later, it received a furious bombardment, but it was not till 7 June that a breach was made in its huge walls. Fortunately, as preparations for its storming were being concluded, the French commander, the Chevalier Sainte Croix, acknowledged he was unlikely to receive any rescue in the form of a force being assembled at Vannes, and offered to surrender, enabling the British to take possession of both objectives on the following day. The excellent working relations between the naval and military chiefs helped secure Belle-Isle as a place of refreshment for the fleet while it was engaged in blockading the French.

In June, the soldier son sent his mother an express with news of the capitulation of the French, promising her a full account of the siege later. He particularly regretted the death on 5 May of a Lieutenant Stone of the Scots Fusiliers who was shot by a sentry of his own regiment. It was early morning after a battle to re-take a section of works when Brydone encountered the Fusiliers' colonel who was dying. He 'had even then the most noble countenance' despite having been shot through the breast and stabbed by a bayonet. Brydone 'took him by the hand', but he was 'speechless and expired soon after'. Among other glimpses of war that Brydone gave his mother was the arrival at the post he was manning of a French deserter, who provided details of the redoubt and its fortifications although still convinced that the Citadel would last out for some months. An invitation to dine with Brigadier-General Thomas Desaguiliers of the Royal Artillery, himself the grandson of a protestant pastor, was also memorable. His host had arrived on the island about the same time as Brydone, and General Hodgson was to put him in charge of the siege of the Citadel. He successfully organised the positioning of thirty guns and thirty mortars which fired 17,000 shot and 12,000 shells into the target, being wounded by a shell five days before the capitulation of the fortress.

Drawing his letter to a close, Brydone privately confessed that it had been a fearsome campaign, revealing that General Craufurd had apparently been captured by the French, along with two aides-de-camp on his way to an English-held position.[9] He did not see 'the light of the sun for three weeks', becoming 'pale as ashes', like all prisoners and all who lived in the trenches, and who were 'little better than mulattos'. The mainland of France could, however, be seen easily with a spyglass. The ground was covered with 'flowers, fine celery growing wild, and samphire plentiful to use as greens (cabbage)'. General Hodgson entertained some of the gentry of the island while other officers were left to 'stave in' fifty or sixty barrels of wine to prevent the men from liberating them.[10]

British forces had been successful in the war, not only in Europe but in the Caribbean with the capture of Dominica. Furthermore, in India, the last French fortress of Pondicherry had fallen. Meanwhile, France was lobbying for support from Spain, her traditional ally. Ferdinand VI of Spain did not immediately respond, and it was only after Charles III replaced him on the throne that his government became more pro-French and entered the war against Portugal. The Spanish hoped to capture Almeida and advance on the Alentejo and Lisbon, both moves which threatened British commercial interests. At the beginning of May 1761, Spanish troops easily took Briança and Miranda do Douro, but their attack on Porto brought matters to something of a halt, with French reinforcements being struck down by disease and Spanish forces held up by floods. In the Spring of 1762, Brydone's regiment was again ordered on active service, this time as part of a larger British contingent. The force comprised two troops of the 16th Light Dragoons (Burgoyne's), the 3rd Buffs, the 67th (Lambert's), the 85th (Craufurd's) and four regiments from Ireland. A number of British officers were also sent to take up commands in the Portuguese army.

France and Spain had agreed that the former would prosecute the war in Westphalia, leaving the latter to overrun Portugal. Spanish armies had already occupied the provinces of Tras-os-Montes in the north-east and Beira, and a third was forming on the frontier of Estramadura, with the intention of penetrating into the Alentejo, the region between Lisbon and the Algarve. The force from Belle-Isle arrived in the Tagus in early May but it was not till June that the regiments from Ireland put in an appearance. With them came the London-born Count Frederick de Lippe-Bückeburg, the Allies' German commander-in-chief (till 1763), and Lord Loudoun, an Ayrshire peer commanding British forces. On August 5, the Spanish began a siege of Almeida, and Lippe wrote to its governor instructing him to resist until a breach had been made in the fortress wide enough for the passage of 30 men abreast. Captain Dawson, Brydone's erstwhile lieutenant, was sent to supervise the defences, but on 25 August a capitulation was signed, after 40 men of the garrison had been killed. Meanwhile, Lippe attempted to relieve the pressure on Almeida by a counter-attack in the south. He determined that the Spaniards should be attacked in camp before they entered Portugal and Brigadier-General Burgoyne was ordered to achieve this.[11] Striking out on a five day march across the mountains, he successfully caught the enemy completely by surprise at Valencia d'Alcantara, taking the Spanish general and a large number of his officers and men captive. Burgoyne did not, however, find the magazines and stores there that he had expected although he raised a contribution from its inhabitants and destroyed many of the arms that could not be removed.

Much of the summer was spent organising defence along the Zêzere River and preventing Spanish forces crossing the Tagus at Vila Velha de Ródão. Lord Loudoun encamped at Sardoal, and Lippe undertook the task of guarding as best he could every road and pass to Lisbon. Charged with defending the pass over the river at Vila Velha, Burgoyne took post on the south side of the Tagus, facing the town. In addition to part of Craufurd's 85th, he had the English grenadiers. Another detachment of Portuguese grenadiers and a regiment of cavalry, under the command of the Count de St Jago, occupied the pass of Alvito. Another detachment was posted at Perdrigal to prevent the advance of the enemy through the mountains and at Vila Velha there were 150 Portuguese under the command of a captain. The pass at Alvito was assumed to be impregnable although the Count de Maceda and his 6000 Spanish forces did not think so.

On the first of October, Count de Maceda attacked the Portuguese forces (and a small post commanded by a major at St Simon) defending the old Moorish castle of Vila Velha. The castle was covered by Burgoyne's fire and held out for a time, but the force at St Simon was easily routed, so putting the Spaniards in a position to attack the Count de St Jago. The latter immediately withdrew, his retreat being covered by Lord Loudoun who had been sent there hastily by Lippe, along with four British battalions and a similar number of field guns, Loudoun had the defences in the pass levelled to stop them being used against him. The force remained high in the mountains till the retreating Portuguese battalions had filed off the road to Sobrina Formosa. Loudoun's force had, meanwhile, been augmented by six companies of Portuguese grenadiers, fifty of Burgoyne's dragoons and as many Portuguese cavalry. St Jago's force was attacked in the rear but the presence of mind shown by Loudoun's men and Major McBean – and the four guns – saved the day, enabling them to retire towards Cardigos without further loss.

Burgoyne nevertheless recognised that the Spaniards now posed a threat to Vila Velha and he ordered a detachment of 100 British grenadiers, 200 of Craufurd's 85th, and 50 light dragoons under Lieutenant-Colonel Charles Lee, to ford the Tagus on the night of the 5th and surprise the Spanish cavalry camp at Vila Velha. Colonel Lee's force had the fortune to get into the encampment without being noticed. Some firing then took place and a good many of the enemy were killed in their tents. The British infantry used the bayonet without

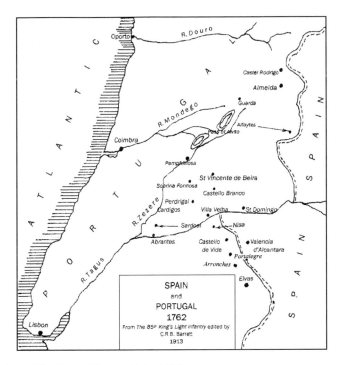

Map of Spain and Portugal in 1762.

firing a shot whilst the only part of the Spanish force that made a stand was a body of horse. These were charged by Lieutenant Maitland at the head of the dragoons and were routed with considerable slaughter. Four guns were spiked, two had been removed. The magazines were burned, sixty artillery mules were brought off, a few horses, a captain and two subalterns of horse, a subaltern of artillery, a sergeant and fourteen privates and a considerable quantity of valuable baggage and loot. The British loss was one corporal killed, two men wounded, four horses killed and six wounded. After what was described as 'this dashing little affair', there was little more fighting owing to the advanced state of the season.

By the middle of October, the Spanish army had retreated back to Spain, with Lippe and Portuguese forces under Lord Townsend pursuing them. Brydone's journal at this point records him undertaking a reconnoitre of Spanish positions north and south of the River Tagus, between Castelo Branco and Nisa. The Spanish had taken two priests prisoner along with other captives from a village. Local opinion was that the enemy had used the ford nearby, but it was now impassable and the river would not go down for many weeks. There was no other ford between there and Vila Velha. Although Burgoyne had been pleased with his report, Brydone went on to say that the horse he had been riding had fallen down a precipice, and luckily 'I threw myself off when I found him going and seized hold of a bush, otherwise I must have been killed'.

On 20 October, after four days of continuous rain, and 'a most dreadful hurricane', there was evidence that the Spanish encampment at Castelo Branco was being evacuated. Deserters were signalling that they wished to surrender. However, with the storm still raging, and 'men and ammunition … in a very poor state', orders came to prepare for action in a day or so. The weakest men were put in charge of hospitals, cattle and baggage. On 27 October, Lippe arrived at Nisa, and two days later, soon after news had been received of a massacre of a joint British and Portuguese party by the Spanish where there had been only one survivor, Brydone reported that the enemy had 'gone into cantonments around Castelo Branco and will probably keep us in perpetual alarms during the winter quarters'.

Two days into November, news of the capture of Havana, an important Spanish naval base in the Caribbean, was celebrated with a *feu de joie*. On the sixth of the month, Brydone was sent with orders for Colonel Vaughan at Elvas, a fortified town in excess of 100 miles away. He was required to march to Arronches, a little to the north, and 'put it in the best state of defence possible'. Brydone had great difficulty in getting a guide, and reaching Portalegre at 10 o'clock at night, he was obliged to wait two hours before the Portuguese would open the gates. To his great surprise he found Colonel Vaughan and his two regiments already there. 'The drum was beat immediately', Brydone said, and 'the poor wretches obliged to march off although they had scarce got into bed after five or six very fatiguing days march from Elvas'. Brydone was given the Prince's lodging in the town where he was received in 'a most pompous manner, and entertained much as Don Quixote at the Duke's'.

Several days later, Brydone found his regiment's camp about 12 miles from Nisa. The general told them at dinner that 'we should have attacked the Spaniards at Castelo Branco' that day, but just before the orders were to have been given out, some deserters arrived and told Count Lippe that the Spanish army had 'set off in such a hurry that they had not even time to carry off their sick men and officers'. A corporal's party with two of the Prince of Mecklenburg-Strelitz's regiment were sent to reconnoitre the place where they found a letter from Pedro de Bolea, the Count of Aranda and Spanish commander-in-chief, 'begging that he would be humane enough to take care of the sick whom he was obliged to leave behind; and if it was ever in his power to show the like generosity, he might depend on his gratitude'. On 8 November Brydone reported the receipt of orders to attack 4000 Spanish on their way to Castelo Branco. A steep hill caused great suffering on account of the heat, and the men had nothing to eat save from the chestnut groves they passed. Moreover, finding that the Spaniards were already on their way to Valencia d'Alcantara, Brydone's party first pitched their tents wherever they could on the mountain above Castelo de Vide in 'dreadful weather', and by the thirteenth of the month, 'all men except a detachment of 30' were ordered into the town, and Lord Loudoun was 'on forced marches from Abrantes' in the west.

Still in continual rain, Colonel Lee 'fell in with the Grand Guard which though vastly superior in numbers, immediately galloped off' whilst Colonel Skinner and his party came back having seen nothing. Meanwhile, deserters had for some time agreed that news of a peace being signed was likely soon. Count Lippe was informed on 24 November 1762 that peace preliminaries had been signed. Emissaries were then exchanged and an armistice agreed.[12]

Patrick had written to his mother from an army camp near the River Tagus the previous August, describing the state of the Portuguese and Spanish armies. He had been upset and angry not only about correspondence being late but the high postal charges levied by the Portuguese. By the end of January 1763, however, Brydone was pleased to discover that he 'might with great ease have (command of) a Portuguese company but the point is not yet determined, whether British officers who accept a Portuguese rank, shall be allowed to retain their other commissions'. The possibility led him to tell his uncle, the Revd Matthew Sandilands Dysart, the minister at Eccles,[13] and to whose letters Brydone's mother had the habit of attaching a postscript, that he might 'stay a year or two' in Portugal. If not, which he was almost certain was the case, 'you will see me in a few months – a poor half-pay subaltern – for no temptation, however great shall ever make me renounce my liberty as a British subject'. The men, he added, were 'sickly, more from the wine of the country than fighting the Spanish'. Then, before handing his letter to an officer who would bring it home, Brydone could not resist making a geographical measurement. It drew attention to the speed of the River Tagus, which at that time of year flowed very fast and 'because of the rains in the mountains a boat can travel the 100 or more miles from their camp to Lisbon in seven or eight hours'.[14]

The 85th passed the winter in quarters among the Portuguese peasantry and in February 1763 the Treaty of Paris was signed. Regiments generally were sent home and on arrival in England the 85th was soon disbanded and the majority of officers relegated to half pay.

With the war over, Brydone and a number of other officers spent a short time in Lisbon, his second journal providing a short commentary about the country in which he had spent the previous year, albeit that his physical and mental tiredness results in its somewhat abrupt ending. In general, he wrote, Portugal was barren but 'this is more owing to the indolence of the inhabitants than the unkindness of Nature, for in many places where the soil is properly cultivated, the farmer enjoys a double crop of corn and oil on the same ground, and that so far as being of detriment to one another, that I have always observed the wheat to flourish most under the shade of the olive trees, owing principally, I suppose, to the richness which must necessarily be communicated to the ground from the quality of fruit that falls every year before it is entirely ripe'. Describing vineyards along the Tagus, as a Scot who had never seen them before, he wrote 'the vine is cultivated with care, and amply rewards the trouble of the husbandman; its fruit varies in taste and quality, not only in every province but in almost every village'. The large American aloe and the Indian fig, plants used for hedging, also came in for special attention. The number of lateral leaves the aloe produced, and 'the progress till the plant is perhaps fifteen or sixteen feet high', made it a useful impenetrable bush, although in the case of the Black fig, 'the prickles are a barrier', it too was a useful plant for gardens and orchards.

Following a comment on the value of a machine operated by a mule which raised and channelled water from wells to the fields, Brydone said there was plenty of game in most parts of Portugal, some forests being the preserve of the Royal Family. It may have been death to any Portuguese of whatever rank to be seen with guns or dogs 'on these sacred plains', but as the ex-soldier said, 'we made no hesitation in breaking through this dread law ... and traversed them with the same freedom as if they had been our own. Although they did not meet any deer or wolves, and found a bird like a turkey which was too fast for them to shoot, no hares, foxes, boar, rabbits or partridges were spared.

Turning to what he called the strongest proof of the national character of a nation, those 'amusements' or 'unheard of cruelties' reckoned to be worthy of the Royal presence, Brydone said that Portugal already had an *auto-da-fé*, the right of the Catholic Inquisition in which the sentence was carried out usually by burning at the stake, and a Bull Feast (the running of the bulls) both of which were 'supported by the same spirit'. Amusement had always been sufficient excuse among those nations who prided themselves on having conquered the ferocity of savages, and who allowed such torture to animals. He had seen these 'feasts' for himself, and held that they were 'the greatest height of barbarism'. Turning more directly to rituals in Catholic countries, a subject which was to be a life-long concern for Brydone, brought up in a Presbyterian environment as he had been, he wrote, 'If a Mexican or a Peruvian were to see one of these feasts, he would imagine that they were sacrifices to the Divinity, but what would be his surprise when he was told that they are the Christian nations that pretend to reform the world, who abhor human sacrifices, and who as a proof of their abhorrence, have butchered the whole Western World because the religion of some of its nations admitted of this ceremony. These are the people who boast of the God which they adore, that his tender mercies are over all his other works. How happily do they imitate this blessed character'!

Murder had become 'a very trifling crime', Brydone wrote, during his service 'there were not less than a hundred of our men that fell by the treacherous hand of the people they were come to protect', adding that 'the churches in Lisbon and the large cities were elegant (and) ornamented with paintings by great masters'. In the smaller towns and villages, it was the relics of saints, skulls, bones and 'wigs with which they decorate the figures of Christ and the Virgin' that caught his eye. He could not remember how many hundred skulls of St Anthony he had seen preserved in different religious houses across Portugal, 'few or none of which allow a day to pass without performing something very extraordinary'.

Noting 'the complete uncertainty' and unreliability of the size of Lisbon's population before and after the great earthquake on All Saints' Day 1755, Brydone said 'it was remarkable that none of the Royal Family, no Prince of the blood, hardly any *Noblesse* perished'. It had been observed that 'the English and all foreign merchants suffered much less than the inhabitants' which he thought 'amazing when one considers the havoc made amongst the buildings that so few lives have been lost', despite the heavy damage in one district where hardly a stone was left standing and magnificent streets were 'laid level with the ground'. Of the 30,000 houses in the capital, he was told on good authority that 'not more than 4,000 (were) in good habitable condition'. The earthquake, he considered, had, however, 'been of service in other respects'. The 'Inquisition was thrown down and several of the inquisitors buried in the ruins'. He believed it would be a blessing for the nation were it to 'never again raise its head' since it, not the earthquake, had been 'the ruin of Portugal'.

In Brydone's opinion, the palace of the King Joseph Emanuel at Belém in Lisbon contained nothing worth seeing, but the gardens were elegant and contained an aviary and a small zoological park where it would seem he had his first encounter with elephants. The appearance and capacity of the opera house in the city was admired, and although the comedies performed were 'insipid', the interludes of singing and dancing were enjoyable, and the machinery used to move trees about on stage, in scenes involving Apollo and the Muses, fascinating. The harbour at Lisbon, the 'epitome of the world where all languages were spoken', all religions professed, and 'all sorts of wickedness's committed', was fascinating. The Alcantara aqueduct with its fourteen arches, which had been built in 1746 to bring drinking water to Lisbon, had survived the earthquake. Visiting the site with a number of his army companions, of whom Brydone named only one, was Dr John Hunter. He had served both in Belle-Isle and Portugal, and was to establish his own anatomy school and become an eminent London surgeon, specialising in the treatment of venereal and diseases associated with the nature of digestion. He made use of a wide range of animal skeletons in his research, and believed, like Brydone, that information documented by experiment and disciplined observation was at the heart of his work.

By the early part of 1764, however, the life of a visitor had palled, and uncertain about what might happen next, he seems to have returned to Scotland by stages, penning his thoughts about the beauty of nature as he meandered through Switzerland and the Alps as an 18th century Hannibal, as if to draw a line under his wartime experiences.

CHAPTER 3

# Becomes a travelling tutor on the continent (1764–1770)

At the end of October 1764, and with Brydone in Scotland looking for a profitable occupation, just how he came to be a preceptor or travelling tutor to the sons of those able to afford his services is not recorded. It was probably a combination of factors. His army experience had boosted his confidence and encouraged a particular thoroughness and care in looking into a broad range of scientific subjects, but whether he could share such matters with others considerably younger than himself, while being paid for doing so, would need to be tested. Such guides, mentors and tutors had certainly accompanied travellers through the centuries, and he may well have heard about Van Bobbart who assisted the education of the Barrett brothers in the seventeenth century, or John Anderson, the eldest son of the minister at Roseneath in Dumbartonshire who became tutor to both Lord Doune and Sir James Campbell. Another Scot who was to become a reputable architect and civil engineer, and who joined his brother on the Grand Tour in 1754, had been Robert Mylne. One Mr Home, a Church of England priest with a living in Essex, had been prevailed upon to become the travelling tutor to one of the sons of the eccentric landowner and MP, John Elwes, in 1763. A year later even Adam Smith, the celebrated professor and later political economist, took up the invitation to travel abroad with the third Duke of Buccleuch.

At first sight, it may appear something of a surprise that Brydone chose to move to Switzerland soon afterwards. The number of

British travellers who visited the country in the eighteenth century was, however, huge with cohorts descending on Geneva, Neuchatel and Lausanne. The country was then enjoying a relatively peaceful period, one which only ended when the French invaded in 1798. The Helvetic Society, founded in 1762, aimed to promote 'friendship and love'. Learned and patriotic societies sprang up across the country and Swiss intellectuals discussed scientific and philosophical ideas, especially those of Diderot, Voltaire and Rousseau. The old towns of Lausanne and Ouchy were 'Bernese-run backwaters', having been under Bernese rule since 1536 and Vaud would not become a canton till 1803. British aristocrats, gentry, well-off bourgeoisie and elegant commoners inhabited numerous places along Lake Geneva, and became typical representatives of Britain so far as the Swiss were concerned. Gibbon deplored the invasion, saying that his adopted town had been invaded by strangers. Other writers, including Addison and Horace Walpole, were matched by a flow of scientists, botanists, physicians, amateur glaciologists and travellers.

Some years later Brydone was to describe Switzerland as this 'little uncouth country ... the very excrescence of Europe', where 'nature seems to have thrown out all her cold and stagnating humours; full of lakes, marshes and woods, and surrounded by immense rocks and everlasting mountains of ice, the barren but sacred ramparts of liberty'.[1] A later comment, by the writer of his obituary, described Brydone climbing in the Alps and the Apennines where he used 'the best instruments that England could furnish, for the purpose of making discoveries as to the precise state and temperature of the air on the summit of the highest mountains in Europe'. He often witnessed phenomena not uncommon in such regions, and once he 'beheld a thunder-storm bursting under his feet!'. The writer concluded by saying that 'his apparatus, and his experiments, acquired for him the reputation, not of a philosopher, but of a conjuror, amidst the habitable recesses of the elevated summits ... while his talents and conversation charmed all he approached'.[2]

At the time of Brydone's arrival, the Swiss travel writer, César-François Saussure, who had visited Holland, Germany and England during fifteen years of travel, was revising an account of his travels which had already passed through numerous hands (including those of Voltaire) and which would become three large volumes for his children.[3] In December 1764, James Boswell was warmly welcomed by an unwell and somewhat reclusive Rousseau. He had been forced to flee when his books were banned, and after making his way with the help of the Duc de Luxembourg, he had found shelter in the village of Môtiers near Val-de-Travers in the Neuchâtel canton of Switzerland, then a protectorate of the Prussian crown. Boswell was also to stay two nights later that month with a seventy-one-year-old Voltaire in a chateau at Fernay in France, four miles from Geneva, where he reigned for nearly twenty years.

Midway through May 1765, Rousseau received another of his frequent visitors, this time from five Englishmen who had been 'unannounced and recommended' to him by Captain Daniel Roguin, a Prussian officer who had toured the continent with Lord Cornwallis. Brydone was one of the privileged five, the others being Lord Kilmaurs, Mr Millekin and Mr Kendrick, friends of James Stuart Mackenzie, Scotland's Lord Privy Seal; and Henry Errington from Sandhoe in Northumberland who had passed the winter in Italy.[4] The last was among those visitors about whom Rousseau 'could not congratulate himself'. In contrast, about Brydone he wrote '*Patrick Brydone est un personnage charmant. homme de science, il s'occupait d'expériences sur l'électricité, et fut un des premiers à se servir de la bouteille de Leyde pour traiter les paralytiques au moyen de chocs*'.[5]

During the winter of 1766–7, Brydone was in Turin where he met Lord Glenorchy, a politician who had just become a member of the Privy Council, and whom he had encountered in Nice and Milan the previous year.[6] His lordship was sitting for his portrait, and together with his lady had been drawn by the same hand, and 'very ably executed'. Her role as a colourful hostess was often reported in the English newspapers. Also there was Sir James Wright, a diplomat and art collector who had just been knighted and was on his way to Venice to take up the post of British minister. An agreeable young Mr Stewart, 'mentioned by Mrs Swinburn' had arrived, and 'taken a place in the Academy for six months'. Flowery compliments were prolific, occasioned by the visit of His Highness of Brunswick (Prince Edward, Duke of York) who was expected to be received at the ducal court. Brydone clearly enjoyed the lively society among British visitors at this time.[7]

After commenting on the power and conduct of the Duke of Savoy, concluding that he was 'a good prince' with a great passion for art and precious stones, Brydone said there was 'very little appearance' that he would have occasion to use the military forces so often invoked by his father 'who had been at more battles and sieges than all the other monarchs of Europe'. A newly established tobacco manufactory near Turin was a good sign. So far as the architectural and ecclesiastical attractions of the city were concerned, Brydone accepted that many of the churches were elegant but few were magnificent. 'That of the Jesuits' he added 'as everywhere else is the richest'. The cathedral was not special save for the chapel, the depository of the most sacred and valuable relict, 'the winding sheet of Our Saviour miraculously preserved for near 2000 years'. He noted the many violent disputes about whether or not it might have been the head of John the Baptist, recalling a dozen of such relics in different churches in Spain and Italy, adding somewhat facetiously that 'the Turin shroud had four Papal bulls to support its authenticity but the one in Rome seven'.[8]

Just when William Beckford (1744–1799) and Brydone met is unclear but it was likely to have been towards the end of 1767. The tutor received a commission from an uncle of the young Beckford to undertake his supervision during a tour of Europe. His father, Richard Beckford, had died in 1756.[9] Born in Jamaica to his father's common-law wife, Elizabeth Hay, William inherited the greater part of his father's hugely profitable, slave-run sugar estates on the island as well as property in Great Britain. Beckford land holdings were scattered over eleven of the nineteen Jamaican parishes but 13,500 acres out of a total of some 42,000 were in Westmoreland. The three plantations of Roaring River, Fort William and Williamsfield produced 450 hogsheads and one tierce of sugar, and 219 puncheons of rum. William was eighteen years old when he matriculated from Balliol College, Oxford, where Theophilus Leigh was the rather uninspiring and long time master, and after three years of studying the classical curriculum, along with Latin and Greek texts, he became a master of arts.

Also joining Brydone's party were William Fullarton (1754–1808) and a Mr Glover, about whom very little is known. The first, whose home had been built in 1745 in the village of the same name near Irvine in Ayrshire, was only five when he succeeded his father. Growing up he successfully cultivated the estate and became known as a man with a penchant for the study of agricultural science. Ten years later, young William spent some time at the University in Edinburgh after which a grand tour was considered appropriate. On his return home in 1771 Fullarton took up diplomacy, having found the early training of a lawyer at Lincoln's Inn not to his liking. He served under Lord Stormont as secretary to the embassy in Paris between 1775 and 1778 and returned to England when hostilities broke out with France, being elected one of the two members of Parliament for the Devon constituency of Plympton Erle in 1779. With his best friend, Lord Seaforth, Fullarton raised regiments from

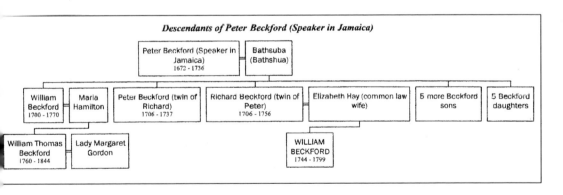

*Descendants of Peter Beckford (Speaker in Jamaica)*

their respective estates, both men becoming Lieutenant-Colonels, one in the 98th, the other in the 100th Foot.[10]

Brydone's third Journal describes the route followed by the three companions and their servants, beginning in 1767 at Montélimar in the French département of the Drôme where they may have assembled. From there they visited Fréjus and Antibes before departing in December from Nice for Turin, the tour's easterly extremity. Their journey took in Sospel, Limone Piemonte and several villages in the neighbourhood. A letter addressed to a Mr Wilbraham, a Lancashire name, at the end of April 1768 tells of the party leaving Turin at six in the morning and passing rice fields 'divided irregularly into squares, triangles, parallelograms and every kind of mathematical figure', each filled with water to a depth of four or five inches.[11] The travellers visited Novara on the frontier between Piedmont and Milan, a district well-known for robbers and where there were skulls on posts beside the road. A river with its origin in Lake Maggiore was 'very fine with a rapid current' and good for fish unlike those whose waters derived from melted snow and which were generally 'thick and muddy'. Away from the rice fields which depended on stagnant water, vineyards and cornfields were mixed and the crops seemed rich.

The party's arrival at Milan in 1768 coincided with the Archdiocese preparing to celebrate a grand festival later in May. At its centre was a nail found in Rome by St Ambrose, the city's fourth-century bishop, and brought back to the city. Brydone's impatience with all ceremonial was soon being expressed, and with the cathedral unfinished after 400 years and five hundred men still working on it, he could only conclude that the money 'thrown away on this mountain of marble would have built twenty of the finest palaces on earth if applied with art and judgment'. Other irritants were the statue of St Bartholomew and the tomb of St Charles Borromeo (the patron saint of learning and the arts) at Arona, richly covered with silver with the saint's body in jewelled robes in a rock crystal case.

The social round included parties (with and without the oft-used fireworks), walks and a variety of chamber concerts in the company of other members of the English aristocracy and gentry in Milan at the time. Among those listed by Brydone were Messrs Dean and Horn, also Richard Aldworth who was to be an MP for nearly thirty years till 1774. He assumed the name and arms of Neville following the death of his aunt, the countess of Portsmouth, in 1762, and undertook negotiations in France for Bute's administration the following year, the only office he was to hold. The party particularly enjoyed hearing a concert given by guitars, harpsichord, flutes, fiddle, lute and archlute at a house belonging to a Count Jambaretti.

Brydone, Beckford, Fullarton and Glover were to return to the Lake of Geneva via the Simplon Pass after a short visit to *Isola Bella*, the beautiful island in Lake Maggiore. Staying at 'a poor inn' at Faragol (probably Fariolo) where there was a beautiful sixteen-year-old girl at a fireside spinning coarse fibre. Brydone made her blush when he took her hand and kissed it. The travellers felt that she was being forced to work by an old woman who was also in the room but they could not decide whether they ought to do anything about it. Leaving the village at five in the morning after complaining about the landlord's charges, the party watched their luggage being loaded, and having mounted their horses set off for Domodossola. The next day they passed a well-known and dangerous cascade with a 'profound abyss' on one side and crossed by a bridge, one of the numerous Ponte del Diavolo. At a height approaching 7,000 feet as measured above the level of Lake Maggiore, the wind was fierce, and after an excellent meal Brydone observed how the snow on the surrounding slopes had been blown about. The 'snow was carried up in the air and formed immense clouds that darkened the sky'. There were marks of an avalanche through a wood about 150 yards wide.

Leaving the Simplon Pass behind them the party eventually arrived at Brig in the Valais where Brydone regretted that they had not time enough to measure the height of a sugarloaf-shaped mountain seen from the village. Despite a problem with a carriage wheel they were soon at Sion, from where they returned to Lausanne, after exploring Martigny and St Maurice.[12] Recalling the expedition later, Brydone told Beckford, 'I remember, after making the tour of Savoy and the Lower Valais, every woman we met in

Switzerland appeared an angel. The same things happened when travelling through some parts of Germany; and you will easily recollect the surprising difference betwixt a beauty at Milan and one at Turin, although these places lie adjacent to each other'.[13]

From the young Beckford, Brydone was to learn something of the history and development of the West Indies, particularly sugar-growing in Jamaica. The production of sugar cane brought together at least two continents. In the eleventh and twelfth centuries, Northern Europe encountered its production in such islands as Sicily and Cyprus, and in the sixteenth century Spanish expeditions brought it to the New World, including Jamaica. It was the Dutch, however, who after bringing sugar production to the Lesser Antilles in the mid seventeenth century, introduced the crop to Barbados. Westmoreland, at the western extremity of Jamaica, with its sixty-nine sugar plantations, was one of the great sugar estates on the Island in the third quarter of the eighteenth century. William Beckford enthused about the salubrity of the climate and the fertility of the soil.

In the mid 1750s, the island's chief engineer and surveyor began the first detailed survey of Jamaica, and the governor saw the opportunity to order planters to undertake an inventory of their assets, an exercise which showed Richard Beckford working four plantations in fee simple and one in leasehold. Debts secured by bonds and promissory notes, along with monies in open account, were in the region of £83,300 (in Jamaican currency) whilst other assets included some £41,000 worth of goods shipped to England on consignment. His total worth amounted to £168,000 in local currency or £120,000 in Sterling. By 1766, the aggregate value of William Beckford's account was £12,700, the bulk of which was from the three sugar plantations. Output had, however, declined to less than a third of that in 1756, one possible cause being the conversion of the Smithfield and Hatfield sugar plantation into a cattle pen and the expiry of the lease on the Shrewsbury Estate.

During the summer of 1768, Brydone seems to have left his charges for a period and returned to Britain. Where he sailed from to reach Coleraine in Ireland on the afternoon of 21 May is not clear but he was immediately impressed by the size of the salmon and eel fisheries, and the methods of trapping used in the River Bann. He was soon exploring the Giant's Causeway which 'fully answered' his expectations, the coast being 'extremely bold and elevated' before dining with a Dr Monk. Lord Antrim's estate he described as reaching 'from the bar of Coleraine to near Belfast and is about twenty miles wide'. His estimate of the estate's worth which he put at £8,000 per year may have been provided by a tenant who entertained him. Then, towards the end of August 1768, Brydone records a journey by boat to Donaghadee, east of Belfast and at the top of the Ards Peninsula. The voyage which was 'very disagreeable' took twenty-two and a half hours and he found the inn, the 'Hillsborough Arms' quite 'indifferent'. In the dining room was a notice put up by his lordship, the first Earl of Hillsborough and scorned by patrons which explained that he had used his power as postmaster-general in Pitt's administration to double 'the price of passage for men and horses'. Dining in Belfast the next day a well-dressed gentleman advised him not to miss seeing Lough Neagh, by far the largest freshwater lough in the world, as he rode to Antrim at its north-easterly edge. Brydone concluded that it was 'good wheat and corn country' and there was plenty of limestone. The price of horses to Belfast was seven shillings and in Londonderry, some ten shillings. His 'good and reasonable' hostelry in Antrim was run by a remarkably handsome landlady. The traveller was delighted to hear that the Bishop was praised everywhere and that his friend Stuart (probably James Stewart 1742–1821) had won election for Co. Tyrone in the Irish House of Commons, especially as he had spent £1,000 on it.[14]

How Brydone spent much of 1769 in Scotland is not recorded, but by the end of September he was en route for Italy where he would re-engage with the earlier party, but without Beckford, and to accompany them to Naples and Sicily. After crossing the Channel to Boulogne on 10 October, he made his way to Paris, Lyons, Turin and Milan, where he arrived on 12 November. The city's Ambrosian Library, with its 50,000 printed volumes and 15,000 manuscripts, immediately fascinated the travellers and in the library's Hall of Paintings, some of Pieter Bruegel, the younger's works. The cathedral, however, was said to be 'the most enormous production of human folly'. Two days later when the party was in the vicinity of the river Po at Piacenza Brydone described a number of boats 'joined together by a very long rope at the end of which (was a) great ferry boat. By pointing the prow of each boat obliquely up the stream, the current plays on the sides of the boats, and without any other power, forces them across the river'. Again the cathedral came in for criticism unlike the quality of the cheeses, due to the excellent pasturage.

With the Apennines soon in sight the party followed the Taro, an ugly river so swollen that they spent half a day in an inn waiting for the water to go down. Eight miles from Parma, the duke's residence, the country was very rich, if 'abominably uniform'. There, Brydone met Padre Pauli, a rather grave and solemn Spaniard well-known for having written an account of the rise and fall of Paestum, and the antiquities of Pozzuoli (both in the south of Italy), and accepted an offer to visit his friends and relations in Lucca. Snow on the mountains prompted Brydone to push on to Reggio Emilia, 'a poor place' but larger than he anticipated, with houses built over arches similar to Modena, and one where the College of the Nobles offered excellent teaching for 250 young gentlemen.

Approaching Bologna, travellers were traditionally invited to see the place where Augustus, Mark Anthony and Marcus Lepidus had formed the second triumvirate in 43BC. Subsequently, Brydone's party visited the museum, described by Brydone as 'the best in the world ... (with) about thirty rooms, all rich in contents, with curious animals, birds and serpents'. He found a piece of stone exactly the same as that he saw at the Giant's Causeway. The party went on to hear a performance of *The Miller of Mansfield* which was 'excellently rendered'.[15] Brydone called it an opera by Baldassare Galluppi, and named the singers involved, which suggests that the Italian took the London piece and adapted it for Italian audiences. Leaving the city on their way to Florence, the travellers passed through Pietramala where Brydone and his companions dug a sample of earth and found soil a foot down of a blue and green colour 'smelling of turpentine'. Their guide set alight to it and 'it burned with a great noise, but (was) not so hot as common fire'. Our tutor thought it might be naphtha, as had been found by Jean-Baptiste Tarvernier around the shore of the Caspian Sea.

The travellers arrived at Florence towards the end of November where the approach was 'glorious', the triumphal arch 'very fine', and the view from the top of the square tower 'perfect'. Brydone was to favour Hellenistic sculptures over the work of Michelangelo and be irritated by the 'ridiculous harlequin appearance' of the different marbles used in the cathedral's entrance. Pictures by Raphael, Louis Carracci, Guido, Rubens, Bruegel and Michelangelo were in Brydone's opinion 'infinitely surpassed' by Titian's 'Venus of Urbino'. Leaving behind the galleries which they recognised as the 'greatest in the world', the party was soon compelled to leave Florence for Siena, the third town of Tuscany, thirty miles through the Apennines. After an overnight stop, on 28 November they continued on to Acquapendente and Viterbo, 'the capital of St Peter's patrimony with about 10,000 souls', as Brydone described it. The travellers were now within 100 miles of Rome, and some 160 miles from their destination, Naples.

Near the end of the town of Ronciglione, Brydone recorded his discovery of a deep romantic glen with a series of cascades and caverns, many inhabited. 'They pretend' he wrote, 'they were miraculously formed there for the first Christians in the time of persecutions, but if they were so, the miracle workers performed their operations with edge tools, for the marks of them are everywhere very conspicuous'. From Lake Vico, a caldera lake amid the area's famous beech forest, the travellers found themselves on the very irregular Emilian Way, the ancient route from Rome to Northern Italy. The country was a 'melancholy spectacle'. The finest fields were 'overgrown with brushwood and briars' and in some districts there was not a house to be seen for miles. Peasants were obliged to sell their produce at prices set by the Farmer's General, a practice which had led to some abandoning farming altogether. Perhaps as the result of a change of plan, or to suit the arrangements made by their friends in Naples, the travellers were to leave their visit to Rome until later. They were there for only two days at the beginning of December and slept the following night at Velletri, where it was difficult to find beds. The inhabitants of

Rome, Brydone concluded, 'look unhealthy and appear indolent', and 'the whole of the Campagna de Roma is now so entirely depopulated that so far as the eye can reach you can hardly see a cottage'. However, he praised the present Pope for his good sense in encouraging trade and hoped that economic recovery might yet be achieved.

The party's eventual arrival in Naples coincided with the start of 1770. It was then the third largest city in Europe. Ferdinand IV, the third son of Charles III of Spain, was on the throne and presiding over a golden age of art, music, science and literature. Furthermore, it was to be a remarkable year in the annals of North European exploration and literary travel books. Vesuvius erupted periodically during this decade, regularly inviting scientists and artists to inspect this natural phenomenon. The first four days of January saw Brydone preoccupied with the volcano which was 'entirely covered with snow' and 'an uncommon quantity of smoke issued from the crater'. A large cloud rested over Pompeii and the Torre del Greco. On one occasion he saw 'a bright blaze dart out of the cloud immediately above the crater … very like the firing of a cannon'. Visiting the circuit of Pompeii which had become 'vineyards, gardens and cornfields', he described the progress that had been made unearthing the main street and the prison at the barracks, commenting on the humorous style of some of the paintings. There was even in a skeleton, Brydone wrote 'an air of tranquillity and resignation'. Herculaneum was buried under 'a solid rock of lava 60–80 feet deep' and according to Brydone the expense of clearing it away would be 'enormous'.

The travellers steadily moved into the Neapolitan social scene, with evening meetings with Lord Tilbury, Madame André and Count Kaunitz, the last being in all likelihood the Austrian statesman and diplomat.[16] Other hosts with whom they dined were Mr Methuen[17] and the Danish ambassador. A performance of Handel's *Alexander's Feast*, in Italian, was given at the home of William Hamilton. The soul of the British colony at this time was Kenneth Mackenzie (Lord Fortrose), MP for Bute and Caithness and later a fellow of the Royal Society, who together with Hamilton and his lady had not been deterred from making an expedition to Sicily the previous summer. They returned 'much delighted with it', but in a letter Hamilton wrote to the Secretary of the Royal Society he admitted 'no great stress should be laid upon these observations, as the many inconveniences we laboured under, and the little practice we had in such nice operations, must necessarily have rendered them very inaccurate'.[18] A diplomat and art collector, Hamilton had arrived in Naples in 1764 to take up his post as ambassador at the Court when Naples was recovering from famine and plague.[19]

It was King Ferdinand's birthday on 12 January, with a great gala at court and 'the queen loaded with diamonds'. Describing people's clothing and appearance at court, Brydone found it 'very pleasing, and the lack of stiff formality … also pleasant'. The travellers spent the whole of the next day with the padre (father) in charge of the *Capodimonte*, a vast palace built by King Charles III of Spain, a little to the north of the city. There, they inspected medals, cameos and paintings. Brydone was especially enamoured by his discovery of a collection of telescopes with very different focuses and magnifying powers which the father had put together, and delighted to be made 'a present of both his books of microscopical observations and the history of Vesuvius'. The next few days were generally cold and Vesuvius quiet but three consecutive nights at the end of January produced 'considerable explosions' and the noise of the mountain was 'very audible'.

It was around nine o'clock in the morning on the first of February that Brydone and his two charges set out to climb Vesuvius, arriving at the top by 1 p.m. There were violent rumblings and explosions during the ascent and near the top the party encountered serious falls of large stones which made them take shelter and run below shelves of lava. In his report, Brydone spoke of three Irish gentlemen, Messrs Malone, King and Tavisden, being so terrified by the falls of rock that they ran away, advising Brydone that his life would be in danger if he went on. He was clearly very frightened and felt a degree of horror 'beyond what any other object had ever inspired'. In his journal he reported that 'I ventured to the top of an elevation near the brim of the great mouth and got a clear view down into the bowels of the mountain which infinitely exceeds all the descriptions I have ever yet heard of either Hell or Purgatory; an immense ocean of fire struggling on all sides to burst out and throwing up waves like that of a sea in a storm'. Retreating, Brydone found their guide praying to St Januarius, the patron saint of Naples. Having gathered a variety of salts, and admiring the scene for upwards of three hours, the travellers set out for Portici, a little to the south-east, and returned to Naples about 8 p.m.[20]

There were almost perpetual explosions from the mountain till the middle of March when the travellers observed thin white smoke rising on the north side that reached almost down to the valley. It was there, in Brydone's opinion, that the eruption had started. The party stayed up all night to watch. The following day, Brydone set off with Messrs Jewl and Hanbury to the Hermitage, two men about whom little is known, which was reached after some three hours.[21] The party left their mules and went on foot to look for lava. This was regarded as very dangerous by the locals. They found the valley between Monte Somma (itself some six miles east of Naples) and Vesuvius, a 'stream of liquid fire'. The guides were frightened by explosions but the party was sure there was more to see and bribed them to continue. A half a mile further on they found a new river of fire, which Brydone described in the following terms: 'We came close to its banks, and indeed the appearance was very terrible. It was sweeping away everything before it, and bushes and shrubs and trees took fire and were consumed immediately on its approach. Nay, they were often in a blaze at several feet distance from the fire'. They had to climb up the side of Mount Somma to escape the flow and heat. When Brydone asked his guide whether anyone had been killed by eruptions in his time, the man said he had heard of one mad Englishman being stifled by going too close.[22]

It was early summer before Brydone and his charges were ready to contemplate leaving for Sicily. Writing to 'Dear Beckford' on 14 May, our tutor recalled having heard the Jamaican sugar planter regret that despite all 'his peregrinations across Europe' he had always neglected the island of Sicily, and spent much of his time 'running over the old beaten track, and in examining the thread-bare subjects of Italy and France'. The itinerary had clearly been a matter of much cogitation and debate, not least since the Italians considered it impossible on account of there being no inns, and

Brydone told Beckford that 'we intend to profit from this hint of yours. Fullarton has been urging me to it with all that ardour which a new prospect of acquiring knowledge ever inspires in him; and Glover, your old acquaintance, has promised to accompany us'.[23]

Although Brydone's party enjoyed their time in Naples, they became increasingly frustrated by the weather. It had been 'abundantly warm' with sudden storms of wind and rain almost every day, such that ships had been unable to leave the harbour for lengthy periods. The party had originally planned to go by land to Regium, and from there to cross over to Messina, but the danger of *banditti* in Calabria and Apulia, and the prospect of wretched accommodation, made them relinquish this. Brydone was convinced that the physicians who had advised him had made a mistake so far as the climate was concerned. Naples was certainly one of the warmest in Italy but it was 'as certainly one of the most inconstant'. From what they had observed, the climate disagreed with 'the greatest part of our valetudinarians (those anxious about their health) but more particularly with the gouty people who have all found themselves better at Rome'. With the wind blowing continually for more than a week, their gaiety and good spirits were in danger of being blown away. A degree of lassitude, 'both to the body and mind', was creeping over everyone. The natives were not exempt from the effects of the wind, declaring that 'a Neapolitan lover avoids his mistress with the utmost care in the time of the sirocco, and the indolence it inspires is almost sufficient to extinguish every passion'.

As a result, Brydone was soon examining the cause of 'this abominable wind', despite finding that it made no difference to the barometer reading. Other experiments led him to the conclusion that 'the best antidote against the effects of the sirocco' was sea-bathing. Viscount Fortrose provided 'a large commodious boat for this purpose'. They met every morning at eight o'clock and rowed about a half a mile out to sea, where they stripped and plunged into the water. Three or four of his Lordship's ten watermen 'generally go in with us, to pick up stragglers and secure us from all accidents. They dive with ease to the depth of forty, and sometimes fifty feet, and bring up shell-fish ... we have likewise learned to strip in the

water, and find it no difficult matter' and 'I am fully persuaded ...
that in the case of shipwreck we should greatly have the advantage
over those who had never practised it'.[24]

Afterwards, an English breakfast was taken with Lord Fortrose,
and followed by a 'little concert' with Emanuele Barbella, 'the
sweetest fiddle in Italy', leading the band. A composer himself, the
brilliant circle around Lord Fortrose included the music historian
Charley Burney who was to publish his highly acclaimed *The
Present State of Music in France and Italy* in May 1771. Interestingly,
Pietro Fabris's painting shows Kenneth MacKenzie presiding over a
concert party, with William Hamilton playing viola, the composer
Gaetano Pugnani, violin, and none other than the visiting Mozarts
providing the keyboard accompaniment. The young Wolfgang
is at the octave spinet and his father Leopold at the harpsichord.
Fortrose's balletic stance, copied by one of his dogs, suggests he
may have been conducting.

Amid his preparations Brydone had to ready his scientific mind
for the benefit of his charges and, at the same time, prepare to make
a full written account of the visit for the eventual benefit of his
friend Beckford at least. He was to show far more than his prowess
as a travel writer and take the reader into the worlds of invention,
electricity, botany, astronomy and vulcanology. All of Brydone's
faculties came into play when he was in an analytical mood, and
long before pen was put to paper. The subject was examined from
the point of its origin, design, development, age and purpose, with
stress put on the extent to which it may or had been changed. It was
as if his mind sought third or even fourth dimensions; anything that
might prise open a diagnosis. Oddities, the unexpected unusual or
the illogical delighted him, inspiring his sense of fun. He examined,
for example, crucifixes on sale in a Sicilian market and immediately
noticed that the amber from which they were made was 'electrical
in a high degree; powerfully attracting feathers, straws, and other
light bodies; somewhat emblematical', as Brydone said, of what
they represented. Some pieces of this amber contained flies and
other insects, curiously preserved in its substance, 'and we were
not a little entertained' he wrote, 'with the ingenuity of one of the
artists who ... left a large blue-bottle fly, with its wings expanded,

exactly over the head of a saint, to represent, he told us, *lo spirito santo* descending upon him'.[25]

Brydone took pleasure in scientific speculation, and was devoted to all manner of measurements, taking particular interest in thermometer and barometer readings. He wanted to account for things and find out how they worked, as the following two chapters will demonstrate. One moment, Brydone would recommend the wearing of 'a waistcoat of the finest flannel', covered by another of silk and producing 'a kind of electric atmosphere around the body that might possibly be one of the best preservatives against the effect of damps'. The next, he would be suggesting that ladies given to wearing long, erect hairpins or wire cap frames should 'ground (earth) themselves during thunderstorms', or be wondering whether childbirth might not be easier at sea-level or in warmer climates. As an ex-military man, Brydone could even spare a moment to advise soldiers to carry a small mirror, not for personal beautification, but with which to practice on sunny days setting distant targets on fire 'by the convergence of the reflections'.[26]

By 15 May the Sicilian expedition was under way, with Brydone and his party aboard the vessel *Charming Molly* off the island of Capri and heading for Messina. A 'fine and brisk tramontane' (or north wind) had replaced the sirocco. After eating a hearty supper at the home of a Mr Walter, and drinking plentifully of his excellent burgundy, they departed from Naples around five o'clock, firing their farewell signals to their friends on shore. As it got dark, the captain made a bowl of grog and promised them a happy voyage. By the morning of 17 May, it was a different story: an 'execrable contrary wind and vile heaving waves' meant that the party had been groaning to one another from their beds for twenty-four hours. It was three o'clock in the afternoon, however, before Stromboli and its adjacent newly emerged island, came in sight, and the ship steadied. Three days later they had a distinct view of the crater, different from Vesuvius and others around the bay as it seemed to be the only one that burned without ceasing. For Beckford's benefit, Brydone described the commercial significance of the Lipari Islands; the great quantities of alum, sulphur, nitre, cinnabar, and most sorts of fruits, particularly raisins, currants and figs in great perfection, which brought in considerable revenue for the King. Then, after recalling that it was Homer who had Aeolus controlling the winds through which they had sailed, Brydone reminded Beckford (another Greek student) that the poets had also placed the forge of Vulcan in Hiera, one of these islands.

The travellers were in calm waters by 19 May, and within half a mile of the coast of Sicily which was 'low, but finely variegated'. On the Calabrian side was the famous rock of Scylla, with Cape Pylorus on the Sicilian, and the straits of Faro between. Brydone told Beckford that the approach to Messina, although not as grand as Naples, was still 'one of the finest that can be imagined'. They were 'just opposite to Cape Pylorus' when they were obliged to wait some hours for the tide to turn. The anchor was eventually cast in the afternoon but not before they discovered that the name of one of their servants had been omitted from their bills of health. According to the captain, a long period of quarantine would certainly result if he was discovered. They 'had just time to get him wrapped up in a hammock and shut down below the hatches with orders not to stir in case of a search'. The fellow was 'in his hole till dark' on account of the consul and people from the health office staying on board 'much longer than we could have wished'. However, they were soon ashore and lodged in 'the most wretched of Inns' – any house appeared 'a palace, and any bit of dry land a paradise'.[27]

It seems that Brydone had intended to post each letter he wrote to Beckford, living north of Naples on the Italian mainland, whenever it proved possible. In the event, there were thirty-eight such items, some bundled up with others and read by his friend at his leisure, whilst a single complete epistolary account of the party's expedition through Sicily and Malta would be published. Writing from Messina on 20 May, Brydone told the story of the whirlpool of Charybdis. He found Aristotle's description of it heavy going and quoted a piece from Homer's *Odyssey* for Beckford's benefit: 'Dire Scylla there a scene of horror forms, and here Charybdis fills the deep with storms'. The scientist wanted to know the causes of such 'an intestine and irregular motion', to say nothing of its sound as 'a voracious sea-monster, perpetually roaring for its prey'. Ships were forced to go as near as possible to the coast of Calabria to avoid the suction generated, a thought which led Brydone to tell his friend about a number of galleys and galliots which had sailed out of Messina's 'beautiful harbour' that morning. They were a picturesque sight 'their oars moving all together, with the greatest regularity … nine or ten men to each oar … the hardest work you can imagine'. Then, Brydone characteristically added for Beckford's edification that 'these wretches are chained to their oars, and sleep every night on the bare benches without anything to throw over them'.

Having found that the governor, the Prince of Villa Franca, was away at his country house, the party was unable to pay their respects or deliver their letters of introduction. After dinner that evening, the party was taken by the British deputy-consul (a Sicilian) to a number of convents where they were received by nuns 'with great politeness and affability'. Brydone described how they conversed for some hours 'but none of them had sincerity enough to acknowledge the unhappiness of their position', adding that he had experienced something similar in Portugal. All pretended to be happy and contented, but 'some of them had a soft melancholy in their faces which gave the lie to their words'. On leaving the convent they observed a great concourse of people on Mount Pellegrino outside the city. The consul told them it was a celebration in honour of St Francis, and an image of the saint soon made his appearance, being carried through the crowd before being returned to his chapel. Brydone went on to tell Beckford that 'the saint performs a number of miracles every day', adding with a smile, 'to all those who have an abundance of money and abundance of faith'. His ministers were, however, 'only a set of poor, greasy capuchins' who did not seem to have enriched themselves.

Out walking the following day, the party observed flowers much admired in English gardens along with a variety of flowering shrubs. The fields about Messina were covered with the richest white clover, intermixed with a variety of aromatic plants. Unfortunately for Brydone, he found his copy of the history of Sicily published by a Dominican friar in 1558, did not confirm what he had been told, how salt produced by the heat of the sun emitted a smell something like violets which perfumed the sea-shore. The party was about to 'sup upon steaks of *pisce spada*' (or swordfish) when Brydone noticed that the sword of the fish they were to eat was 'about four feet long ... a formidable weapon ... not unlike a Highland broad sword'.[28]

With the absent Prince of Villa Franca now returned, the party was given an audience and received with 'a good deal of state'. The governor decided that his wisest course of action was to provide them with guards for their protection during the forthcoming journey, men they might entirely rely on 'who were people of the most determined resolution'. They were shown off, clothed in the Prince's livery of yellow and green, with silver lace, and wore a badge of their honourable order. An 'upper servant' of the Prince also ordered their muleteers to be ready at daybreak the next day. It was at this point in his report, however, that Brydone asked Beckford to consider who these 'trusty guards' really were – 'the most daring, and most hardened villains, who in any other country would have been broken upon the wheel'. A local banker, a 'very sensible man', had told him that in the east of the island 'it had been found impracticable to extirpate the *banditti* on account of the mountainous terrain. In fact, magistrates had often been obliged to protect them, and even to pay them court, as they were so determined and vindictive. On the other hand it was never known that any person who had put himself under their protection had cause to repent it. Those of their number who 'enlisted in the service of society' were 'known and respected by the other *banditti* all over the island'.

Telling Beckford that the party was almost ready to leave Messina, Brydone felt he could not do so without paying homage to Count of Jerba (1245–1305) in freeing the island from the yoke of the Saracens. He had 'fixed the seat of government in Palermo and put the political system of the island upon a sound basis'. Suspecting that a 'most extraordinary phenomenon', often observed near Messina, was similar to the *aurora borealis*, Brydone also explained that 'in the heat of summer, after the sea and air have been much agitated by the winds and a perfect calm succeeds, there appears, about the time of dawn, in that part of the heavens over the Straits, a great variety of singular forms, some at rest and some moving about with great velocity'. Linking it to an electrical cause, he told Beckford that 'the air, strongly impregnated with this matter, was confined betwixt two ridges of mountains' being 'at the same time, exceedingly agitated from below by the violence of the current', which produced a great variety of forms.

Promising to leave his epistle for Beckford at the next post, and to write again once the party reached Catania, if they escaped 'unhurt from all the perils of Etna', it was *Adieu*.

CHAPTER 4

# In Eastern Sicily and Malta (May 1770)

By 22 May Brydone was able to tell Beckford that the party had enjoyed 'a delightful journey' down the rich, well-cultivated east coast of Sicily to the area around Tauromenium (or Taormina). They had left Messina early in the morning with a baggage-train made up of six mules for themselves and servants, and a further two for their baggage. He admitted it made 'no contemptible appearance when you call to mind our front and rear guard'. Two great Drawcansir figures, in the mould of the blustering bully character in the second Duke of Buckingham's satirical play, *The Rehersal*, were armed from head to foot, with a sword worn at their side, two enormous pistols, and a long arquebus. 'They recounted', Brydone wrote, an 'abundance of wonderful stories of robberies and murders' so that he was persuaded that 'they themselves were the principal actors'. The cost of dinner for eleven men, including three muleteers, and feed for ten mules and horses, did not amount to half a guinea. With umbrellas holding off some of the heat, and an occasional swim, the party explored Tauromenium's ancient Greek theatre where the seating generally faced towards Etna, and had boxes reserved for women. Their guards found rooms for them, not in the town but in Giardini, a village at the foot of the mountain where they had 'an excellent supper and good wine'.[1]

Having perhaps written excessively about the theatre, Brydone told Beckford he would try to avoid unnecessary 'mensuration of antique walls' although he despaired of success. He admitted to his friend that few things in writing were more difficult than *s'emparer de l'imagination*. The objective was to 'make ourselves masters of the reader's imagination, to carry it along with us, through every scene, and make it in a manner congenial with our own'. Every prospect should open on the reader 'with the same light, and arising in the same colours, and at the same instant too, as upon us'. Where descriptions failed in this, 'the pleasure of reading them must be very trivial'.[2]

The travelling tutor was soon already 'two days in arrears' with his record on account of the party's exhausting climb of Mount Etna. After another early start, and leaving the Catania road to their left, the party went through the first region of Etna as they ascended the mountain, where 'there had been eruptions of fire all over this country at a great distance from the summit'. In the village of Piedmonte were 'craters and stones of a large size scattered all around'. The road was difficult and the first ten miles 'took near four hours to travel it'. Brydone's barometer reading showed a fall from 29 degrees and 10 lines on the coast to 27 degrees and 3 lines. The Fahrenheit thermometer 'made by Mr Adams in London' gave a reading of 73 degrees. People were 'extremely inquisitive and curious' to know the reason for their visit and gave them 'an excellent supper and good wine'.

Following an aqueduct which the Prince of Palagonia had built 'at great expense to supply Piedmonte with water', the party found the ascent steeper as they arrived at a woody region.[3] Part of it had been destroyed in 1755 when a torrent of boiling water issued from the crater during an eruption but their 'conductors' (guides) were able to show them something of the recovering 'verdure and vegetation'. The common opinion, Brydone told his friend, was 'that this water was raised by the power of suction through some communication betwixt the volcano and the sea, the absurdity of which is too glaring to need a refutation'. He imagined that it might be accounted for either by a stream of lava falling into one of the valleys of snow, or more probably, some melted snow lodged in a cavern on the mountain till the excessive heat from the lava below burst its sides, so producing this phenomenon.

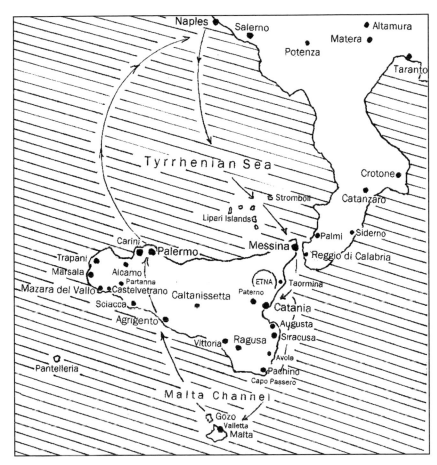

Sketch plan of the route taken by Brydone in 1770 in Sicily and Malta.

Climbing through woods of cork and evergreen oak, five or six miles further on, the party came across a number of great chestnut trees, some of enormous size. According to Brydone, one, called Il Castagno dei Cento Cavalli (the Chestnut Tree of a Hundred Horses) by Jean-Pierre Houël the French artist, was 'by much the most celebrated'. Glover, whose name is only mentioned four times in Brydone's account, measured it separately and found it had a girth of 204 feet. If it had once been 'united in one solid stem', said Brydone, 'it must, with justice indeed, have been looked upon as a very wonderful phenomenon in the vegetable world'. Turning to the climate of the region, the tutor found the barometer had now fallen to 26 degrees and 5 lines which meant 'an elevation of very near four thousand feet; equivalent', as he told Beckford, and 'in the opinion of some French academicians, to eighteen or twenty degrees of latitude in the formation of a climate'. The high nitrate content of the Etna ash also contributed greatly to 'the luxuriance' of the vegetation, and the air too, created a constant supply of salt – the 'food of vegetables'.

At sunset, the group descended to Jacireale (Acireale) in the valley of the Demons where, after what had been a very tiring journey, they took lodgings at a Dominican convent. Brydone had been especially surprised by the vast extent of 'the last lava we crossed before our arrival here … I thought we never should have had done with it; it certainly is not less than six or seven miles broad, and appears in many places to be of an enormous depth'. It was a realisation that was to influence his subsequent thinking greatly. He had been keen to see what form the lava took when it met the sea, discovering that it 'had formed a large black high promontory where before it was deep water'. Canon Recupero, the elderly historiographer of Etna whose *Storia naturale e generale dell'Etna* was to be published in 1817 after his death, told Brydone that the very same lava was mentioned by Diodorus Siculus, and that it burst from Etna at the time of the second Punic War (218–201 BC). In the lowest part of Etna the harvest was almost over but near the 'confines of the *Regione Sylvosa*' it would not begin for several weeks. Along the road, however, the reapers abused the travellers 'from all quarters; and more excellent blackguards' Brydone had yet to meet, but their guides were 'a full match for them' and 'we could not help admiring the volubility and natural elocution with which they spoke'.[4]

It was 25 May when the party set out from Jaci, as it was known locally, to Catania, and Brydone began another letter to Beckford. Eight mountains formed by eruption, some very high, and others 'of a great compass' were counted. Once at the 'noble and beautiful' ancient city of Catania, founded in the eighth century BC, Brydone and his friends 'were amazed to find … there was no such thing as an inn. They were taken to a house they called such but it was 'so wretchedly mean and dirty' that they were obliged to look elsewhere. However, with the assistance of Canon Recupero, to whom they had letters of introduction, they soon found themselves comfortably lodged in a convent. The Prince of Biscari and governor of Catania, a 'person of very great merit and distinction' whose family had ruled from the late seventeenth century, returned the visit they paid him and made the party the 'most engaging offers'.

Recupero, who obligingly became what Brydone called 'our Cicerone' (a word for a guide which came into occasional use in the seventeenth century) was soon showing the party several curious items of antiquity which were so 'shaken and shattered' by the mountain that hardly any were unbroken. Nevertheless, Brydone explained to Beckford how some geologists had 'pierced through seven distinct lavas one under the other, the surfaces of which were parallel, and most of them covered with a thick bed of rich earth' and 'the eruption which formed the lowest of these lavas, if we may be allowed to reason from analogy, must have flowed from the mountain at least 14,000 years ago'. The canon admitted to Brydone that he had been 'exceedingly embarrassed by these discoveries in writing the history of the mountain – that 'Moses hangs like a dead weight upon him' so blunting all his zeal for enquiry. Brydone concluded that the priest did not have the conscience to make the mountain he was writing about as young as Moses had made the world. The bishop had already warned Recupero to 'be on his guard, and not to pretend to be 'a better natural historian than Moses'.[5]

The following morning the party visited the house and museum of the prince. Its antiques were only inferior to those of the King of Naples at Portici. His family, which comprised the princess his wife, a son and daughter, whom Brydone described as happy, resembled nothing he had met with on the continent. They seemed to 'emulate each other in benignity'. Soon afterwards, the party discovered 'a convent of fat Benedictine monks, who were determined to make sure of a paradise, at least in this world, if not in the other'. A visitation 'to these sons of humility, temperance and mortification' followed, in the company of Recupero, where they were received and entertained with 'great civility and politeness'. Their museum was only a little inferior to that of the governor and the monks' apartments were 'much more magnificent'. The walks were broad and paved with flints, with vegetation benefiting from soil that must have been brought from a distance as the surface of lava there was 'as hard and bare as a piece of iron'.[6]

Several days of visits followed, to another great theatre, the ruins of an aqueduct, eighteen miles long, and the ruins of several temples, and were combined with preparations for what Brydone called, 'one of the greatest objects' of the expedition – 'the examination of Mount Etna ... the venerable father of mountains'. Recupero warned him, however, that the season was not far enough advanced yet which would probably mean that they would not get near the summit. Nevertheless, the travellers set off at day-break on 27 May and at Nicolosi, twelve miles up the mountain, their landlord gave them an account of the fate suffered by the beautiful country at Hybla, nearby on the southern slope. Recounting it, Brydone said 'It was so celebrated for its fertility, and particularly for its honey, that it was called *Mel Passi* (or a stopping place for honey), till it was overwhelmed by the lava of Etna; and having then become totally barren, by a kind of pun its name was changed to *Mal Passi*. In a second eruption ... it soon reassumed its ancient beauty and fertility, and for many years was called *Bel Passi*'.[7] It was with considerable difficulty, Brydone told Beckford, that he persuaded the local inhabitants that 'they had not come to search for hidden treasures'. Two men followed him, and 'kept a close eye on every step' he took. They were, he said, 'likewise a good deal surprised to see me pull out of my pocket a magnetical needle and a small electrometer which I had prepared at Catania to examine the electrical state of the air; and I was at first afraid they should have taken me for a conjuror ... but luckily that idea did not strike them'.

An hour and a half later, after walking over barren ash and lava, they were again in the *Regione Sylvosa*, a 'heavenly spot'. The woody region went on for eight or nine miles and that night the party passed through little more than a half of it before arriving at their lodgings which was 'no other than a large cave, formed by one of the most ancient ... lavas', called the *Spelonca del Capriole* or the Goat's Cave. As soon as it was dark the party retired, but they were awake at eleven o'clock after a nap. Melting down some snow they boiled their tea kettle and made a hurried meal to prepare themselves for the remaining part of their expedition. 'We were nine in number', Brydone recorded, 'for we had our three servants, the Cyclops (our conductor), and two men to take care of our mules'. Their conductor took them 'over antres vast and deserts wild' (a slight misquotation by Brydone from Othello) where 'scarce human foot had ever trod'.[8]

Soon the prospect before them was an expanse of snow and ice that alarmed them exceedingly, and 'almost staggered our resolution'. The high mountain was 'vomiting out torrents of smoke' and appeared altogether inaccessible. Their diffidence was increased further when the Cyclops told them that 'the surface ... being hot below, melted the snow in particular spots and formed pools of water where it was impossible to foresee ... danger'. He, nevertheless, told the party 'after taking a great draught of brandy' that they had plenty of time and could take as many rests as they pleased, that 'the snow could be little more than seven miles, and that (they) certainly should be able to pass it before sunrise'. Accordingly, each man took 'a dram of liqueur which soon removed every objection'.

They were encouraged by the thought that the emperor Adrian (Hadrian) and the philosopher Plato had undertaken the same climb. Moreover, just before dawn they arrived at the ruins of an ancient structure called *Il Torre del Filosofo*, supposed to have been built by the Greek philosopher Empedocles who had taken up his habitation there to be able to study the mountain better. Others supposed it to have been the ruin of a temple to Venus. There, Brydone told his friend, 'a fresh application to our liqueur bottle' was made and, with the sky clear and the vault of heaven appearing 'in awful majesty and splendour', the mood changed. The party observed that the number of stars seemed to 'be infinitely increased, and the light of each of them appeared brighter than usual. The whiteness of the milky way was like a pure flame that shot across the heavens, and with the naked eye we could observe clusters of stars that were invisible in the region below'. They did not recall passing through 'ten or twelve thousand feet of gross vapour that blunts and confuses every ray before it reaches the surface of the earth'. Brydone exclaimed with a flourish, 'What a glorious situation for an observatory!

Had Empedocles had the eyes of Galileo, what discoveries must he have made!'

Arriving at a place where there was no snow, and there was a 'warm and comfortable vapour' from the mountain, the travellers were induced to make another halt, allowing the usual thermometer readings to be taken before they left for the summit which was three hundred yards away. Looking at 'the most wonderful and most sublime sight in nature' Brydone immediately had to admit that 'description must ever fall short ... neither is there on the surface of this globe any one point that unites so many ... sublime objects – the immense elevation from the surface of the earth, drawn as it were to a single point, without any neighbouring mountain for the senses and imagination to rest upon, and recover from their astonishment (on) their way down to the world'. The body of the sun was seen rising from the ocean, the islands of Lipari, Panarea, Alicudi, Strombolo and Volcano appeared under their feet, and they 'looked down on the whole of Sicily as on a map'. Every river, Brydone said, could be traced 'through all its windings, from source to its mouth'. In Malta, nearly two hundred miles away, he said, 'they perceive all the eruptions from the second region' (where agriculture was possible). Interestingly, Brydone did not know the height of Etna, saying that it would be easy to 'calculate the extent of its visible horizon; and vice versa, if its visible horizon was exactly ascertained, it would be an easy matter to calculate the height of the mountain'.

The party then turned its attention to the fourth region of the mountain, the region of fire. The immense crater was about three and a half miles in circumference, 'shelving down on each side'. From many places, volumes of sulphurous smoke issued and near the centre of the crater was the great mouth of the volcano, 'that tremendous gulf so celebrated in all ages'. It was with a mixture of pleasure and pain that they left 'this awful scene' and although in hope of seeing a thunderstorm 'under their feet', something which Brydone had seen in the Alps, the wind had risen and clouds were beginning to gather. At this point, and having been told of the effect produced by discharging a gun at the top of mountains, our tutor discharged his pistol and was 'a good deal surprised to find that instead of increasing the sound, it was almost reduced to nothing'. It sounded like 'the stroke of a stick on a door', showing that the thinner the air was, the less was its impression on the ear, 'for in a vacuum there (could) be no noise'.

During the descent, Brydone's leg folded under him while running over the ice, spraining it so violently that 'in a few minutes it swelled to a great degree' and, as he told Beckford, 'I found myself unable to put my foot to the ground. Every muscle and fibre was at the same time chilled and froze by the extreme cold, the thermometer continuing still below the point of congelation'. He lay on the ice for a considerable time in great agony, telling Beckford that 'in these exalted regions, it was impossible to have a horse or carriages of any kind, and your poor philosopher was obliged to hop on one leg, with two men supporting him, for several miles over the snow'. Meanwhile, the two 'wags' (Fullarton and Glover) enjoyed alleging that he had left the greatest part of his philosophy behind him – for 'the use of Empedocles's heirs and successors'. Happy to get back to his mule, Brydone could only describe the bed of leaves waiting for him in a cave (*Spelonca del Capriole*) near the village of Nicolosi, some twelve miles up the mountain, as 'paradise'. The travellers left the summit about six o'clock and it was eight at night before they reached Catania where they immediately went to bed. Brydone was confined to his room for some time as 'the abominable sprain' held him 'fast by the foot' and he was 'obliged to drop all further thoughts of climbing mountains'.[9]

After 'contemplating that electricity would probably soon be considered as the great vivifying principle of nature', Brydone told his friend about several travellers in the Alps who 'were caught amongst thunderclouds, and to their utter astonishment, found their bodies so full of electrical fire, that spontaneous flashes darted from their fingers'. Fearing that Beckford would laugh at the story he was to tell, Brydone assured him that he was never more serious in his life before describing how an amiable lady of his acquaintance, Mrs Douglas of Kelso, 'almost lost her life by one of those caps mounted on wire'. Standing at an open window during a thunderstorm, 'the lightning was attracted by the wire, and the cap was burnt to ashes' but happily her hair was in its natural state, without powder, pomatum or pins' so preventing the fire from being conducted to her head. It doubtless reminded him of how near he probably came to disaster when conducting his own youthful experiments. Then, in what was Brydone's eleventh letter to Beckford, the invalid complimented their 'facetious and agreeable companion', Canon Recupero, for being kind enough to sit with him a good deal during his 'confinement'. Both men went on to enjoy a long valedictory discussion about Etna's lesser-known caves and lakes, its former wild beasts, its flowers and trees, the *Palma Christi*, from whose seed castor oil was made, the 'esteemed' horses and cattle of the region along with its porcupines and land tortoises.[10]

It was the last day of May 1770 when Fullarton, Glover and Brydone set sail aboard a felucca, a traditional sailing boat with a crew of two or three and one or two lateen sails, from Catania for 'the mighty Syracuse', some 30 to 40 miles away. The view of Etna from the sea was 'more complete and satisfactory' than anywhere on the island. They passed the mouths of several rivers, the first being the Simeto or the river of St Paul, and after a few hours sailing the city of Augusta came in view, with its impressive fortifications. Some time before their arrival in Syracuse, the sea fell to a dead calm, and they brought on board a fine turtle which had been fast asleep on the surface. Although their intention to cook it was frustrated when the creature made an escape, it did not stop Fullarton asking Brydone whether he would prefer to eat 'a little of the calipash or the calipee', the former being an edible, gelatinous, greenish substance below the upper shell of a turtle, and the latter a similar but yellow substance lying beneath the lower shell. When both men called for *pazienza* and shrugged their shoulders, Glover exploded, saying that 'all the *pazienza* on earth was not equal to a good turtle'.

They rowed round the greatest part of the walls of Syracuse without seeing a soul, the very walls, as Brydone told Beckford, that had been the terror of Roman arms, 'from whence Archimedes had battered their fleets, and with his engines lifted their vessels out of the sea, and dashed them against the rocks'. There were no inns as usual and, having searched all the monasteries and religious fraternities for beds and found them 'wretchedly mean and dirty', they bedded down on some straw, only to be 'eaten up by vermin of every kind'. Their letters for Count Gaetano produced no offers of accommodation although in other respects he was to show them every civility. A gentleman of good sense, who had written several treatises on the antiquities of Sicily, he also gave them 'the use of his carriage, in explaining the ruins ... and letters of recommendation for Malta'.

Despite the catacombs, 'a great work: little inferior either to those of Rome or Naples', and the celebrated fountain of Arethusa dedicated to Diana whose temple was near by, and being shown 'the spot where Archimedes' house stood', it did not take long for the party to lose interest in Syracuse. Of all the wretched places they had seen, it was the most wretched. Its inhabitants were extremely poor and beggarly, producing a dismal contrast with the city's former opulence and power – *sic transit gloria mundi*. Not being able to find a table upon which to write in the 'dirty hovel' where they were living, Brydone had been obliged to 'lay a form over the back of two chairs' as a *succedaneum* (a substitute). Worst of all, they could find nothing to eat and 'might have starved ... if we had not brought some cold fowls along with us'. Such circumstances dictated a quick departure and the party had soon negotiated the hire of a Maltese *sparonaro*, a small, six-oared boat. However, made entirely for speed to avoid the African pirates and 'other Barbaresque vessels', it was so flat and so narrow that they were forced to keep near to the coast. It was daybreak on 2 June, when the party left the Marmoreo, the great port at Syracuse, but the wind became exceedingly violent around noon and the crew was forced to ground the vessel for a while before continuing to Capo Passero, the most southerly point of Sicily.

It was to be some time before the travellers could embark on their 100-mile voyage to Malta. There being no habitation they could use on the small island on which they found themselves, they camped in a cavern with a good swimming place nearby. After dinner their pilot advised them to get aboard the boat and row some hundred yards out to sea and anchor, so avoiding local peasants who might be tempted to rob and kill. Wrapped in their cloaks the men spent a disagreeable and uncomfortable night. The *sparonaro* was not big enough for all six of them, and they had 'nothing but the hard boards to lie on'. Fortunately, they made 'the happiest discovery' for under the shelter of a rock was 'a great quantity of fine, soft, dry sea-weed … intended by providence', Brydone wrote, 'for our bed'. They agreed to stand sentry by turns, with Fullarton's double-barrelled gun well-primed and loaded for the reception of the enemy. While breakfast was being prepared the following morning, a fishing boat arrived bringing with it some excellent fish which was soon on the fire while others were 'roaring for their cold fowl'.[11]

In spite of the unfavourable prognostications about the weather, the party had little time to wait and was able eventually to get under sail around six o'clock in the afternoon. Passing down the coast two hours later they landed to cook some macaroni they had purchased from their sailors and shoot something for their sea-store. With the wind absent, they were soon being rowed into what sailors called the Malta canal where the sea was very high, and the coast of Sicily began to recede. At midnight, their sailors began a hymn to the Virgin: 'the music was simple, solemn and melancholy, and in perfect harmony with the scene and with all our feelings'. It was about two o'clock on 4 June that a fine breeze picked up, and after three more hours sailing they arrived in Valletta where they were met by an officer from the health office who obliged them to swear an oath as to the circumstances of their voyage. He behaved 'in the civilest manner and immediately sent us Mr Rutter, the English consul, for whom we had letters of recommendation'. The consul then conducted the party to an inn which had the appearance of being a palace, where they had an excellent supper, a good burgundy, and drank the health of H M George III on his birthday. They were soon 'going into clean comfortable beds – in expectation of the sweetest slumbers'. It was 'a new world indeed'.

The Knights of the Order of St John came to Malta in 1522 after their loss of Crete, After a four month siege by the Turks in 1565 the Grand Master decided to construct the fortified harbour of Valletta which, in the event, was never put to the test. By the time the Aragonese Grand Master, Perrellos, died in 1720 the order was in decline. Unparalleled ostentation had replaced the ideals of its founders. The knights were an anachronism to all save their bankrupt protectors, the Popes in Rome. When the fourteen-year autocratic reign of Dom António Manoel de Vilhena ended in 1736, King Philip V of Spain's son, the Bourbon Charles VIII, united Naples and Sicily and crowned himself the autonomous king of the newly created Kingdom of the Two Sicilies. An uneventful five-year reign by the Majorcan Ramon Despuig was followed by the long reign of Pinto, the Portuguese Grand Master, between 1743 and 1773. Not a man content with mere titles, he had attempted in 1763 to reduce Malta's dependence on Sicily by trying to acquire Corsica from the Genoese, but after much haggling it was the French who bought it five years later, a year before Napoleon's birth there.

Although Brydone's arrival in the new world of Malta had been met by some enjoyable hospitality, and writing that night to Beckford he had reminded him that true luxury was 'only to be attained by undergoing a few hardships', the party's banker, a Mr Pousilach, arrived the next morning with an invitation to join him at his country house. 'Noble entertainment' followed, with an elegant dessert and a great variety of wines. In the countryside, peasants were bringing in the wheat harvest but Brydone was soon reporting that the crop they depended on most was cotton which was manufactured into stockings, coverlets and blankets. He also noted that sugar-cane was being successfully grown but not in any quantity. Impressed by the noble churches in every village, he noted the statues of marble, rich tapestry, and silver plate. Towards the end of the day, the party was invited to enjoy the entertainment provided by the departure of a Maltese squadron to assist the French against the Bey of Tunis. It comprised three galleys, the largest with 900 men, each of the others with some 700, along with three galliots and several *scampavias*, literally runaways, used for their speed. There were about thirty knights in each galley, all 'making signals ... to their mistresses who were weeping for their departure from the bastions'. Brydone concluded by saying that 'after viewing the show from the ramparts, we took a boat and followed the squadron for some time, and did not return till long after sunset'.

The next day the three travellers inspected many of Valletta's buildings, including the palace of the Grand-Master, where they were introduced to Fra Emmanuel Pinto ('a clear-headed, sensible, little old man'), the infirmary and the great church of St John, in fact the co-cathedral. Listening to a service in what was clearly a 'magnificent church', Brydone thought it 'more over-charged with parade and ceremony' that he had ever observed. 'The number of genuflexions before the altar, the kissing of the prior's hand, the holding up of his robes by the subaltern priest ... the throwing incense upon all the knights of the great cross and neglecting the poorer knights ... appeared to us ... highly ridiculous'. It was all 'so different from that purity and simplicity of worship that constitutes the very essence of true Christianity'. The mass had been held as a thanksgiving for their deliverance from a 'terrible conspiracy by some Turkish slaves' who, having taken an oath to kill their masters, had poisoned some fountains twenty-one years previously. Our tutor had apparently heard how the plot had been discovered by a Turkish-speaking Jew who overheard a 'discourse that he thought suspicious' in the coffee house he kept.[12]

On 7 June, as Brydone's sixteenth letter to Beckford was being written, the three men travelled through the island in coaches drawn by one mule each, going first to see the ancient city of Melita. Their guides could only speak Arabic but they were received by an officer responsible for the city who received them politely and showed them the old palace. Brydone was particularly impressed by what had been achieved by a hundred and fifty thousand people on the islands of Malta and Gozo . Valletta obtained its water from an aqueduct composed of some thousand arches which had been constructed and paid for by one of the grand-masters, and the nation supported a substantial naval fleet with several vessels of galleys, galliots, four ships of sixty guns, all of which were supplied with excellent artillery.

Not withstanding the supposed bigotry of the Maltese, Brydone described how the spirit of toleration was so strong that a mosque had lately been built for their sworn enemies the Turks. However, our tutor was surprised to find that Malta permitted duelling by law, albeit with some curious restrictions. Duellists were obliged,

Brydone told Beckford, 'to decide their quarrel in one particular street of the city, and if they presumed to fight anywhere else, they are liable to the rigour of the law'. Not less singular was the obligation 'under the most severe penalties' to put up their sword when ordered to do so, by a woman, a priest or a knight. Three months previously, two knights had had a dispute at the billiard table. One used a good deal of abusive language and added a blow but to everyone's astonishment refused to fight his antagonist. When he refused a second time 'still he refused to enter the lists'. The poor wretch was condemned to make *amende honourable* (being originally a punishment in France which required the offender to be led barefoot and stripped to his shirt, with a rope around his neck, to beg pardon) in the great Church of St John for forty-five days successively.[13]

It was still warm in the early evening of 7 June, and the thermometer in the mid-seventies when Brydone told Beckford that they were making preparations for a long voyage, and it would be 'not easy to say from whence he would next write'. They eventually left Malta in another *sparonaro* which they hired to take them to Agrigento (Agrigentum that was), midway along Sicily's long south-west coast. They passed the islands of Gozo and Comino four days later, both covered with redoubts and fortifications of all kinds, and as night came on they found themselves once more at the mercy of the waves. Their rowers began their evening song to the Virgin, beating time with their oars. Their offering, Brydone wrote, 'was acceptable for they had the most delightful weather'. Wrapped in their cloaks, and on mattresses acquired in Malta, they slept most comfortably. A little after dawn they saw part of Mount Etna smoking above the waters, and by ten o'clock they had sight of the coast of Sicily. Brydone could not help giving his own thanks: sailors regarded this passage as one of the most stormy and dangerous in the Mediterranean. Given the smallness of their boat, and the great breadth of this passage, he told Beckford 'we could not help admiring the temerity of these people who, at all seasons of the year, venture to Sicily in these diminutive vessels; yet it is very seldom that any accident happens'.

The party arrived off Sicily a little before sunset and found a convenient sandy beach in the vicinity of Ragusa. While the servants prepared a supper, our travellers amused themselves bathing and collecting shells, but with the wind particularly favourable they were soon back aboard their barque. Brydone told Beckford that they had expected to find the nautilus (a cephalopod) for which Ragusa was famous 'but in this we did not succeed'. At about noon the next day, they arrived in Agrigento where the captain of the port accompanied the party up to the city which was about four miles from the harbour and some 1100 feet above sea level. Large American aloes grew on both sides of the road, with their flower stems between twenty and thirty feet high. The city of Agrigentum, called *Girgenti* by the Sicilians, made a noble appearance, only inferior to that of Genoa, but its population had fallen to some twenty thousand and its houses were mean and the streets dirty. Fortunately, Canon Spoto, whom they had met in Naples at Hamilton's home, gave them hospitality and lodged them comfortably in his house, a welcome change from the cramped quarters aboard their *sparonaro*.[14]

An examination of numerous ruined Greek temples followed. Not one of the columns of the Temple of Concord had fallen down and half of that dedicated to Venus remained, similar to the condition of the Temple of Juno on its elevated site. The tutor recalled the Greek artist, Zeuxis, and his famous painting of the women of Agrigentum who had been ambitious of the honour of appearing before him. Then, fearing that his correspondent might be bored by more tales of antiquity, Brydone rounded off his letter by turning to the geology of the area. The city's wall, and the catacombs and sepulchres were all very great, and had been built from rock, as mentioned by Polybius, the historian. The whole mountain on which Agrigentum had been, he said, 'composed of a concretion of seashells run together, and cemented by a kind of sand or gravel, and now become as hard, and perhaps more durable than even marble itself'. He promised Beckford to bring home some piece of white stone, unexposed to the air, 'for the inspection of the curious'.

A week after their arrival the travellers received a deputation from the bishop inviting them to 'a great dinner' at the port. The location was a little puzzling and Brydone turned to Tommaso Fazello for help. The sixteenth century Dominican friar had written the first printed history of Sicily (*De Rebus Siculis Decades Duae*) at Palermo in 1558, and Fazello's text confirmed the city's reputation for hospitality. Brydone told Beckford that 'we dined with the bishop according to agreement, and rose from the table convinced that the ancient Agrigentini could not possibly understand the true luxury of eating better than their descendants, to whom they have transmitted a very competent portion both of their social virtues and vices. I beg their pardon for calling them vices. I wish I had a softer name for it; it looks like ingratitude for their hospitality, for which we owe them so much'. They had been thirty at table but they had not less than a hundred dishes of meat and 'nothing was wanting that could be invented to stimulate and to flatter the palate ... the company was remarkably merry'. Brydone had to ask his friend what he thought of 'these reverend fathers of the Church?' One had said 'we have exploded from our system everything that is dismal or melancholy; and are persuaded, that of all the roads in the universe, the road to heaven must be the pleasantest and least gloomy; if it be not so, God have mercy upon us, for I am afraid we shall never get there'.[15]

The party's worrisome sea journey was followed by a pleasant and relaxing stay with Canon Spoto, but indecision now set in and the question posed to the travellers in Agrigentum was whether to go to Palermo by land or sea.

CHAPTER 5

# The travellers arrive in Palermo (June 1770)

Two days later, our chronicler told Beckford that the party's plans to travel onward by sea to Trapani, just beyond Marsala in the north-west corner of the island, had been abandoned. Minds had been changed and they 'were determined to put no more confidence in that element'. Instead, they chose the cross-island route and by 16 June were 'about halfway towards Palermo', the capital of Sicily. When the travellers left the high mountains they still had one more night to spend on the road, and another fifty miles to travel on 'cursed, stubborn' mules, over rocks and precipices. It turned out to be a relatively comfortable night although 'the fleas, the bugs, and the chickens did all that lay in their power' to deprive them of it. Their two guards came to awake them before five, 'apostrophising their entry with a detail of the horrid robberies and murders that had been committed in the neighbourhood', all on the very road they were about to travel. By the time they had originally intended to leave, the 'whole squadron' was ranged in order of battle, and when they began their march they were 'attended by the whole village, man, woman and child'. On this occasion, they travelled till about midnight when they decided to sleep on a straw-covered floor in a wretched village, resuming their journey before day-break. Brydone described the seventeen year-old Fullarton as 'strong as a lion', and despite the fatigue of the journey and three days without undressing, he was fit to begin … another march'. Having eaten breakfast under a fig tree, the party was soon approaching Palermo.

The seventeenth century had been an unhappy one for Sicily, being followed in the eighteenth by the departure of many landed aristocrats not only from the cities of Palermo, Catania, Messina and Syracuse but the countryside too. Large estates were left in the charge of *gabelotti* who played the role of *padrone* to the local peasantry, helping settle disputes and protecting them from bandits, becoming in effect the ruling class in rural Sicily. When Charles II, the last Hapsburg King of Spain and ruler of large parts of Italy died in 1700, the succession passed from the Hapsburgs to the Bourbons, a move which other European powers contested during the War of the Spanish Succession. The outcome saw Spain ceding the Spanish Netherlands, the Kingdom of Naples, the Duchy of Milan and Sardinia to the Hapsburg monarchy whilst Gibraltar and Minorca became British. Sicily, on the other hand, was given to the Duchy of Savoy under the Treaty of Utrecht and Victor Amadeus II of Savoy ruled the island from Turin. In 1719, however, the Duke who had become King went to war with the Austrians, anticipating support from Spain.

Spain chose to recover Sicily for herself, a move which eventually saw Austrian and Spanish forces in June that year fighting a decisive battle at Francavilla di Sicilia, near Taormina. When the Austrians withdrew they left 6,000 dead and wounded whilst the Spanish casualties were some 2,000. The Austrians later besieged Messina, with the war continuing till a peace treaty was signed at The Hague in February 1720, and Emperor Charles VI of Austria's possession of the island confirmed. Spanish forces were evacuated back to Spain by the British Navy. Indirect Spanish rule, through what has been called 'a pampered, parasitic, and corrupt nobility', resumed in 1734 when Sicily passed into the control of Charles de Bourbon after his forces occupied Naples in May and Palermo in September. Charles decided to rule from Naples which gave Sicily and Italy south of Rome a beneficial autonomy, to say nothing of late Baroque palaces and churches all over the island. In 1759, Charles I left Sicily to succeed to the Spanish throne as Charles III of Spain, and thereafter his young son ruled in Naples as Ferdinand IV.

There being no choice, Brydone and his party had been 'indifferently lodged' in Palermo's one inn, at a cost of five ducats a day. There was no keeping the noisy, troublesome French landlady out of their rooms, and she plagued the party by telling them how such a prince or such a duke had 'been so superlatively happy' in her establishment. Everyone seemed to be in love with her, a feeling which obliged Brydone to tell her that they were a 'very retired sort' of person and did 'not like company'. Her esteem for the party immediately fell. Passing through the kitchen on one occasion Brydone heard her exclaim: Ah, *mon Dieu*! Comme ces Anglais sont sauvages. Although she had been in Palermo for twenty years, she was as perfectly French 'as if she had never been without the gates of Paris'.

It was 23 June when the tutor gave his correspondent notice that he would have a great deal to tell him about Palermo – 'we are everyday more delighted with it'. Their letters of introduction had been duly delivered, in consequence of which they 'were loaded with civilities'. Describing the two great streets which intersected each other in the centre of the city, Brydone was impressed with the 'elegant uniform buildings' and the way they formed the square called the *Ottangolo*. In his view, the *Porta Felice* was the handsomest of four elegant gates to the city, each at a distance of about a half mile from the centre. The *Marino*, which started from the *Porta Felice* was 'a delightful walk' and one greatly enjoyed by the nobility of Palermo. In its centre, 'an elegant kind of temple' had been erected which, in the summer months, was made use of by an orchestra. Night was turned into day, 'the better to favour pleasure and intrigue', and as the clock struck midnight, 'the symphony' struck up and the order that 'no person, of whatever quality, shall presume to carry a light' came into effect. With the flambeaux extinguished at the *Porta Felice*, where the servants waited for the return of the carriages, Brydone said, 'the company generally continue together in utter darkness, except when the intruding moon, with her horns and her chastity, comes to disturb them'.

'Sicilian ladies', Brydone told his friend, 'marry at thirteen or fourteen' and sometimes were grandmothers before they were thirty. A few days previously, a Count Stetela presented them to his cousin, the Princess Partana (more probably Partanna), with whom they talked for a half an hour. She had borne twelve children, the eldest being a fine girl of fifteen, and was still in her bloom. She assured them that she 'never enjoyed more perfect health than when she was in child-bed' and 'during the time of pregnancy she was often indisposed but that immediately on delivery she was cured of all her complaints'. Brydone lamented how England lost many of her finest women in childbed, and that 'even the most fortunate and easy deliveries were attended with violent pain and anguish'. The princess could only 'thank Heaven that she was born a Sicilian'.

The influence different climates had on childbirth puzzled Brydone, despite it being a matter for the learned to decide. In cold, and particularly mountainous countries, births were difficult and dangerous, and easier in warm and low places. He speculated that the air of the first hardened and contracted the fibres, whilst that of the second softened and relaxed them. He thought, nevertheless, that 'one may easily conceive what a change it must make upon the whole frame, to add the pressure of a column of air of two or three thousand feet more than it is accustomed to; and if muscular motion is performed by the pressure of the atmosphere, as some have alleged', Brydone argued, 'how much must this add to the action of every muscle'. However, if this hypothesis was true, he added, the strength of those who had climbed Etna should have been diminished by a third, and this did not appear to be the case. Our traveller said he often thought that physicians paid too little attention to such considerations. They sent people with the same complaints to Marseilles and Aix, one at sea level, the other at near six hundred feet above it.[1]

The travellers' fondness for Palermo was increasing every day. The Sicilians were 'frank and sincere … and their politeness (did) not consist of show and grimace like some of the polite nations of the continent' The Viceroy, Giovanni Fogliani d'Aragona, Marquis of Pellegrino, set the pattern of hospitality which the nobles followed. An amiable and agreeable man, he was as much beloved and esteemed 'as a viceroy to an absolute monarch can be'. He had been in England in his youth and had read many authors with whose works he seemed well-acquainted. Brydone described his position in regard to Naples as not unlike what the lord-lieutenant of Ireland was to England – with one trifling difference.

His absolute authority meant that Sicilian patriots had gained few arguments and no votes, a position not dissimilar to that held by Lord Townshend, the Irish envoy, but without the power. Brydone added that he hoped Beckford's 'Hibernian squabbles', about which they had heard so much, 'even at this distant corner, would soon have an end'. Although his correspondent, and Mrs Beckford, were to leave Europe for Jamaica in February 1774 and remain there for thirteen years, there is no evidence that they were in Ireland at this time, if ever. The reference to 'squabbles' might, however, have been associated with the 'rum business', the removal of customs duties refunded on Jamaican spirits first imported into England and then re-exported to Ireland.

Describing Sicilian cookery as a mixture of French and Spanish, Brydone pictured a circle of *fricassés*, *fricandeaux*, *ragoûts* and *pet de loups* (edible puffballs), with olive oil preserving 'its rank and dignity' at the centre of the table. In their ordinary living, Sicilians were very frugal and temperate. Their reputation for being very amorous was not without reason since 'the whole nation are poets, even the peasants; and a man stands a poor chance for a mistress that is not capable of celebrating her praises'. In music, as well as poetry, soft amorous pieces were generally styled *Siciliani* and used 'to play all night under their mistresses' windows, to express the delicacy of their passion'. Serenading was not now so much in fashion. 'Ladies', he wrote, 'are not now so rigid … neither do they require the prodigious martial feats' once in favour. In truth, said Brydone, 'gallantry is pretty much upon the same footing here as in Italy'. A breach of the marriage vow was no longer looked upon as one of the deadly sins, and confessors now fell 'upon easy and pleasant enough methods of making them atone for it'. Husbands 'are content; and, like able generals, make up for the loss of one fortress by the taking of another. However, female licentiousness has by no means come to such a height as in Italy'.

At the end of June a visit was paid to the celebrated convent of the Capuchins, a mile or so outside the city. It contained nothing very remarkable but the burial place proved a great curiosity. A vast subterraneous apartment, divided into large commodious galleries, had been hollowed out into a variety of niches, each filled with dead bodies, fixed upright upon their legs. There were about three hundred of them, all dressed in the clothes they usually wore. Many of them had been there for two hundred and fifty or more years, yet none were reduced to skeletons. Whilst Brydone was not sure whether the practice had anything to recommend it, the people of Palermo paid daily visits to their deceased friends. Some of the Capuchin friars slept in the galleries every night but as the interdiction written in large characters over the gate, said 'no woman is ever admitted either dead or alive'.

No sooner had our travellers left the convent than their carriage broke down, and as the act of walking was 'of all things, the most disgraceful', both in Palermo and Naples, they risked having their 'characters blasted for ever'. Consequently, their Sicilian servant, Philip, took care to make such a noise about it that their dignity did not suffer. He kept a little in front of them, 'pesting and blasting' all the way, bawling out to every person he met that there were no coaches to be had, no carriages of any kind, either for love or money. Fortunately, Philip knew the geography of the town well and conducted them through lanes only known to himself. Eventually finding a coach, Brydone could only question why 'an Italian nobleman is ashamed of nothing as much as the use of his legs'.[2]

For a few nights the party viewed the course of a comet, seemingly the first people in Palermo to take an interest in it. 'It had no tail', Brydone wrote, 'but was surrounded by a faintish ill-defined light that made it look like a bright star shining through a thin cloud'. He thought in all probability this was due to an atmosphere around the comet that caused a refraction of the rays, and prevented them from being seen with the clearness observed in bodies which had no atmosphere. Two nights previously the party had had the good fortune to catch the comet just passing close by a small fixed star, whose light was not only considerably dimmed but they thought they saw 'a sensible change of place in the star, as soon as its rays fell into the atmosphere of the comet – owing no doubt to the refraction in passing through that atmosphere'. The 'profound astronomers', as the Palermitans called the travellers, tried to trace the line of the comet's course but as they could not find a globe, it was not possible to do it with any degree of precision. Its direction was almost due north, and its velocity 'amazing'. Brydone estimated that it had travelled 'more than 60 million miles in a day, a motion that vastly surpasses all human comprehension'. He went on to explain to Beckford that the nearer the comet approached the sun, the greater was its acceleration. They attempted to find whether it had any observable parallax but its speed of travel made this impossible.

To the common observer, Brydone mused, it must be hard to conceive that gravity always got the better of centrifugal force, and that 'the sun, like an electric body, after it had once charged the objects that it had attracted with its own effluvia or atmosphere, by degrees loses its attraction, and at last, even repels them', or that 'the attracting power like what we observe in electricity, does not return again till the effluvia imbibed from the attracting body is dispelled or dissipated'. He thought that if the system of electricity, and of repulsion and attraction, had been known in Newton's day, he would undoubtedly have called it to his aid. Extending his commentary at this point, Brydone then postulated that the tails of comets, like kites, were their atmospheres, rendered highly electrical by either the violence of their motion or their proximity to the sun. He had been long convinced about this since any kite sent up to twelve or thirteen hundred feet with a small wire about its string, at all times will produce fire. Bringing his lesson to an end, Brydone had to admit that his comet had led him a dance. Moreover, feeling that he had irritated Beckford unduly with his lengthy comments about comets and astronomy, Brydone asked his pardon, saying humorously that, 'I am sure, whatever this comet may be to the universe, it has been an *ignis fatuus* to me; for it has led me strangely out of my road and bewildered me among rocks and quicksands'.

During the first week of July, the party took its leave of their French landlady after Count Bushemi (Buscemi), a 'very amiable young man', arranged an alternative 'lodging on the sea-shore, one of the coolest and most agreeable in Palermo'. The cathedral, or *Madre Chiesa*, was a venerable, large Gothic building, supported within by eighty columns of oriental granite, with a great number of richly decorated chapels, the most important being that to St Rosalia or *La Santuzza*, the patroness of Palermo, and whose feast was soon to be celebrated. The relics of the saint were preserved in a large silver box, studded with precious stones, and 'used to perform many miracles ... being esteemed the most effectual remedy against the plague'. The Flemish court painter, Anthony Van Dyck, travelled to Sicily from Genoa in 1624 to paint Emanuele Filiberto, the viceroy, at whose invitation he had come. He stayed in Palermo for some time, particularly enjoying the company of the nobility. Other riches of the church were some bones of St Peter, and a whole arm of St John the Baptist. In the Sacristy, there were some robes embroidered with oriental pearl that were near four hundred years old and yet looked as fresh as the day they had been made. Another church, at Monreale, about five miles from the city, was next in dignity to that of the cathedral. It was nearly the same size and encrusted with mosaic, 'at an incredible expense'. It had been built by William II (1155–1189), known as 'the Good', whose memory was still held in great veneration by the Sicilians.[3]

With construction of stands for the fireworks and other preparations for the festival very much in hand, Brydone told his friend about the investigations he had been making into who exactly St Rosalia was, having found that nobody locally could give him 'a tolerable account of her sainthood'. He had been to every bookshop but could find nothing but an epic poem, written in the Sicilian language, of which she was the heroine. Notes accompanying it said that at fifteen she 'deserted the world' and withdrew to the mountains. Little or nothing was then heard of her for five hundred years till 1624, when a holy man had a vision that her bones were in a cave near the top of *Monte Pelegrino*. He also promised an end to the plague if her bones were carried thrice round the walls of the city. As a result, the magistrates authorised a search and St Rosalia became the greatest saint in the calendar. Brydone, on the other hand, thought it altogether much more likely that the bones belonged to 'some poor wretch that had been murdered, or died for want in the mountains'.

Our travellers came to the conclusion that fashionable folk in Palermo regarded ordinary people 'in great contempt' so far as matters of religion were concerned. This led Brydone to speak of the 'silly books, that have been written by weak, well-meaning men, in defence of religion' who he was confident had made more infidels than all the works of Bolingbroke (the Tory politician and philosopher), Shaftesbury (the third earl, philosopher and author), or even Voltaire himself'. These 'grave, plodding blockheads', as the people of fashion were described, did all they could to make people think there was 'little or nothing' to be said for religion. The universal error of these gentry was, Brydone said, that 'they ever attempt to explain, and reconcile to sense and reason, those very mysteries that the first principles of our religion teach us are incomprehensible'. Brydone recalled having once heard an ignorant priest declare that he did not find the least difficulty in conceiving the mystery of the Trinity, or that of the Incarnation; and that he would undertake to make them plain to the meanest of capacities. 'Don't you think', roared Brydone to his friend, 'that a few such teachers as this must hurt religion more by their zeal, than all its opponents can by their wit?' Had such heroes stayed behind the bulwarks of faith and of mystery, Brydone argued, 'their adversaries never could have touched them'. They had been foolish enough to abandon these strongholds ... 'a sad piece of generalship indeed: such defenders must ever ruin the best cause'. Educated people in Palermo despised the wild superstitions of the vulgar, yet went regularly to mass.

On Sunday, the eighth of July, the long-expected sirocco arrived. The first blast of it felt like 'burning steam from the mouth of an oven'. Shutting the door of their new lodging, Brydone called out to Fullarton that 'the whole atmosphere was in a flame'. The air was thick and heavy but the barometer was little affected. It felt 'somewhat like the subterraneous sweating stoves at Naples'. Wet blankets were being hung on the inside of open windows. Some gentlemen from the country spoke of finding the grass and plants that had been green the day before, were become quite brown, and crackled under their feet as if dried in an oven. The previous day, the travellers had been entertained at the palace of Prince Partana, from whose balcony the viceroy reviewed a regiment of the Swiss Guard. Describing them as a really 'fine body of men' Brydone said they had two field pieces on each flank and 'the evolutions were performed with more precision and steadiness than one generally meets with, except in England and Germany'. The grenadiers were furnished with false grenades, and when during the entertainment some fell among 'the thick crowd of nobility' there was an entertaining scene as they defended themselves with their hats, and threw them very dextrously upon their neighbours. No damage was done save for the singeing of a few wigs and caps.

The company at Prince Partana's had been 'brilliant, and the entertainment noble', consisting of ices, creams, chocolate, sweetmeats and fruit; half of the company played cards, the remainder amused themselves in conversation, and walking on the terrace. The young prince and princess, who were very amiable, played with several of their companions at 'cross-purposes, and other games of that kind'. The young ladies had been 'easy, affable and unaffected, and not (as on the continent) perpetually stuck up by the sides of their mothers who bring them into company, not for their amusement, but to offer them for sale'. Brydone thought that the mothers of Palermo had proper confidence in their daughters, and 'allowed their real characters to form … and ripen'.

Meanwhile, 'the whole world was on the very tip-toe of expectation', the feast of St Rosalia was to start on July 12 at about four o'clock in the afternoon. A 'most enormous machine' would be drawn through the centre of the city, from the *Marino* to the *Porto Nuovo*, preceded by a troop of horse with trumpets and kettledrums, and all the city officers in their gala uniforms. The triumphal chariot, measuring seventy feet long, thirty feet wide, and upwards of eighty feet high, overtopped many of the tallest houses but Brydone was puzzled by the absence of any visible means of enabling the vehicle to change direction. 'The form of its under part' wrote Brydone, 'was like that of the Roman galleys but it swells as it advances in height, and the front assumes an oval shape like an amphitheatre, with seats placed in the theatrical manner'. A great orchestra filled the rows, one above the other, and a little behind, there was a large dome supported by six Corinthian columns, adorned with figures of saints and angels. On the top of the dome was the gigantic silver statue of St Rosalia. This vast fabric was drawn by fifty-six huge mules. The triumph was finished in about three hours and succeeded by beautiful illuminations. Offshore, all manner of galleys, galliots and other shipping ranged in a semi-circle opposite the viceroy and his party and duly fired off their artillery and water-rockets, producing a very noble effect.

A firework display followed in the evening when 'a vast explosion of two thousand rockets, bombs, serpents, squibs and devils' filled the atmosphere. Later, as the viceroy sailed out to sea in a richly illuminated galley, Brydone and his friends watched the seventy-two oarsmen send it 'flying with vast velocity over the waters'. The following day, festivities began with the first of several horse races through the city, with six horses in each. The 'gaudily dressed' jockeys were boys about twelve years old, with no saddle or bridle, using a small piece of cord as a bit to guide their animal. The noise of a cannon set them off through the streets of the city with the winning post coming into view after exactly a mile. Having timed a race at one minute and thirty-five seconds, Brydone thought it impressive 'considering the size of the horses (scarce fourteen hands)'. That evening two orchestras and two bands played in the garden of the Archbishop, putting our tutor in mind of the atmosphere in London's Vauxhall Gardens. The next night an ornamented *Piazza Ottangolare* became the venue for more entertainment, this time provided by still more orchestras and bands.

On the evening of 16 July, the 'first man of the opera distinguished himself very much' when the travellers went to hear several visiting opera stars and dancers. Brydone thought the great mezzo-soprano castrato, Gaspare Pacchierotti, was one of the 'most agreeable singers' he had ever heard and one who in a few years would be 'very well celebrated' – a prognostication which proved correct when he sang at the *Teatro San Carlo* in Naples. A second soprano, Giuseppe Campagnucci, was preferable to most singers that he had heard in Italy. The first woman soprano had been Caterina Gabrielli, and 'with sopranos such as these' Brydone told his correspondent, 'the opera here will not be a despicable one … the opera dancers are those you had last year at London; they are just arrived'.[4]

It was around this time that Brydone realised he had not told Beckford about a hiccup in the party's plans for the return journey to Naples. He had hired a small vessel, had their baggage and sea-stores put aboard, and even taken leave of the viceroy and had their passports returned, when they were set upon by their friends. They pleaded with them to remain another fortnight with 'so much earnestness and cordiality' that he had 'discharged their vessel and sent for their trunks'. It was, as a result, hard for Brydone to say how long they might stay, 'indeed, had we brought our clothes and books from Naples, it is hard to say how long we might have stayed'.[5] He had, nevertheless, sent to engage another vessel and the probability was that they would not leave for five or six days, thereby giving the party time to enquire further into the island's antiquities.

The day before more performances of opera were due to start, the party walked up *Monte Pelegrino* to pay their respects to St Rosalia. The road was very properly termed *la scala*, or the stair, and they found the saint lying in her grotto, 'her head gently reclining upon her hand, and a crucifix before her'. The statue was the figure of a lovely girl of about fifteen in the act of devotion, in the finest white marble and of the most exquisite workmanship. A church had been built around the damp cave where it was located and priests watched over the relics. From the top of the mountain, the 'beautiful and extensive prospect' stretched across to many of the Lipari Islands, and a large proportion of Mount Etna could be seen although it was almost the whole length of Sicily away.

Palermo or Panormus, as the Phoenicians called it, lay within two miles of the foot of the mountain, near 'the extremity of a kind of natural amphitheatre'. Next to Chamefeno, it was generally supposed to be the most ancient city on the island. Explaining that the bishop of Lucera had translated a Chaldean inscription which was over one of the old gates into the city, and which Brydone thought a great curiosity, he told Beckford that it meant: 'There is no other God but one God. There is no other power but this same God. There is no other conqueror but this God whom we adore'.[6] The son of Fazello, the island's historian who had preserved it and another inscription, had been indignant when he found two masons demolishing such a precious relic.

Interestingly, Brydone asked Beckford to show this letter to their mutual friend, Mr Crofts, and obtain 'his sentiments on these etymologies and antiquities', adding that he should 'tell him I have not forgot his commission, and shall procure him all the oldest and most unintelligible books in Palermo'. On those conditions, Brydone said, 'I send him a most valuable fragment' – part of a Chaldean inscription that had been copied from a block of white marble in ruins nearby, and which he wanted to have translated. The friend could have been the Irishman William Crofts (1726–1784) who married Elizabeth Beare in 1754, by whom he had 12 children.

In his thirty-third letter to Beckford on 24 July, Brydone said he was never in better spirits despite the heat, and ready to give an account of the island's fisheries. On 'such a day as this in England we (would) be panting for breath, and no mortal would think either of reading or writing'. The catching of tuna fish constituted one of the principal amusements during the summer months; and the curing and sending them to foreign markets was an important branch of the island's commerce. The fish did not make their appearance till the latter end of May, at which time the *tonnaros*, as the nets were called, were being prepared. At great expense, a 'kind of aquatic castle of strong nets was formed, fastened to the bottom of the sea by anchors and heavy leaden weights'. These *tonnaros* were erected in the passages among the rocks and islands known to be frequented by the tuna. As soon as the fish got into the 'hall', or first apartment of the net, the fishermen standing sentry in their boats, shut the outer door to prevent the fish from escaping. Some *tonnaros* had a great number of apartments, each with a different name – the saloon, the parlour, the dining-room, but the last apartment was always styled *la camera della morte*. Armed with a spear or harpoon, the fishermen then attacked 'the poor, defenceless' fish.

The taking of the swordfish was, to Brydone's mind, 'a more noble diversion'. No art was made use of to ensnare him. It was 'exactly like whale fishing in miniature'. The abundantly superstitious Sicilian fisherman used a chant, rather as a charm, to bring the fish nearer their boats. It was their only bait. However, Brydone quickly added, for the benefit of his correspondent, how the fish would plunge under the water immediately if it heard a word of Italian spoken, to 'appear no more'. In addition, he spoke of the *morena* eels much favoured by the Romans which were prolific in the sea near Messina. Other fish included mullet and mackerel which were usually caught at night by two men in a small boat, one of whom held a lighted torch over the surface of the water while the other stood with his harpoon poised. Brydone said he had seen great quantities killed in this manner both in Sicily and Naples. A 'large fleet of boats employed in this kind of fishing', he wrote, 'makes a beautiful appearance on the water on a fine summer night'. The people of Trepani to the west of Palermo were considered to be the most ingenious when it came to coral fishing. One of their inventions Brydone described was a 'great cross of wood, to the centre of which is fixed a heavy hard stone, capable of carrying the cross to the bottom'. Pieces of small net were tied to each limb of the cross so that as soon as the fishermen felt the contraption touch the bottom, the rope was fastened to their boat, and they began to row about over the coral beds. The great stone then broke the coral from the rocks and fish in the area were entangled in the nets.[7]

The life led by fishermen prompted the tutor's concern for all who suffered from the oppressive Neapolitan government. Some were obliged to 'invent branches of commerce that nature seemed to have denied them'. Sugar-cane was much cultivated on the island but 'the farmers are already ruined', duties on it forced many to abandon the crop. Furthermore, were they under a free government, Brydone thought their wheat crop alone would be 'sufficient to render this little nation one of the richest and most flourishing in the world'. The ministry in Naples, or rather that of Spain, he wrote, had taken this method 'to humble the pride of Sicilian barons'. Complaint was universal, and Brydone considered that 'if the ministry persevere in these rigorous measures, there must be either a revolt or they must soon be reduced to a state of poverty as well as servitude'. He believed most of them would readily embrace any plausible scheme to shake off their yoke, as in general they appeared to be 'people of great sensibility with high notions of honour and liberty'.

Our tutor felt that the people's spirit had in great measure kept them free of the Spanish inquisition since the barons, experienced in exercising despotic government themselves, could not bear the thought of becoming slaves 'to a set of ignorant Spanish priests'. The laws of Sicily, Brydone wrote, were 'scattered in a great number of volumes', and although the King of Sardinia had intended to abridge and collect them into a single code he was not long enough in possession of the island to achieve this work. The power of the viceroy, he admitted. was 'pretty absolute'. In addition to command over all military force, he had 'unbounded authority in all civil tribunals', and the right to nominate all offices of state, both civil and ecclesiastical. The military forces of Sicily consisted of about 9,500 men of whom 1,200 were cavalry. Forts and signal towers between the many small ports along the coast helped alert the local populace of any invasion, particularly from the Barbary side of the island. Fires were kept ready for lighting, with a person to watch at each of them, so that the 'whole island could be alerted, they assure us, in the space of an hour'. The nationalist (or even colonialist) in Brydone reminded Beckford that 'if this island were in the hands of a naval power … it is evident that it must command the whole Levant trade'.[8]

'We have now got everything ready for our departure', wrote Brydone on 26 July, 'and if the wind continues favourable, this is probably the last letter I shall write you from Sicily'. Two chebecks (or sabaks) had sailed for Naples that morning. Of Arab origin, these three-masted vessels, with full lateen-rig, carried eighteen oars to assure mobility during calm weather and had a distinctive stern platform extending over the sea. They had been offered a passage but explained they had already engaged 'a little ship for themselves', and this was expected. As matters turned out, three more letters were to be written from Palermo between 27–29 July, and the correspondence concluded in Naples on the first of August.

Being obliged to kill time on account of the wind not being from the right direction for the arrival of their transport, Brydone swept his mind to find subjects he had forgotten to tell Beckford about. Among a potpourri were Sicilian customs, the art of animated conversation, superstitions and the marriage ceremony, the islanders' fondness for study, hot mineral waters and sulphurous baths, the use of liquorice for colds, land utilisation on the island and, in addition to methods of preserving grain, notes on the much-cultivated soda plant, great quantities of which were sent every year to supply the greenhouses of Venice. Other memories were the island's beautiful forests, the flocks, the game, the tar, the cork, the honey, along with the variety of marble quarried and caverns providing a variety of minerals and other material such cinnabar, mercury, sulphur, alum, nitre and vitriol. It was, however, 'the beauty of women' that posed the greatest problem for Brydone.

Sicilian ladies married very young and frequently lived to see the fifth and sixth generation. In general our tutor described them as 'sprightly and agreeable' and in most parts of Italy 'they would be esteemed handsome' but to a Piedmontese they might be declared 'very ordinary', perhaps also to 'most Englishmen'. The problem lay in the vagueness of man's ideas of female beauty, Brydone concluded. They changed in every climate and a criterion was 'nowhere to be found', prompting an Alexander Pope-like quotation:

> Ask where's the North? At York, t'is on the Tweed;
> In Scotland at the Orcades, and there,
> At Nova Zembla, or the Lord knows where.

Recalling some of his own earlier encounters with the female sex, he said 'I remember after making the tour of Savoy and the Lower Valais, every woman we met in Switzerland appeared an angel'. It was a similar story when they were travelling through some parts of Germany, and thinking that Beckford would easily recollect it, he mentioned 'the surprising difference betwixt a beauty at Milan and one at Turin' despite their proximity geographically.

Thoughts about women's hair and heroism followed. Sicilian ladies had 'remarkably fine hair' and they understood 'how to dress and adorn it to the greatest advantage'. Although now only an embellishment, in former times it had been a protection for their country. After a long siege by Saracens, Palermo had been reduced by famine and what distressed the citizens still more was the absence of materials for making bowstrings. As they were about to surrender 'a patriotic dame stepped forth', and proposed that they should all cut off their hair, and twist it into bowstrings – an action which was immediately complied with, and which led to the assailants being beaten off and the arrival of re-enforcements. A local poet had written that the hair of our ladies now 'discharges no other shafts but those of Cupid, and the only cords it forms are the cords of love'.

It was the twenty-ninth of July when the travellers finally said their *adieus* to the viceroy. Brydone had to admit there was 'little or no probability' that they would see their hosts or Sicily again, or that they would ever have it in their power 'to make any return for the many civilities' they had received. Two days later the party went aboard their ship and after a further 'two days delightful sailing' they arrived in Naples where they found the worthy friends they had left behind.

# CHAPTER 6

# Brydone becomes a successful writer (1771–1773)

Our thirty-five year-old tutoring polymath and his two pupils, appear to have left Rome for Lausanne, and ultimately England, on the first of April 1771. The next day they were passing through Tivoli and six days later were at Frascati. After visiting Civita Castellana on 20 April, the party continued first to Terni, then Foligno and Loreto (by Ancona) to Senigallia. Then, leaving the Adriatic coast for the environs of Bologna, they eventually arrived in Venice at the end of the first week of May for what was to be a stay of some sixteen days. Thereafter, their route took them to Milan, and following a stay in the region of Lakes Garda, Como and Lugano, they next reached Airolo, on the southern side of the St Gotthard pass. Only foot traffic and pack animals could make the journey till 1775 when the first carriage made the climb and descent, but by 5 June, Brydone's party was in the land of the Swiss, reaching Luzern via Erstfeld, on 8 June. Two days later they were in Bern from where they travelled to Lausanne via Payerne. Later that summer there were expeditions to the Lakes of Thun and Brienz, and to Frutigen, and subsequent travels to Lauterbrunnen, Grindelwald, Meiringen, Interlaken and Spiez.

Brydone had told Beckford in his final letter that his intention was to 'leave the parched fields of Italy for the delightful cool mountains of Switzerland, where liberty and simplicity, long since banished from polished nations, still flourish in their original purity' and 'where the temperature and moderation of the climate, and that of the inhabitants are mutually emblematical of each other'. He also admitted never sitting down to write 'these enormous epistles' without seeing his friend on 'the opposite side of the table' but he could foresee a time when 'we shall be heartily tired of art, and shall begin again to languish for nature. It is she alone that can give any real or lasting pleasure, and in all our pursuits of happiness, if she is not our guide, we can never attain our end'. Then, having said his personal *adieu* to his 'dear friend', Brydone added, 'you have been our faithful companion during this tour, and have not contributed a little to its pleasure. If it has afforded equal entertainment to you, we shall beg of you still to accompany us through the rest of our travels. A man must have miserable imagination indeed, that can be in solitude while he has such friends to converse with'. In signing off, Brydone hoped Beckford would 'still submit to be one of the party' as they went through other parts of the Kingdom of Naples.[1]

William Beckford would appear to have lived in Rome for a period, returning to England in 1773 before he and his wife Elizabeth went back to Jamaica the following year. His principal task was to restore his properties to their earlier profitability and reduce debts which had accrued in his absence, but his lawyers had been negligent and conditions in the market had not been helped by the American War of Independence. Notwithstanding these problems, he had become the patron of several artists, including Philip Wickstead, a portrait painter and pupil of Johan Zoffany, whom he had met in Italy and who went to stay with his patron in Jamaica. Another was George Robertson, who had studied at Shipley's art school near Fountain Court in The Strand.[2]

In Scotland, Brydone resumed a largely rural existence, broken occasionally by a number of scientific experiments. He would doubtless have been well aware of the several scientific papers which Sir John Pringle, published in 1772. These included work on such subjects as *Experiments on Septic and Antiseptic Substances and Observations on the Diseases of the Army in Camp and Garrison*. Elected president of the Royal Society that year, Pringle delivered a set of discourses which were subsequently published.[3]

On the evening of Monday 10 February 1772, Brydone had apparently been riding through the town of Tweedmouth, in

England, just south of the Scottish border, when he noticed that the atmosphere was suddenly illuminated in a very extraordinary manner – 'The light of the moon, which was about half full, seemed to be extinguished by the blaze; and I saw my shadow projected on the ground, and almost as distinct, and well-defined, as in sunshine'. Turning round to see where it had come from he 'beheld a long, bright flame, moving almost horizontally along the heavens. It was of a conical form, and from the base to the apex could not be less than six or seven degrees ... but it descended gently, and appeared to burst about five or six degrees lower. Its course was from north-west to south-east and seemed to have an inclination to the horizon; but this might be only a deception'. The light it gave out was brighter than that of Venus and its colour resembled 'the flame of burning camphire', an archaic name for henna.

Having previously observed similar explosions from meteors of this kind Brydone described how he pulled out his watch (which had a second hand) to measure the exact time the report took to reach him. He waited for upwards of four minutes, then: 'despairing of any report, I rode on, but had not got to the middle of the bridge, when I was stunned by a loud and heavy explosion resembling the discharge of a heavy mortar, at no distance, and followed by a kind of rumbling noise like that of thunder. I examined my watch, and found that the sound had five minutes and about seven seconds to reach me; which, according to the common commutation of 1,142 feet in a second, amounts to the distance of at least 66 miles'. Brydone explained to Sir John how he had expected to have seen some account of this phenomenon from Newcastle as, from its direction and distance, the meteor must have burst 'pretty near to the zenith of that city', but he had found no notice of it in the newspapers.

About a week later, Brydone mentioned what he had seen to Sir John Paterson of Eccles, a member of Parliament, who told him he had been on the road between Greenlaw and his house, in the company of Mr Thomas Cockburn of Edinburgh. They had not only seen the meteor but as they had been travelling to the south they had seen it from its first appearance. When it first became luminous, it was almost vertical, but it went off 'descending to the south-east'. Writing to Sir John, Brydone was anxious to stress that as these gentlemen were at least 20 miles to the west of the spot where he had made his observation, and the appearance and height of the meteor seemed to have been nearly the same to them as himself, it was 'probable that it was at a very great distance from the earth, and much beyond the limits that have been assigned to our atmosphere'. He went on to recall how he had frequently observed smaller meteors (or falling stars) from the mountain of San Bernard, and how lately he had had 'the good fortune to see several of them from the highest region of Mount Etna'; an elevation still more considerable, and probably the greatest accessible one in Europe'.

Our astronomer said he was inclined to believe, from their frequent appearance during the last frost, that the air had been 'in a very favourable state for electrical purposes'. To prove it to himself, Brydone recalled the back of a cat, which, as was well-known, often exhibited strong marks of electricity. He then cut a quantity of harpsichord wire into short pieces of five or six inches, and tying them together at one end, made the other diverge like the hair of a brush. He then took a large metal pestle of a mortar for his conductor, to the end of which he fixed the brush of wire, insulating the whole by placing it on a couple of wine-glasses. Putting a cat on his knee, and bringing her back under the wires, Brydone began to stroke her gently. As the animal continued in good humour, he had the satisfaction of seeing the conductor so much charged that it emitted sparks of a considerable force, and attracted such light bodies as were brought near it. Eventually, 'the passage of the electrical fire from the hair of her back (the cat's) to the small wires occasioned, it seems, a disagreeable sensation, and she sprang away in fright'. A second experiment, this time with a young lady holding the feline collaborator, followed. The back of this woman's hand was covered with a piece of dry silk so that none of the electric fire communicated to the wires might be lost, and soon after she began stroking the cat, the conductor appeared fully charged.

Not wholly content with his experiments, Brydone finally enlisted the help of yet another young lady, probably the 'Mrs Douglass of Kelso' mentioned in a letter to Beckford from Etna.[4]

The conductor was insulated as before and the lady placed herself such that her head almost touched the brush of wire. Her sister was then asked to stand on a cake of bees-wax behind her, and as soon as she began to comb the hair of the former, the conductor emitted sparks of the largest size hitherto achieved. The hair was extremely electric, and when the room was darkened, Brydone described how they could perceive the fire passing from it along the small wires to the conductor. The young lady who was on the wax was not a little surprised to find that the moment she began to comb her sister's hair, her own body became electric, 'darting out sparks of fire against every substance that approached her'.

The day following, and with the weather hazy and the frost greatly abated, several more heads became the subject of experimentation. Brydone was able to conclude his report to Sir John Pringle (and readers of the Royal Society's 'Transactions') by saying that 'we found that the stronger the hair, the greater was the effect; whereas, soft flaxen hair produced little or no fire at all'. However, he thought it might 'not be improper to mention that these experiments were made in a warm, dry room, before a good fire, and at a time when the thermometer in the open air was at six or seven degrees below the point of congelation (a word often used in his letters to Beckford). The hair which succeeded best was perfectly dry, and no powder or pomatum had been used on it for some months before'.[5]

A letter written on 3 June 1772 by David Hume, the philosopher, shows that plans were afoot to have Brydone's account of *A Tour through Sicily and Malta in a series of letters to William Beckford Esq. of Somerly in Suffolk*, made into a book, and that he played a part, albeit a small one, in its publication. Hume, who as a young man had to chosen to sit on a stool in a merchant's office rather than accept a travelling tutorship, was living at home in a corner of St Andrew's Square Edinburgh when he wrote to William Strahan, a printer and buyer of authors' copyrights and a close friend in London, who published all his and many of Samuel Johnson's works. He left the letter unsealed so that he could read it before passing it on to Thomas Cadell, the printer and publisher with whom he had an occasional partnership. Continuing, he wrote:

There is a friend of mine, Captain Braiden, who has writ, in the form of letters, his travels through Sicily and Malta. They are very curious and agreeable; and I as well as others of his friends have advised him to publish them; and I also advised him, to carry them to you. If you read them I hope we shall agree in opinion. I conjecture they make one volume, a little less than a volume of the *Spectator*.[6]

What happened during the next six months is a matter for conjecture but it seems likely that Beckford would have been among 'others of his friends' encouraging the project. In November, Benjamin Franklin nominated Brydone as a fellow of the Royal Society. Having served for a year as a member of the Society's council on four occasions, Franklin had had a hand in recommending at least thirty-seven candidates for election as fellows. So far as eight of these were concerned, he wrote their names in his own hand and gave a brief indication of their residence and special interests.[7] Brydone's proposers were John Pringle, Benjamin Franklin, John Hunter, Thomas Dundas, Rod Valtravis and J W Huck, and the excellent company he found himself in spoke for itself:

John Winthrop (1714–1779) – 1765, Cambridge Mass., astronomer, mathematician
Arthur Lee (1740–1792) – 1766, Williamsburg Va., physician
Charles L'Epinasse – 1767, London, mathematician
Jan Ingenhousz (1730–1799) – 1769, Vienna, physician at court, physicist
Alexander Dalrymple (1737–1808) – 1770, London, mathematician, geographer
Patrick Brydone (1736–1818) – 1772, Berwickshire, electrician, traveller
William Henly (died 1779) – 1773, London, linen-draper, electrician
John Coakley Lettsom (1744–1815) – London, physician, philanthropist

The first edition of Brydone's 115,000-word book appeared in 1773 as two 8mo volumes published by Strahan and Cadell in the

Strand. It was to be Brydone's only literary work and be recognised as a major work about the Grand Tour, and the first of its type about Sicily. Quarter-bound in tan brown calf, with tan paper boards and the spine tooled in gold, the copy presented to the king incorporated a George III monogram stamped at the head of the spine.[8] The *Tour* was Strahan's third publication that year. He paid Brydone £75 for a half share in the work which was printed in April. Some 1,250 copies of the first edition were sold, followed by another 500 and 1,000 copies of the second and third editions respectively printed in September. A fourth edition of 1,000 copies appeared in July 1774. In August 1775 the fifth edition of another 1,000 copies was produced whilst in October 1776 yet another 2,000 copies of the sixth edition appeared. A total of 6,750 copies were sold in less than four years.

Interestingly, the 'Advertisement', a prefix to volumes common at that time, and in which the publisher introduced Brydone's book to the reader, throws some light on the timing of its publication:

> The author wrote them for the amusement of his friends, and as an assistance to his memory ... One principal motive ... was the desire of giving to the world, and perhaps transmitting to posterity, a monument to his friendship with the gentleman to whom they are addressed.

The advertisement went on to explain that when Baron Johann Riesdesel's book *Travels through Sicily and that part of Italy formerly called 'Magna Graecia'* first appeared in a translation by John Reinhold Forster, a German naturalist with Scottish connections, Brydone's work had already gone to press. He had shown some concern but, as the publisher wrote: 'On perusal, he had the satisfaction to find that the two works did not much interfere. In transcribing them for the press, he found it necessary both to retrench and to amplify; by which the ease of the epistolary style has probably suffered, and some of the letters have been extended much beyond their original length'. Finally, readers were asked take account of 'the very inconvenient circumstances ... in which many of them were written'. Brydone had not attempted 'to re-model them' as what might be gained in 'form and expression' would probably be lost in 'ease and simplicity'.[9]

Charles Wesley had been one of William Strahan's earliest customers and he expanded his business twice from premises in the parish of St Bride's, whose church had long been associated with newspapers and the print trade. Always someone who would buy copyrights from authors, Strahan's attendance at London trade sales led to him completing at least 330 transactions for sets of copyright shares in 411 books between 1751 and 1780.[10] The occasional partnership of Thomas Cadell, an eminent London bookseller and publisher with William and later with Andrew Strahan, proved beneficial to both men. His successes included such works as Gibbon's *Decline and Fall of the Roman Empire* and the sentimental novel *The Man of Feeling* by the Scottish author, Henry Mackenzie.[11]

One of the earliest compliments Brydone received was in May 1773 when a writer in *The Gentleman's Magazine* said that his 'travels are entertaining in a high degree. The author seems to possess the two grand qualities necessary to a good traveller – curiosity to see, and ingenuity to describe'. Another was from Fanny Burney, daughter of Dr Charles Burney, the composer and music teacher whom he met at a concert given at the family's London home. The Burneys had enjoyed 'a most heavenly evening' with Guiseppe Millico, the Italian castrato, a 'judicious performer and worthy man', Eligio Celestini, that 'sweet violinist', and Antonio Sacchini, the opera composer. In a reference to Brydone's book, Fanny told readers of her diary for May 1773 that: 'I have received very great entertainment from this book; it is written in an easy, natural, and lively style, and full of anecdotes, observations, and descriptions, and in many places is very philosophical. It discovers throughout a liveliness of imagination, an insatiate curiosity after knowledge, and the most vehement desire of instruction. I very much wish, that the author may continue his acquaintance with my father; for I am sure he must be very agreeable'.[12] William Cowper, the letter-writer and poet, soon followed giving Brydone similar praise in a letter to Joseph Hill, his closest friend at that time, when he described him as 'a gentleman who relates his travels so agreeably that he deserves always to travel with an agreeable companion'.[13]

In July, the *Tour* was the subject of favourable comment by the *Monthly Review* (or Literary Journal), a periodical about which the *London Evening Post* said when it first appeared, 'gave an account with proper abstracts of new books as they came out'. Its founder, the non-conformist bookseller Ralph Griffiths, spoke of Brydone as 'at once the gentleman, the scholar, and the man of science: a rational observer, a philosophical enquirer, and a polite and pleasing companion'. He wrote of his language being free and flowing, though not always correct. The punctilious editor took exception to the use of 'so soon' in place of 'as soon as', also such slips of grammar as 'the collection of metals, cameos and intaglios are very princely', and assumed that such errors would be corrected in the second edition. Brydone's manner was, however, 'cheerful and lively; yet properly varied' to suit the reader.

Its initial comment suggested that the *Monthly Review* had not fully grasped who the 'happy cast' had been during the 1770 *Tour*. There were, it said 'slight intimations, *en passant*, in certain parts', that Brydone travelled 'in the character of governor to some young man of fashion; whose friends seem to have made a happy choice in the person whom they entrusted with so important a charge as that of guarding the morals and forming the manners of youth'. Griffiths went on to tell his readers that despite 'the great encomiums on the air of Naples' they were used to hearing about, Mr Brydone's account was altogether different. He stressed, for example, the contrasting temperatures in Rome and Naples, and his belief that though much colder in winter, Rome was the healthier climate, even for those with gout. Naples was more eligible in summer on account of the refreshing influence of the sea breezes.

The review told how Brydone had looked in vain for some account of the nature and cause of the Sirocco wind, noting in the book's second volume, that although much more violent in Sicily, there it seldom lasted more than three days. He also concluded that someone with 'a reflecting mind, like Mr Brydone's, could not but be struck with the melancholy change which this fine part of Italy had experienced since the times of its ancient splendour and happiness'. The picture Brydone had drawn of the bay at Naples had been 'quite enchanting' and, if not unique, one that at least inspired the reader with its 'prodigious variety of mountains, valleys, promontories and islands, covered over with an everlasting verdure, and loaded with the richest fruits' – all 'the produce of subterraneous fire'.

Matters were not so straightforward when the reviewer reached the incident in Catania already described, where Canon Recupero confessed to Brydone that, when writing the *History of Aetna*, he found 'Moses hanging like a dead weight upon him', and he questioned what would 'become of the book, or its author, if he dare publish it'. The canon had measured the stratas of lava in a draw-well on Etna and used them as an argument to prove the great antiquity of the volcano (at least some 14,000 years ago), not allowing his conscience 'to make the mountain so young as that prophet (made) the world'.[14] Numerous clerics questioned whether the story of creation was to 'be overturned by an uncertain remark such as this?'. Brydone's suggestion that the earth was as old as it was proved shocking to many, even blasphemous. It was this passage that Dr Johnson had in mind when he met Fullarton in 1778, and remarked, that Brydone would have been a better author 'if he had been more attentive to his Bible'.[15]

The commentary also drew attention to the 'degree of wildness and ferocity' Brydone found in the inhabitants of Etna and compared his account with that of Baron Riedesel, whose travels had been the subject of an article in the *Monthly Review* in March and April 1772.[16] Riedesel had found them 'good-natured, civil and honest people such as are to be met with in all places'. To account for what he called 'this difference of representation', Griffiths could only say that each had spoken of the people as he found them, and suppose that 'Baron R ... met only with decent people, and Captain B happened to fall in with the mob'.

The *Monthly Review* found the description Brydone had given of his journey up to the summit of Etna 'very entertaining'. The whole mountain was divided into 'three distinct regions ... the fertile, the woody, and the barren'. Although different 'both in climate and productions', they were similar to the three zones of the earth, something that the reviewer was pleased to join Brydone in styling as the torrid, the temperate, and the frigid zones. After describing a few of their characteristics, the reviewer had to admit that his abridgement was in danger of injuring the original account, obliging him 'to pass over a thousand curious particulars'. He was, nevertheless, determined not to omit 'the author's ingenious observations relating to the latent fires of this stupendous volcano'. The lower region of the great parent mountain was covered with a multitude of lesser hills, 'every one of which was a volcano', so encouraging the reviewer to comment on the singular beauty of one by the name of Monpelieri, in an area where the possessions of nearly 30,000 people had been destroyed.

In its August edition, the *Monthly Review* chose to conclude its critique, having the previous month left the travellers 'to the enjoyment of their repose, on their bed of leaves in the cavern of goats in the middle or woody region of Mount Etna'. This time Griffiths invited Brydone to tell the story of the party's lengthy climb up the volcano. He ended his piece by concluding that 'Captain Brydone's *Tour* contains more good sense, more knowledge, more variety of entertainment, than is to be found in most works of the kind; in truth, we cannot at present recollect *one* that can be put in competition with it'.[17]

No sooner had the first edition of Brydone's book appeared in the bookshops than two more versions of the *Tour* were being printed in Dublin. A Mr J Potts, who had published Richard Twiss's *Travels through Portugal and Spain*, and which had been much-criticised on account of its lengthy quotations from other authors, was the first. Another edition was printed by Mr R Marchbank for Mr R Moncrieffe, a bookseller who had just published the *History of Ireland*.

In the early part of 1774, Strahan and Cadell produced a two-volume 'corrected second edition'. A third edition, with a folding map, followed later and as the year progressed, Brydone would have been made aware of two more editions emanating from Dublin. In 1775, it appears that Strahan and Cadell had another edition produced for them, and four of the Dublin booksellers and printers combined to produce a corrected and enlarged edition for the United Company of Booksellers. The London partnership that had first launched what was becoming a best-seller produced 'a second edition' in 1790. Yet another edition appeared in 1806, printed for Cadell and a new partner, William Davies in the Strand, whilst 1807 saw two editions. Vernon, Hood & Sharpe in London had one printed in Edinburgh by Abernethy & Walker, and H D Symonds of Paternoster Row, another. By 1809, others in the trade were developing the genre and Richard Phillips of Blackfriars and T Gillet, his Fleet Street printer, produced A *Collection of Voyages and Travels*, the 18th volume of which summarised Brydone's visit to Sicily and Malta. Then, in 1817, R Chapman of Trongate in Glasgow printed a two volume edition of the *Tour*. In 1840 'A *Tour through Sicily and Malta* by P. Brydone FRS, with a biographical memoir, and notes prepared for the present edition' was published by the Edinburgh firm of William and Robert Chambers, and a 'new and complete' edition of the *Tour* by F.(*sic*) Brydone was published by George Clark and Son of Aberdeen in 1848.

Bookshops enjoyed a good trade from the *Tour*. Libraries also saw it in good demand. At the Bristol Library, where it was the third most popular item with borrowers (and borrowed 100 times) between 1773 and 1775, only one other book was in greater demand during the next eleven years. Alexander Donaldson was a particularly important Edinburgh bookseller and printer at this time. He had just invaded the London market, the result of which was a struggle between all the leading booksellers who made claim to their copyrights in perpetuity whereas the Scottish book trade generally accepted that copyrights were limited to the maximum term of twenty-eight years, as established by Queen Anne in 1710.[18] The aristocratic patronage of writers had almost disappeared, being replaced by the practice whereby publishers paid writers for the copyright of their works. Few of the many hack writers were well paid but more important writers, such as Samuel Johnson, who declared that 'Nobody but a blockhead ever wrote except for money', made £1,575 from his *Dictionary* in 1755. The *Wealth of Nations* was to produce £500 for Adam Smith, and Alexander Pope received £4,000 for each of his translations of the *Iliad* and the *Odyssey*.

It was not long before Brydone's work was being given a boost by other publishers abroad. In America, Joseph Bumstead was an eminent printer for Boston publishers such as John Boyle, Ebenezer and Benjamin Larkin, James White and David West, a number of whom came together in 1792 to produce a new edition of the *Tour*. Six years later, Thomas Dickman, a Massachusetts printer and bookstore owner who had been the first postmaster in Greenfield, published a two-volume edition. Three years after the turn of the century, Evert Duyckinck, a man of Dutch descent who lived in New York and his printer colleague from the Bowery, J C Totten, began their part in widening Brydone's customer base, producing in 1813 a version of the *Tour* based on Strahan and Cadell's 1775 edition.

Having watched as his book was bought, read and reviewed, Brydone then found that it was being translated into several European languages. This affirmed the genre of travel books in spite of some translators who, for example, made starkly obvious mistakes with the spelling of the author's name, or omitted pages which they considered undermined religious devotion. An early Dutch edition was produced by Jacob Yntema and Jacob Tieboel of Amsterdam in 1774, and five years later the printer and another publisher again put it on the market. In 1776, *la Société Typographique* of Neuchâtel, Switzerland, published the two-volume *Voyages en Sicile et à Malthe, soigneusement corrigée sur la seconde édition angloise, augmentée de notes intéressantes par M. Derveil*, and translated into French by Jean-Nicolas Démeunier (1751–1814), a writer who supported the Revolutionary cause in America. The following year, a German translation was published by Johann Friedrich Junius in Leipzig, entitled *P. Brydone's Reise durch Sicilien und Malta in Briefen an William Bedford* (sic).

In 1782, Count Michel-Jean de Borch arranged for the publication of a three-volume French translation of the *Tour* by *les Frères Reycends* of Turin, with twenty-nine engraved plates, numerous double pages and folding maps, bound in marbled calf and decorated in gilt. The volumes were, however, 'deemed very imperfect'. Twelve months later, Borch produced a German edition under the title *Briefe über Sicilien und Maltha*. It was 1805 when *Reize van Paulus Brijdone in Sicilie en Malta, ondernomen in het Jaar 1770* appeared the Netherlands, a Dutch translation by J B J

Breton who had earlier translated the works of Joachim Heinrich Campe, the linguist, educator and publisher.

By this time the main impetus had declined, but in 1831 the German publisher *Verlag der Schbuchhandlung of Braunschweig* launched an abridged translation, made by Campe before his death in 1818. In 1844, Alfred Mame & Cie of Tours, published *Voyage de Patrick Brydone en Sicilie et à Malte* in French, following it with another edition two years later. Seven years later, the year of the Great Exhibition in Hyde Park, Alfred Mame produced a fourth, 'quality' edition, again using the Campe translation from which certain passages had been removed on account of their unsuitability for young readers, adding 'a few notes to bring up to date the historical tales of the author'.

The fact that Brydone appears not to have offered any of his subsequent writing for publication may have been due to the price he achieved for his book's copyright from Strahan and Cadell, and the way the trade subsequently seems to have exploited the *Tour* to its own interest. There is little doubt, however, that the tutor's reputation had been made. His standing in the scientific community was given a considerable lift by his literary achievement. It also increased and broadened the already large pool of his acquaintances and well-wishers, particularly among the aristocracy. One book may have been enough for Brydone but his appetite for travel had not been diminished, albeit that his journal-writing reverted to its original form as an *aide-memoire* rather than being an opportunity to express what one American academic described as his 'finely-crafted similes' or 'delicately wrought descriptions and occasionally moralised episodes'.[19]

CHAPTER 7

# Travels to Vienna and thence to Berlin (1775–1776)

Although Brydone generally welcomed the responsibility and duties involved in his tutoring of such men as Beckford, Fullarton and Glover, he was soon to be the escort of the occasional malcontent. Furthermore, as time went by, he rather wished he had another source of income to help him break the constant cycle of peregrinations. Experience taught him that the paymaster, usually the parent or uncle of one of his charges, could behave just as badly as their young, particularly where money was concerned.

In the summer of 1774, the thirty-eight-year old Brydone set out on several short visits from Lausanne, apparently alone and by way of local exploration. The first was to the Lake Constance region of the country, passing through or stopping for a day or so at Avenches, Bern, Zug and Zürich on the way. His journal describes another brief expedition on the Rhine in July when he embarked at Stein, a pretty village where Lake Constance becomes the river again, and disembarked at Rhinefelden. He was soon back in Lausanne by way of la Chaux-de-Fonds after staying overnight at Soleure (Solothurn) and Neuchâtel. His motive for this second expedition nearby may have had something to do with Franz Mesmer, a German physician then working in Vienna, who was not only interested in astronomy but had performed several sensational cures involving the use of magnetism at places along Lake Constance.

In August, and with some late summer mountain trekking in mind, Brydone again left Lausanne south-eastwards, spending a night at Bex (the site of the famous salt mine), and then at Sion (or Sedunum as the Romans called it). His route to Interlaken took him through Visp to Oberwald, the source of the Rhône, where he stayed at an inn before going across the mountains northward to Guttannen in Schweiz. From there he reached his destination after passing through Meiringen and the town of Brienz.[1] A month later, according to his journal, Brydone seems to have enjoyed a short diversion to Vallorbe and the area around Les Charbonnières and le Pont, with its Lac de Joux. After visits to Cossonay, Nyon and Versoix, he returned to Lausanne after a brief stay in Geneva.[2]

Among Brydone's summer visitors in 1775 was Alleyne Fitzherbert, later 1st baron St Helens (1753–1839), a man of great wit, very pleasant and beloved, who was to become a diplomat, and be posted to the court of Catherine the Great at St Petersburg eight years later. He received a scholarship from Cambridge to travel to France and Italy, and seems to have been on his way south in the company of Sir Francis Kinloch of Gilmerton, East Lothian, the sixth baronet.[3]

By the late autumn that year, however, Brydone was making preparations for what would be a busy 1776 in charge of two new gentlemen, Lord Lindsey and William Morton Pitt, a kinsman of the prime minister.[4] Unfortunately, Brydone says nothing about who specifically recommended him as these gentlemen's tutor or what influenced the choice of Eastern Europe as their destination, one that he had not previously visited. The young lord, then in his twentieth year, was Robert Bertie, the only son of General Peregrine Bertie (1714–1778) and Mary Panton. He was to prove a handful for all who came to know him. It seems that he served for a short time in the army as a volunteer in North America, becoming the fourth duke and the seventh Earl of Lindsey on the death of his father in August 1778. The following year he held the office of Lord Lieutenant of Lincolnshire and in February was invested as a Privy Counsellor. He died unmarried in July 1779 at the age of twenty three. According to Emma Elliot in her *Memoir of the Right Honourable Hugh Elliot* he was one of those Englishmen 'bent on volunteering for the army' but long 'prevented from doing so by the commands of his father and the tears of his mother'.[5] The second young gentleman, William Pitt, had been born in 1754 and educated at Queen's, Oxford. He was to spend five years travelling in different parts of the continent before becoming MP for Poole and declining the offer of a diplomatic appointment at Berlin in 1782. He subsequently represented Dorset till 1826 and died ten years later.[6] According to the *Gentleman's Magazine* he was 'beloved of his family, esteemed by his friends, he passed through life distinguished by the possession of the purest virtues and by the exercise of a diffusive philanthropy, and extensive practical benevolence'.

On 14 December 1775, the party left Lausanne for Vienna, taking almost exactly a month to reach the capital of Austria and the Hapsburg Court. They stopped en route at Augsburg and Munich, the latter having been the subject of comment by Hugh Elliot, the second son of Sir Gilbert Elliot and envoy-extraordinary to the Elector of Bavaria, when he began his diplomatic career and settled in Munich.[7] In 1774, nothing could exceed the poverty and misery of the people, nor the extravagance and gaiety of the court. In a letter to the President of the Board of Trade in September that year, Hugh had written that 'to draw any picture of the state of this country would be to go back two ages in the progress of society. They are in nothing on a par with the rest of Europe, except in music and debauchery ... Trial by torture is the ordinary method in this Electorate, of convicting criminals'. More clouds appeared in the spring of 1775 and his disgust at the 'venal creatures who preyed upon the court' made the diplomatic novice even gloomier. In the city itself 'the dread word Reform was heard ... and received ... much as the blast of the last trumpet' might be hereafter. The most cheerful aspect of life was the occasional presence of young English travellers who, he said, 'amid such folly and vice, were not wholly unmindful of better things'.[8]

In Vienna, Maria Theresa, the only female ruler of the Hapsburg Empire, had begun her reign in 1740 when her father, Emperor Charles VI, died. He believed she would surrender power to her husband, Francis Stephen of Lorraine (1708–1765) and did not introduce her to the workings of government. In fact, after giving birth to sixteen children between 1738 and 1756 she became a 'courageous, generous and kind' reforming ruler. She strengthened the army by doubling the size it had been in her father's reign and re-ordered the country's fiscal income. Austria's conflict with Saxony began the Seven Years' War which ended when she signed the Treaty of Hubertusberg in 1763 and recognised Prussia's possession of Silesia. After regulating the dues paid by serfs to their lords, she reformed the education system in 1775 and the following year saw the burning of witches outlawed and capital punishment replaced by forced labour.

When Lord North, the future prime minister, had arrived in Vienna in 1752 during his grand tour, he and Lord Dartmouth, his step-brother, found a society greatly given over to pleasure, a gay city 'almost in a continual hurry'. The following year, Henry Herbert, the 10th earl of Pembroke recommended the Austrian capital 'for cheapness' and so far as travel was concerned. 'I wish you not to take post, but to use the carriages of the country, which, though slow, are much cheaper than the post and not very much slower than the German Post carriages, except it be between Prague and Vienna, where they drive vastly fast on the finest road possible'.[9] He was also to recommend a visit to Pressburg as 'worthwhile'.

Some twenty-four years later in the middle of January, and having been on the road from Lausanne for sixteen days, Brydone's party approached Vienna through vineyards and woods on smooth roads of hardened deep snow. He particularly noticed the country houses on its outskirts, some defended against the bitter cold by 'double windows', the seals of which he later tested with a lighted candle, along with the working of stoves used to heat rooms. The social round started almost immediately, and with Britain's envoy-extraordinary, Sir Robert Murray Keith KB, temporarily in England on leave of absence after the death of his father, the travellers were entertained by the Spanish and French ambassadors. The first gave a masked ball for the children of some of the 'better' families, and the second, a ball where there was 'a prodigious number of very fine women dressed with great taste and elegance'.

The British envoy was extremely able. He became well-regarded by Empress Maria Theresa and Joseph II, her son, who became emperor in 1764 after the death of his father Francis. Born in

Edinburgh, Keith had been sent to a military academy in London from where he joined a Scots brigade, and becoming a captain in the 73rd Regiment of Foot, he was made aide-de-camp to Lord Sackville, fighting at the Battle of Minden in 1759. Despite the post being a difficult one, and one that required him to entertain British visitors at his own expense, and the well-known ill humour of the court, he was highly regarded for the manner in which he carried out his duties, his political sagacity, wit and *bonhomie*. Subsequent to matters arising from his father's death, Keith found himself elected MP for Peeblesshire in 1775.[10] William Robertson, the principal of Edinburgh University and Scottish historian, and someone yet to appear in the Brydone story, occasionally asked him for assistance with his research. Although he never attended the Commons and remained a member of the House until 1780, he was unable to return to Vienna till June 1776.

It was at ten o'clock in the morning on Sunday 21 January that Brydone was presented to the Emperor, and to the Empress at noon. The following week saw Brydone dining in 'prodigious magnificence' with Franz Josef, Prince of Liechtenstein and later with Prince von Kaunitz, the Austrian chancellor and foreign minister who, having trained as a lawyer, had been a life-long enemy of Prussia and was to again become involved in war with that state over the Bavarian succession in 1778–9. Welcomed by Prince Hieronymus von Colloredo, prince-archbishop of Salzburg, Brydone rather ungraciously commented afterwards that his hospitality was 'very magnificent but not equal to Prince Liechtenstein's'.[11]

Parades and exhibitions of horse-drawn sledges were very much part of Viennese life once the snow had arrived and, when it had not, quantities were brought in from the country. On one occasion, the Horse Guards galloped through those streets to level the area where the *traineaux* were to pass and a large machine drawn by six horses and mounted on a sledge provided a platform for a band. Another party of nearly thirty sledges, one with four horses belonging to the Empress and her son, Emperor Joseph II, made 'a fine appearance' when they returned at night with flambeaux burning. By the end of Brydone's first week, it was 'dreadful cold', as the rest of Europe had been discovering, and Brydone described another sledge party with the cream of the court, and ladies 'in furs and diamonds'. The cost of fitting it out, with the dress of the footmen and other ornaments was as much as seventeen thousand florins or two thousand guineas, and sometimes more. The parade lasted about two hours, and despite the many furs, the occupants were almost frozen at the end. Next morning, a heavily wrapped-up Brydone took a walk in the street and reported several sentinels frozen to death, along with several ordinary people.

Among the entertainment offered to the travellers was a performance of *Zémire et Azor*, a comic opera by the Belgian composer André Grétry which was to have its first performance at the King's Theatre in London three years later. Philip Stanhope, who had become Lord Chesterfield in 1773, and was to study at Leipzig University before becoming a diplomat, arranged a concert. Such occasions, along with a play and masquerade in the suburbs, led Brydone to say that 'I never was in any place where the people are so fond of what is called pleasures as at Vienna'. People, he added, who 'are constantly running after pleasures very seldom find them'.

On the second day of February, the travellers went six or seven miles upstream to see the Danube. Brydone concluded that there had probably been a thaw somewhere well to the West as there were unbroken pieces of ice 'as large as houses' opposite them. He could not understand how such mountains of ice, some not less than thirty feet, had been raised. The surface resembled one of the glaciers in Switzerland and at a distance it looked as if its surface had been 'violently agitated by wind and suddenly condensed when it was raised into high and irregular waves'. No sooner had they digested the view than the decision was taken that they would take rooms near the river so as to be present when the thaw started to move the ice and threaten, if not sweep away, the nearby wooden bridges, and even houses. Hundreds of workmen used to replacing bridges and damaged property were standing by.

A small zoo which was not opened to the public till 1779, the menagerie of Emperor Francis I, in the grounds of the Schönbrunn palace, became the subject of lengthy comment by Brydone. Wild animals were seen from a circular amphitheatre, with three rows of 'boxes', the animals being kept in dens underneath. A number of animals were baited by ferocious dogs, a camel, a wild bull, tiger, bears and wolves. One dog was 'an overmatch for the tiger, and the two would very soon have been killed if they had not been separated'. The men who went into the arena (keepers) were 'armed with blunt pitchforks' and there was 'a tree in the centre' where they could escape danger. Being told that the next fight would be between a goat and some wolves, their inclination was to depart, and they were leaving when, to their astonishment, they saw the goat stood firm and stamped his feet. The first wolf that approached received such a knock on the forehead that, stunned, he retired much faster than he had advanced. Three wolves soon had their backs against the wall, the last two declining all combat. Also in the amphitheatre, Brydone added, was 'a large band of martial musicians ... with trumpets, kettledrums, horns, clarinets, hautbois etc'.

Almost daily excursions were arranged for the author by members of the aristocracy or academia. English authors, Brydone noted, were well-known and 'the most agreeable place to visit' was the salon of the Countess von Thun und Hohenstein 'where the personality of the hostess ensures that no-one is ever bored'. Hugh Elliot said that she had 'everything but beauty. I have never seen a more agreeable or sensible woman'. A performance of the hymn *Stabat Mater* by 'the cream of the town's musicians' at the home of the countess at the end of March was followed by Mme de Waldstein, her sister, playing many pieces on the piano where 'her personal modesty only added to the delight of the audience'. A week later, the travellers enjoyed the playing of a celebrated composer/violinist, and a lute player, but their names were left blank in Brydone's record.

On the first Sunday in March a jubilee celebration required the streets to be laid with boards as the whole court were to have marched in procession to the church but unfortunately it was a very rainy morning, and they went in carriages. New Year's Day, Brydone explained, was 'the only fixed day of gala', the birthdays of the royal family were 'not even known, and give no embarrassment to anybody'. This led to the tutor questioning the meaning of the word 'jubilee' which, in a play by Farquar meant 'rejoicing' although said Brydone, rather inaccurately, 'it is a penance and mortification to obtain indulgence'. Referring to Mount Calvary Church, south of the city, where penitents carried up figures representing the story of the crucifixion, the tutor was scornful of the idea that this would win them freedom from their sins.

The palace at Schönbrunn was commended as 'elegant and not over-loaded with gilding'. Paintings by members of the Imperial family were of a standard equal to those by the best masters. One artist had been sent to the Tyrol by the Empress to paint landscapes, later becoming the curator of the Emperor's gallery in Vienna. Work in the palace gardens, including a colonnade and terraces, employed over 600 men. Numerous water features were under construction with groups of statuary being sculpted from white Tyrolean marble. There was to be a pheasantry and further additions to the menagerie. Other works being built or encouraged by the Emperor were improvements to the porcelain factory, a half an hour's walk from town, which produced goods 'not inferior to Dresden or Berlin'. Then, as Easter arrived, archdukes and duchesses in the presence of the Emperor performed the ceremony of washing the feet of twelve old men and a similar number of old women, elderly paupers. With a purse of money round the neck of each, 'a good dinner was provided and the remains sent to their homes'.

Although the length of Brydone's eventual three-month sojourn in Vienna was determined largely by weather that prevented long-distance travel, and society was 'more pleasing than almost any other place', life there was a matter of 'spending, or rather killing time'. Recognising that Vienna was 'certainly a good place to form what is called a man of the world' Brydone nevertheless said 'this kind of life is to me one great void that hardly leaves one pleasing or satisfactory idea behind it. And every night that I come home at twelve or one o'clock from great and numerous companies I ask myself what I have gained, and I find that I am not one idea the richer'. He bemoaned the sameness of social life, and the inability of having time alone. 'How different this is from retirement where I have my books and a few select friends whom I love, and who love me'. Even a little later, after reaching Berlin, the tutor wrote that 'after a succession of breakfasts, dinners, suppers and balls' he liked to have evenings in summer to himself, that was 'almost perfect solitude'. Furthermore, if those who 'bemoan their low station in life could see the dull uniformity that is almost always attendant on (those of) high rank, they would be thankful they had avoided it'.

The forty-one year old Brydone and his party crossed into Hungary on 9 April 1776 for what could only be called a short excursion lasting barely a week.[12] Hapsburg control of Hungary continued to be largely ineffective. By 1767 the increasing poverty of the serfs who struggled to make a living from the land and who made up 90 percent of the population, had led to Maria Theresa issuing an urbarium or revised table of feudal obligations. Instead of improving the situation, landlords began making greater demands on their tenants, forcing many serfs off their holdings. It was only to be with the arrival of Maria Theresa's son, Joseph II, in 1780 that Hungary began to benefit from a programme of modernisation.[13]

The journey to Pressburg, the largest and most important town in the kingdom of Hungary (today Bratislava in Slovakia), took a little under twelve hours and Brydone described it as flat until the last three leagues where it was 'mountainous and romantic'. After a good supper at the famous Swan Inn, the tutor joined Pitt who 'had already gone to bed' and slept soundly. The next day saw the party on the road to the silver mining town of Shemnitz, south of the major gold and silver mining area at Cremnitz, both in the shadow of the Carpathian mountains. They passed through Neutra (Nitra) and Tyrnau (Trnava) and across the fast-flowing river Vagus which started life in the Tatras Mountains. The climb into the mountains involved fourteen hours in the chaise and Brydone concluded that 'agriculture seems well understood here' and the ground 'very well ploughed'. Given the poverty of the peasantry they were 'extremely polite and obsequious and pulled off their hats ... yards off, and stood hat in hand till we passed'.

At a place referred to as Baha Banya, situated 'on the side of a mountain', Brydone enquired the distance to Shemnitz and found they still had four long hours on the road.[14] Surprised to be greeted in Latin by people in the street, they responded in like fashion but as it was then near seven o'clock in the evening, and beginning to rain, the party decided to stay, concluding that if the villagers thought it was a four hour journey, it would probably prove at least two hours longer. In the event, and armed with letters of introduction, they set out very early next morning and arrived after three hours despite the journey being 'almost all uphill'.

The buildings housing the mine and the workers were spread over the mountainside, but looked 'very romantic'. There was plenty of evidence that these mines had been worked for thousands of years. Tools used by prehistoric miners at the locality called *Spania Dolina* have been dated to 2000–1700BC. With the help of Baron Mitrowski, the superintendent, who had been at Cremnitz when Brydone's party arrived, and who immediately arranged for an intelligent overseer to conduct the party to the subterranean works, they put on some miners clothing, consisting of a jacket which came down near the knee, an apron … fixed behind instead of before, and a Hungarian cap of black cloth 'something like a grenadier's cap but flat on the top'. So equipped, they followed different galleries in the mines for nearly three hours.

Describing the size of the mine, Brydone said there were 6,000 men working there, some receiving 12 *kreutzers* (a silver coin) for an eight-hour shift and others on piece-work. Near the main vein, the heat and smell of sulphur was everywhere and men worked naked, often using gunpowder to break up the rock. In addition to an academy in the town for mechanics, chemistry and mineralogy where students undertook a three-year course, various models of the equipment used on site were inspected, the most interesting of which, Brydone wrote, being a model of the mountain itself, the external form of the hillside on one side, and a representation of all the galleries and machines in the interior on the other. He was particularly impressed by the mine's use of water to drive the machinery, and the many reservoirs, dams and channels that had been built at 'enormous and incredible expense' to minimise its loss of power in dry summers. Passing one reservoir which was still 'frozen to a great thickness', he was told it would not melt for perhaps six weeks more.

On their return to Baha Banya, the travellers found there was no food to be had, but showing their landlady a cake or two of something edible they had with them, she boiled it into an acceptable soup which, after tasting it, her family thought excellent. Passing through Tyrnau, the party returned to Pressburg on 14 April, looking down from the castle on the Danube, its ferries and the town below. The streams of the river united in a single vast flow, sometimes upwards of 80 feet deep, and whilst the extensive plain to the east was visible, as were some fortresses on the mountains to the west, the view Brydone had been told there would be of the steeples of Vienna was absent. However, they were soon back in Austria but not before he had made a note of the ferry's convenience. A stage of wood was laid over two large boats which were then joined to a rope reaching a great way up the river. 'When the side of the boats are opposed to the stream', Brydone wrote, 'the current soon forces it across the river, and this by so gentle a motion that it is hardly perceived'.[15]

Once back in Vienna, it only took Brydone a few days to prepare for the second leg of his journey to Berlin and eastwards, this time one of considerably longer duration. However, no sooner had the party left for Prague than Lord Lindsey and Pitt had 'a very ugly accident', presumably involving their carriage but about which Brydone gave no details. Their ten hour journey to the village of Deutsch-Brod went through country 'rather barren, arable with poor soil and fir tree woods everywhere'. Wooden covered bridges were like those in Switzerland and roads were very rough. The country around Prague looked fertile, but as Brydone said, it was 'strange that such a country should be subject to famine', and that the death of some 300,000 people only four years before had been from 'an epidemical distemper occasioned by the scarcity of provisions'. The travellers nevertheless reached the outskirts of the capital of Bohemia on 24 April and breakfasted with Countess Maria von Thun, a mile from the town. The countess and others whom they had met in Vienna had, according to Emma Elliot, been concerned about Lord Lindsey's behaviour so much so that 'an active profession was the only chance of saving him from a wasted and disgraceful life'. The countess hoped that when her own son grew up she would not be 'blind to his real interest', whilst Brydone acknowledged her help in inspiring Lord Lindsey 'with some of that generous and noble patriotic zeal which you alone seem capable of communicating to all who converse with you'.[16]

The party met several Austrian officers and Count Harrach from an old Austro-Bohemian family in Prague, and subsequently went to see a German tragedy, in a small, dark theatre which was 'not elegant ... and not crowded': it was 'poor entertainment and the ballet rather worse'. The next day Brydone was taken round a military clothing store by Major Sullivan, which he described as 'an excellent establishment'. The clothes for the whole of the Bohemian army were kept there, and a great deal of them made there. 'Vast cellars' Brydone wrote, 'were filled with cloth all arranged in order with the names of the different regiments' to which they belonged. The materials were made into clothes in rooms above the cellars. In one there were sixty to seventy tailors and in another as many shoemakers with all the tradesmen being former soldiers, with two field officers, four captains and a dozen or so subalterns in charge. 'These gentlemen', recorded Brydone, 'are either infirm or have been wounded in the service and this is considered as a retreat for life as they retain their full pay'.

The next stage of the journey was from Prague to Lobositz where Brydone considered taking a boat to Dresden on the River Labe, a 'fine river, more attractive than the Danube at Vienna', but discounted it when he learned it would have taken twenty hours or so. The road chosen on the side of a high mountain overhung by horrid rocks and precipices, and the noble and majestic river flowing at the foot of it, were soon as daunting as the water had been. There were several forts and castles on the summits and vineyards producing 'a rich wine, much esteemed' on the south banks of the river below. The road into Dresden lay in a fertile valley watered by the Elbe and although Brydone had to admit that the journey through nine post stations had taken more than twenty-four hours, far longer than they were told it would, it 'was the handsomest city I have yet seen in Germany. The streets are broad and straight, and the houses in general good, four stories high (with) several handsome squares' but 'it was impossible to walk the streets of this as well as Prague without feeling the greatest indignation against the tyrant (the King of Prussia) who reduced them both to ruin'.

Two hours after their arrival in the capital of Saxony, Brydone received an invitation from Count Sachem, the elector's first minister, to dine with him the next day, 1 May. Brydone described the occasion in the following terms: 'We dined ... at a table of 30 covers composed of the foreign ministers etc. There were only five or six ladies, and none of them handsome. The dining hour here is one o'clock'. Also joining them in Dresden, having arrived from Vienna, was Lord Chesterfield, a fellow member of the Society of Antiquaries, who a day or so later made Brydone a present of a cup and saucer.[17] A performance of *Il geloso in cimento* (Jealousy at its height), a comic Italian opera by Bertati with music by Amphossi was 'very pretty' but there was not one good voice in the theatre. The house was small and although the whole family of Elector Frederick Augustus, a strong supporter of the Enlightenment, was there, Brydone did not think there were more than sixty people present.[18]

Rough sketch map of Eastern Europe in the last quarter of the Eighteenth Century (including the Holy Roman and Austrian Empires, and the Russian Empire).

After viewing a collection of local porcelain the next day, including a breakfast set costing about 140 ducats (or £70), the travellers drove out to the elector's impressive country house, the Schloss Moritzburg, and its park, the latter being about six miles in circumference and containing cornfields, wilderness, lawn and gardens. Much of the property had suffered at the hand of the King of Prussia who had encamped for some time in the park, but it was the great church built of Rouen stone in 1743, the Lutheran Frauenkirche, that caught Brydone's eye with its dome (a section of an oblong spheroid) 'so built that all the Prussian bombs and cannon could make no impression on it'.

Dinner at court two days later, a 'very cold day', was the sequel to the party's formal presentation to the Elector, Frederick and his Electress, Amalie of Zweibrücken-Birkenfeld. In the evening they joined the Electress in her apartments as she had not been well, although as Brydone recorded, 'her vivacity was not lessened'. Writing his journal as usual that evening he said 'although all the Electoral family is Catholic, all sects of Christians are tolerated here, but none can buy property but Lutherans, the established religion of the country. All religions are received in the army'. Overnight there was a great deal of snow, and probably to their surprise, the party was again invited to dine at court that evening, Saturday 4 May. Brydone found himself on the Electress's right, and wrote: 'She is extremely gay, talked and laughed a great deal. A good but not luxurious dinner of two covers. The Elector likewise talked very much'. The next day, after being presented to the Duke of Courland, he told of how both played whist, with visitors taking turns to sit at the tables. The rest of the court stood round the tables, it being, said Brydone, a 'very formal and a very tiresome ceremony, though all the family are very affable'.[19]

As it was a Sunday, the travellers chose to attend the Lutheran Church (the *Kreuzkirche*) 'a very singular building'. There were, wrote Brydone, 'four fronts and a door at each angle. The inside is like a great theatre. There is a large pit with circular benches. Many galleries are over the other seven or eight I should think, and a number of boxes. The ascent to the top is by a gentle slope round the dome'. In the evening, they 'supped at the minister's and played whist', Brydone noting that although the Prince's subjects were of the Lutheran and Catholic faith they intermarried happily, with sons being bred in their father's religion and daughters in their mother's. Unlike what had been seen in Bohemia, crime was low and 'they saw no gibbets or wheels' (on which people were broken).

It was half past five on the Monday morning when, with the bill of twenty five shillings a day paid 'for very good lodgings', the travellers, accompanied by Lord Chesterfield, left Dresden for Leipzig after their five-day stay. The first change of horses proved to be at Meissen where the huge collection of porcelain models they had seen earlier in the Palais d'Hollande came from. The party arrived at 9 p.m. after driving through rich fertile country with handsome villages and 'good-humoured looking people'. There were no lodgings but Lord Chesterfield found apartments in a merchant's house and the next day Leipzig was revealed as 'a pretty little town' on the Elbe, 'full of shops for every kind of merchandise'. The university intrigued Brydone and he wrote that although on a par with the greatest elsewhere, 'there is no public building. The professors give their lectures at home and the students, about 1,000, I am told, lodge in private houses. They have no particular dress to distinguish them, and as they are so scattered about the place, they are not generally acquainted with each other'. 'The streets', he continued, 'are ill-paved and with very small stones. There is only a row of large stones in the middle'. This enabled the riotous student to 'appropriate' a supply of stones for his own purposes and was 'a constant cause of quarrels'.

Leipzig was in the middle of its three-week commercial fair, first mentioned in 1165, during which the meeting place for the *beau monde* was what Brydone called 'an ugly square filled with jewellers' shops'. He was clearly surprised to find that some of the merchants trading linen, silk, horses, carriages, cattle and books had come from England. The following day, the traveller went to see an art collection owned by a Leipzig businessman, Daniel Winkler, who had some 600 originals mostly of the Flemish school, including, it was said, one Rembrandt, and nearly 8000 drawings and prints. This was followed by a performance of the melodrama

*Ariadne auf Naxos* by Heinrich Wilhelm von Gerstenberg. Brydone admitted to not understanding a word of what the two characters spoke 'accompanied by a full orchestra, but not in recitative'. Nevertheless, the 'variety and expression of the music was amazing' and the performance, he said, 'drew tears from many of the audience'.

Later that week Lord Chesterfield gave a party in a village outside Leipzig at which Brydone met Professor Christian August Clodius who had become full professor of philosophy at the university in 1764 and married Julie Stölzel in 1771.[20] Being the time of the fair it was a holiday. Dr Hubert, another professor, was also there, and their discourse was 'witty and learned without being pedantic' The house where they dined was a rendezvous for many fashionable people, with the young men resembling students at Oxford or Cambridge. It was 'a charming retreat' that used to belong to Lord Chesterfield, with a flower garden, set amid shady walks, green fields and rivers winding through what was generally flat country. As the conversation flowed, Professor Clodius related how Brydone's description of Mount Etna in the *Tour* had encouraged him to write a tale describing the sentiments of two travellers after their descent from that mountain.

After a long solitary walk in the wood near the town on Friday 10 May, Brydone joined the company to sup at what he called, 'the public table' which was provided during the time of the fair. There was as great a variety of food as there were people at the tables (counts, princes, valets, grocers and others) and the cost was about one crown (or Thaler) a head. Those at the gaming tables, Brydone said 'seemed to lose or win with the same phlegm and indifference'. Having eaten at Professor Hubert's the next day, the last of the fair, their host took him to meet Mr Zollicoffer, a Lutheran minister and a 'very learned and worthy man' who had translated the *Tour through Sicily* into German.[21]

The travellers' journey to Berlin took little more than two days in spite of their carriage breaking down on Sunday 12 May and their being forced to spend most of the night on the road outside Wittenberg. This provoked Lord Lindsey and Mr Robertson (who may have been his man-servant) to set off for the town independently. Repairs took till midday on the Monday but they reached Beelitz, a village some dozen miles south of Potsdam, at nine in the evening. Crops on sandy land looked 'hardly worth cutting down' and the woodland was mostly fir and birch. When they were being searched at one of the posts, they found an English soldier who had been taken prisoner by the Prussians and forced to enlist. He was waiting for an opportunity to desert. Finding that there was 'nothing tolerable to eat' at the inn, the party went to bed supperless, but managed to arrive in Berlin during the early afternoon of the following day.

The party's presentation to King Frederick II (who had been on the throne from 1740), and his consort Elisabeth Christine of Braunschweig-Wolfenbüttel, was 'the most agreeable that can be imagined'. The king and queen, however, lived separate lives and had little in common. Brydone was struck with 'the softness of his voice and the nobleness of his manner'. He said 'many very obliging things', and in French, '*Il y a longtemps … que j'ai eu le plaisir de faire votre connaissance. J'ai lu vos lettres avec beaucoup de plaisir et je suis bien aisé de vous voir ici*'. Many of his questions, the author of the *Tour* wrote, showed him 'to be intimately acquainted both with the antient and modern state of Sicily' adding that the letter which amused him the most was that describing the Bishop's dinner at Agrigentum'. When Brydone expressed surprise at his majesty's interest in his letters, the monarch said '*Non, assurement il mérite tous les étages qu'on en a fait*' and, after retiring briefly, did him the honour of saying '*Le publique Monsieur, vous est extrêmement redevable et moi en particulier. Je vous remercie pour le plaisir que vous m'avez donné*'. All this was said in front of the whole court – a gathering of at least 150 people comprising princes, generals, officers, ministers of state and foreign ministers many of whom, as Brydone said, would have totally ignored him had the king not said what he did.

With hardly a day without invitations to various events, Brydone became a little tired of 'this bustling, bowing, noisy and insipid life'. The feelings he had for Vienna had been transferred to the Prussian capital. Berlin's population was to increase from 6,000 people in 1648 to 170,000 by the turn of the 18th century. Military defence had been a priority of Frederick the Great's father, and during the Seven Years' War when the city was briefly occupied by Russian and Austrian forces, the population reached 100,000, of which 26,000 were soldiers. Brydone described the duties of the garrison as to guard the walls and prevent desertion, saying 'if a deserter gets over the wall and is returned, he is made to say where he crossed … and the sentries there … punished. The rolls are called at night, and a cannon sounded if anyone is missed'.

The Hohenzollerns built a palace on the Cölln side of the river Spree and the design and construction of a grid of streets a little to the west of the palace followed. A further boost to Berlin's expansion was given by the construction of important architectural landmarks along and around the *Unter den Linden*. The latter developed from a bridle path laid out in the sixteenth century to access the hunting grounds of the Tiergarten, and replaced in 1647 by a magnificent boulevard of linden trees which crossed from the *Stadtschloss* to the gates of the city. It was, however, not till 1792, that the road from Berlin to Potsdam was opened as Prussia's first paved highway. Prominent new buildings included the Opera House (1742), Prince Henry's Palace (1756) and the opening of St Hedwig's Cathedral three years before Brydone's visit, followed four year later by completion of the Royal Library.

A Plan of the City of Berlin in 1776, published by John Stockdale, and drawn by John Andrews, a man of unknown origin who, according to the *Gentleman's Magazine*, was an able scholar, historian and politician

Fifteen miles to the south-west was Potsdam, on the river Havel and then separate from Berlin, not unlike Windsor outside London, the residence of the Prussian kings (and later German Kaisers). The relatively modest palace of the *Sanssouci* in the rococo style used by Frederick, like the *Neues Palais*, was in Potsdam and had been built to celebrate the ousting of Austria from its long role as the dominant power in German affairs. *Monbijou* palace on the north bank of the River Spree, the residence of Queen Frederika Louisa till her death in 1757, was unused at the time of Brydone's visit. The Potsdam Stadtschloss, another royal palace, had been built near its Old Market in the mid-1660s and became Frederick the Great's winter residence. Nearby was the much newer City Hall, designed by the Dutch architect Jan Bouman, with its circular tower and other buildings in what came to be known as the Dutch quarter. Three gates provided access into Potsdam, the oldest the Jägertor being built in 1733, the *Neuener Tor* not far from the Dutch quarter, and the ornate *Brandenburger Tor* which had been completed five years before Brydone's visit, not to be confused with Berlin's similarly named triumphal arch on the *Luisenplatz* built in the 1730s.

Diplomatic hospitality began to be extended to the travellers on the last day of May. 'Mr Harris' wrote Brydone, 'gave us two breakfasts, with dancing after them till four or five in the evening'. After leaving Oxford in 1765, spending a year at Leyden, and unconventionally travelling through Prussia and Poland during his grand tour, in 1769 James Harris became chargé d'affaires at the embassy in Madrid and minister plenipotentiary three years later. By the time he came to Berlin in 1772 he was still only twenty-five years old, and within a month of his arrival he had achieved the coup of being the first foreign diplomat to reveal an agreement to partition Poland signed by Frederick the Great and Prussia's ally Russia.[22] Brydone was impressed with the twenty or thirty ladies Harris assembled on both occasions; there were 'hardly two or three that were not handsome'. He 'did the honours of the English nation with great taste and magnificence, and to the universal satisfaction of every lady'.

The envoy-extraordinary had a house in which it seems Brydone, if not the other travellers stayed, and a garden that Brydone much admired. The weather was to become very hot and the party swam in his purpose-made pool. The temperature in Brydone's room was 72°F, later rising to 79°F and very different from the 45°F it had been at the end of May. Harris, who married the following year, used his prestigious social occasions to influence those with power and authority, telling the tutor that English country dances were popular at these functions. Waltzing was gaining favour, a trend which Brydone disapproved of.

As their first week in Berlin came to an end, Brydone wrote that 'Pol and I' (possibly a reference to William Morton Pitt) were invited to sup with the Princess Royal, then 62, the sister of Frederick the Great and Margravine of Brandenburg-Ansbach, at the *Schloss Monbijou*. On the northern bank of the River Spree and within sight of the city, it had served as the summer residence of Queen Sophie Dorothea till her death in 1757, and remained uninhabited for a long time. The evening was attended by the Princess Royal, Prince Henry, the thirteenth child of King Frederick William I, a soldier and diplomat who always lived in the shadow of his elder brother the king, numerous other princesses, diplomats and the chamberlain, and started with a walk in the garden. Dinner passed in quiet conversation but, with the dessert on the table and the band playing, Brydone was suddenly conscious that he was not wearing clean gloves (then a common etiquette) and about to go through to a large hall which opened on to the garden, where the assembled party would dance till early morning.

The Prussian Academy of Sciences held its annual meeting on 6 June. Founded at the beginning of the eighteenth century, it had seen considerable change during Frederick the Great's reign, including the passing of a law requiring it to invite the public to suggest unsolved scientific problems for its academicians to solve, and the construction in 1753 of its own laboratory. Although overshadowed by the Royal Society in London and the *Académie Française* in Paris and divided by internal rivalries in the first half of the eighteenth century, it developed an international reputation. Ten years before Brydone's visit, the king had replaced its director Leonhard Euler, a Swiss mathematician and physicist, with Joseph-Louis Lagrange, another eminent academic in similar fields who was to hold the post for twenty years. It was this scientist to whom Brydone was presented before 'a discourse was read, principally an eloge (an encomium or panegyric) of the king'. The tutor seems to have expected a competition of some sort to have been on the agenda but, as he wrote, 'due to an administrative failure ... a discourse was read on the poets who succeeded Homer. It was full of fire and imagination, and equally displayed the ingenuity and erudition of the author'. The gathering lasted two hours, watched by the five-year-old Prince Frederick of Brunswick.

One afternoon three days later, Brydone and his party were in the garden of the Queen's country palace at Schönhausen in Pankow, outside the city gates to the north of Berlin. The gathering was without much ceremony or fuss, more English than French in style, with much 'shade and verdure ... agreeable in a hot summer'. Her Majesty 'was very pleased when they praised the attractive country nature of the place'. Returning to Berlin between nine and ten o'clock after what had obviously been a congenial event, the party was joined there by a Mr Lewis and Sir John Stepney, the eighth baronet and MP for Monmouth who had just become envoy to Dresden. It was not until 3 a.m that they were back in Potsdam, having travelled the last leg in Mr Pitt's wagon.[23] Next day, the enlarged party went to visit several palaces and gardens in Potsdam, including the Sanssouci, designed for Frederick so that he could be 'without cares' and relax away from the pomp and ceremony at court, but which they found smaller than expected 'with only a few little apartments'. Even the king's own chamber was 'very small and indifferently furnished. Books, papers and music were lying about in great confusion' but Brydone noted a convenient writing table, and a neat music stand with some of Johann Quantz's flute solos on it.[24] The chairs, on the other hand, were 'old and ragged and would not be admitted to any decent house in England'. Brydone considered Sanssouci which had been built in two years at a cost of £120,000, 'magnificent ... very much for show'. From the belvedere in the garden there was a fine view of the river 'which swells out in many places and gives life and variety to the scene'. After dinner the party observed a very large bustard in a field near the road, seeming much larger than a turkey, whereupon Sir John Stepney nearly shot it 'but missed by a foot'.

The travellers had been in Berlin for nearly five weeks when they at last left for Oranienburg on 18 June, the first leg of their 120 or so mile journey to Strelitz, the home of the Duke of Mecklenburg-Strelitz.[25] The party passed a royal castle falling into ruin by the river

Havel on 'a country road of deep heavy sand', and at Oranienburg looked at the palace and garden, 'neither of which was worthy of notice'. The next change of horses was at Zehdenick where the country became less heavy with 'tolerable rye in the fields but no wheat'. Fine woods and numerous 'beautiful birds' were visible as the travellers approached Fürstenberg and its lake, belonging to the duke.

Determined to reach Strelitz in one day, the party arrived an hour after midnight. Despite its reputation as one of the backward regions of the empire, Brydone had an introduction to its anglophile ruler and clearly wanted to meet him, having learned about the economic and social improvements he had begun to introduce. His immediate reaction was, however, that attractive as the town's location was beside the lake, it was still 'capable of improvement'. The park had some deer and the smaller lakes were well-stocked with fish. They were shown an English china service 'beautifully painted with birds and insects' and 'no two pieces alike' at the palace which was undergoing repair, necessitating that the duke lived at Neubrandenburg, some 50 miles from the Baltic Sea.

Travelling northward on 20 June to meet the Duke in his temporary home, the travellers passed varied country and several lakes, one 10 or 12 miles long. Nightingales greeted them as they walked along the bank of a lake to stretch themselves. Brydone was inclined to believe that 'the further north these birds inhabit they have the greater variety of song'. The lake was 'smooth and clear as glass. All nature enjoyed a perfect calm'. At last the tutor had some 'perfect solitude'. On their arrival, and finding that the duke was lodged on the market place in 'a house with two chimneys something like a Scotch manse only there (were) some miserable statues and two sentinels before the door', the party sent in their names and were invited to dinner.

Pitt and Brydone dined at court with Duke Karl and his wife Princess Friederike, along with three ladies and two gentlemen-in-waiting. Mystery remains regarding the whereabouts of young Lindsey, who was last heard of on the road to Berlin. Their highnesses spoke a great deal, 'with benignity and goodness', he lamenting his inability to give Mecklenburg peasants more freedom since he could not bring other nobles round to his point of view. He admitted the great poverty, explaining that his land was in sequestration and the £1,000 per year allowed him by the Council of the Empire did not allow him to support the dignity of his court. The Diet, he explained was held each year in the middle of winter, with separate tents being pitched for the Dukes of Mecklenburg-Strelitz and Mecklenburg-Schwerin, with 'the nobles made to appear bare-headed even in the deepest cold'. Princess Friederike, who was a good musician and played the German flute very well, said they had entertained few English people. The Duke of Hamilton and the Duke of Devonshire had paid visits but she could not make the latter 'open his lips'. Brydone concluded that 'They seem to lead a miserable and uniform life, and are slaves to etiquette even without knowing it, for the Duke told me that he had destroyed every kind of etiquette and ceremony the moment after he had got out from under his canopy of state'.

Returning south, Brydone left Berlin and Potsdam on 29 June by way of a large park which stretched 'almost to Charlottenburg', finding it 'very pleasant and varied'. Although similar to the gardens at Versailles, he said they were greatly neglected on account of the king never living there with some water features beginning to 'be covered with verdure' and the statue of Neptune looked 'ridiculous, rising from the grass'. For Brydone, Potsdam was 'one of the handsomest towns in Germany, but when you were admiring a fine Corinthian front it (was) ten to one' that a soldier would show himself from a window 'hanging out his waistcoat or breeches to air, for almost the whole (was) a barracks'.[26]

# CHAPTER 8

# In Poland and the Russian Empire (July to November 1776)

Unfortunately, there were times on the next leg of what was a lengthy journey eastwards when he appears to have had neither the time nor space on the small sheets of notepaper he used to keep a note of events, furthermore, he rarely names his companions. At the end of a gathering in Berlin given by a Lord M to allow Brydone to say his farewells, which lasted four or five hours and where he was 'charmed by his gaiety and good humour', they ate brose (a Scots oatmeal porridge) and 'no roast meat', and listened to Scottish airs and reels being played by a piper at the door of an adjacent room. Brydone also called on others who had entertained them, walking for two hours with the Prince Royal who was 'familiar with every play of Shakespeare and expressed much goodness and humanity' but 'detested the character of the Polish nation'. In the evening, Brydone went to a concert he gave where he also played the cello, 'well for an amateur', adding that 'their highnesses talked to me the whole time as I was the only stranger, and pressed me very much to stay for the fetes' promised by the Grand Duke in July.

Having passed through Fürstenwald, some 35 miles from Potsdam, Brydone was soon in the small 'neat' town of Frankfurt on the river Oder, where 600 students attended its university. The wooden bridge over the river was protected by breakwaters that helped to split large blocks of ice before they could damage the structure. Travelling through numerous villages Brydone could only conclude that 'The people of this miserable sandy country who have never had an opportunity of seeing any other probably imagine that all the world is made of sand and … (as a consequence) are perfectly pleased with their condition'. The Swiss and Scotch Highlanders were, he admitted, 'more subject to *malaise du pais* than any other'. At Grosse Glogau in Silesia, a small town with a river that often overflowed and which had been returned to Prussia in 1745, the country became much richer with 'excellent wheat and many fruit trees'. An officer from a British regiment was kind enough to ask whether he could be of any service. The inn, which proved to be 'as good as any in England', had a double spit for roasting or smoking meat over a large fire which so fascinated Brydone that he drew a small sketch of it.[1]

As Brydone left Prussia and entered what had been Poland, there were signs that the border differed by several miles from that marked on any of the maps he was using. Poland was the carvery of Europe. The massacre of Jews, Poles and Ukrainians in 1768 at Uman in the Polish-Lithuanian Commonwealth by Ukrainian rebels, where in excess of 20,000 had been killed, had led to Polish nobles agreeing to build a fortress at Bar in Podolia to protect the Commonwealth against Russian influence. It was typical of such bloody times that between 1769 and 1771 both Austria and Prussia had seized various border territories. In February 1772 they partitioned the Commonwealth and by August, Russia, Prussia and Austria occupied those parts they had agreed upon. It was an important success for Frederick the Great and the first of what was to be three partitions. East Prussia and Brandenburg were brought together, and Prussia added 600,000 people to her population. Three-quarters of the newly added urban populace were German-speaking. Russia received the largest, if least important addition to her territory along with 1.3 million people.

In October 1773, the Sejm, the lower house of the Polish parliament, and the king, Stanislaw August Poniatowski, a protégé of Russia, established the first Ministry of Education which was charged with reshaping the educational system and replacing the monopoly held by Jesuit schools. Three universities were opened in Warsaw, Vilnius and Krakow. The next two years saw Austria and Russia making light work of invading and annexing Poland, the latter with an army of 150,000 men. Warsaw was to fall to Austria along with other major cities, and Britain who was still technically at war with Poland stormed Gdansk in 1775. By 1776, when Brydone arrived, the new Polish government had just settled in. The Polish-Prussian commercial treaty of March 1775 had been 'an exercise in piratical mercantilism, designed to turn Poland into a source of cheap raw materials for the Prussian economy and a captive market for Prussian exports'. Another threat to the new state was the king himself. He had a habit of upsetting experiments, and traditionalists and those with Russian interests wanted him shackled. He became not so much a king as 'the honorary president of a new executive'.[2]

The journey to Warsaw, a distance of well over 300 miles was to take more than a week and involved passing through or staying a night in such towns as Poznan and Kutno. At first the countryside was barren, but soon 'there were many windmills and much corn' which was exported to Brandenburg. Hops were being grown in some places but no fruit and 'no running water.' The cottages were composed of a 'wooden-frame fill'd up with clay' and the furniture of those Brydone entered consisted of a 'long narrow table of fir tree forms, two or three earthen pots, a tub for water and a straw bed'. Most of the peasants they met were 'bare-footed men and women, and ill-clad, as humble as the nobles appear proud.' At Poznan, 'not a handsome town' in spite of a few tolerable buildings, there was news of a disturbance and with a Baron Puget, an officer in the Prussian service, as his Cicerone, Brydone noted several cannon ready in the market-place in case of trouble. He was to be later awoken by kettle drums and trumpets and to watch some Russians at exercise.

Once in Warsaw, introductions were effected, initially to Count Moglin, a large landowner from Brandenburg, along with the Princess Marechale, Izabella Lubomirska, née Czartoryska, wife of the Grand Marshal of the Polish Crown, Stanislaw Lubomirski. She was one of the Polish aristocracy who were often called 'by their office more than their names.' This took some time and 'a stranger' Brydone wrote, 'is long in learning all their names and often makes blunders.' His first formal dinner was with the princess at the Wilanów Palace some five miles outside the city, built a century before by King Jan Sobieski. Pleasantly situated by the banks of the Vistula, there was a canal which had been built partly to surround the garden. Prince Adam Kazimierz Czartoryski, a writer and critic, had compared the country scene there with the Elysian Fields. 'As you advance,' Brydone wrote, 'you observe a neat village composed of a number of small thatched houses. Every cottage has its garden and a little green. Lambs and kids are seen skipping about, and every tree and bush is pregnant with life and music'. The creation was called 'Povonskai'.

Brydone added Polish noblemen to his list of the richest and most powerful of any in Europe, and the peasants the poorest and most wretched. He had been told that several Polish families had an income of upwards of £100,000 a year whereas few among the poor had 100 ducats. Those with authority, whom the tutor called 'the Nonces', enjoyed very great privileges much greater than members of parliament at Westminster and their persons were 'so sacred that any injury offered to them, even the slightest blow, is death'. Twenty years before, he added, 'their splendour was prodigious' and many had thirty or forty horsemen attending them. Emphasising the present resentment between rich and poor, he described how two large wooden houses burned to the ground in three hours and nobody rushed to help but stood in doorways viewing the sight.

Turning to the military, the ex-soldier reported that there were about 30,000 Russian troops in Poland, 'now well-behaved' but they had not always been so. The Poles had 'not above five or six thousand effective men'. Several questioned him about General Charles Lee who was fighting with rebel forces in America and who had served for a time after the Seven Years' War in the Polish army of King Stanislaw II. There had been trouble in a small town nearby where the Russians had massacred many Poles who had come to vote. About 50 of the local gentry and 9 Russian soldiers had been killed, along with 12 or 14 wounded. On 18 July, Brydone encountered some Russians, six carts full of them, 'they were all cut either on the head, the arms or hands'. He was told by the Jews driving the carts that there had been a dispute at the election on account of the 'nonce', or candidate chosen, having been nominated by the Russians. Then, one of the Polish noblemen railed against the pusillanimity of their decision in choosing 'a representative appointed by their tyrants'. The Russian commanding officer told him to be silent. High words followed and the Pole drew his sabre and wounded the officer. This was enough, and the Russian troops charged the Polish nobles with their bayonets. Some defended themselves with their sabres, others 'had pistols in their boots'. It had been a very unequal engagement.

The following day, the court chamberlain gave the Brydone party an 'afternoon entertainment at his country house, with fruit, ices, coffee and tea'. It made use of a 'most luxurious little retreat ... a rotondo lit only from above'. Nearby was a lake with some boats, and a grotto at one end. While visiting the king's summer palace and park at Lazienki, Brydone was particularly charmed by several Chinese paintings, including one showing a view of Canton. Another guide who was prepared to talk to the travellers about the feudal state of agriculture in the country, and show them samples of corn from his own land, was General Franciszek Branicki who had been ambassador in both Berlin and Moscow. The traveller's only regret from his brief tour of Warsaw was the absence of any public walk, particularly one through woods similar to those enjoyed by the aristocracy. The Garden Saxe, the only public garden, had been opened in 1727, but it was small, formal and attached to a palace.[3]

Brydone left Warsaw northwards for Riga on 26 July, first visiting Bialystok, considered the Versailles of Poland where he was given a dinner of 'fat woodcock bred in the marshes roundabout'. Then, in extremely hot conditions, he stopped fo a while at Grodno (or Hrodna), the second town of Lithuania on the substantial and navigable river Neman, an important centre of trade and commerce. A place of culture, it had several castles, one of which had been the residence of Stephen Báthory, a King of Poland in the second half of the sixteenth century. It had been severely ravaged by fire some twenty years before and many of the palaces were falling into ruin. The head of the Grodno annexe of *L'Académie du Corps des Cadets de la Noblesse* which had been founded in Warsaw by the king not much more than ten years before, showed Brydone the school's collection of sea shells found in the Indian Ocean, together with many precious stones, including diamonds, rubies, aquamarines and topaz found there.

Twenty miles beyond Grodno, the fore axletree of the traveller's coach broke. Accidents involving the iron bar connecting the opposite wheels of a carriage were common, especially where the roads were constructed from tree trunks placed across their width. After finding that the smith in the next village was only a locksmith, they had to return to Grodno 'by slow stages ... a great inconvenience in the heat and dust'. Having time to stare, Brydone described a typical Lithuanian cottage – one large room sometimes seventy to eighty feet long, with animals and people in it. Walls were made from tree trunks and holes filled with moss, the roof being of fir roughly split. Less explicable was that the language people used to their horses was the same as that used in Scotland.

On the last day of July, and after passing through Merkiné, the travellers at last found themselves in Kauno (now Kaunas), some 115 miles north of Grodno. Brydone was tired out, having had no sleep for four nights in the carriage. He described it as 'a pleasant little town on two navigable rivers, admirable for an active commercial people, but here is little or no trade, and all the best houses (are) going to ruin'. The town, he said, was known for its honey, 'better than that of Majorca, and its hydromel, called Lippetz'. Russian guards were everywhere with cannon and ammunition wagons but the tutor received no reply when he addressed them in French.

Along the road to Riga the party encountered 'fine corn country'. They stopped a while in Jelgava, the capital of Courland 'a neat town with wooden houses painted red, white and green, where Peter von Biron, the last Duke of Courland, had encouraged its development as a centre of culture. He lived outside the town in an impressive palace, despite it being in a state of 'very bad repair'. Travelling the last 30 miles through a great deal of heathland and brushwood where the River Lielupe was shallow, they were soon in Riga where they were received very politely by Count von Browne, the governor-general of Livonia, and Brydone was given his 'very necessary passport'. The count, an Irish soldier of fortune who had been a full general in the Russian service, explained that the journey through to St Petersburg would take a day more than usual on account of the road being very busy with the duke's couriers.

Encountering an atmosphere of illegal money-making where travellers were concerned, Brydone complained about the efforts of the post master to impose six instead of four horses on his carriage, threatening to go to the governor. Mariana Starke, in her *Information and Direction for Travellers*, published in 1824, explained that a Russian postillion could not demand more than one copeck a horse per verst (about two-thirds of a mile) but travellers often paid more. The law required that three horses were to be put to every carriage containing two or three people. No one was allowed to travel post without having first obtained an order for post-horses, signed by a governor, civil or military, a *podaroshna*. The consequence of low prices for post-horses was that foreigners frequently found it difficult to find them. In winter, it was usual to travel in sledges which were fast, when a journey of 250 versts might be accomplished in twenty-four hours.

With a long way yet to go Brydone's party soon left Riga, and on Saturday 3 August, they were 'past a lake, and … along a high bank by a fine river', the Daugava, when their postillion nearly caused an accident with a peasant, 'by sheer carelessness'. The next morning it was cold enough for Brydone to note that the temperature in the carriage had fallen to a cool 43°F although by ten o'clock it was 'burning hot' at 75°F. His wearisome mood returned and the list of his complaints lengthened by the minute. Charges for part-versts were 'always rounded up', the military paid 'only half the post charges', he was being 'attacked by fleas and bugs' and 'charged five English shillings for a dish of coffee'. Travelling beds and sheets were absolutely necessary in Russia, something of which he would have been told. A bed was a scarce commodity even in the cities and quite unobtainable at country inns, and the carrying of provisions was strongly advised.

Reaching Tartu on 6 August, 170 miles from St Petersburg, then known as Dorpat, Brydone was surprised to find a town, formerly built of stone, was 'now built of wood, the result of sieges and fires in the recent past'. The peasants about the town were 'in the most poor and abject state imaginable'. He felt deeply for their misery, having 'seen their tyrannical masters beat them with the most inconceivable cruelty when all the defence they could offer was throwing themselves on their knees with their hands and eyes lifted up to heaven imploring mercy'. At Narva, a further eighty-five or so miles, where good-sized vessels could load, the story was of 'a disagreeable town' but one with impressive sawmills receiving logs that had been floated down the river from Lake Piepus where 'one man can do the work of thirty'.

The travellers arrived in the Russian capital on Friday 9 August 1776, the journey from Warsaw having taken fifteen days. Founded by Peter the Great (1672–1725), St Petersburg became the seat of the Romanov dynasty and the Imperial Court of the Russian Tsars. Catherine II, the most renowned and longest-ruling female leader of Russia, came to the throne in 1762 following a *coup d'état* which she engineered together with the officers of the Royal Guard and which supposedly involved the assassination of her husband Peter III. An enlightened despot, she was to be a reformer, and a patron of the arts who presided over the Russian Enlightenment. She spoke French fluently and became an avid art collector, filling the Winter Palace (later becoming the Hermitage Museum) with priceless masterpieces. Catherine also wrote plays and essays, being what the Prussian king, Friederich II, described as 'very proud, very ambitious, and very vain'.

The catastrophic fires which St Petersburg had experienced forty years before Brydone arrived had led to the establishment of a redevelopment commission under Count Burkhard Christoph von Münnich, a Danish-born, German military engineer. The plan it produced divided the city into five boroughs with its centre in the Admiralty borough between the Neva and the Fontanka rivers. Three radial streets, now known as Nevsky Prospekt, Gorokhovaya Street and Voznesensky Prospekt, accommodated buildings initially in Baroque style but after the 1760s in neoclassical architecture. There were no permanent bridges across the Neva, only pontoons, and the Obvodny Canal (not completed till 1833) became the southern boundary of the city.

Brydone was to add his name to the dozens of Scots and their families living in and around St Petersburg at this time, and the hundreds of other foreign nationals. Early evidence of a 'Caledonian Phalanx', as it came to be described, was provided by Scottish vessels trading with Poland and Prussia in the fifteenth century, followed in the next century by armed Scottish merchantmen clashing with Hanseatic vessels.[4] The port of Leith had strong connections with the eastern Baltic and the names of a growing number of Scottish soldiers, sailors, master-craftsmen and merchants, soon appeared among St Petersburg visitors and residents. Typical among numerous soldiers were John and Andrew Wood who transferred their loyalty to Russia at the beginning of the seventeenth century after initially being in the Polish army whilst Patrick Gordon, born in Aberdeenshire, fought in the Polish and Swedish armies before finding his way to Moscow, where he became a confidant to Peter the Great and a general serving in the Ukraine.

Among Russian sailors in the seventeenth century was another Aberdonian. Admiral Thomas Gordon served the Scots Royal Navy till 1707, the British Navy after the union with England, and the Imperial Russian Navy between 1717 and 1741. Another former Royal Navy recruit was Samuel Greig who after fighting in the Seven Years' War obtained the rank of vice-admiral and became commander of Kronstadt, then more commonly called Cronstadt. His huge achievement was in constructing its arsenal, docks and lengthy fortifications on the seven-mile long Kotlin Island, which greatly impressed Brydone. He was also pleased to note that the Carron Iron Works in Falkirk had supplied fire pumps to help remedy the 'awkward and unwieldy' drainage associated with the great canal built by Peter the Great (known as the Maritime Canal). Although doctors in Russia were scarce, and generally German, some were Scottish. In 1621, Arthur Dee had arrived in Moscow having been appointed chief physician to Tsar Michael Romanov, a post he held for fourteen years. During Tsar Peter III's short reign in 1762, John Rogerson, a doctor from Dumfriesshire, was given permission to practice and, having settled into fashionable society in St Petersburg during the reign of Catherine, was appointed physician-in-ordinary in January 1776 with a salary of 4000 roubles a year, and elected to the Imperial Academy of Sciences. He was subsequently elected to the Royal Society in London for promoting Anglo-Russian scientific links.

An architect, Charles Cameron, whose grandfather came from Edinburgh, was to arrive at the court in St Petersburg in 1778 and become the private architect of Catherine, working only for her and the heir to the throne, Grand Duke Paul. After completing a hanging garden and a Chinese ensemble in the palace and gardens of Tsarskoye Selo, near St Petersburg, he designed and built the model town of Sofia as part of the landscaping of the park. Having worked among bricklayers, stone masons and smiths he next became director of the Alexandrovsk textile mill and mint master of the Izhorsky iron works in Kolpino. All such craftsmen would have been inspired by 'the Livonian carpenter' as Donizetti's opera of 1819 described Peter the Great. His masterful use of timber scaffolding, with wide ramps several hundred yards long enabled other trades to access buildings as they rose. Incoming ships were required to bring in stone and other material used by the army of prisoners deployed in the city's construction.

Among other travellers undertaking the 'Northern Tour' about this time, and who put their first impressions of St Petersburg and its populace into print, was Sir Nathaniel William Wraxall. Earlier in the decade he had visited Portugal and Scandinavia, publishing *Cursory Remarks made in a tour through some of the Northern Parts of Europe* in 1775 where he reported 'everything is on a vast and colossal scale, resembling that of the Empire itself. The public buildings, churches, monasteries and private palaces of the nobility are of an immense size, and seem as if designed for creatures of a superior height and dimension to man'. In a reference which echoed something of what has been called his 'self-consciously chivalric' style, he went on to say that he had been told 'that the style of loveliness here, is not a little different from ours; and that in order to possess any pre-eminent degree of it, a woman must weigh at least two hundred weight'.

Described as 'a vast canvas of historical and guide-book material', Coxe's *Travels*, published in 1784 by Thomas Cadell, ran through six English editions. The historian and clergyman, William

Coxe, who had George Augustus Herbert, the future eleventh Earl of Pembroke, in his care, wrote how he had been 'filled with astonishment that so late as the beginning of this century, the ground on which Petersburg now stands was only a vast morass occupied by a few fisherman's huts'. In an early comment about the Russian male, Coxe reported that despite the edicts issued by Peter I against the wearing of beards, it was:

> a barbarism in which the bulk of the people still continue. I am ready to allow that the principal nobles are perfectly civilized, and as refined in their entertainments, mode of living, and social intercourse as those of other European countries but there is a wide difference between polishing a nation, and polishing a few individuals. The merchants and peasants still universally retain their beards, their national dress, their original manners and, what is most remarkable, the greatest part of the merchants and burghers of the large towns, even the citizens of Petersburg and Moscow, resemble in their external appearance and general mode of living, the inhabitants of the smallest village ... Notwithstanding the rigorous edicts issued by Peter I, I can venture to assert that of the 11,500,000 males which form the population of the Russian empire, at least nine million wear their beards.

Rising from the marshy delta of the river Neva, St Petersburg had become a city of extraordinary beauty and the showpiece of a new Russia. The 'Venice of the North' was soon vying with Amsterdam for the title but floods were, and remained, a constant threat. The basin of the Neva, with Lakes Ladoga and Onega, was fed by twenty to thirty rivers from the White Sea, an inlet of the Barents Sea. When construction began in 1703, canals and pounds for drainage had to be dug out, the extracted soil being used to raise the level of buildings. By the end of the nineteenth century there were nearly fifty waterways and one hundred and one islands. The Citadel, now referred to as the Fortress, was the first structure to be built, originally of clay then by 1730, of stone and the Peter and Paul Cathedral nearby, with its spire of copper gilt, was completed three years later.

Brydone's initial focus in his journal was on The Admiralty building in St Petersburg, which was 'a mighty mystery'. No stranger was allowed to see it, he reported, perhaps because it was 'not worth the seeing', a presumption Brydone used in the case of mysteries. Mrs Starke drew attention to its quarter of a mile facade, six porticos and gilt dome in front of the dockyard. In an octagonal house built for the purpose, 'the traveller found an Archimedean sphere, about twelve feet in diameter and representing the heavens, with every constellation and every considerable star'. Brydone felt it to be 'an admirable method of studying astronomy. The outside is the teraqueous globe. Motion is given it by a handle within', but it did not appear ever to have had any regular motion by clockwork to represent the appearance of the heavens.

The trade carried on throughout St Petersburg, 'the centre of this immense empire', was an object of singular curiosity on Brydone's part. He found 'the commodities of almost every district of it are easily conveyed by water carriages from the centre to the very extremes of the empire'. The Ukraine, he wrote, 'the country of the

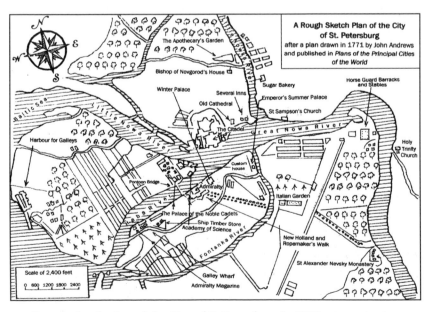

Rough sketch plan of the City of St Petersburg in 1771.

Cossacks is the most fertile region. Large barges are towed up the Volga till the descent to the Baltic is reached, when they are carried by the current'. He told how goods were taken past cataracts by teams of men who were punished if they damaged or lost them. Albeit that shipping was seasonal, varying with the height of the river, which was dependent on the snow melt, he was astonished at the speed with which goods were transferred; vessels were often sold in St Petersburg when they were unable to return up river. As he adjusted to local conditions, enquiries about the origin of the tea that was sold in shops elucidated the fact that it was brought overland from China. The finest was, however, no longer available and they drank English tea, as that from India was called, at about fourteen shillings per pound.

Brydone was soon picking up information from a variety of sources, one being Dr Matthew Guthrie, the son of an Edinburgh lawyer. After an apprenticeship with William Inglis, a surgeon, and a brief period at sea in the employ of the East India Company, Guthrie had returned to Scotland to take a course in medicine at the University of Edinburgh. Once qualified, and after practising for while in London, he went to Russia only to find that he would have more opportunity with higher qualifications. As a result, he returned home to take MA and MD degrees at St Andrews, and in 1770 he was appointed to the Admiralty in St Petersburg. Following service in Moldova during the first Russo-Turkish war, he returned to the capital in 1776 where he was to spend the rest of his life as chief doctor to the Land (First) Cadet Corps, and be awarded hereditary noble status.[5] Brydone enjoyed listening to Guthrie's comments on all manner of things. On one occasion, after mentioning that he had learned that the machine used to convey warships built at St Petersburg to the naval base at Cronstadt across the bay was called a 'camel', Guthrie recalled his own encounter with such animals. Speaking of 'the killing wind' experienced in the region around Belsova, the physician said, 'the camels and animals can feel it coming and put their heads to the ground'. He had seen animals killed from wind.

In St Petersburg, 'lodgings, carriage and servants are dear', Brydone explained. Two good rooms at the Hotel de Londres cost one rouble a day or twenty a month.[6] A carriage and pair was 46 roubles a month or 2 roubles per day, but if Brydone used his own carriage, the cost was halved. Many people used four-horse carriages owing to the city being so spread out. Merchants were very hospitable to visitors carrying introductions. The English colony all lived in one place and seemed very comfortable. They were, Brydone thought, 'on a better footing with the court and the nobility than any merchants' that he had seen, and were invited everywhere, and treated well by the Empress. Nevertheless, Brydone was convinced that any traveller who wished to avoid 'inconvenience or embarrassment' should not come to Poland or Russia. The entry process and customs inspection was very long and just as complicated on departure. The paperwork required and the necessary bribes required careful scrutiny. He himself waited more than two weeks for his passport, and was fortunate to have William Morton Pitt nearby when his charge, who read Cyrillic script, spotted that it had been made out for sea travel only, not the mode of travel Brydone had asked for.

So far as the affairs of the Russian Empire were concerned, Brydone said that the impetus they had received from Peter (the Great) was still evident, but 'if any person were to examine the manner in which public matters are now conducted, they would probably find it extremely slovenly. Everything is made a job of, the Empress is cheated on all hands, and the only consideration in any department is how much money they can pocket'. He said that when rear-admiral Sir Charles Knowles, who had been chief of the surveying branch of the Russian navy between 1770 and 1774, returned to England, he described the courtyard of the Admiralty as being 'covered with filth and rotten trees ... that might be removed at an easy expense'. The Queen 'ordered it to be done, and a sum of money was allotted for paving it, but on clearing away the filth it was found to be paved already, though nobody knew of it'. Furthermore, Brydone said that on the island where Peter had intended to build his city, the streets were still discernable but covered in grass. The church where the imperial family were buried was nearby.

It was at this point that Brydone referred to the steeple of the old cathedral which had been recently struck by lightning and burned.

The travellers climbed the scaffolding to view the prospect, the branches of the river flowing through the city and only uniting as they fell out into the Gulf of Finland. To the west the view ended with the steeples and fortifications of Cronstadt. They then inspected the clock which was being built for the church before visiting the small wooden hut, now referred to as the 'cabin of Peter the Great', where Peter lived at the start of his work. It was 'surrounded by another building to preserve it' and greatly admired by Brydone. Among construction work recorded was one 'enormous palace, two or three times the size of Versailles' but not elegant, and another which the Empress was having built for General Count Grigory Orlov, who had distinguished himself during the Seven Years' War and by whom she had an illegitimate son. Because there was a plethora of timber, scaffolding was made of it and was, as Brydone said 'often more beautiful than the building itself'. Houses were of wood or brick, but plastered to resemble stone.

The rites of the Greek Orthodox Church came in for criticism from the innately Presbyterian Brydone when he described them as surpassing in absurdity 'everything that is possible to imagine'. The rites of Rome were 'reason and common sense' in comparison. Worst of all, they were 'not only so overcharged with ceremonies but so insufferably long that no patience is able to stand it. There is a great deal of horrid uncouth barbarous singing which is the only music that is allowed'. Sometimes, he wrote, 'they stand bowing and making the sign of the cross for near a quarter of an hour together'.

Having seen an artillery regiment encamped outside the city where, by way of a compliment to the ladies present, they 'threw a good many shells with very tolerable precision', the ex-soldier caught sight of a passing funeral cortege, 'the coffin having a hat at one end, spurs at the other, and a sword along its length'. Guns were also mentioned when Brydone met Count Ivan Osterman, the son of a famous father, and at that time a senator, who recalled that twenty-five years previously 'the best place for snipe shooting was where the shops now are'.[7] Another member of the nobility maintained that Russians, or the aristocracy at least, did not live to old age, explaining that by the time they were Brydone's age they were aging, and seldom lived beyond sixty, hot baths in the ubiquitous bathhouses contributing to this. To such scraps about the habits and behaviour at one end of the social ladder the traveller added several deeply felt remarks about Russian peasants, praising their 'ease and grace' and their command of language. Calling them 'natural actors', Brydone thought it would now be wrong to assume that 'this talent belongs to the warmer southern climate, and that northern nations are slow and phlegmatic'. Drunkenness was, he thought, 'more prevalent than in any other place, even Switzerland', and many horses sensing a drunken stupor behind them, found their own way home. Since Russians habitually travelled on straw mattresses in their carts and slept on many journeys, it was not surprising that some 'took their entire fortune with them, strung in roubles and half-roubles round their neck'.

The scientific community in St Petersburg was represented by men such as Franz Aepinus (1724–1802). Born in Rostock, and later admitted a member of the Prussian Academy of Sciences, he had settled in St Petersburg in 1757, becoming a professor of physics, a member of the Russian Academy, head of the cryptographic service of Russia and tutor to Empress Catherine's son, Paul. His predecessors had been George Richmann (1711–1753) who died carrying out experiments on atmospheric electrical charges, and Mikhail Lomonosov (1711–1765) a polymath who undertook important Polar expeditions and temperature measurements across the Empire. Aepinus' discussion of the effects of parallax in the transit of a planet over the sun's disc had excited a great deal of interest in 1764 and two years later, as an acknowledgement of the contribution St Petersburg academics had made, Benjamin Franklin sent him his own work on physical and meteorological observation. With his own experiments almost twenty years before much in mind, Brydone would have listened closely when, as the only eye witness, Aepinus gave him an account of the death of Professor Richmann from electrocution. The two men evidently got on well, sharing their thoughts about the experiments Adam Braun at the university and Mikhail Lomonosov had conducted in 1759, obtaining solid mercury by freezing a thermometer in a mixture of snow and nitric acid. Brydone had not at first given credence to

Braun's experiments, since 'the shape of the equipment used had affected the outcome'.

Adjacent to the Customs House on the riverside at St Petersburg were the city's extensive warehouses about which Brydone noted that 'no fire or light of any kind' was permitted on account of a great number of them having been burnt down; the doors were now made of iron. Among Russia's commodity exports, hemp accounted for more than a quarter, and significant trade was done in bar iron, linen and flax (19 per cent, 10 per cent and 5 per cent respectively). By the end of the Seven Years' War, Russian hemp for rope accounted for 90–95 per cent of the hemp imported into Britain, nearly all of it coming from the Baltic and being handled through the St Petersburg office of the London firm of A Thompson and G Peters. The average 'clean hemp' exported between 1764 and 1782 was more than 21,000 tons per annum, of which 19,000 tons, rather than the 11,000 tons mentioned by Brydone, went to England.

During the period 1765 and 1779 about a third of timber exports, made up of cut pieces of deal, went to the British market, some through St Petersburg, but the majority from Viborg. In the first four years of Catherine's reign, deal exports through St Petersburg and Cronstadt averaged 57,000 pieces, with British ships transporting more than 90 per cent of the trade. Two years before Brydone's arrival, however, exports had increased to about 182,000 pieces, with the trade being shared with Riga which had found its niche in the mast trade in the early part of the eighteenth century.[8]

Towards the end of his stay, Brydone visited Tsarskoye Selo, the royal country residence fifteen miles south of St Petersburg, and a similar distance from Strelna (shown above) which Catherine I and her daughter Empress Elizabeth had started to build, and which was still undergoing work in 1776. The road was 'a fine paved one', but it and part of the road to the Peterhof palace, were the only 'made ones in the Empire, apart from those made of wood'. The 'Tsar's Village' was, however, 'by no means pleasing'. Brydone said 'The front, and its external as well as internal parts, is so covered with gilding that if the architecture had been good, which it is not, the effect would have been destroyed. It is full of windows and I am told the apartments are by no means agreeable. However,

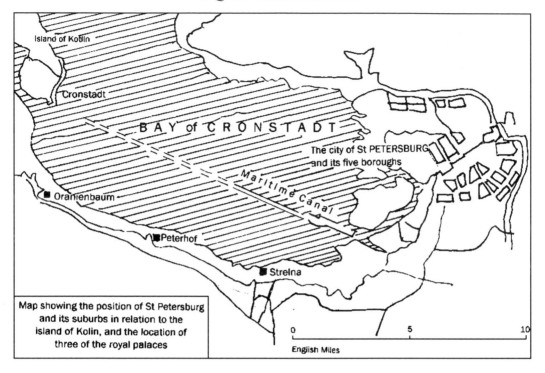

Map showing the position of St Petersburg and its suburbs in relation to the island of Kolin, and the location of three of the royal palaces

it is her Majesty's favourite residence and all her other country palaces are almost abandoned, though for both its prospect and air, Peterhof and Oranienbaum are certainly superior'. In Brydone's view, none of them was comparable to Strelna, the choice of Peter.[9] The gardens contained monuments raised by the Empress to commemorate her generals and favourites, including Prince Orlov, and those killed in the Turkish War of 1768–74. The war, Brydone added, had given Russia a respectable name through Europe but in fact it had been very deleterious to the nation. Upwards of 200,000 had died of the plague around Moscow, whilst 300,000 Culmucks, a branch of the Mongolian race, had been forced to move from Astrakhan to China, quite apart from an 'incredible number' being lost in campaigns.

Throughout his visit to the capital of the Russian Empire, Brydone clearly lacked formal introductions to the Empress or any of her closest family. It seems unlikely that he would have neglected the opportunity of a meeting with Catherine had one been possible. Why it never took place would certainly have been bound up with the absence of the ambassador when Brydone arrived. The previous summer, Sir Robert Gunning (1731–1816), the British envoy-extraordinary and plenipotentiary at the court of Catherine, had been asked by London to establish whether General Panin, the Russian foreign minister, would look favourably on Russian troops being made available for service in North America. Receiving a favourable response, and the support of the empress herself, all had looked promising till an objection to the 20,000 force being under the command of a British general, and their being transported to Canada on British ships, brought negotiations to a close. Despite praise for his efforts from Lord Suffolk, the secretary of state, Gunning felt bound to press for his recall on grounds of ill-health. He had left St Petersburg in February that year and was at home in England.[10]

This resulted in Brydone being more than usually dependent on merchants and members of the British community to guide his itinerary and contacts. There is no mention in his journals of him meeting Richard Oakes who took charge until the new envoy-extraordinary Sir James Harris and his sister Katherine arrived in December 1777.[11] Brydone and William Morton Pitt had, however, enjoyed their visit enough for Pitt to be invited to join the Harrises in the summer of 1778. During a trip to Moscow at that time he wrote warmly to Sir James to say 'how perfectly surprised' he had been 'to find the country so agreeable'. A month later, he had changed his mind after being marched off to prison for intervening in a dispute involving his footman where the heat, smell, lice, filth and conversation were 'the amusements of this place'. On his release the next day, Pitt was urged by friends in St Petersburg to write an account of his experience of being locked in a dungeon with seven men and a woman, some chained. Pitt told Sir James that he had been 'confined by treachery and without foundation' and only later had discovered that an officer should have been there, the rascal had forsaken his post. The head of police in Moscow had, nevertheless, 'sacrificed his room ... very politely' so that he could write to the envoy.[12]

When towards the end of the first week in September preparations were being made for the travellers' departure, and their return home, there were 'numberless delays'. Brydone would have been advised to ensure that the names of those in his party appeared some three times in the official gazette. This was an important requirement which, added to the formalities associated with the podaroshna (the right to requisition and the right of way, issued by the tsar) and passports often took a long time to complete. In the event, there was some trouble obtaining horses but no delays on leaving the country and they were able to travel at fourteen versts an hour 'until the front horses were for some reason frightened, leapt into a ditch and overturned them'. The return journey towards Riga was nevertheless worse than the journey to the city. Describing the peasants whose animals had been requisitioned, Brydone said they were starving by the roadsides. Rooms at inns were taken by officers and soldiers, and at every stop Brydone found neither 'space in a room or any civility by these subalterns although they saw my distress, and that I was a fellow officer'. At one post house, the two sons of Field Marshal Romanzow, who had been in overall command during the Turkish War, apologised to him for the troubles he was suffering. Even the arrival of their father did not produce any horses and a two-day stay at a nearby house was 'miserable'.

The experience of travelling in Russia caused Brydone to change the opinion he had held of the nation as a generous one which had been based on acquaintanceships he had made previously in Europe. He now admitted that the whole nation was 'not of the same stamp' and felt especially angry that the rules of hospitality were so completely disregarded, and travellers were always treated badly in comparison to local nobility. Postillions generally rode on the right hand horse, 'contrary to the practice of all other nations', and although it was rare to see horses stumbling or falling, they went too fast, particularly downhill 'where we would put on the drag'. At post houses, 'their own gentlemen' get away long before a stranger's party, and 'in the course of my life', Brydone wrote, 'I never found so great an occasion for temper and patience, and I have often thought how extremely happy it was that Lord Lindsey did not come into this country, for his natural impetuosity, and violence on seeing himself ill-used, must have got him into many quarrels'.[13]

Nine days were spent on the road to Riga where Brydone was shown much politeness by Baron Campenhausen, a member of another noble Baltic-German family who, as next in command to the governor, had procured his passports. However, about two or three hours after his arrival Brydone was seized with a giddiness and violent fit of fainting. 'Everybody thought' wrote the tutor 'I should have expired. It lasted for several hours, however, by a very plentiful bleeding and after two days that I kept my bed I was almost well, only a slight headache remaining'. Once well enough he was given a dinner and supper by three men from the Ledov Pottery factory, Messrs Green, Pearson and Wale.

As a result it was the middle of September when the party eventually left for Warsaw and the countryside was in the middle of harvest despite occasional heavy rain. South of Jelgarva, Brydone noticed that the inns were built so that carriages could be sheltered overnight, with a door often leading from the shelter into the inn building, which as he said was 'more satisfactory than having to hire a guard for the night'. The road deteriorated, becoming 'horrid ... (being) made of fir logs tied together and much broken'. At an indifferent inn Brydone tasted a dish of the common red fungus which grew at the root of fir trees, and found it very good. On 21 September, the travellers met Baron Charles de Bagge, a collector of instruments and composer, who although born in Latvia, had lived in Paris in the Place des Victoires for some considerable time and who invited Brydone to call on him. It was at this point, and after dinner together, that the travellers entered Poland and after paying twenty one ducats for the hire of a voiture and four horses, they found themselves in the port of Memel (Klaipéda) on the Baltic coast. Describing it as 'a small dirty port', the tutor's adjectives only reflected the rolling sand banks between the town and the Baltic thrown up by storms and violent seas. A large trade in flax, linseed, timber and hemp went through the port where seven or eight hundred vessels loaded each year, the majority being English. Finding the brother of a friend who was consul there, Brydone spent a short time with him and his wife who gave him some provisions for the journey together with the present of a fine piece of amber.

After the village of Rossitten (Rybachy) situated along a fresh water lake just behind the brackish sea of the Baltic, and about halfway between Memel and Königsberg (Kaliningrad), Brydone shot two brace of snipe and one and a half of woodcock in twenty minutes. Being very tired, the travellers stopped to sleep at Sarkau, on the coastal road at the end of the lagoon just six miles north of. Königsberg where they found 'as good an inn as any on the road from Petersburg'. No sooner had they reached the port at the junction of the two streams making up the river Pregola than they were told how the amber trade which produced an annual income for the king of about £6,000 was organised. People dragged it from the bottom of the lagoon and lakes nearby using nets on long poles whilst some, usually of inferior quality, was found inland by digging. After looking around what was a very old town, Brydone was saddened by the absence of any old architecture of note in Königsberg, due to frequent fires and unattractive new buildings. Only three English business houses traded in the hemp and linseed, two of whom were Mr Collins and Messrs Hay and Barclay, the latter's well-known partner, Robert Hay, havng been a founder member of the English Club in St Petersburg. Leaving the city, the party appears to have been given directions by General Anhalt-Dessau[14] and they were soon travelling through Bartenstein (Bartoszyce), Shippenheil and Rastenberg (Ketrzyn) where the roads were terrible, the only consolation being that the weather was dry.

The country became wild and more beautiful but it was taking six or seven hours to cover five miles. At Pultansk (Pultusk) on the River Narew some 40 miles north of Warsaw, the 'postmaster ran a slovenly house' and had nothing for them to eat or drink. He wanted 110 florins to take them to Warsaw and Brydone decided to complain even if it meant waiting longer, believing it to be another instance of peculation. A local judge showed sympathy with their case, and offered them his own horses for a sum a little less than the postmaster's. Soon across the river Bug in a large boat, the party arrived in the Polish capital on 3 October.

The city was showing its greatest brilliance, with balls, assemblies, plays and concerts every night due to it being the time when the national diet met. Against such a background, it was understandable that Brydone noted that duelling was allowed so long as it took place 'at least three miles from the king's residence'. Among the most agreeable houses were those belonging to the Prince Palatine of Russia, that of the Russian ambassador, and General Ogiñski. The serious playing of cards in such company, especially at night, and where two or three hundred ducats could be wagered on a single card, was frowned on by Brydone. So far as dancing was concerned, it was a different story. The polonaise was 'very attractive', unlike other dances which were 'nothing more than a man and a woman walking round the room'. Ten days or so later, after noting that there were 1,500 Russian troops encamped just outside Warsaw, and reminding himself about the composition of the permanent council of the diet in his journal, the travellers were again on the road.[15]

On the night of 13 October, instead of returning to Berlin in the direction they had come, directly westward, Brydone's party was making its way along the river Vistula towards its mouth when they were almost immediately held up at a bridge, and obliged to bribe customs men. Thinking they were back on the road, they were surprised moments later to be attacked by another bunch of customs men from whom they learned that they were in fact on an island in the middle of the river, not at the border. They had to shout for boatmen, and wait an hour in 'piercingly cold' weather till they were put on shore. However, much relieved, they eventually found Culm (Chelmno) on a 'high bank of the Vistula, with a pretty view' where there was 'a fair that day, selling cloth, furs and fruit'.

With signs of increasing German or Prussian influence as they neared the Baltic, the travellers passed through Marienwerder (Kwidzyn) and Gdañsk (Mottlau), the regional capital where there was a long wait for horses, and which the travellers left on 18 October, they were soon in Berlin. The penultimate leg of the journey seems to have taken nearly three weeks. Its highlight for Brydone was the water feature in the grounds surrounding Weissenstein Castle above Kassel. The young landgrave, Charles, had been responsible for the city providing shelter for nearly 2,000 Huguenot refugees in 1685 and had ordered the construction of the Oktagon and the Orangerie under the direction of an Italian architect. The park itself, except for the terraces, was only to be interrupted by straight avenues. In the event, development at Weissenstein and the Karlsberg, as the area was then called, was interrupted by the death of Charles in 1730. Not surprisingly, Brydone compared the area and volume of the Weissenstein of his day with those at Versailles and Peterhof, finding in favour of the property in Hesse-Kassel.

The tired travellers reached Calais on 16 November, only to find that a wreck was blocking the harbour and weather in the English Channel was generally bad. Spirits would have been lifted temporarily by their finding that the young third Duke of Dorset, a keen cricketer who had presented the Vine Cricket Ground to the people of Sevenoaks in Kent two years before, and a number of his friends, were also there among those prevented from taking passage to Dover.[16] Brydone and his charges had, however, been on the road one way or another since they left Lausanne almost a full year before, and would hardly have been at their ease. The expedition to St Petersburg had not been as successful as he had hoped and expected. The fact that he was forced to depend on the hospitality and guidance of members of the British business community and only a few of the nobility, in the absence of effective diplomatic intervention on his behalf, greatly influenced the direction and character of the visit. His programme, skewed as it was, nevertheless gave him greater experience of Russian life at levels sometimes well below that lived by its all-pervasive aristocracy than he might have expected. By its very location on the Neva, the nature and character of the buildings in St Petersburg became an important aspect of Brydone's commentary. The peasantry, 'the natural actors', certainly won his respect, but despite sharing the general British esteem for Peter the Great, he left Catherine's Russia disappointed and irritated by the 'much-boasted civilisation of this nation' where he had not found 'any native whose name has been distinguished in the world for any fine art or science'. 'Big was not better', persistent and universal bureaucratic delays, and the deep-rooted bribery also left their mark on the travellers. It was a society in conflict.[17]

Following their departure from Vienna in early April, Brydone and William Morton Pitt had travelled in excess of 3,500 miles, or approximately 500 miles a month, over roads and in conditions that were often extremely dangerous and uncomfortable. Despite this, the younger man was to return to Russia almost immediately and spend some five years in total travelling on the continent. He became a captain in the Dorset Militia in 1778, and five years later inherited Encombe House on the Isle of Purbeck. At the end of the decade he succeed his cousin as county Member of Parliament, achieving much for the people of Dorset over the following thirty six years. Brydone on the other hand, now 40 years old, would have been relieved to be coming home.

# CHAPTER 9

# Becomes tutor to the Prime Minister's sons (1777–1778)

Writing to his elder brother Matthew, a prosperous fish merchant from Berwick-on-Tweed specialising in the salmon trade, from New Street, Hannover Square, London in April 1777, Brydone thought he would have reached 'the other side of the Tweed long ere this time' but there had been so many things to be done before he could consider leaving London. He had had 'several temptations to go abroad again' but he had 'as yet resisted them all'. On the subject of settling down, he said, 'I wish I knew of some snug pleasant little spot that was either to be let for a number of years or to be sold'. He thought it highly probable that he would be a purchaser 'for although I cannot easily get out of London, I by no means like the London life and should not visit it often'. With few capital resources and a meagre income from what had been an almost continual flow of tutoring assignments, Patrick compared his plight with someone on an unproductive treadmill or tread wheel. In asking Matthew about the number of captains he now employed, and expressing the hope that he was 'now getting as rich as a Croesus', Brydone showed some family envy, but he was also as much concerned about their younger brother, Robert. Telling Matthew that Bob's affairs were 'in very bad order', which was surprising, particularly since he had never had 'any loss or misfortune in trade', he could only suggest that there had been some 'negligence or mismanagement'. After warning him not to mention his concern to Robert personally, Brydone praised Matthew for all the news his letters contained. He also mentioned meeting up with William Fullarton, who was just back from Portugal. He hoped to go with him to Bath for a few days.[1]

The tutor was not afforded his wish. Having acquired a masterful knowledge of who and what was worth seeing in Europe, on top of the publicity given him by the publication of the *Tour through Sicily*, it was understandable that the treadmill Brydone hoped had ended, quickly restarted. The only compensation lay in the fact that there was less likelihood that the new client he had contracted with would behave as badly as some of his predecessors had done. As Journal No.10 shows, he was back in Calais by 19 July 1777 having 'had an agreeable crossing of five hours' from Dover in the company of Lord North's two older sons. The decision of the prime minister to employ Brydone as travelling tutor to George Augustus (1757–1802) and Francis (1761–1817) was almost certainly influenced, if not taken, by the boy's grandfather, Francis, first Earl Guilford, the wealthy caretaker of the family's morals, money and property.[2] Brydone's reputation had evidently gone ahead of him, and his subsequent relationship with several generations of the North family was to raise his social standing to a new level, and greatly improve his finances. It was to be a halcyon summer during which the two North boys were to be introduced to the natural world, no exertion travelling over unknown roads in the peace of the mountains.

War in America, ever-increasing pressures at Westminster, and the forthcoming entry of France and Spain into the conflict, so battered Lord North's physical and mental energy that he was in danger of losing some of the solace he had enjoyed within the family. Writing to his father in the middle of August from the family seat at Wroxton Abbey in Oxfordshire, he told him that the situation 'has sunk my spirits, weaken'd my understanding, impaired my memory, and filled my heart with a kind of uneasiness from which nothing can deliver me but an honourable retreat', or resignation.[3] His eldest boy had just come down from Trinity College, Oxford, and Francis, after attending Eton, was to go into the army as a cornet later in 1777.[4] Lord North had himself undertaken the Grand Tour with his stepbrother on leaving Oxford, visiting Vienna and Milan before studying for a time at Leipzig University, and acquiring 'the polish it was the purpose of the exercise to impart'.[5]

The tutor and his new charges were soon on the road across France towards the Swiss cantons where they would spend the summer. It was not unknown for people to travel to or through enemy countries in time of war, provided they had passports and they were well-connected. Wars were considered to be between states, not individuals. Passing through the small village of Ardres, south east of Calais and near Henry VIII's 'Field of Gold', the party visited the abbey of Saint-Bertin at St Omer. With the tiresome and often inhospitable roads of Prussia, Livonia and Russia replaced by a better well-trodden path, and the intelligent company of one twenty-year-old youth and another still in his teens, Brydone could begin to relax and contemplate a period of peace by the lake at his favoured Lausanne. A gentle introduction to the artistic sights and sounds around them included a performance in Lille of Molière's *L'Ecole des Femmes* and a one-act comedy by Louis Anseaume called *Le Milicien* where despite very tolerable performances the audience hissed the leading actress, 'a beautiful creature' who 'did her part extremely well'. At Rheims, while walking round the cathedral, Brydone succumbed to telling his charges that the phial of holy oil there had been brought down from heaven by a dove, 'the Holy Ghost no doubt', to anoint Bishop Clovis and his successors. More seriously, he shared the description given of the phenomenon of a shaking pillar in the building, caused most probably by vibration set up by the movement of one of the cathedral's four bells. No expert had been able to account for it. After a long day's journey, passing through Chaumont and Langres on 26 July, described by Brydone as 'the Birmingham of France' on account of their economic growth, the party spent the night at Champlitte.

Crossing high ground, six or seven miles from Pontarlier on the Franco-Swiss border, Brydone used his barometer to estimate their height above sea level as about 4000 feet. He was also able to show George and Francis a periodic spring whose intermittent flow rose and fell 'in as little as five or six minutes', not dependent on rain or drought and caused perhaps by the terrain creating a syphon effect. The next day, 30 July, the travellers arrived in Lausanne, the Brydone's welcome base, where the process of getting to know the boys better and discussing their itinerary could begin in comfort. Within a few days they were crossing Lac Léman to the small French town of Évian-les-Bains; the crossing was 'smooth but lengthy'. A mile to the west of the town they found another spring, this time the Sainte Catherine chalybeate spring whose medicinal value the Marquis de Lessert would publicise in 1789. Whether Brydone, or his charges, knew that another member of the North family had discovered the chalybeate spring at Tunbridge Wells in 1606, is not recorded.[6]

Ten days or so into August, Brydone set off with the boys, having arranged for them to undertake some physical exercise climbing in the vicinity of the Rhône glacier. En route the travellers visited the salt works at Bex in the Valais, near Aigle, where they were caught in a thunderstorm. The building where water was evaporated was struck by lightning and a round hole made in the roof, shattering some tiles. Further damage was only prevented by the dampness of one of the roof beams. Arriving at St Pierre-de-Clages, where they stayed the night with the local priest, the tutor recorded all the trees in full leaf, noting that the beautiful verdure of the Valais appeared 'to be still growing'. Then as Brydone caught sight of a rainbow, 'bright and beautiful beyond conception', and several times rode into the very thickest of its vapour, he was soon 'wet to the skin'. In that situation, Brydone explained, 'the rainbow forms a complete circle of vivid ardent colours (more) than any ever formed by the prism'. His horse 'tho far from being skittish, was frightened when he saw this beautiful appearance round him'.

Simple lessons in meteorology and other subjects helped broaden the interests of his charges, and having spoken to them about the four great rivers of North America all rising within a few leagues of each other, he referred to a not dissimilar pattern in Europe with the rivers Rhine, Rhône, Danube and Po. A visit to the Rhne glacier followed on 14 August, with guides and mules aiding the climb where it was particularly steep. Melt water normally went into a basin after flooding down the mountainside but that season the water had made a passage through and under the ice so that the basin was empty. Coming across a shepherd who attracted his sheep with salt, Brydone was almost knocked over when holding out his hand to some sheep. They went on to look at the monastery of St Bernard on the pass of that name, where there were four or five different nationals in the church, 'two thirds of them (were) asleep with fatigue'. The fact that there were 'too many people' was given as the reason for not going further.[7]

Lord North thanked Brydone from Bushy House, a property overlooking Bushy Park near Teddington which had been provided for him by the king, for 'the great pleasure' his letters had given the North family, insisting that his 'fellow travellers' had also been good correspondents. George and Francis had written three letters from Lausanne which had been greedily read. 'They may be assured', their father wrote, 'that there are few authors whose writings afford their readers completer satisfaction than theirs do'. He hoped they would be much improved by their residence at Lausanne and that Brydone would be as pleased with them as they were with him. Their letters, Lord North said, were 'full of the happiness they enjoy in your company', and a sign that they were behaving in a manner that deserved Brydone's approbation. He felt 'the objects of their application should be few, and well-chosen … and a certain proportion of each day should be set aside for their studies and exercises which should never be diverted to any other purpose on any account'. Furthermore, 'if they frequent the best company in Lausanne, their conversation in the afternoons will be a means of acquiring much useful knowledge, and especially of making a proficiency in the language'. The boys, he hoped, were convinced that 'the two or three years which they have before them are of the most decisive consequence to their future welfare and reputation' but feared that 'too many travellers recollect nothing but the loss of money and loss of time'.

At this time Lausanne, like Geneva, had attracted a social *mélange* drawn from the nobility and aristocracy of northern Europe. Although a town of only eight or nine thousand inhabitants, it boasted no less than eighteen playhouses where regular actors and travelling troupes performed. It was common practice to give two performances each night, a play in the first part of the evening, followed by an opera, usually a comedy or *opéra bouffon*, in the second. Opera made its debut in 1755 and by the 1782–1783 season, eighty performances were being given with the repertoire drawn from works by Monsigny, Rousseau, Gossec, Philidore, Dezède, Piccinini and Barre. Lausanne was no mere watering-place for groups of foreigners passing through, it catered for those young who were coming to the end of their formal education and preparing to take their place in society. It also exerted a fascination over writers, free-thinkers and those whose knowledge and horizons needed to be broadened, thereby providing opportunities for the more mature and able intellectuals to share their experiences.

Lord North next wanted the tutor's 'best idea … of the additional expense' that had been caused by Francis having come along with George, suggesting that he had not originally been included in the plan. He wanted to know what proportion of their expenses fell to him as he wished to make 'proper arrangements' for furnishing Brydone with 'a regular and sufficient supply of money'. He also enclosed a letter for Brydone which his Lordship said 'has lain for about three weeks upon my table at London, and has been forgot amongst the multiplicity of business that has lately occupied my attention'. To remedy this, Lord Noth suggested that correspondence should be directed to John Robinson, his secretary and secretary to the Treasury, in Downing Street. This would enable letters to be 'better taken care of, and less liable to be delayed'. Then, responding to some remarks the tutor had made about the war, Lord North said: 'You have, I perceive, been alarm'd by articles in the French papers relating one or two defeats of the King's troops in America. The whole is false … It is true, that we wish for something more decisive than any event which has happen'd but the news we have hitherto received in the course of this campaign has been in our favour'. There was every reason to believe that General Burgoyne had taken Ticonderoga and a revolutionary officer, Major-General Prescott, had been 'lost' to their cause after showing unpardonable negligence by sleeping unguarded at a cottage two miles from his army, and being 'carried off in the night'.[8]

It was Lord Guilford's turn at the beginning of December to thank Brydone for the good account he had given of the boys' progress at Lausanne.[9] Writing to Brydone at the home of Mr Porta in Lausanne, the boys' grandfather said that George was 'well-satisfied with the sort of life you lead and nothing can be more for his advantage than having leisure to think'. So far as Francis was concerned, he had unluckily scalded his leg while at a dance. The accident had been more serious than his father first thought, and the boy had resolved to take more pains with his dancing. He also confessed to making it 'worse by eating and drinking too much'. Lord Guilford particularly welcomed Brydone's intention to have the young men perform a play in French as although George 'had laid some foundation' in the language, Francis had 'still to work hard with his French master' and needed 'that advantage'. His Lordship had come up to London on 26 November to attend the christening of Princess Sophia, the fifth daughter of King George III and Queen Charlotte on the first of December, by the Archbishop of Canterbury in the Great Council Chamber at St James's Palace. Many members of the family had been present, 'some with colds' but everyone in the country was 'impatient for news from America'. The 'want of it', he told Brydone, 'was an awkward circumstance to the administration on the opening of parliament', but the spirit of faction seemed to be declining, and the general ardour for prosecuting the war with vigour, and maintaining the dependence of the Colonies on their mother country, 'made it no disadvantage'.[10]

Three months into 1778 there was political news from Lord Guilford. 'The war', he wrote, 'of which there has been so much talk in France, seems now coming in earnest. The King of France's sending a very offensive declaration of his having concluded a Treaty of Amity and Commerce with the Americans, has raised a violent resentment here and Lord Stormont, has orders to withdraw from the French court'. The British ambassador had married his second wife, Louisa Cathcart, during his service in Paris and was to become secretary of state for the northern department at the Foreign Office in London in October the following year. The marquis de Noailles, the French ambassador, had 'gone from hence'. Turning to matters at home, he told Brydone of the 'very long days' in the House of Commons where, the previous Friday, Charles Fox's motion of censure against Lord George Germayne, the Secretary of State for the Colonies, had been defeated.[11] Referring to Francis as the Captain, Brydone's commendation of him made Lord Guilford think it 'inbent' upon him to pass on the compliment in his own correspondence with him. Also, the Swiss carrier was about to depart, he proposed to send Brydone 'some of the little plates' he wanted.

The second expedition undertaken by Lord North's sons in June and July, on horseback for a circular tour of over 500 miles around Switzerland's furthest boundaries in the north-east and to the Italian side of the Alps in the south, was again to test their resilience and physical fitness. It had, however, few of the time pressures imposed by the journey to and from Russia that Brydone had made, and allowed the boys to give closer attention to a wider range of studies without exhausting their guide. According to Journal No 11, they set off on Saturday 20 June, following a route which Brydone knew well. A visit to the rooms and gardens at the Madeleine Hermitage near Fribourg was followed by an examination of the curious collection of the Revd M Sprüngli's stuffed birds in Bern, including a bearded vulture found at Glarus in Eastern Switzerland. At Solothurn, on the left bank of the Aar, the party visited the churches of St Peter and St Ursen, and the nearby monastery. Passing through Olten on 26 June, they reached the old-fashioned town of Baden the following day whose baths were mentioned by Pliny and Tacitus but did 'not appear to be much altered since their time'. The source was very abundant and so hot, Brydone was told, that 'it boils an egg in five minutes'. Taking a bath with another gentleman out of curiosity, they both found themselves doubting at least some of the claims that had been made.

Describing the abbey at Einsiedeln outside Zürich as 'the Loretto of Switzerland', Brydone was forced to report that the building was 'very fine though tawdry with gilding and painting. The ex-votos (or votive offerings) are innumerable, and the book giving an account of the miracles is the grossest and most abominable insult that was ever offered to common sense'. An 'infinity of shops' were selling trumpery which was 'very paltry and very cheap'. Returning to Zürich by boat, the party breakfasted the next day (the first of July), with Dr Johann Kaspar Lavater, a notable Swiss pastor and physionomist. He was for a time a friend of Goethe, and the son of the city's bürgermeister, Hans Konrad Heidegger. The party then called on Salomon Gessner, the poet and printmaker who had been one of the founders of the Helvetic Society. He was in bed but rose to receive them. The partnership Gessner had in the porcelain and faience business made it easy for the travellers to tour his factory on 3 July at Schooren in Kilchberg where they saw 'beautiful figures' designed by him. In the town library, Brydone recorded, they found the original letters of Lady Jane Grey to Luther 'written in elegant Latin and beautiful characters'. Another of their hosts was Hans Caspar Hirzel, the eminent Swiss physician and writer on rural affairs, known as the 'Rustic Socrates', and the older Professor J Wilhelm Ludwig Gleim. Both men were in their working clothes and the visitors were received with great cordiality and were shown over Hirzel's farm. 'I really believe', wrote Brydone, 'he is one of the most perfect workings of God upon earth. All flattery and the attention, all the adulation that has been paid him, has never made him forget himself one moment. He pretends to no knowledge

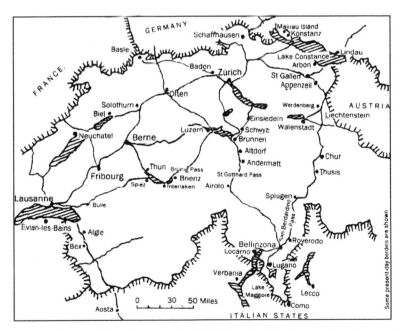

Rough sketch map of the places visited in Switzerland and elsewhere by Brydone and Lord North's two sons, in June and July 1778.

but that of a farmer, but his natural eloquence and elocution is astonishing on every subject on which he talks'.[12]

The party left Zürich for Lake Constance (Bodensee) on 3 July after going to bed at 9 pm the previous evening when the town fell silent. Clocks there, and in Basle, were an hour faster than the sun 'to make the people go sooner to bed'. Having greatly admired the falls of the Rhine, a little to the south of medieval Schaffhausen, the travellers hired a boat for the journey along the river into the lake. It took four men eight hours to row the distance of nearly thirty miles. A little to the north of the German town of Konstanz, just offshore, was the well-wooded island of Mainau belonging to one of the richest Commanderies of the Teutonic Order where the party was given a tour of the wine cellars and tasted what resembled 'good Rhenish', before returning to the *Adler*, their tavern.

Travelling through rich fertile country the next day, Monday 6 July, where the corn was grown among fruit trees and the local population maintained that no harm came to either crop, Brydone arrived at the small town of Arbon on the Swiss side of the lake. The towers of the German town of Lindau were just visible on the other side. The scene had a particular charm with a family of storks and their chicks that had a nest on the chimney of the building opposite the travellers' inn, but they stayed only one night. Their road to St Gallen passed through Rorschach which was partly flooded, up to the belly of their horses in some places. Fortunately, the next six or seven miles uphill was a broad turnpike to the town, a 'very unusual thing but important'. As they approached St Gallen, then with a population of about 8,000, cloth was spread out on bleaching greens, evidence of the 'industrious and flourishing' state of its textile industry. In 1714, it produced 38,000 pieces. Once again the party only stayed one night, and a visit to the Abbey and the cathedral which had been constructed in the late Baroque style between 1755 and 1768, and which was still being added to, was given priority. There were two fine organs and the Abbey library, recognised as one of the richest medieval libraries in the world, contained over 2000 manuscripts, some on bark, some on papyrus, and one which they were assured was as old as Cicero, written on a wax tablet. The prince-abbot then was Beda Angehm who served from 1767 to 1796, not the son of a peasant as Brydone said but of a surgeon who initially studied at the Jesuit College in Konstanz.

On leaving, the party found itself trapped in the village of Teufen by a sudden and fierce storm late in the day. An inn gave the three travellers a delicious supper, with the innkeeper and the guide who joined them at table providing 'excellent company'. The following morning at Oberried in the Rhinetal, Brydone and the boys went to see Hans Ulrich Grubenmann, a tall fine-looking man whose looks greatly belied his seventy years, and who had been consulted on the design of bridges in many parts of Europe. He showed them over his house, and some of his plans, which they admired greatly.[13] Later, they rode westward to Appenzell, encountering 'enormous difficulty on the roads with stakes along the way, which troubled the horses very much'; nevertheless, the view of the Rhine was 'a worthy reward for the journey'. Below Lake Constance it was 'smooth and slow' and at Werdenberg 'impetuous and muddy ... and full of stones and gravel'.

Having come through an attractive valley on 9 July, the travellers arrived at Walenstadt in the dark with a thunderstorm going round the mountains above them. At 5 am, they went down to the lake and were much impressed by the isolation of the area and the seemingly impenetrable mountains. After viewing the 2,000 ft cascade at Pfeffersbade, and 'the celebrated *engoufrement*', the party had more than 40 miles to go before it arrived at Thusis, the confluence of the Hinterrhein and Nolla rivers. Nearing what turned out to be 'not a handsome town', they helped themselves to the red and black cherries, but on arrival they could only sympathise with the peasants who were mourning the loss of crops and property damaged by floods. By 14 July, the party was a dozen or so miles further on at Splügen, another small community of barely four hundred Italian and Romansch-speakers.

Although there had been a mule track over the San Bernardino pass since the fifteenth century, and a road for wheeled vehicles had opened eight years before, both the ascent and descent proved difficult for the travellers, with their horses losing shoes. The top, at 6,700 feet, was 'very barren, but with shepherds and their flocks everywhere'. They passed a glacier and a high lake before descending into the valley, arriving at Roveredo where they spent the night. Arriving in Bellinzona on 16 July, where the women were happier than on the north side of the mountains, and there were no beggars to plague them, the party was impressed by the three castles that dominated the town. The next day six men rowed and sailed them from Magadino at the top end of Lake Maggiore down to the three small Borromean Islands in the Italian part of the lake between Verbania and Stresa, a journey which took nine hours there and eight back. 'The banks of the Maggiore', Brydone wrote, 'exhibit every beauty in nature; the water is clear and there are more than twenty kinds of fish'.

The gentlemen were, however, soon again on their way, reaching Airolo late on 19 July after passing through Giornico where, it being a Sunday, there had been a festival. The climb up the St Gotthard pass to the Hospice proved steep, in exceedingly cold weather. Two Capuchin monks lived in the rest house with its six small rooms which had only recently been built. Staying on the descent at the 'White Cross', an inn at Amsteg, the party arrived in Altdorf on 21 July. There the travellers were shown 'much civility' by the town prosecutor, a Mr Epp who had worked for a long time in Spain and Naples before retiring to Flüelen on the south-easterly tip of Lake Luzern. He and his son accompanied them into Luzern the next day and Brydone enjoyed discussing the mistakes he had spotted in local maps. Since none of all of the lake's channels could be seen from one point, and some maps showed they could, they must be inaccurate. General Pfeffer, who had acted as their guide for the last part of their journey, told them of the work he had done surveying the mountains in this part of Switzerland. Occasionally, his life had certainly been in danger, especially where the local peasantry thought he intended to show his findings to the King of France who might use them to invade.

Leaving Luzern on 24 July, Brydone, George and Francis embarked in a boat near the foot of Mt Pilatus at the south-westerly tip of the lake, and rowed for two hours to Alpnacht. From Lungern they set off on horseback over the Brünig pass which was tiring, but they had the reward of the view from the summit: 'the whole valley of Hasli is spread out like a map' wrote Brydone. The night

1. The Old Priory in the coastal village of Coldingham where Brydone was born. (Photograph by Bob Thomson)

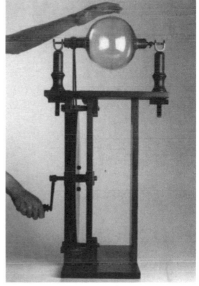

*Above left*: 2. Cottages near the Bogan burn where Coldingham gingham was woven. (Photograph by Dr Michael Fently)

*Above right*: 3. A reproduction of Francis Hauksbee's frictional electricity machine devised by him while in London in 1706–8. (Science Museum/Science & Society Picture Library).

*Above left*: 4. Portrait of Sir John Pringle (1707–1782) by Sir Joshua Reynolds in 1774. (The Royal Society, London)

*Above right*: 5. A detail of a mezzotint portrait of an elderly Patrick Brydone by William Ward, after Andrew Geddes, published by Colnaghi & Co. in 1818. (The Trustees of the British Museum)

*Above left*: 6. Engraving of Thomas Cadell, the elder (1742–1802), bookseller and publisher, by Henry Hoppner Meyer. (National Portrait Gallery, London)

*Above right*: 7. A portrait of the printer and publisher William Strahan (1715–1785) by Sir Joshua Reynolds. (National Portrait Gallery, London)

*Above left*: 8. Charles Turner's mezzotint of Frances d'Arblay (1752–1840); 'Fanny Burney' as she was known. (National Portrait Gallery, London)

*Above right*: 9. A pastel of William Cowper (1731–1800), painted in 1792 by George Romney. The letter-writer and poet was one of the first to congratulate Brydone on the publication of his book. (National Portrait Gallery, London)

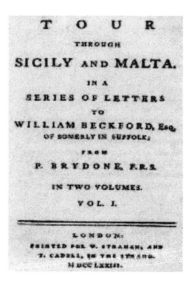

*Above left*: 10. An engraving of Ralph Griffiths (*c*. 1720–1803), the owner of the *Monthly Review* which drew the literary world's attention to Brydone's book. (As shown in the *European Magazine*, 1803)

*Above right*: 11. Frontispiece of Volume 1 of Brydone's *Tour* as published by Thomas Cadell in 1773.

12. The cathedral of Notre Dame in Lausanne facing the Savoy alps, the small town on Lake Geneva where Brydone lived when he became a tutor.

*Above left*: 13. The elderly William Morton Pitt (1754–1836) who was in Brydone's charge in 1776 and who became an MP in 1780. (From the *Swanage Post*)

*Above middle*: 14. Robert Bertie (1756–1779), the young Lord Lindsey; another of Brydone's charges. He died at the early age of twenty-three. (Grimsthorpe and Drummond Castle Trust Ltd)

*Above right*: 15. An engraving of Alleyne Fitzherbert (1753–1839) who was visiting Lausanne in the company of Francis Kinloch when Brydone met him in 1775. (National Portrait Gallery, London)

*Above left*: 16. A portrait of Empress Maria Theresa (1717–1780), the last ruler of the Hapsburg Empire, by Jean-Étienne Liotard, a French-Swiss painter. (Museum of Art & History, Geneva)

*Above right*: 17. A drawing by Georg Decker of Kaiser Joseph II (1741–1790), Holy Roman Emperor between 1765 and 1790. (Albertina, Vienna)

*Above left*: 18. Franz Josef I, Prince of Liechtenstein. His portrait was painted by Alexander Roslin, a Swedish artist. (Liechtenstein, The Princely Collections Vaduz-Vienna)

*Above right*: 19. Jean-Étienne Liotard's portrait of Prince von Kaunitz, the Austrian Chancellor, another of the tutor's hosts. (Bridgeman Art Library, London)

*Above left*: 20. An engraving of King Frederick II (the Great) to whom Brydone was presented at Potsdam in May 1776. (Universal Images Group)

*Above right*: 21. Frederic Reclam's portrait of Elisabeth Christine Braunschweig-Wolfenbüttel (1715–1797), the consort of Frederick the Great. (Stiftung Preussische Schlösser und Gärten, Berlin-Brandenburg)

*Above left*: 22. Portrait of Duke Karl II of Mecklenburg-Strelitz who married Princess Friederike of Hesse-Darmstadt eight years before Brydone's visit. (The Royal Collection Trust © Her Majesty Queen Elizabeth II, 2014)

*Above right*: 23. A portrait, attributed to Johan Zoffany, of Sophia Charlotte, daughter of Duke Karl Louis Frederick of Mecklenburg-Strelitz, who became Queen of the United Kingdom and Hannover in 1761. (Holburne Museum, Bath)

*Above left*: 24. Thomas Gainsborough's portrait of Francis North (1704–1790). (Image courtesy of the Witt Library, Courtauld Institute of Art, London)

*Above right*: 25. A portrait by Nathaniel Dance of Frederick North (1732–1792), prime minister between 1770 and 1782. (National Portrait Gallery, London)

*Above left*: 26. The portrait of George Augustus North (1757–1802) by George Romney. (Coutts & Co, London)

*Above middle*: 27. An 1821 mezzotint portrait of Francis North (1761–1817) by Charles Turner after Sir Thomas Lawrence. Francis went into the army and became a playwright. (National Portrait Gallery, London)

*Above right*: 28. An engraving of Frederick North (1766–1827), the prime minister's youngest son, published by Edward Orme from a drawing made in Ceylon. (National Portrait Gallery, London)

*Above left*: 29. A portrait of Prince Nikolaus Esterházy, a decorated soldier and patron of the composer Haydn. Esterházy's influence and character fascinated Brydone. (Bridgeman Art Library, London)

*Above right*: 30. A portrait of Prince Albert of Saxony, painted two years before the travellers' visit to his castle in 1779. (Kunsthistorisches Museum, Vienna)

*Above left*: 31. A detail of Sir Henry Raeburn's portrait of John Campbell (1762–1834), whose tutor in Switzerland, Horace-Bénédict de Saussure, Brydone recommended. (Scottish National Portrait Gallery)

*Above right*: 32. A portrait of the third Earl of Breadalbane (1696–1782) by John Wootton. He became John and Colin Campbells' tutor the year before Brydone met them in Switzerland. (UK Government Art Collection)

*Above left*: 33. Oelenhainz's portrait of Johann Kaspar Lavater, a Swiss pastor, whom Brydone met in 1778 while in Zürich. (Pestalozzianum-Stiftung für Bildung, Schule und Dialog, Zürich)

*Above middle*: 34. Horace-Bénédict de Saussure (1740–1799), a noted Swiss naturalist and scientist, and tutor to the Campbell boys. (Museum of Art & History, Geneva)

*Above right*: 35. Portrait of Salomon Gessner (1730–1788), poet and printmaker, by Anton Graff. (Swiss National Museum, Zürich)

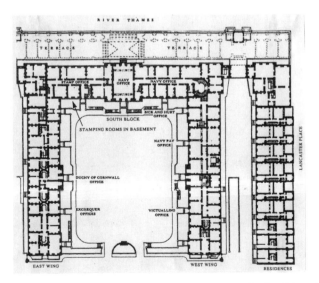

36. The Ground Plan of the New Somerset House, with the River Thames and the location of the stamping rooms in the top left-hand corner of the building. (From 'Creating a Good Impression' by H. Dagnall)

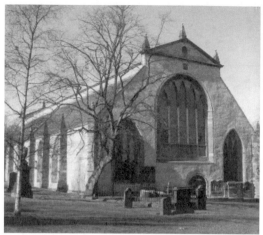

*Above left*: 37. Portrait of Revd William Robertson (1721–1793), historian and Principal of Edinburgh University, painted by Sir Joshua Reynolds in 1772. (Scottish National Portrait Gallery)

*Above right*: 38. Brydone's father-in-law, the Revd William Robertson, was minister of Old Greyfriars Kirk, Edinburgh between 1761 and his death in 1793. He is buried in the churchyard.

*Above left*: 39. John Opie's 1803 portrait of Charles Stanhope, third Earl Stanhope (1753–1816) who read Brydone's paper about a remarkable thunder-storm to the Royal Society in February 1787. (Science Museum/Science & Society Picture Library)

*Above right*: 40. John Home (1722–1808) whose portrait was painted by Sir Henry Raeburn, had trained for the ministry with William Robertson and became a tutor to the Prince of Wales. (National Portrait Gallery, London)

41. Wroxton Abbey, the Jacobean home near Banbury in Oxfordshire of Francis, the first Earl of Guilford (1704–1790), the father of Lord North.

42. Bushy House, Teddington, Lord North's country home near London.

43. Lennel House as it became in the 1820s, Brydone's home just north of Coldstream on the river Tweed, where Beatrix Potter subsequently spent a summer.

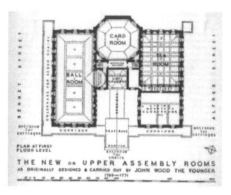

*Above, left & right*: 44. The entrance and floor plan of John Wood, the Younger's new Upper Rooms, Bath, the Mecca of Georgian Society. (From *The Georgian Buildings of Bath* by Walter Ison)

45. A drawing by Robert Woodruff of The Circus in Bath, opening into Bennett Street, where the Brydone family experienced a violent snow storm after attending a concert at the Upper Rooms. (Victoria Art Gallery, Bath and North East Somerset Council)

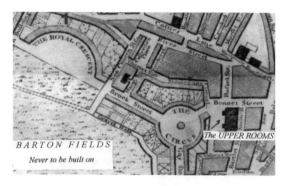

46. A modified plan showing Bennett Street in relation to the Upper Rooms (the original being from *A Guide to all the Watering and Sea-Bathing Places for 1813* by John Feltham).

*Above left*: 47. A portrait of Gilbert Elliot (1751–1814), governor-general of India, painted by James Atkinson, a surgeon. (National Portrait Gallery, London)

*Above right*: 48. James Scott's mezzotint portrait of Anna Maria Amyand (1752–1829), after Sir Joshua Reynolds. She became the wife of the first Lord Minto. (National Portrait Gallery, London)

*Above left*: 49. A detail from G. Zobel's mezzotint of Gilbert Elliot (1782–1859), after Sir Francis Grant, shows him as the diplomat and minister he was to become in the 1830s. (National Portrait Gallery, London)

*Above right*: 50. Mary Elliot née Brydone, when she was the second Countess of Minto, from a miniature by Sir William Ross taken in 1851, two years before her death.

*Above, left & right*: 51 and 52. Sir Samuel Romilly, painted by Sir Thomas Lawrence, (Tate Gallery, on loan to the National Portrait Gallery, London), and his wife 'dear Anne' by John Hoppner, who stayed at Minto in 1812. (Bridgeman Art Library, London)

*Above left*: 53. Dugald Stewart (1753–1828), a philosopher and mathematician, gave a series of lectures in Edinburgh attended by Gilbert Elliot in the winter of 1809. (Scottish National Portrait Gallery)

*Above middle*: 54. A pencil drawing of Dr William Somerville (1771–1860) by Sir F L Chantrey. Born at Minto, Somerville became a military surgeon and in 1811 he met Brydone's son-in-law on manoeuvres in Jedburgh. (National Portrait Gallery, London)

*Above right*: 55. Dr Adam Clarke, the Methodist minister, criticised Brydone's religious writings as 'a sneer against revelation'. His portrait by Thomas Blood was published as an engraving in 1816. (National Portrait Gallery, London)

56. Eden Farm in Kent to which Lord Minto travelled through 'cold drizzling rain' for the funeral of his brother-in-law.

57. The memorial tablet in Westminster Abbey to the first Earl Minto who died in June 1814. The name of his brother Hugh Elliot was added in 1830. (Dean & Chapter of Westminster)

*Below left*: 58. Dr Samuel Spiker (1786–1858), the Berlin journalist and writer who passed near Coldstream in July 1816. (Bildagentur für Kunst, Berlin)

*Below middle*: 59. Thomas Mitchell's watercolour of Francis Rawdon Hastings (1754–1826) around 1804. As the second Earl of Moira, he replaced Lord Minto as governor-general of India. (National Portrait Gallery, London)

*Below right*: 60. Detail of a portrait painted by Sir Thomas Lawrence of Queen Caroline of Brunswick, who entertained Gilbert and Mary at Blackheath. (National Portrait Gallery, London)

61. The Höhenweg near Interlaken in 1830, painted by Jules-Louis-Frederic Villeneuve. The population of the village of Interlaken at the time of the Elliot family's visit would have been considerably less than 1,000 people.

62. A mezzotint portrait of an elderly Patrick Brydone by William Ward, after Andrew Geddes, published by Colnaghi & Co. in 1818. (The Trustees of the British Museum)

was spent at Brienz, on the lake of the same name, after what the tutor called one of 'the most interesting days of the whole journey, for the experience of the scenery, the cascades and the beauty of the mountains'. They were soon in the Simmental, homeward towards Lausanne at the end of their exhausting journey. At Bulle, in the district of Gruyère, Brydone scribbled his closing notes, praising the peasants of the region for their style of life when compared to town dwellers, citing the higher death rate in cities as proof of the peasants' good judgement, and praising the way both men and women sang traditional songs. There had been few worrying times and his charges had seen much natural beauty and some good examples of architecture. He could only hope that their father would appreciate his efforts.[14]

In the event, it was Lord Guilford who wrote to Brydone, first on 19 August and then on 24 September, acknowledging the pleasure he'd derived from the tutor's letters written in Chur and Luzern. Guests at Wroxton were Brownlow North, the prime minister's half-brother and bishop of Winchester, along with Mrs North who joined 'in love and compliments' to the young men in Brydone's care. Lord Guilford had been 'well-pleased with the rational entertainments' that the tutor had arranged during their travels, but he was a little concerned that Francis had lost the journal he had been keeping, and that he had been mistaken for a young lady. The old earl who was related to the Ancasters, also shared the news of three deaths which had occurred in quick succession, one being that of General Peregrine Bertie, the third Duke of Ancaster. The second, the death of the Duchess of Ancaster's mother, which caused her a 'great deal of terrible agitation', had been followed by the drowning of young Lindsey, Brydone's 'late pupil', in the lake of the family property at Grimsthorpe in Lincolnshire. Imagining that Brydone had heard how Admiral Keppel 'had been much beaten by the French' Lord Guilford concluded by telling him that 'we are satisfied here that he has beaten the French, but not near so much as we hoped he would have done. We have ... got home our trade to a great value which would not have happened had not the French been a little disconcerted'.[15]

The second letter from Wroxton heaped the praise of the young men's parents on Brydone. They were 'very sensible how much their doing well' had been the object of his 'care and attention', The old lord thought it impossible that his grandsons could 'pass their time this winter so much to their advantage as at Lausanne, in the same way as they did the last'. He agreed with Brydone that the eldest grandson's 'tendency to indulge inaction' was 'almost his only fault', and judged well when he made George the expedition's treasurer. Anyone who was going to 'manage a good estate' would find 'full employment and no leisure to indulge a disposition to inaction', adding that by the expense of your journey being much greater than he (George) expected he will see he must always leave a latitude in his calculations'.

It also became clear that in making arrangements for a credit of £300 to be sent to Monsieur Porta, and another £200 when he was to be in London the following week, the earl had been asked by his son to take full control of the purse strings. Both sums were in addition to the £300 already given to Brydone by the prime minister. Moreover, with Brydone accepting probably irregular or only part-payments from the Duke of Ancaster for his services, he expressed much concern that the tutor had 'taken up money in London' (or a commercial loan). He said that the delay in sending him his tutor's fee had been due to him not knowing where or to whom it was to be sent, but he knew how important money was to the tutor. In closing, Lord Guilford explained that his son had just returned from a visit to the west of England, and he proposed going to London for a few days before staying a little time in Kent.[16]

Another of Brydone's friendships had also flourished in 1778. He at last met the two young men about whom their mother, Mrs Elizabeth Campbell, had written to him at the end of 1775. A widow, she lived at Craig's Court near Charing Cross with her sons, John (1762–1834) and Colin (1763–1793) who both attended Westminster School nearby. Her husband, Colin Campbell of Carwhin had died in 1772. Wanting Brydone's advice about a tutor for her boys on their travels abroad, he had been able to tell her that Horace-Bénédict de Saussure, a Genevan aristocrat, was about to set out for London and would be a suitable candidate. Born near Geneva in 1740, his botanical studies had been followed by an interest in the geology and topography of the Alps, and he had offered a reward for the first ascent of Mont Blanc.[17] In sending his good wishes to the young gentlemen, should they come into de Saussure's care, Brydone had advised them not to look on him 'so much as their governor as their friend and companion'. As matters turned out, the Campbell boys spent their next summer holiday in England and Scotland being guided by their uncle, the elderly third Earl of Breadalbane, who felt he could help on that occasion.[18] He nevertheless agreed with Mrs Campbell that de Saussure should 'accompany our young men to a foreign university, and afterwards on their travels' and, 'if he answers the character Mr Brydone gives of him, which I have no reason to doubt, he will be more a companion than a tutor and will make himself very agreeable to them'.

In the autumn of 1778, Mrs Campbell's two boys and their entourage were living near Lausanne, to the west of Morges, a pleasant old lakeside town in the centre of the vine-growing area on the northern edge of Lake Geneva. They told their mother how they had 'the pleasure of seeing (her) friend Mr Brydone'. Colin Campbell spoke of 'beginning to understand the French', whilst John reported that he had not fully recovered from a sprain but was much better. Brydone could be confident that the boys' introduction to society had been taken forward. 'At every ball ... we have found some English', he reported. Dancing the *allemande*, a dance peculiar to Switzerland, had become a frequent feature of their teaching, and a group of about twenty gentlemen and ladies from the age of sixteen to twenty four met every Sunday evening 'at cards, blind man's buff, dances, and all the oddest games you can think of'. Brydone gave the boys English newspapers to read as a treat, but they found little in them of interest until, with Britain again at war with France, they could identify with Captain Lockhart Ross, a Scottish naval officer who had served with distinction in a battle off Ushant. John Campbell told his mother 'he is a brave man, and I dare say he will behave well and better than Keppel or Howe'. However, towards the end of the year, and with 'only three Englishmen besides Lord North's sons in Lausanne', but others expected, John admitted that he liked 'this place better than I did, as I begin to understand the French which makes it more agreeable'. Dining with Brydone on 15 December, it seems both boys had become bored by 'the sameness of the place' at Morges, and now preferred Lausanne.[19]

# CHAPTER 10

# A Third Tour with George and Francis North (May to October 1779)

It seems that Lord North's father only heard of what he called 'George's plan' for a German tour by chance, early in April 1779. Writing to Brydone the following month, he said it was a matter about which 'we are entirely ignorant'. Moreover, he showed some annoyance that Brydone had not made it clear where letters of credit were to have been sent or to whom they should be made out. Lord Aylesbury, the elderly great intriguer, asked Lord Bruce to carry Guilford's letter to Lausanne.[1] It was hoped it would arrive there before the party left but, if not, he assumed Brydone's Monsieur Porta would know where he could be found. As to 'George's plan for his German tour', the earl could only say that 'as you have settled it together, I dare say we should approve it', a comment reflecting the close eye he kept on all that was going on as well as on financial matters. Lord Guilford was certain that Sir Robert Keith, the British ambassador, would make 'it as agreeable and advantageous to the young men as possible' despite the fact that they would see the court 'at some disadvantage', given that nobility were apt to go out of town for the summer, as they did in England. Lord North thought the party could be 'well-assured of receiving much service … from … ministers in every court' they visited. Then, basing his information on a letter young George had written to one of his sisters, and which he had seen, Lord Guilford imagined Brydone and his party would leave Lausanne about the middle of the month.[2]

It was in the middle of May that Sir Robert Keith, the extremely able British envoy in Vienna, wrote to Lord Pembroke, telling him that 'I expect Lord North's two sons very shortly from Lausanne, along with Brydone, and they shall be made most welcome. If you hear anything of them at Munich or Salzburg, and can tell me the precise time of their expected arrival in Vienna, you will do me a great pleasure'.[3] Meanwhile, in London, the North family were impatient for good news of the war from Admiral Barrington, in command of the Leeward Islands squadron. Having 'given the French a little rap on the fingers', there had been some delight when Sir James Wallace drove them into Cancale Bay instead of St Malo and took or destroyed three frigates, along with several boats due to be used against Jersey. Speaking for his son, Lord Guiford said that both men were relaxed about the French conquest of Senegal, 'they seem to be much pleased'. He then asked Brydone's opinion of 'Mr Necker's desire to retire'; the French finance minister's friends had apparently not given a national war loan any great support. So far as the boys' life in Lausanne was concerned, their grandfather was especially pleased to learn that they had received the sacrament of Holy Communion in Lausanne. He felt they had not been 'frequenting divine service so often as they ought'. Lord Guilford thought he had received benefit from his journey to Bath but passed on the fact that the opposition in Parliament were very disagreeable in both Houses 'endeavouring to do any mischief they can to their country'. Finally, he said, he could not remember whether he had told George that he had been unanimously elected in his absence as an assistant of the Corporation of Banbury which gave him a voice in the election of the mayor, and asked Brydone to convey his congratulations on the honour.[4]

It was two o'clock in the afternoon of Sunday the thirtieth of May, when George and Francis again left Lausanne for what was to be a tortuous three-part journey across Europe, and the last for their tutor. The first leg which took a route into France, a rare destination for Brydone, suggested that he had little hand in its selection. However, by the beginning of June the party was in Lyon, France's second city, where they found lodgings at the *Hôtel de York*. After visiting St John's cathedral where the fourteenth century astronomical clock it contained was not liked, on account of the ugly figures which surmounted its twenty-foot square plinth, the travellers noted that there was a public execution in the square. The offender's crime, for which he had been tortured, had been the theft of a piece of grey cloth. Coolly, those in the crowd going to the opera then went on their way. The next day the travellers watched a religious procession of perhaps seven to eight thousand people from the upper windows of the Town House which was followed at six in the evening by another, with children in costume as angels, and 'a toddler as the Lamb of God'. It was only with much difficulty that their gravity was maintained as she 'waddled past' them, but Brydone admitted there seemed to be 'a great deal of devotion among the people'. Driving out in the evening amid large numbers of the population sauntering in squares, avenues and quays, the travellers could find no merriment or any dancing, which they thought 'curious on such a day of celebration. However, the theatre in Lyon was a disappointment: 'in short we saw no piece that was a proper entertainment for a rational audience'.

An establishment which received unstinting praise from Brydone for its ground-breaking scientific and anatomical work was the École Vétérinaire, the world's first veterinary school. Claude Bourgelat became so concerned about the various diseases afflicting French horses, particularly one known by its German name of rinderpest, that he gave up the law, and in 1761 founded the school. Brydone was less enthusiastic about some aspects of the textile industry. Silk weaving had been an important industry since the sixteenth century but the tutor found the method of weaving velvet in Lyon unduly complicated: 'the loom requires three months to mount', and the cost of made-to-measure clothes was 'huge'. He was, nevertheless, greatly amazed by another process which involved a silver ingot being 'first covered in gold, the gold bonded to the silver, and the ingot then thinned down (drawn) through smaller and smaller holes (dies) till the resulting wire stretches for three or four hundred miles'. Such insights evidently contributed to a theory Brydone had about productivity at work. Those in sedentary occupations such as weaving, were people who 'pull down the natural spirits' and were 'much less gay', whilst those who cultivated the ground were 'the happier'. To everybody's amusement, on the chimney of one workshop were the words: '*Il n'y a rien tant à craindre de gens occupés que la visite de ceux qui n'ont rien à faire*' or 'There is nothing that busy people fear more than a visit from someone with nothing to do'.

Then, on 8 June, the travellers departed, having explored an island three miles up the Saône river the previous day, 'in pleasant countryside' where the boats were 'piloted and rowed by women, who do their work excellently'. Two nights on the road were spent at a good inn at Montluel and Bourg-en-Bresse. In a suburb of the latter town, the party visited the church monastery of Brou which had been built in the sixteenth century by the daughter of Marguerite of Bourbon, the wife of Philip II of Savoy. Richly ornamented on the outside and with remarkable architecture inside, they found it 'curious'. Outside the church there was a dial on which the months of the year were written, and if a man stood on the mark which showed the month of the year, becoming in effect the gnomon of the dial, his shadow showed the hour of the day. Brydone thought the Royal Saltworks at Arc-en-Senans near Besançon which they passed, and which had only started production about twenty-five years before, would 'not last much longer'. The supply of wood from nearby forests, and used in the manufacturing process, was being progressively denuded.[5]

For several leagues, the hills and roads on the way to Besançon were covered with a great many small black frogs about a third of an inch long. Brydone could only assume that the rain of the previous day and night, after a two-day drought, might have had brought them about. Once beyond the principal town in the Franche-Comté, and Belfort, transferred to France at the end of the Thirty Years' War, where the Duke of Württemberg's court was celebrating the birth of a young Prussian prince, their route took the party along the banks of the River Doubs. There the tutor noticed an absence of rounded river stones in the valley, all the rocks and stones being angular and pointed.

By Sunday 13 June, the travellers were in Basle from where they 'saw the top of Mont Blanc perfectly, about 150 miles in a right line'. With the road 'covered with river stones', travel had been most uncomfortable, so much so that Brydone noted that the French postmasters had petitioned the *intendant* at Strasbourg to have them removed. The weather was unseasonably cool, the thermometer showing 53°F and there had been a sharp shower of hail. Despite this, the boys were soon being guided towards Holbein's 'Dance of Death', a piece of fantastic medieval art, an allegory of the *danse macabre* in a series of woodcuts showing 'Death' in many disguises.[6] In saying that the work had 'not much merit, and is not by Holbein', Brydone reflected the view then held by the erudite English antiquary, Francis Douce, that with the Alphabet and the Dance of Death being published without Holbein's name, and the engraver's name, Hans Lützelburger, appearing on many of what were called 'printer's proofs', Holbein was unlikely to have been the originator of the works. There were, however, some other works of his in the university library, one which, in Brydone's view, the artist's painting of the punishment of Christ, which was 'highly valued' locally and worth seeing.

Described by Brydone as 'an ugly town, but celebrated for its École Militaire', on 15 June the travellers passed through Colmar, some forty miles, south south-west of Strasbourg, and on the River Lauch. Founded in the ninth century, and taken by a Swedish army in 1632, it had been finally conquered by France in 1673. The land near the principal city in Alsace, Strasbourg, was fertile and the people were growing 'a great deal of Indian corn, wheat, tobacco, rye, hemp and rape seed'. In the city's Lutheran church of St Thomas, the travellers marvelled at the mausoleum of Count Maurice de Saxe, a German who served in the French army and became a Marshal of France. Only created the year before, it was 'a great monument ... a masterpiece'. The catholic Bishop who, as the tutor recorded, was always a member of the de Rohan family, had a palace 'superior to that of most sovereign princes'.

The following day the travellers arrived in a town famous for the peace to which it gave its name. Rastatt, on the Murg river above its junction with the Rhine, had been the residence of the margrave of Baden-Baden until 1771. In the eponymous, sprawling castle they were shown the room in which he had died, it being explained that his widow did not use that side of the palace. The present Margrave rarely stayed there but they met an English officer in his service, a Mr Burdett. A day later, 18 June, found the party in Mannheim which had been virtually destroyed both in the Thirty Years' War and again in 1689 by the French army. It was only by 1760 that the elector, Charles III, completed the construction of his palace and the Jesuit Church. During the eighteenth century, Mannheim became the home of several composers and under Carlo Grua the court orchestra had a good reputation; but the court had just left the city when the travellers arrived.

Staying overnight at *Le Cour Pallatin*, a 'very good inn', Brydone concluded that Mannheim was 'one of the best organised and attractive towns in Europe, with good fortifications and a guard of about three hundred'. There were a few good tapestries, one of the Gobelins having been a present from the King of France, and there were a few 'capital' items among the pictures in the palace worth seeing but nothing 'outstanding'. The opera house was both 'elegant and commodious'. It held three thousand people who all entered without charge paid for by the Elector. The library, with its 50,000 volumes, was open two days a week to scholars and those known to the authorities, the size of the collection in the print room astonishing the tutor. In the Hall of Antiquities, Brydone said, 'all the best statues of Florence and Rome can be seen, and Mr Verchafeldt (the keeper) has mounted them on wooden pedestals so that … young artists can study them at any angle'.

The Professor of Experimental Physics and Mathematics at the Physics Institute which had been founded at Mannheim in 1756, Christian Mayer, a Jesuit father, took the party round his observatory. Among his mainly English instruments 'there was a very fine quadrant by Bird' of 8 foot radius.[7] Before the travellers left, they were taken to the palace of Igersheim, probably the rebuilt Burg Neuhaus castle west of the city and south of Würzburg, which was considered 'neat and comfortable but not special'. They were allowed to glimpse the electress and the young prince at dinner through a hole in the door. Mannheim had been a delight for the polymath and his pupils. In Mainz, their next brief destination, the day was spent looking at more palaces, 'none of them remarkable'. As a child of the manse, Brydone was pleased to find that the prior who took the party round the churches of St Peter and St Ignatius seemed 'very contented'.

The party's passage through Hochheim and the vineyards of the region brought them to Frankfurt, at the confluence of the Main and Rhine rivers, on 22 June. The cathedral and the town house were the only buildings shown to the public. 'The emperor', Brydone wrote, was 'crowned in the first and dines in the second'. The tutor's oft-expressed concern for the Jews again became apparent. He could only find one street in which they could live. 'They are' he said 'locked up here from ten each night, and all day until six o'clock on Sundays'. As in Mainz where the Jewish community dated from the tenth century, and in other parts of Europe, outbreaks of the Black Death were often blamed on them, and the massacres which resulted contrasted violently with other periods during which peaceful co-existence was possible.

Before turning south for Darmstadt, the party moved to Hanau, also in Hesse and in a bend in the river Kinzig, a little to the east of Frankfurt. The journey had only taken two hours but Brydone had been irritated by his unreliable odometer again breaking. Brydone liked Hanau and felt it would probably become 'one of the foremost watering places of Germany'. Protestant refugees from the Netherlands and France in the sixteenth century had helped establish it, bringing with them their skills as goldsmiths. With Frederick II's thirty-six-year-old son William away from home when Brydone's party arrived, the travellers were taken to the nearby chalybeate spring in a *voiture de conversation*, described by the tutor as 'a kind of char-a-banc on springs'. The establishment had three lodging houses for those taking the waters. Afterwards they all returned to the palace for supper and everyone retired at half past ten.

The following day was a Saturday, 26 June, and the party again dined and supped at court, where Prince William, a 'stout, active man', expressed his devotion to the English nation in terms which caused him to weep. 'His mother' he said 'had been English, and brought him up as a member of that nation. His great ambition was to lead a joint action of his own and English troops against the French. He knew he had not enough experience as yet, but hoped very much that the day would come when he was able to show this proof of his attachment to the nation'. Unusually, Brydone spent three days enjoying life in and around the gardens of the spa, with architectural visits for once left aside, but not all was to his liking. He found the style of card playing at court one he was not used to in Lausanne, and on another occasion in the presence of both George and Francis, Brydone felt he had to contradict the prince who, after describing the campaign he had fought in with the King of Prussia, referred to General Burgoyne as being 'haughty and dismissed by his officers'.[8]

With supper on the first day of July behind them, the travellers took their leave of the court, being 'truly affected by the sentiments expressed on their departure'. The next two days spent in Darmstadt were 'the happiest ... of their life'. Once established at the Angel Inn, they introduced themselves to the grand court marshal and were immediately invited to dine with Prince George, the second son of Landgrave Louis VIII, who had married Maria Louise in 1748. Servants and équipage were sent to escort them, and the meal was most agreeable. After tea, the travellers were driven into the country where several gardens were shown, one having been laid out professionally. Supper with the family followed, and the next day they watched a church parade of 1,500 'fine fellows'. Nearby was an 'Exercise House', some 240 feet long and 150 feet broad, with 'no pillars or other visible support for the roof, except walls of immense thickness'.

On the last occasion the party dined and supped at court there were about fifty at table, and Brydone found the prince 'rather grave but agreeable and sensible'. The young, eighteen-year-old princess Louise Henriette, who was in 'full bloom ... beautiful, and full of talents', had been engaged in preparing two dramatic productions to celebrate her father's birthday on the eleventh of July. The Abbé from Mannheim who was a fine harpsichord player had written the accompanying music. Brydone wrote that he did not think it possible that 'two days acquaintance could have me regret a place so much, but we were as easy and as well-acquainted as if we had been some months'. Pressed to stay longer, and 'with very heavy hearts', the travellers nevertheless took their leave.

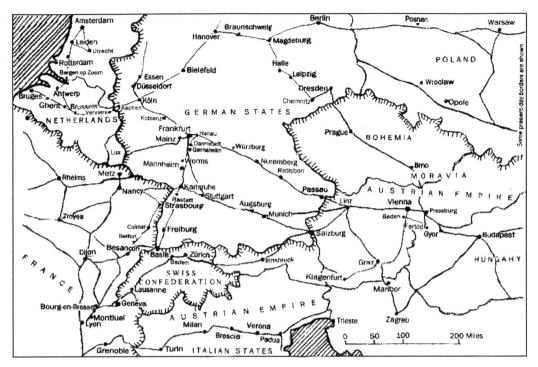

Rough sketch map of Europe showing the areas visited by Brydone and Lord North's sons, George and Francis, between May and October 1779.

A journey of three hours the next day brought the party to Gernsheim on the east bank of the Rhine. Breaches in the castle defences made by the French had yet to be repaired. The Baroque church of St Mary Magdalene, referred to as the cathedral by Brydone, stood out with its curved onion dome from quite a distance. Two days later the travellers arrived in Stuttgart after a journey which followed the Neckar valley. The roads in the Duke of Württemberg's dominion were excellent. Brydone wrote a card to Count Richter, the grand chamberlain, and he at once sent an express to Hohenstein, forty miles or so to the south of Stuttgart, to ask when they might be presented. In the meantime, they visited the Academy, 'a vast establishment of 350 students' where only sixty or seventy paid, and students benefited from everything being 'clean and well-ordered' despite being separated by social class.

The Duke's influence was everywhere. Pictures of Charles Eugene honoured the patronage he gave the arts, but Brydone told a story that showed him in a different light. He kept a string of mistresses by whom he had fathered eleven children, and had persecuted a loyal servant of the family after the father had refused to give his daughter to the Duke. 'The entire family and all who had tried to help them' Brydone recorded, 'were reduced to starvation until Prince Louis made them a small pension which he himself could ill afford'.

Schloss Solitude, to the west of Stuttgart, which had been recommended to the travellers, proved a disappointment. Brydone could only write that 'nature has been most cruelly tormented'. Much money had been spent on it but she (nature) most obstinately resists every effort to embellish her'. The Chinese House in the grounds was 'pretty', their guide explaining that only English visitors were permitted to see it, and then only on an express order from the Duke. Brydone wrote later, not without a quiet smile, that 'we were not extremely vain of our prerogative'. Equipment for the outdoor theatre had never been used and 'the supports for the bushes and trees of the scenery were about to collapse'. The visitors' disillusionment continued when they found the court apartments in the palace unfinished and 'the gilding on the roof done several times at vast expense'. The party left Stuttgart on 9 July with little regret at not seeing its master.

Arriving in Munich on Sunday morning, 11 July, the travellers were immediately presented to the Elector and supped with him at the Nymphenburg Palace, to the northwest of the city. Built in 1675, partly to the design of an Italian architect, it became a favourite summer residence of the rulers of Bavaria. At the time Brydone's party arrived, the Elector of the Palatinate was Duke Charles Theodore who reigned from December 1777 to February 1799.[9] He was 'very polite and attentive, speaking to all his guests' of whom there were about sixty at table. After an elegant meal, people either played cards or walked in the magnificent palace gardens. Supper lasted two hours and a half, the Elector then retired, and everyone else went to their carriages. This, Brydone wrote 'makes a good appearance on the road at night with a number of servants on horseback with flambeaux'.

The travellers soon met and dined with Count Sinsheim before going with him to the casino. Although Brydone came to regard this member of a family from south-western Germany as a friend, the party soon concluded that of all the agreeable people they met on their travels, none was Bavarian. 'It's true', Brydone said, that 'they are civil to strangers and give very good dinners, but the society at their tables, the only sauce which can make these dinners agreeable, is very defective'. The count and the tutor were soon discussing the extraordinary claims of a faith healer whom the former had seen in action, and who had cured him of any belief in miracles for all time. Apparently, Franz Mesmer, a Viennese physician with a taste for showmanship, whom Brydone had probably heard of four or five years previously when he had been in the vicinity of Lake Constance, had gone to Paris. Recalling a man 'who pretended by natural means to perform all the miracles of Gassner (a Catholic priest and exorcist) by magnetism and music' had found Vienna 'no longer a proper theatre for his absurdities'. Even so, Brydone had to admit that when he was last in Germany it was 'not to be believed the number of proselytes he had made to his system'.

Brydone, George and Francis set out for Vienna at the start of the last week of July. It was a fine day and they put the servants in the coach and themselves in the post wagon. In the street, Brydone saw a lady whom he had met the previous evening, a rich widow about forty years old, to whom he bowed and kissed her hand. She promptly assumed 'a stern aspect, not liking to be greeted by someone in a post wagon' but he continued to salute her till they were past. Turning back, and laughing to his companions, the tutor said 'I cannot say I heard it, but I am almost certain I saw her say to her sister, an old woman who is a *dame d'honneur*: "a very pretty conquest truly which I have made last night"'.

On their arrival, the travellers 'found excellent apartments at the *Boeuf Blanc*' for which they paid four florins a day, and later met Prince Schwarzenberg at dinner.[10] Brydone's last visit to the capital of the Hapsburg Empire had been in 1776, and in winter. On this occasion the temperature remained as high as 86F for several days, bringing on a violent storm lasting several hours, with some flooding in the streets, but 'the dust was flying' again soon afterwards. When the party was presented to Joseph II, the Holy Roman Emperor, he spoke much in praise of Lord North and said he was happy to see his sons. Then around six o'clock that afternoon, the court went hawking, the gentlemen on horseback, and the ladies in carriages, the target being heron and some hare. The emperor, Brydone noted, was always ready to attend his mother's needs. Despite taking very little exercise, having almost lost the use of her limbs, Maria Theresa was still much occupied with hearing complaints and receiving petitions every morning from six o'clock. It seems that she never fully recovered from an attack of the smallpox she had suffered in 1767 and, in addition to shortness of breath and insomnia, she had developed dropsy or oedema as it was then called. Talk at the emperor's table was about the defeat of the French fleet in the Caribbean, reported but unconfirmed. A month before, it had been as if war had arrived in Austria when a powder magazine in the lines just a mile from the city had exploded, killing nearly 300 people.

On 27 July, on the way to being presented to the Empress and other members of the court, her coach passed the travellers and they could see clearly how very unassuming it was, 'not at all like a nobleman's'. The peasantry, however, recognised her and knelt as she passed and threw coins to them. The court theatre, also known as the Burgtheater which opened in 1741, and which was to have a chequered career for much of the eighteenth century, had been built next to Maria Theresa's palace at her request. Brydone described its interior as 'neat but not magnificent, with only three boxes'. The nobility sat in the front four rows of benches and anyone else could occupy the rest of it. 'The players and wind orchestra were good', he said. The following night it was the party's turn to hear another performance of *Ariadne auf Naxos*, this time a melodrama by Georg Benda, a Bohemian composer and conductor, at Prince Schwarzenberg's 'small and ill-contrived' theatre at his palace in the suburbs. It was 'tolerably well done' despite the ballet being 'execrable'.

At the end of the first week in Vienna, Brydone saw the new gardens of the Schönbrunn palace which had been constructed since his previous visit. The fountains were impressive and the ruin of a triumphal arch, known as the 'Ruin of Carthage' and later the *gloriette*, which had only been built the previous year, looked as if it really was ancient. Returning to the Prater, the public park in the centre of Vienna, originally a small island in the Danube and an area where the Emperor allowed coffee houses to be established, the travellers watched a display of fireworks. With Joseph II moving among the crowds, and appearing pleased that no one took notice of him, Brydone wrote 'he certainly has more enjoyment of life than any prince in the world. He has that of a sovereign and that of a private person'. Admiringly, the tutor went on to tell how the Emperor apparently had obtained detailed plans about navigation on the Danube despite constant obstruction from the Turks.[11]

As their stay drifted into August, the tutor's record was reduced to tittle-tattle and gossip as the court ladies babbled on. The Emperor's first wife, Princess Isabella of Palma, who had a presentiment about of her own death, was said to have been responsible for the unhappiness of his second wife, the Princess of Bavaria, who was carried off by smallpox. Such tales led Brydone to mention that in Vienna, a 'wife takes the title of her husband, even if it is lower than her own. The people are no longer slaves to etiquette, but they are still slaves to rank and family. Classes marry within themselves'. Families 'dare not marry out of their class', or the children of such a union would not be allowed at court. This would be 'the end of privilege'. The story was told about a Count Palus, a very rich man who thought to buy his way into high rank by marrying a girl from a good but poor family. The poor wretch became an object of pity and contempt, said Brydone: he is now 'too proud to associate with those of his former rank, and the nobility is much too proud to associate with him'.

On 10 August, the party de-camped to the small spa town of Baden, fifteen miles south of Vienna. Its season had been in May and June so that it was now not overfull of company. At the foot of beautiful mountains, there were several sources of mineral water and with a temperature of around 95°F, conditions were most agreeable. Brydone bathed his legs and feet only once, finding himself overheated for several days after. The Emperor had built 'an *écluse* (or lock) of great strength on the river' and when the floodgates were shut the river rose, forming a lake. It was covered with timber when the travellers saw it, as the forest which provided firewood for the town was situated there. Brydone examined the course taken by the timber when the gates were opened and found that the piles of logs formed a barricade seven feet high. On the side of an adjacent mountain, the Calvarienberg, which was largely composed of dolomitic limestone, was a representation of Christ asking that the cup might pass from him, and faced by an angel which the tutor found 'arch'. Further to the south where there were some remains of *Thermae Pannonicae*, the Roman settlement, the party was given much-enjoyed hospitality by a baron who owned a country house there. His garden was a mixture of the English and Dutch styles.

The next destination seems to have been planned by Brydone to show his two charges something of the Hungary he had visited with Lord Lindsey and William Pitt three years before, including Pressburg which had always been a favourite of Lord North. En route, the travellers visited Eszterháza (today part of the town of Fertöd, 60 miles south of Vienna) where Prince Nikolaus Esterházy had built a palace in the 1760s. He had been a successful Austrian general in the Seven Years' War. Brydone described his Baroque castle, developed on land owned by the Esterházy family since 1622, as 'magnificent and the profusion of gilding and embroidery great' even if the 'paintings and statues were execrable'. There were 'chairs which entertain you with a symphony when you sit on them, and there are trinkets everywhere', all suggesting to the tutor that the owner 'wished to protect himself from boredom'. In fact, as Brydone soon discovered, he was then busy building a road through the swampy banks of a large lake which would shorten the journey to Pressburg by seven or eight hours.

When the party met the Prince, they found him 'very shy', a man who 'wished to be incognito in his own house' and 'a slave to his caprice', as Brydone put it. When they were presented to him, he talked easily but offered no hospitality. Not only his son, Count Weissenwolf, later Prince Anton, who had served in his father's regiment, but the Countess along with General Jerningham and his wife were 'hurt beyond measure' that he did not invite the travellers to dinner.[12] Such matters were soon forgotten when the tutor learned more about the Prince's orchestra and theatres. The eminent composer Joseph Haydn, lived in a four-room flat near the palace when not working in Vienna as Kapelmeister, both Paul Anton Esterházy and his brother being appreciative of his work, and the latter becoming his patron. Haydn had his own small orchestra, along with responsibility for the Prince's two opera houses, the second being a puppet theatre where plays and opera were acted. Given the man Nikolaus Esterházy was, Brydone was a little relieved to find his much preferred residence was Mon Bijoux, a 'pretty little house' although the interior contained 'execrable and immodest paintings'.

In a village then called Jahrndorf, a few miles to the south of Pressburg, the travellers had to rescue one of their servants from a Hungarian with a pistol. Brydone explained how he had got out of the carriage 'to feast on grapes at the side of the road' when a robber threatened him. By the time they approached the town itself it was dark and they were 'entertained by two beautiful balls of wildfire or Will-o'-the-wisp'. The tutor said 'they moved gently near the surface of the earth and came very near the road where we were. Then they rose a little into the air and seemed to play round each other, appearing to be mutually attracted, and then repelled'. Describing the twenty minute display as 'this Castor and Pollux', he went on to admit that that he did not know whether they had appeared first over marshy ground, the traditional location in folklore. He thought it probable but 'the day had been hot and sultry without a cloud and the night was clear'.

Memories of the Pressburg that Brydone visited in 1776 were soon being shared with the North brothers, not least those of the ferry with its 'vast platform on two large boats' which was 'pushed over from bank to bank by the current (of the Danube) pushing against the side of the boats'. It was as if the older military man wanted the young soldier to learn something about how an army might bridge an important river. On this occasion, there was time to visit the castle where they were shown paintings of the region by Archduchess Maria Christina and excellent drawings by her husband, Prince Albert of Saxony who had been made the Royal

Governor of Hungary in 1765. Thereafter, the travellers backtracked to Vienna which they left on 13 September.

Overnight stops were made at various places. The Imperial Diet to which British diplomats were credited at this period met at Ratisbon, the name then given to Regensburg, seventy miles from their next destination.[13] It was, Brydone wrote, 'very ugly and dangerous at night' and its inn 'indifferent and costly', but the travellers arrived safely in Nuremberg on 17 September. It had probably been the longest uninterrupted leg of their journeys. The following day in Würzberg, the shape and colour of 'a magnificent Aurora Borealis' raised the travellers' spirits. Passing through Aschaffenburg in North West Bavaria, the travellers arrived back in Hanau on the twentieth of the month where their reception was most cordial, and again they were invited to dine at court. They spent the afternoon with their highnesses at Wilhelmbad, the spa nearby where the Prince was making improvements.

Although the Rhine was rarely travelled for pleasure, the original plan had been to take a boat down the river from Hanau. Vessels carrying people rather than goods, which were to become known as Wasserdiligencen, the post-ships, were to be developed from the skiffs which carried goods from the countryside to cities. Leaving Hanau, their boat managed to reach Schwalbach, a little to the north of Frankfurt, before the poor autumnal weather forced them to return to the land. By 23 September, they had passed Koblenz and Andernach, close to a narrows in the river referred to by the Romans as *Porta Antunnacensis*, reaching Köln, which they thought 'a very ugly city', a day later. From Aachen, they rode on through Verviers to Spa, with its mineral springs in a valley of the Ardennes, They found the waters 'very insipid' at Chaudfontaines but 'the place was well frequented in the season. This was followed by a 'ball at Vauxhall', an oblique reference to a jolly visit to the casino where there was very little dancing and 'Pharaoh', or the card game 'Faro', seemed to be most popular with the company. The triumvirate slept the night at Liège before going on to Brussels.[14]

Nothing is known about Brydone's stay in Brussels but, in what appears to have been the draft of a letter to Lord North, and later included by Brydone in Journal No. 21, the tutor refers to:

the Dutch people's love of and instinct for ... oeconomy. What indeed can you expect from a country where nothing is attended to but profit and loss and where an arithmetician is in higher estimation than a poet or a philosopher. Indeed we must own we had not much opportunity of studying the genius of the people. Oeconomy, their great cardinal virtue, renders it inconsistent with their national character to have any commerce with strangers except a commerce by which something is to be gained, and as we were altogether out of that line we had no commerce with them at all except in their inns where we cannot boast.

Also at this point in his record, Brydone added, rather blandly in the light of what soon happened, that a Mr Gordon had engaged a yacht to meet the travellers in the port at Antwerp so that he could have a chance of examining the course of the River Scheldt.[15]

It had taken the party six hours to reach Antwerp from Brussels and the town of Michelin, where lace of that name was made, through country which was pleasant despite its flatness. Once in city, the travellers particularly admired the masterpieces of Paul Rubens, in spite of his 'Flagellation of Christ' in the Church of St Paul which produced in Brydone 'a sentiment of horror rather than anything else'. Soon afterwards, as they continued to explore Antwerp, Brydone told of a lady's death from hydrophobia having been bitten by her dog, and the sadness the men felt, knowing that they carried Hill's antidote for the bite of a mad dog, and knew nothing of it. At daybreak on 6 October, however, the group embarked aboard the yacht provided by Mr Gordon, and excellent time was made down what today is the Oosterscheldt till the vessel became stranded on a sandbank. With plenty of good wine provided by Mr Gordon, worries were wholly absent, and the party took the opportunity of examining the bed of the river at ebb-tide, observing the appearance of the channel as the water went down and vast flats of mud and sand emerged around them.

Some of the crew explained that a great dam or dyke was being built to increase the availability of useable land in the region. Zeeland and the port of Walcheren had been increasingly settled and many of Antwerp's prosperous Flemings had moved north. Asked whether they could inspect the construction work, the sailors said this would mean wading 'through mud up to their waists'. When the yacht, or more probably a galliot or fishing smack, was re-floated, the wind had changed. Unable to reach Dordrecht, which was then called Dort, the party spent the night near Tholen, then on the island of the same name. The next morning they were again held back by a strong wind and anchored off the island of Duiveland, a little further north-west, where they landed on the dyke to examine the soil formations thrown up by the river. Seeing people using the sods next to the sea to firm up bundles of straw and reeds to make it 'more firm and tenacious', Brydone concluded that 'the defence formed of such very slight materials had a great effect in defending it from the force of the waves'.

When the travellers' pilot and some of the crew went into the village to buy provisions and did not return when expected, Mr Gordon and a member of the upper chamber, referred to by Brydone as 'Lord L', thought there would be no difficulty in going back on board the ship without their assistance as both the wind and tide were in their favour. However, 'just as they pulled a little out from land a large Dutch brig made her appearance, coming full sail down upon them'. 'To avoid her' Brydone continued 'they were obliged to return to the dyke, by which manoeuvre they were driven considerably below our vessel. Although they pulled with great power and assiduity, it was in vain they attempted to regain the ground they had lost. The wind and tide were both against them and bore them off as an easy conquest'.

'For some time' Brydone wrote 'I enjoyed this scene of confusion from the top of the dyke, and laughed heartily at their embarrassment as they had held me very cheap when I objected to the expedition and refused to accompany them on account of their want of skill as navigators. However, at last observing their strength was nearly exhausted, I went to some Dutchmen who were at work on the dyke and offering them money, the only argument with a Dutchman, begged they would wade in and pull the boat up to the landing place'. When his offer was contemptuously dismissed it seems Brydone himself eventually accepted the task. Next morning, and with a favourable wind, the party was able to sail from Dort to Rotterdam, gliding down the river Meuse as it drained into the North Sea. Brydone was 'delighted by the intermingling of tall ships with the trees, steeples and windmills in the city'. After dinner they went on to The Hague where the party stayed the night. A final excursion to Broek in Waterland, a village just to the north east of Amsterdam followed.[16]

The party was soon to reach England, closing what Brydone thought would be his long travelling life. Always happy to be crossing boundaries, whether of science or belief, none at that moment could have been more pleasurable than the journey across the Channel. The North family now awaited their return. Lord North having told his father he had written to both his sons and 'pressed them to contrive to be in England within the month of October'.

Both George and Francis had written to their father and grandfather at intervals during the two years they had been away, and Brydone responded regularly to Lord Guilford's requests for reports, and occasionally to the prime minister himself. One such letter to Downing Street from Munich told him that 'the two Mr Norths continue to enjoy the most perfect health, and to require the friendship, esteem and affection of every worthy person in the different courts to which they visit'. Brydone felt convinced that the princely household of Hanau and Darmstadt would 'ever remember them with great pleasure'. The young gentlemen had been presented to the Elector Palatine and had just returned from supper at the palace with his Highness, who mentioned having seen their father at Mannheim twenty-five years earlier, probably at the conclusion of Lord North's own grand tour.

Then, having told Lord North that they would probably stay in Munich for only four or five days before going directly to Vienna, Brydone had reported to his patron how the season had been 'exceedingly wet, and the roads deep as in winter which retards us considerably, yet the crop of corn is greater than it has been for many years. That of hay has been lost in many places by the flood, whilst the Rhenish vintage promised to be exceedingly plentiful'. His report also spoke of the people of Munich being 'very happy from the restoration of peace, a reference to the War of Bavarian

Succession, or the Kartoffelkreig, which had ended in May that year. In coming to a close, Brydone passed on 'the two gentlemen's desire to pay their duty to Lord and Lady North, and their love to their sisters'.[17]

Lord Guilford, Lord North's father, wrote regularly to Brydone at roughly three monthly intervals and in August he had arranged for an additional credit of £200 to be sent to Messrs Smitner, the party's German bankers, to 'make you quite easy'. He had heard from all quarters of the 'improvement, good conduct and proper behaviour' of Brydone's charges, and 'was sensible of the share' the tutor had had in it. Mindful, nevertheless, that George's proclivity towards fashion might occasionally lead him 'out of the way', his grandfather had advised him 'to set and not follow examples, and to have the courage to form a character of his own' as a good foundation for his happiness. Among family news he passed on while waiting to hear of the travellers' safe arrival in Vienna was the move to an estate in Wales of the 'poor Duchess of Ancaster', following the death of her husband. He also hoped Mr Montague Burgoyne, the younger son of Sir Roger, the ninth baronet, had joined them.[18]

Brydone's good account of 'our young men' had also been acknowledged by Earl Guilford when he wrote to him at Dresden towards the end of September, but these were anxious times in London. While the threat of a combined French and Spanish fleet in the English Channel hung over the country, the prime minister had been unable to leave London or visit his father. However, Lady North and Lady Drake, the wife of an admiral, arrived at Wroxton for ten days during which time Lord North 'contrived just to come and make his bow to his constituents' in Banbury. It had been a very short visit but it gave his father great pleasure, and 'I think I never saw him appear in better health'. The prime minister was 'mighty glad' that Brydone planned to include Mecklenburg-Strelitz, the German duchy, in the itinerary 'which he would have been very sorry to have you omit'. So far as financial matters were concerned, the earl assumed that Brydone had received a £500 credit on his arrival in Vienna, along with two subsequent credits of £200 each. He went on to suggest that the safest way home would be by Harwich but 'a good deal of precaution must be used', and he concluded with the wish that they had 'a prosperous journey'.[19]

In November, with the travellers safely home, Brydone wrote to Lord North from Somerset Street in the region of London's Aldgate, enclosing a statement of expenses. The cost of the party's journey to Lausanne had been £36 13s, whilst the money drawn from his personal bank accounts there and in Vienna to meet daily expenditure was shown as £917 17s. In total, £1,392 6s had been spent, but two sums 'due to Brydone', one for £511 2s and another for £474 9s, had taken some time to be paid, causing the tutor much concern.

Brydone had, however, come to an important decision about his own future and clearly wanted to give his patron not only a full account of the crossroads at which he found himself, but something of the mental anguish he had and was still experiencing. When he 'returned with the late Duke of Ancaster', Lord Lindsey, and before he accepted the prime minister's invitation, his 'determined resolution' had been 'to bid adieu to travelling'. He had been wandering over the continent of Europe for 15 or 16 years and 'was indeed heartily sick of it'. He had received numerous 'solicitations' to make another tour but, as Brydone said:

My resolution was taken, and I then thought that no temptation could have made me alter it. His heart was set on the enjoyment of that retirement, tranquillity and ease of mind which I had so long, and so ardently, wished for but which I never could command. I was now advanced in life, and an old bachelor had ever appeared to me as the most wretched and foolish of beings. That period was fast approaching and I own I saw it with horror. On the other hand, I had considered domestic enjoyments and the pleasures of a family as the only source of true and genuine happiness, a sentiment which increases every day and which has been greatly fortified since I had the honour of knowing your Lordships

His plan, Brydone continued, had been:

to go directly to Scotland, and as I had almost a universal acquaintance in the country, to endeavour to form a connection with some agreeable family. The only objection was that the state of my finances did not entitle me to expect a very advantageous match. I was, however, determined to try, and just as I was preparing to set out I received your Lordship's invitation of travelling with Mr (George) North. This, I own, was a temptation I could not resist for many reasons but really believe it was what I had heard of his son, being of extraordinary and incomparable character, that determined me, for if I know myself at all, without this consideration, no interested motive whatever should have prevailed on me, so much had I suffered from having neglected it. I, however, consulted my friends and found them as I expected, altogether unanimous. They represented my fortune as made; even beyond my wishes, if I should have the happiness of receiving your Lordship's approbation. They quoted me many instances of people raised to affluence and even dignity from similar connections, and by men of much less power and influence than your Lordship ... These considerations made me perfectly indifferent as to terms, even after it was determined to send Mr Francis along with us. I refused the advice of some who wanted me to stipulate an annuity for life as I had done with the Duke of Ancaster, but others represented that your Lordship could easily reward me better without costing yourself so much, and I thought it more liberal to depend on your Lordship's free act than any previous stipulation.[20]

Brydone's only wish was to see himself in a situation where he could execute this plan, on which he said, his future happiness depended. He no longer expected to find the success he had previously enjoyed but neither did he have any intention of working for such people as Ancaster who did not keep their promises.

All things considered, the second half of the 1770s, and more particularly the last two years, had been a remarkable period in Brydone's life. At least, circumstances allowed him to retire from travelling rather more graciously than would have been the case had he done so after his return from Russia. What the tutor now expected, and when 'domestic enjoyments and the pleasure of a family' might happen, were a different matter. The gratitude of the North family for the services he had rendered had certainly been expressed, and the delicacy with which he had handled the diplomatic back-cloth to so many visits, had been much appreciated, but were they worthy of an accolade or honour? The gratitude of the North family would, however, be expressed in another way although Brydone would have been surprised to know what was in store. The prime minister had never been a rich man, and it was only when his father died ten years later, and he became the second earl, inheriting the family properties of Bushy House, Wroxton Abbey near Banbury, Dillington House in Somerset, Waldershare Park near Dover and the London town house in Devonshire Square, that his own financial position improved.

# CHAPTER 11

# Accepts employment with the Stamp Office (1780–1784)

By the middle of November 1779, with his report in the prime minister's hands, the 44 year-old bachelor would have been hoping for some of the tranquillity and peace of mind, and for the opportunity to find a wife which he had contemplated three years before on his return from Russia. Instead, Brydone would have been greatly amazed to learn what the *Morning Post* told its readers on Monday 13 December, little more than three weeks later. The public heard that the King at St James's Palace had been pleased to appoint Patrick Brydone Esq. to the post of Accountant and Comptroller-General of Stamp Duties, in place of Morgan Vane Esq. deceased. The change in Brydone's fortune was also carried in the *Morning Chronicle and London Advertiser*, *St James's Chronicle*, *The London Chronicle* and from Chester, *Adam's Weekly Courant*. His predecessor, the Hon. Morgan Vane, who was in his early seventies when he died on 14 November 1779, was the son of Gilbert Vane, second baron Barnard of Barnard Castle. After qualifying as a barrister-at-law at the Middle Temple, he married and became comptroller of the Stamp Office in 1729, a position he held for half a century.

Employment at this level in the London Stamp Office of the early 1780s was in many ways a sinecure, and typical of governmental benefices. Given the numerous matters Brydone had to attend to in connection with his years as a travelling tutor, and a swathe of important events which undoubtedly occupied his mind, it would probably have been some time before he could give full attention to his new responsibilities. Among residual requests awaiting Brydone's attention was one he had received the previous year was one from the eldest son of Leopold II, the Prince of Anhalt-Dessau. The anglophile was concerned about an escaped prisoner-of-war of the French, a Mr John Macdonald, who, being destitute of money had been prevailed upon to enlist in the Prussian army and who after serving seventeen years now wanted to return home.[1]

Brydone turned to Sir Robert Murray Keith for help since from what he had learned, there was a possibility that McDonald was once in his regiment and he thought the ambassador might recommend him for a small pension. However, 'none of our Scotch population' in London, wrote Brydone 'seem to know him' and although he had made enquiries at the Admiralty, they had yet to answer. Taking the opportunity of thanking him again for his goodness to the party while they had been in Vienna, and knowing that Keith would have been greatly concerned about the 'terrible defeat' suffered 'last night, or rather this morning', Brydone explained what had happened. John Dunning MP had put down a motion in the House of Commons on 5/6 April that 'the influence of the Crown was too great and ought to be abridged, which was carried, I think 233 to 216', adding that 'it seems to be a desperate game' that the opposition was playing. So far as Lord North's two eldest sons were concerned, he reported that Francis, by then a captain, had left for Litchfield to join his corps and seemed 'to like his business very well', and George had asked that his 'best compliments' be sent to the ambassador for a memorable visit.[2]

In May, the country's hopes for the war in America had been temporarily raised when Charleston was taken by British forces, but by June, the initial and peaceful anti-Catholic protest against the Papists Act of 1776 turned into the Gordon Riots and the mood altered. Some 40–50,000 people marched on the Houses of Parliament, and supporters of Lord George Gordon, the Protestant Association's president, disturbed the proceedings of both houses, where many of the members were attacked. Brydone explained to Sir Robert that a mathematician who happened to be there had assured him that tens of thousands of people had marched from St

George's Fields in Southwark. The streets 'were everywhere filled with them and many were already armed with clubs'. On the night of 7 June, they burned down Newgate Prison and several private houses, including those of Sir George Savile and Lord Mansfield, the Lord Chief Justice. The London home of Lord North was also attacked. However, 'only very few of the light horse who were placed in the square charged full gallop down the street and they then dispersed in a moment'. On the following day, the mob set fire to the King's Bench prison near Bridewell, the Fleet and many private houses. Brydone spoke of the appearance of 'all these fires in the different quarters (being) very tremendous'. As Lord North's house was threatened a second time, he went to assist in defending it, where, 'we had several false alarms during the night but to our disappointment no attack was made for we were well prepared to receive them'. Although the rioters lurked in corners for a time, Brydone said he did not believe 'they would ever dare to come forth again'. Consternation was, nevertheless 'universal and all the shops were shut at five o'clock'. Lord George Gordon, who had led the anti-Catholic protest, found himself charged with treason. Believing that Gordon was being sent to the Tower, at the very moment he was writing to Keith, Brydone thought 'they should have sent him to Bedlam long ago', adding that 'you would not know London, were you here to see it at present'.[3]

The newly appointed employee of the Stamp Office enjoyed more contact with his patron and benefactor in October. The son of another prime minister, Horace Walpole, an author and patron of the arts, who had set off on his own grand tour accompanied by a school friend more than forty years before, and who was to become a waspish letter writer, described an evening he spent at the house of a Mrs Keene in Richmond. 'Last night', he wrote, 'I passed the evening with Lady Hertford at Mrs Keene's. Lord and Lady North were there, *en cour plénière*, with Miss Catherine North, the eldest of the Norths' daughters, members of the Williams family, and Brydone, the Sicilian traveller who, having wriggled himself into Bushy will, I suppose, soon be an envoy, like so many other Scots'.[4]

It was a new world that Brydone now inhabited, and he had much to learn, especially at work. An Act of Parliament in 1775 had authorised new premises for the Stamp Office and it would be December 1787 when John Brettell, secretary to the Board, announced that its business would in future be conducted from Somerset Place, known today as Somerset House.[5] The office that Brydone was to know best during his period of service, along with those used by the Navy, Navy pay and victualling, was in a stupendous and magnificent structure built on the site of the old Palace, erected by the first Duke of Somerset in the reign of Edward VI. It also contained the offices occupied by the auditors of impress, clerk of the estreats, and the duchy courts of Lancaster and Cornwall. Besides houses for the treasurer, paymaster, and six commissioners of the navy, there was one for the commissioner of stamps, along with commodious apartments for others.[6]

Stamp duties possibly had their origin in Spain but in the 1620s, a Dutchman, Johannes van der Broecke, had been successful in a Dutch competition to find a new tax. It was copied by France in 1651 and England in 1694. The first Stamp Act, passed in William and Mary's reign, granted their Majesties 'several duties upon vellum, parchment and paper for four years' during the war with France. The act ordered the setting up of a Stamp Office, its premises being initially in New Square, an extension to Lincoln's Inn. The first Stamp Duties (charged at rates between one penny and forty shillings, and using stamps embossed on to paper) were levied on copies of wills, writs, judgements, summonses, certificates of matriculation, proceedings in Court, probates of wills and Royal grants of honours, promotion or pardon. Historically, stamp taxes were a means of revenue raising and administered by the Board of Stamps. The Stamp Act of 1765 imposed on the American colonies required many printed materials to be produced on stamped paper carrying an embossed revenue stamp.

The Stamp Office had extended its remit in 1711, stamping commodities used by the public rather than just those of the legal profession. It was to become a means of making money from undesirable and antisocial activities. A start was made with a tax on dice and playing cards. Other duties followed – on almanacs and newspapers. This meant that all paper for newspapers, even for Scottish ones, had to be taken to the Stamp Office, unwrapped, stamped, and taken away to the printers. It was becoming the tax point for all matters of knowledge and in 1786 'every packet, box, phial, or other enclosure containing any hair powder' was included. The board was to merge with the Board of Taxes before becoming part of the Inland Revenue Board in 1849.

Among the stamp duties collected were those on the book trade. There had been animosity over the imposition of taxes on knowledge since 1712, and newspaper stamp duty was to increase firstly, from one and a halfpence to two pence in August 1789, and to three and a half pence on the outbreak of the war with Napoleon. Most newspapers had a brownish-red tax stamp in the lower right-hand corner of the first page. Increases resulted in both newspaper publishers and writers campaigning. As early as April 1725, the Exeter printer, Andrew Brice, inveighed against the new stamp tax in *The Postmaster*, claiming that 'we shall be obliged for the future to print on stamped paper'. He anticipated paying His Majesty an extra one thousand pounds per year, and hope that his customers would not take it ill if he increased the price of his papers 'in measure proportionable (sic) to the heavy charge' of a halfpenny on each paper.

The 'Royal Kalendar' for 1782 shows the five commissioners in overall charge of the Stamp Office to have been James Bindley, William Baillie, William Waller, G J Cholmondeley and Richard Tickell, who were each paid £500. The secretary was John Brettell, from a well-known Birmingham family, who received £300. Bindley, a self-avowed 'incurable Bibliomaniac', who owed his appointment to the Office at the beginning of 1765 to his brother, had served on the board of excise. His diligent service, and his compilation of the statutes extant at the time and affecting the board's work, had accounted for his promotion to senior commissioner in 1781. He died at his official apartment in 1818 and when his books, prints and medals were sold, they fetched a total of some £21,000. Given his friendship with many writers, and the continental tour he had undertaken with Louis Dutens in 1763–4, it is hard to think that he had not read Brydone's *Tour through Sicily and Malta* with some relish.[7]

William Baillie, who had been appointed a commissioner in 1773 was an art dealer and print maker who originated from

Ireland and who had completed his education at Middle Temple in 1742. Law was, however, soon displaced by service in the army and he served at Culloden. He retired with the rank of captain in 1761, and returned to collecting works of art. Baillie specialised in imitating drawings by old masters and prints. Among the works he sold after his appointment as a commissioner was a Rembrandt print which he reworked and sold to subscribers for four guineas each. By 1803, a year before his death, John Boydell, the most important employer of engravers in London, was selling Baillie's complete works, including impressions from Rembrandt's plates and becoming the target of much criticism. He died in 1810 at his house in Lisson Grove, Paddington.

Little is known about William Waller but George James Cholmondeley, a Whig peer and the fourth earl of Cholmondeley in Cheshire, had been a colonel in the army in 1779, who went on to hold the office of envoy in Berlin between June and September 1782 before becoming Captain of the Yeomen of the Guard and a Privy Counsellor. Two years later, however, Cholmondeley was no longer a commissioner. Richard Tickell, the fifth commissioner, entered Middle Temple in 1768 and after being called to the bar he had been appointed a commissioner of bankruptcy. But a complaint against him by another lawyer deprived him of this responsibility and it was left to his friend William Brummell, Lord North's private secretary and father of George (known as Beau Brummell), to find him the post of commissioner at the Stamp Office in August 1781.

A dozen years later, the 'Royal Kalendar' illustrated one or two changes in the organisation's hierarchy. Originally, the 1694 Act had determined that seven commissioners would form the board, headed by one of their number as chairman. In 1794, Bindley and Baillie were still serving but John Byng had replaced Cholmondeley, Edward Fawkener had joined the board, and there was one vacancy. Byng was to serve the board from 1782 to 1799. He was a diarist and the nephew of the admiral who was executed for failing 'to do his utmost' to prevent Minorca from falling to the French in 1757. After serving in the Seven Years' War, he was made a lieutenant-colonel but financial difficulties prompted his resignation from the army in 1780.[8] The Fawkener listed was probably one of the two sons of Sir Everard Fawkener (1684–1758) who was a London merchant, knighted in 1735, who became a joint post-master and the inspiration and banker for the Chelsea china manufactory. John Brettell continued to be the Board's secretary.[9]

The London Stamp Office employed about 170 people in the years approaching the new century, a figure which rose to 232 in 1817 and 343 just prior to the merger with the Office of Taxes in 1834.[10] The highest paid employee at this time was the Receiver-General, John Ross Mackye, who was paid £600 a year. He was followed by Brydone, the Comptroller, with a salary of £400 and six clerks under him who were each paid £60 p.a. except for a J. Lloyd, whose salary was £100. Perquisites were few and far between, but conditions of employment good and salaries attractive. In addition to salaried staff, there was a group of individuals who worked for the office as distributors of stamps.

Provincial stamp offices were to be opened across the country. That in Edinburgh opened around 1712 and in 1792, Thomas Blair became Deputy Controller in the Scottish capital. Others at Manchester, Liverpool, Birmingham, Hull and Bristol were often sometimes housed in Custom Houses controlled by the Revenue. Private stamp distributors were key players in income generation. Scattered across Britain, they were supported by what were called their under-distributors. Usually paid on a poundage basis these individuals developed their own *esprit de corps*. William Wordsworth, the poet, became a distributor for the county of Westmoreland, for which he was paid £400 p.a. His promptness in paying over outstanding balances to London at the end of a quarter earned him, and others whose example he had followed, official recognition and praise. It was also not unusual to find boys as young as eight years old being recruited, or employees being searched for dies or other items occasionally purloined.[11] As one academic has written: 'The stamp duty was the simplest of all the imposts, since the taxpayers would go to their local stamp office to purchase the stamp they needed on their document, or the stamped paper or to have a document impressed with a stamp. The official distributors simply ensured they provided the stamps the public requested, and collected the duties as stamps sold'.[12]

The presentation of each year's accounts was the highlight of Brydone's working year and involved his personal attendance. It required him to account for 'money payable to His Majesty in respect of duties granted by several Acts of Parliament, upon stamp vellum, parchment and paper', together with an account of arrears 'of all and every sum of money due and payable' for stamp duty.[13] Handwritten and formatted in such a way as to explain a large number of sub-totals, all for which Brydone was responsible as comptroller, the account was made on continuous sheets of rolled parchment. Reflecting modern practice in a chairman's report, the text rarely lost an opportunity to praise those indirectly and directly involved, for their honesty and loyalty in handling such matters as over-credits, over-charges and returns of useless stamps. Distributors and their agents, warehouse keepers and the rolling press keeper, along with deceased personnel and messengers, were given due credit. During the thirty-eight years of Brydone's service there were, however, constant changes of practice, reflecting the need for tighter auditing and control, and it was some time before the financial year became fixed. The 1790 year, for example, ran from July 1789 to 2 August 1790 whilst the year end for the 1801 year was 5 January 1802. The amount of revenue raised by the Stamp Office during this period was impressive, particularly given the fact that the salaries paid to the commissioners, their officers and clerks were an infinitesimal percentage of that brought in – a cost of £27,342.16s in 1802. Revenue rose from approximately £3 million to £5.8 million in 1790 and 1802 respectively.[14] By 1856 it would reached £7 million and £13 million in 1891.

Brydone would have noted the final act of Lord North's ministry in March 1782 with sadness. In February, the ministry had been defeated on a motion to end offensive war in America but, still believing he might gain the king's permission to negotiate a peace, he did not resign. However, when a group of independent MPs withdrew their support, it became clear that he would lose another vote in the House. His resignation, which had been most reluctantly accepted by George III, was followed by a brief coalition with Fox but by the Spring of 1784, William Pitt (the Younger) was in power, having only made his maiden speech at the beginning of 1781.

One of his first initiatives had been directed against the evasion of customs duties, particularly on tea from the East. Success led to him lowering duties on other goods such as wine and spirits, and the power of revenue officers was strengthened by the Manifest Act of 1786. Overall, Pitt was to achieve a revenue increase of nearly £2 million at this time. Even a cursory look at the accounts of the Stamp Office reveals the extent to which the populace were affected. Important elements were the duty on fire and sea insurance, the 'post horse duty', or the hiring of horses to go one or more stages and changing horses in the process, on advertisements, newspaper stamps, hats, gold and silver plate, to say nothing of those on pamphlets, licence and receipt books, and all manner of penalties.

Commissioners, staff and Brydone were undoubtedly well aware of the corporate benefit afforded by successful anti-fraud action, but a large swathe of the public, particularly in London, saw those employed by the Stamp Office and other government departments as beneficiaries of a dishonest system. Some holders of sinecures had a paid office with few or no duties attached to it. Writing in 1806, Brydone was to refer to 'a strong surmise that many of the patent and sinecure offices had been condemned'. They would, he said 'expire with their present incumbents but whether one or both of mine were of the number, I never have been able perfectly to ascertain'.[15] Referring to his own salary, Brydone said 'The Comptroller-Generalship of Stamps is just £100, paid every quarter with the usual deductions, without any perquisites as it was deprived some time ago of the patronage of the clerkship when the salary was advanced to £430 neat'. He thought the controller of Bristol's port was 'considerably better and depends on the increasing trade of that city'. An improvement there may have been, but a Samuel Worrall who worked at the Stamp Office in Bristol, was to explain later some of the methods and practices used by those making money for and from the Treasury at this time. A good financial reward could be made from selling authorised but privately printed shipping documents, and inflating their price without warning. Also, when Worrall passed 'his right in the patent to his son George, all orders (were) desired to be left for him with R. Henley, at the Stamp Office'. The new beneficiary continued publishing the forms used as bills of lading till 1819 when the patent was bought up by the Customs Fund.[16]

Brydone also referred to the appointment of deputies who sometimes could undermine the role of their seniors, and whose conduct or bad behaviour could bring trouble to both parties. During a parliamentary debate in the Lords on the Sinecure Offices Bill of 1813, Lord Grosvenor was to say that it 'aimed to regulate those offices which were not sinecures, but where the duties were executed by a deputy, and where the emoluments were much too large', He argued that 'there was not in the whole practice of the constitution a greater monster than this system of sinecure offices, where the holders were paid for doing nothing'. Although it might be said 'they were necessary for rewarding merit and services' he thought 'they were very ill-calculated for that purpose'. In asking their Lordships to support the bill, he said the word sinecure was very unpopular, as Brydone and the staff at the Stamp Office were well aware, and 'only an unnecessary expense to the public'.[17] Looking back over his time at the Stamp Office, he was to write that 'I always chose to take the Minister's recommendation at a considerable loss perhaps, but with the advantage of keeping my mind at ease'.[18]

With the traveller now a privileged government employee, able to settle back to life in Scotland and be in receipt of a regular income, it was not surprising that Brydone's name appeared in *Lloyd's Evening Post* in March 1781, among those who subscribed to a Bank of England loan of £12 million. Having assumed the character of a banker's bank, rather than just being the government's bank, its new charter obliged the bank to keep enough gold in its reserves to pay its notes on demand. Brydone was shown investing some £5,000, one of well over a thousand subscribers. Individual sums ranged from £500 to £55,000 (Thos Buckley), £100,000 (John Dorrien), £240,000 (Messrs. Crofts & Co.) and £320,000 (Directors of the East India Company).[19]

North of the border, Brydone had found the 'snug ... pleasant spot' which he had longed for, and by the summer of 1782, he was living at Lennel House in the hamlet of Lennel, a mile and a half north-east of the small town of Coldstream, on the north bank of the River Tweed, and not far from Berwick-on-Tweed. It had been built on an ancient site forming part of the medieval earldom of Dunbar and which belonged to the Norman, Edgar and Liddell families in the period between the twelfth and fifteenth centuries, eventually becoming a seat of the earl of Haddington. The present building, part of which is now a nursing home, was built around 1820 and succeeded the earlier house and farm tenanted by Brydone. To ease his way into this new rural life, orders were soon being sent to booksellers requesting maps and books on gardening, all to be delivered by the Coldstream carrier.[20]

Soon afterwards, however, it seems Brydone left for Nice on the Mediterranean with Lord North's youngest son, Frederick. Clearly, the successful chaperoning of his two older brothers had enabled arrangements to be made for Brydone to now become more his carer than tutor, without this having any detrimental effect on his work at the Stamp Office. Writing from Walmer Castle, Lord North's grace and favour Kentish home as Lord Warden of the Cinq Ports, his son George told Brydone how much his father felt himself obliged to the tutor 'for consenting to accompany Frederick. The time must be your own, but the sooner the better, without hurrying yourself. Frederick will stay here or at Waldershare till you set off'. George had apparently just received an *amende honourable*, a reparation or apology from the artist, Charles Brandoin, after a packet of some of his drawings which were due to be delivered to him in London had been left behind in Lausanne by the person charged with their delivery.[21]

Frederick's health had always been poor as a child, but at Eton in 1782, where the young scholar had been for seven years, and on a day when he had been 'sent up for good' (an outstanding piece of work, had been lodged in the school library for posterity), Frederick wrote his father a letter which showed him capable of a jolly mood, full of youthful affection. He referred to 'all the fine sights' of the summer, including visits by 'those impudent girls', the prime minister's three daughters, his sisters, Catherine, Anne and Charlotte. He also spoke of his surprise that his grandfather, whom he described as 'Old North', had 'taken it into his head to walk so much as he has done', not knowing how active he still was. Turning to his soldier brother, he mentioned how he would have liked to have seen Francis 'riding on his prancing steed before the Lord Lieutenant'.[22] Election as a student at Christ Church, Oxford followed, but he was in residence there for only one term (Michaelmas 1782) before having to take indefinite leave of absence, and he eventually resigned his studentship in 1786.

Abroad with his charge, Brydone had intended to have no connection with Frederick's money matters as 'they were always attended with a good deal of trouble' and generally 'with some loss'. He had, however, sent Lord North an account of the expenses of the journey to Nice which he thought amounted to something under £120. Frederick took charge of money matters till he became very ill, whereupon Brydone was obliged to assume the responsibility. Hoping that the discipline of paying out money might help his charge, Brydone wanted him to pay the posts and travelling expenses, but he soon 'tired of this office and gave me back the purse'. The result was that Brydone then had 'to account to his Lordship for £300 which we received on leaving Nice, and £100 at Bordeaux', confirming that Frederick's illness had put back the planned date of their departure for England.

Admitting that he should have sent his account to Lord North much sooner, Brydone said there had been little time since his return owing to the great confusion in which he had found the accounts in his office. Thankfully, Brydone had now 'got them finished', so enabling him to 'set out for the Tweed'. Although it was 'about six weeks beyond the time limited by Act of Parliament', he did not suppose any advantage would be taken of it 'to his prejudice'. About Frederick's health, he told his patron that he had never changed his opinion, believing that a cure depended upon himself, 'a doctrine he does not much like'. Brydone explained that Frederick's stomach had a tendency to produce excessive phlegm which was the origin of all his complaints 'but temperance and constant exercise would forever prevent it, and probably in a year or two, by the assistance of bitters ... the cause would be entirely removed'.[23]

As the year came to an end there was news that Lord North's eldest son, George, had encountered family disapproval at his choice of Miss Maria Hobart, the daughter of an MP as a wife, on account of her bringing no dowry. Telling his father that he understood 'the impossibility of a present union', and denying any 'intentional deception', George admitted 'his own happiness and comfort' might be threatened by his passion but, rather naively, that he could live easily within a 'very moderate income'. Fortunately for all concerned, Lord Guilford did not put his personal allowance of £800 per annum at risk, and the couple were married in 1785.[24]

A few days later, and with Brydone and Frederick back in Nice, Lord North heard that Frederick had 'got free of all his disagreeable feelings' and was enjoying 'the most perfect health'. The seventeen-year-old had been treated principally with decongestants but 'great moderation and caution both with respect to the quantity and quality of food'. Regular and moderate exercise, both riding and walking, were recommended together with 'slight and short application to study', and 'very early hours ... without medicines (or perhaps a few bitters or chalybeates to strengthen the tone of the stomach) would be altogether sufficient'. Frederick had apparently often expressed a strong desire to see a little of Spain and Brydone went on to make a case for them going to Barcelona in the Spring. The climate was not dissimilar to that in Nice and the country round and about was sufficient to satisfy his charge's curiosity. It would be 'no great detour to return to France by Navarre and Bayonne, and so prosecute the rest of our journey according to the plan your Lordship proposed'.

The timing of such a proposal produced something of a problem. As Brydone explained to Lord North, he contemplated leaving Nice at the end of February, or the beginning of March, so arriving in London early in May if he allowed for a stay of eight or ten days in Paris. If he were unable to attest the annual accounts in London as his employment at the Stamp Office required, Brydone could only rely on his 'Lordship's interference and protection' if he arranged for someone else to perform this duty. Closing his letter with news that Frederick had dined with the son of the second Earl of Dartmouth, Lord Pembroke and several other friends of the North family, he added that William Morton Pitt, now MP for Poole, was expected 'every hour'. The weather in Nice continued 'fine, though interrupted by frequent rain; thermometer generally about 60, that of the seawater 64'.[25]

It was February 1784 when Lord North agreed that Brydone should come to London to render his account and 'let me know what further credit you conceive to be requisite to enable you to finish your tour'. In a warm and familiar letter from Lower Grosvenor Street, his patron spoke frankly, saying 'I ask a thousand pardons for not having answered your very obliging letters, and I can only refer you for my excuse to the busy and turbulent state of the times, which are, I am afraid, too well-known all over Europe for you or any other person to be ignorant of them. Your letters certainly deserved every attention from me, as they made me extremely happy by the good accounts they brought me of the health and conduct of my dear boy'. All the correspondence he had received from Nice seemed unanimous in commending Frederick's progress, which he hoped would 'carry him with equal success and reputation through this troublesome world, for a troublesome world will he find it'.

His lordship had 'not the smallest objection' to Brydone leaving Frederick 'for a while at Nice by himself, as I know that I can confide in his good sense and discretion'. Although he would be called on in England to live on a much smaller income than he had received while abroad, Lord North also acknowledged that he had learned 'every decent degree of economy'. Explaining how futile and impracticable it would be to relate 'any part of our political squabbles in a letter' he promised Brydone he would 'have it all when I see you here'. Lord North also spoke of 'the secret I can tell you' and which Brydone should only communicate to Frederick in confidence, that 'I shall probably not return ... to office, whatever may be the fate of my late colleagues'. This consideration gave him the idea of a meeting with the tutor in Paris on their return, and he added 'We will talk upon this project when we meet. All is now uncertain' – and so. the letter ended.[26]

The statement of expenditure Brydone later submitted shows the travellers having travelled directly to Bordeaux when they left Nice on 15 March 1784. He divided the bill by thirty seven, the number of days taken on the journey to London, and reported a cost of 'somewhat more than four pounds a day'. The bill for one night at Calais was left unpaid, but there were two small bills which Brydone's servant had incurred in respect of the chaise's harness, along with a sum of £8 3s 6d due to him for arranging for Mr Frederick's chaise to be brought from Grosvenor Square to Walmer Castle in Kent. The total paid out during the journey home, 'errors excepted', wrote Brydone, had been £210 17s.[27]

Three months later, Lord North again wrote to Brydone in especially warm terms, giving him the assurance he had wanted about the way the accounts at the Stamp Office had been presented and approved. 'I hope and believe', he wrote 'that you will be no more troubled upon the subject ... and with regard to the accounts you have sent to me, (his and the party's expenses), they are perfectly satisfactory. I am sorry that you have had so much trouble about them, and am more sorry that in your accounts with me, there remains due to you a balance of gratitude which I am much less able than willing to repay'. North went on to readily acknowledge his obligations, saying that he had done everything in his power to show his 'sense of them'; it would have given him 'real happiness to have done more' but he hoped that what had passed had established a friendship and connection between them and their posterity 'that may long subsist to the comfort and happiness of us all'. With 'great truth and regard', he wished Brydone a good journey.[28]

In the autumn, a new deputy comptroller of the Stamp Office in Edinburgh was appointed, a colourful character whom Brydone may well have known. Thomas Blair was a short and rotund gentleman who attempted to offset his lack of height by wearing a high-crowned cocked hat and having his wig frizzled and powdered and then so wired that it sat an inch higher on his head. The staff at the office apparently enjoyed an annual dinner at Fortunes's tavern in Old Stamp Office Close where the diminutive trencherman was said to have managed to 'accomplish with ease, the demolition of a sirloin' or 'the dissection of a capon'.[29]

At the close of 1785, Brydone asked his patron how he should go about appointing a deputy to act in his absence as comptroller at the Stamp Office. He had been told that the First Lord of the Treasury would expect a friend of his to be nominated but Brydone would have to pay him from his own pocket. Lord North's lengthy and sympathetic reply reflected his deep knowledge of the ways of the Treasury's mandarins. Writing from Bushy Park on 26 December, he told Brydone that he had done all he could to help him at present. It was unlikely that that the Board of Excise and Customs would alter their practice on his recommendation and it would have been 'very improper' for him to suggest or propose it to them. However, he wrote, 'If I remember well, the First Lord of the Treasury always thought he had a right to recommend to the officers of the Customs, their deputies', adding that he thought 'the best way to prevent any disagreeable altercation' would be to apply to Mr Dundas, the solicitor-general for Scotland 'through Mrs Brydone's friends', referring to an event which had happened earlier that year. North had no doubt the solicitor-general would do what he could to help 'as he knows it would be agreeable to me'. It was obvious, he said 'that I cannot apply personally to him but I believe that, as he knows it would be agreeable to me, he will the more readily engage in the business for you, and do what he can in your behalf. I will, in the meantime, privately enquire whether anything can be done at the Custom house through my friends there, but I do not expect any success by that channel'.[30]

# CHAPTER 12

# Brydone marries at last (1785–1805)

In March 1785, Brydone received congratulations and warm felicitations on his impending marriage from Lord North, now out of office, and several friends, including the twice-married Lord Binning, a member of Edinburgh's convivial Poker Club, and James Bucknall Grimston, an Irish peer who sat for St Albans in the House of Commons.[1] On the fourth of April, Patrick (of St Andrew's Parish) married Mary (of Old Greyfriar's Parish), the eldest daughter of the noted historian, Principal Robertson of Edinburgh University.[2] She was thirty-three years old and her husband, in his fifty-first year. Burns, who was to meet her at Lennel in May 1787, described Mrs Brydone in his diary 'as a most elegant woman in person and manner', and 'the tones of her voice remarkably sweet'. Dugald Stewart in 'An account of the life and writings of William Robertson' in 1829 said that his eldest daughter was 'married to Mr Brydone, the well-known author of one of our most elegant and popular books of travels'. The *General Evening Post*, a London newspaper, carried a report recording the date as Monday, the sixth of the month.

Despite his fear of remaining a wretched old bachelor, and that even the improved state of his finances might not produce the longed for 'very advantageous match', Brydone's plan had worked; he had married into 'some agreeable family'. His father-in-law, the Rev William Robertson (1721–1793), had been educated at Dalkeith Grammar School with class-mates such as John Home,

John Erskine and William Wilkie, in rooms where the versatile Sir John Pringle taught some of the elements of moral philosophy. In 1751, when he was beginning to make his mark in the general assembly of the Kirk, he had married his cousin Mary, the daughter of James Nisbet, one of the ministers at the Old Kirk in Edinburgh. Among the first members of the Select Society, Robertson debated many literary and social issues, some of which helped him develop his concept of history. Graduating at Edinburgh University as a Doctor of Divinity in 1758, he became an active churchman and much-respected historian. The following year he published a two-volume *History of Scotland during the Reigns of Queen Mary and King James VI, till his Accession to the Crown of England.*

Dr Robertson secured a vacancy at Old Greyfriars Church in 1761 with less demanding parish duties which allowed him more time for his writing. Then, with the support of Lord Bute, secretary of state for the northern department, he became Historiographer-Royal for Scotland, a post that was revived for him but which carried no formal responsibilities or salary beyond an allowance of £200 annually. In March 1762 the following year, and heavily

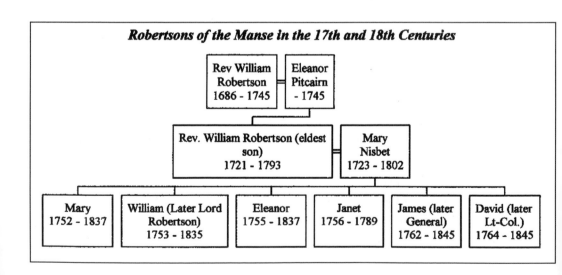

| *Robertsons of the Manse in the 17th and 18th Centuries* |

Rev William Robertson 1686 - 1745 = Eleanor Pitcairn - 1745

Rev. William Robertson (eldest son) 1721 - 1793 = Mary Nisbet 1723 - 1802

| Mary 1752 - 1837 | William (Later Lord Robertson) 1753 - 1835 | Eleanor 1755 - 1837 | Janet 1756 - 1789 | James (later General) 1762 - 1845 | David (later Lt-Col.) 1764 - 1845 |

influenced by his connections and literary reputation, Edinburgh town council elected Robertson Principal of the University. His duties included wide-ranging responsibility for appointments, budgets and regulations in regard to magistrates, on account of the university having been founded as a civic institution. His election as moderator of the general assembly twelve months later further strengthened his position and in a number of addresses he congratulated the king on the outcome of the Seven Years' War.

In 1768, the minister and principal-cum-historian had been in London to hear that William Strahan and Thomas Cadell, his and Brydone's publisher and printer, had agreed to pay him the extraordinary price of £3,500 for *The History of the reign of Charles V*, the French king, in three volumes, along with another £500 for a second edition. Robertson was also to publish *The History of America* in 1777, again with Strahan and Cadell, having harnessed the university's stock of books on the subject. Generally, critics regarded it more favourably than his earlier work on account of its dramatic style and colourful prose. He had, however, suffered physically from his labours, and soon after preaching a sermon in London the following year he fell seriously ill, and increasingly withdrew from public life. Nevertheless, early in the 1780s, and having by then become a fellow of the *Real Academia de la Historia* in Madrid, an academician in Padua, and a fellow of the St Petersburg Academy of Sciences, the principal took the lead in proposing the establishment of an academic society in the Scottish capital, although he was never a very active member. Towards the end of 1783, Brydone had been among one hundred and sixty five gentlemen, the founding Fellows of the Royal Society of Edinburgh, some fifty seven of whom had been members of its precursor, the Edinburgh Philosophical Society.

At the time of his eldest daughter's marriage, Dr Robertson (now sixty-four) appears to have felt strong enough to revive earlier plans for the University's Old College building which were to be implemented four years later. How Patrick and Mary came to meet is unknown but her father and the Rev Robert Brydone, who died in 1761 and was an alumnus of Edinburgh University, probably knew each other. Among the earliest letters exchanged between Brydone and his father-in-law was one written by the latter ten days after the wedding when he recalled how Brydone had admitted that 'alacrity in corresponding' was not one his chief virtues. Dr Robertson assured his son-in-law that 'this being our first intercourse since our new connection ... the more I reflect upon that event, I am the more satisfied'. He was not only a happy man and one without any anxiety about the happiness of his daughter but, as he said, 'I trust that the eve of my own life will be rendered much more comfortable by your friendship and kindness'.

One 'commission' it seems he had earlier asked Brydone to do for him turned out to be the sale of 'a collection of curious and uncommon Spanish books' which he had bought for £110 during research into his *History of Scotland*. Having sent a list to a London bookseller and received no reply, he wanted Brydone to obtain the advice of 'our friend Mr Strahan' about what to do. With the couple in London, Principal Robertson closed his letter with a few items of family news in Edinburgh where his daughter Janet's ill-health continued to be a problem, and looked forward to hearing of their 'safe arrival in the great city'.[3] Mrs Robertson had been understandably worried on this score but she hoped the new Mrs Brydone would write often, and had 'a great desire' to see her in London. The collection of Spanish books was apparently sold when the library of the Rev Jonathan Toup, a classical scholar who died at St Martin's rectory near Looe in Cornwall, came under the hammer the following year.[4]

The couple made their home at Lennel House near Coldstream where Robert Burns acknowledged being given 'an extremely flattering reception' two years later. Sir Walter Scott, the poet and novelist, described Lennel as 'a Cistercian house of religion, now almost entirely demolished ... now the residence of my venerable friend, Patrick Brydone Esq., so well known in the literary world',[5] going on in 1808 to mention it in Marmion:

> Where Lennel's convent closed their march:
> There now is left but one frail arch,
> Yet mourn thou not its cells,
> Our time a fair exchange has made;

Hard by, in hospitable shade,
A reverend pilgrim dwells,
Well worth the whole Bernardine brood,
That e're wore sandal, frock or hood.

At the end of the year, when his wife may have been with her parents at the family house in Edinburgh, and Brydone otherwise involved in England, her husband wrote to tell her about the narrow escape of a 'Daredevil Aeronaut'. The young, flamboyant Italian called Vincenzo Lunardi had flown his great air balloon, made from 500 yards of green, pink and yellow silk, from various Scottish locations, including a flight from St Andrew's Square in Glasgow to Hawick, some 100 miles to the south. An ascent he made on 20 December from the grounds of Heriot's Hospital in Edinburgh, and which attracted a large crowd, was more successful than the one he had tried the previous month. Unfortunately, a strong wind caught the balloon and Lunardi was forced down into the sea after a flight of some seventy minutes. He was, however, picked up by a fishing boat and landed at North Berwick.[6]

Adding to his previous advice, Lord North wrote to Brydone on 26 December, offering his 'best compliments to Mrs Brydone' and saying how delighted he had been to hear that 'you continue to enjoy your office with the same emoluments which were connected to it at the time I had the happiness of procuring it for you'. Apologising for his careless and illegible scribble, he explained that he had done 'all that I think I can do with propriety or hopes of success'. He had written to a friend at the Board of Customs 'to desire him to prevent your being hurried or pressed in by this business, and that you may have a little time given you to determine what you had best do upon this emergency'. Without elaborating on the latter, his patron told him to apply to Mr Dundas. He, or perhaps Mr Pitt, might have a friend who they would wish to appoint Deputy Comptroller at Bristol, but that could not be done if the salary was taken away, and 'they should understand that you will not be able to afford to pay a deputy, but must go to Bristol and perform the duty yourself'. Recalling his own experience, he went on to say that 'This being the case, and there being, I believe, many friends of Mr P and Mr D who have been long waiting for some mark of ministerial favour, your application may perhaps be successful, as the saving to be gained by the suppression of the Deputies' salaries cannot be considerable, and some political convenience may certainly result from adopting the alteration proposed by the Commissioners of Customs'.[7]

In mid-January it became clear that there had been an embarrassing oversight. Brydone reminded his patron how important it was to him that the expenses relating to Frederick's stay in France should be paid. With money taking on a new meaning for him, he felt very strongly that, generous as Lord North had been, he should still settle his debts. 'I have always flattered myself', wrote Brydone, 'that I never should have been in a situation so humiliating as to render the proposal I have made unavoidable, but your Lordship must have seen from the beginning that unless you provided sufficiently for me, I must fall into your hands at last; and I have given up every other interest and pursuit, and have nothing else to lean to. I am far from wanting to be rich, and all I wish is only to be abler to live like a gentleman; and I am sure your Lordship could not permit that I should ever be in a different situation. I gave up the most perfect certainty of it to serve your Lordship and those recommended in my place are now in much better and more easier circumstances than I am myself. I shall be contented with whatever your Lordship shall think proper, but something must be done before I can return to Scotland'. Then, before ending his letter, Brydone added that he had never seen Mr Dundas, and yet he had received an order to appoint a Mr Harford as his deputy, possibly a merchant, brass manufacturer or banker. He could only say that if his Lordship did not come to Town soon, he would 'have the honour of making a visit to (him) at Bushy, before (he went) north'.[8]

In 1786, the old friend for whom Brydone had written the *Tour through Sicily* arrived back in England from Jamaica, having visited the Cayman Islands and landing at Grand Cayman on the way. Now forty-two years old, William Beckford, had proved himself an exceptional planter with a great love of education and art. Unfortunately, within days of reaching London, he had found himself taken in charge by a bailiff and incarcerated in the Fleet prison as a debtor, due apparently to his having stood security for a friend whose misfortunes had originated in the great Atlantic hurricane of 1780. Brydone would also have had news about another member of the Beckford family. William Thomas Beckford who married in 1783 was, however, bisexual and had been obliged to go abroad in July 1785 on account of allegations of homosexual misconduct. He had taken up residence at *La Tour-de-Peilz* near Vevey, close to Brydone's erstwhile base on Lake Geneva, where his impressive oriental novel *Vathek* was published in 1786, but without a series of related tales which he had hoped to see included.

Although his travelling days were behind him, Brydone gently merged a continued interest in all matters scientific during 1786 with an increasingly active domestic life during part of which he was able to enjoy riding for pleasure. The polymath's personal obsessions were, however, pushed aside as a long-awaited romance bore fruit, and in April, a daughter was born to Patrick and Mary, amid much rejoicing in both households. In the Robertson family it seems Mary was sometimes called Molly. Two years later, the birth of a boy, christened Frederick in honour of the North family was celebrated, only for him to die aged four years at Grange House near Edinburgh, the lease of which Brydone's father-in-law had taken to ease what he called his shuttling to and from Edinburgh and the college.[9] To the couple's horror and pain, his brother William Robert, their second boy, was to have a short life as well as his sister Robina who died according to the *Oracle and Public Advertiser* on 20 December 1792 at St Andrew's Square. There was not to be a male heir, but happily, the couple's three daughters, Mary the eldest, Elizabeth (born in 1790) and Williamina, flourished and each married well.

In London, Brydone's name was again being mentioned at the Royal Society. Charles, the third Earl Stanhope, a fellow and father of Lady Hester Stanhope, a great traveller and Arabist, rose to read a paper at the beginning of 1787, entitled *Remarks on Mr Brydone's Account of a remarkable Thunderstorm in Scotland*.[10] He opened what was to be a twenty-page paper with a reference to the fact that no storm of lightning had ever produced effects more curious to contemplate than those about which Brydone had spoken in 1772. It contained facts 'so perfectly inexplicable by the principles of electricity' that it deserved particular attention'. Apparently, a man named James Lauder 'sitting on the fore-part of a cart drawn by two horses, was suddenly struck dead, as also the horses ... and that the cart itself was much injured by electrical fire, although no lightening fell at, or near, the place where this accident happened'. Another labourer in a cart behind confirmed the incident. It 'was not occasioned by any direct main stroke of explosion from a thunder-cloud, either positively or negatively electrified ... since no lightning did pass from the clouds to the earth'.

Stanhope came to the conclusion that electricity had caused the fatalities, accepting that 'no electrical fire did pass immediately either from the clouds into the cart ... or from the cart into the clouds'. From the effects mentioned in Mr Brydone's paper, it was evident that there had been 'a violent motion of the electrical fluid in all ... of the bodies of the man and horses' although there was no lightning. He referred his listeners to the type of electrical shock he had distinguished in his treatise, entitled *Principles of Electricity*. This had been called 'the electrical returning stroke'. Stanhope recalled Brydone describing how 'the shepherd belonging to the farm at Lennel Hill was in a neighbouring field when he observed a lamb (only a few yards from him) drop down, although the lightning and claps of thunder were then at a great distance from him. He ran up immediately, but found the lamb quite dead; nor did he perceive the least convulsive motion, or symptom of life remaining, although the moment before, it appeared to be in perfect health'.

The earl concluded that the thunder-cloud's electrical pressure on the day James Lauder died 'must have been immense'. His cart had been 'higher on the bank' than the one that followed, thus accounting for the second man not having felt the returning stroke. It was extremely fortunate Brydone 'should have been upon the spot at the time ... to give the world so clear and interesting an account'. The state of the ground where Lauder was killed had been remarkably dry 'and of a gravely soil', according to Brydone, something particularly adapted in Stanhope's opinion, to 'the production of the electrical returning stroke'. Then, for the benefit of his audience, the earl 'enumerated eleven necessary requisites' when erecting conductors to secure buildings against damage by lightning, adding that 'this information must be particularly interesting to the Board of Ordnance, on account of the security of … their powder magazines at Purfleet'.[11]

The author of the *Tour* through Sicily would hardly have missed seeing a piece of opportunist publishing by George Kearsley which appeared in 1788.[12] Entitled *The Present State of Sicily and Malta*, his 262 page volume contained 'an advertisement' explaining that it had been originally compiled by a person of distinguished abilities, for the use of some young people. He claimed that the work included all that was interesting in Mr Brydone's *Tour*, in Mr Henry Swinburne's *Travels in the Two Sicilies*; the very curious observations of Sir W. Hamilton, and the substance of René Vertot's *The History of the Knights of Malta*.

The first statute to protect the rights of authors rather than printers had come into effect in April 1710 during the reign of Queen Anne. It granted publishers of a new book, legal protection for 14 years, and 21 years in the case of a book already in print. What came to be known as the Statute of Anne encouraged reading and writing, and confirmed a bargain between authors, booksellers and the public. After several notable legal cases had been brought in attempts to extend the copyright term, the Law Lords decided against perpetual copyright, a decision which opened the market to cheap reprints of works by Shakespeare, Milton, Chaucer – and books such as Kearsley's compilation. Between 1772 and 1802, the number of London booksellers and publishers rose from little more than 100 to 308.[13]

In 1789, another German translation of the Brydone's *Tour* appeared, and in November, Principal Robertson sent his son-in-law some books from Edinburgh, supposing him to have begun some 'serious winter reading', including two volumes of 'Coxe's Travels', whose itinerary was not dissimilar to that of his son-in-law, and Gibbon's *Essai sur l'Etude de la Littérature*. The latter essay which gained the young historian such approbation had been published in England in 1761. Removed from Oxford on becoming a Roman Catholic, Gibbon only reconverted to Protestantism following a period in the care and tutelage of a Reformed Church pastor in Lausanne. Robertson hoped that the volumes from his library by William Coxe would afford Brydone 'some amusement, at least by recollecting to your remembrance places and persons you have seen'.[14]

The following year, Brydone's friend Beckford published *A Descriptive Account of the island of Jamaica: with remarks upon the cultivation of the sugar cane throughout the different seasons of the year, and chiefly considered in a picturesque point of view.* He had occupied himself with writing from the start of his time in prison, his first work being a paper describing the situation of the negroes in Jamaica. Deemed 'impartially made from a local experience of nearly thirteen years in the island', today's reader may have found it a naïve account of the benefits of slavery. He was not unsupported by friends and Dr Charles Burney, the musician and author, wrote from Chelsea College in 1791, saying how he intended trying 'to get Sir Joshua (Reynolds) and Sir Joseph Banks, his old acquaintances, to visit him there with me'. His *History of France from the death of Louis XVI* followed in 1794 while he was still in prison and he died aged 55 in February 1799 while staying in Wimpole Street, at the home of the Earl of Effingham, nephew to Thomas, the second earl who had married a sister of Lord Mayor Beckford in 1744.[15] The *Gentleman's Magazine* stated that 'his pecuniary losses had probably led him to sell his property in Suffolk', describing him as 'late of Somerley Hall', originally a Jacobean mansion situated a few miles north-west of Lowestoft.[16] In 1844, it was substantially re-modelled in the Anglo-Italian style for a railway magnate, and became known as Somerleyton Hall.

Later in August 1790, the Principal wrote to his daughter from Newcastle where he and Mrs Robertson had arrived after a stay at the 'Four Crosses' at Cannock Chase in Staffordshire, a well-known hostelry built in 1636. Disappointed not to have had more news of life at Lennel, he told Mary that they hoped to be at Lennel for breakfast on Saturday, the twenty-eighth, calling at Morpeth on the way. At the end of September, and with the visit over, Principal Robertson spoke of never being more at ease 'or more happy' than when under his son-in-law's roof. There was, however, much work to be done preparing his papers for print which could only be done at the principal's house some distance from where the new college was being built. As a consequence, the two men would have to meet soon in the College. 'We can accommodate you all with ease' wrote Robertson, and 'if you bring your black mare to town you will get your usual exercise'. Enthusiastically, he explained that young Mary, then in her fifth year, would be able to keep up her acquaintance with old friends, the children having 'ready access to walks'. Pressing his invitation still more, his father-in-law advised Brydone not to defer his visit too long as the roads to Lennel 'become almost impassable after a fall of snow'. John Home, the Church of Scotland minister and playwright then nearing his seventies, had dined with them the previous evening.[17]

In October, Brydone's father-in-law responded from Grange House to the Lennel household's need for a gardener, suggesting William Murray. Said to be about thirty and 'a discreet sober lad', he had served his apprenticeship in Angus and had spent three years working for Lord North at Bushy Park and William Fullerton of Carstairs. Principal Robertson told Brydone that all were better and he continued 'to make ground' after the death of his grandson the previous July, and a conference he had had with Dr Black. Having occasion to write to the minister at Newbattle the previous day he had enquired *sub rosa* about 'the wise-woman in his parish', in the event perhaps, that her activities might appeal to his son-in-law's perennial interest in anything unusual or extraordinary. His letter closed with good wishes to Molly and the two children Mary and Wee-Wee (William Robert).[18]

Two letters in April 1793, one each from Brydone and Robertson, may have been their last exchange before Robertson's death. A short note from Brydone on the first of the month concerned his father-in-law's generous conveyance to him of his 'right to hold stock in the proposed canal between Edinburgh and Glasgow', being his 'subscription of five guineas to the (cost of) the survey'. In making a gift of it to Brydone, he explained that he had also given a security that exempted his son-in-law from any other calls that might be made as a consequence of his 'subscription to the survey, and from any other expense whatever'.[19] Work had started on the impressive Forth-Clyde canal project in the late 1760s with John Smeaton, the great civil engineer who had played an important role in the re-construction of Eddystone lighthouse, supplying the plans. The canal was well under way by 1771 and in 1785 money from forfeited Jacobite estates was used to finance the 28 mile link and its twenty locks. Five years later it was open between Grangemouth on the Firth of Forth to Bowling on the Clyde, with several extensions to the system being added between 1793 and 1822.

Although Principal Robertson experienced no acute pain or sickness at this time, his constipation was debilitating and unlikely to have been helped by the exercise he took 'daily in the carriage'. The whole family, meanwhile, were concerned about the outcome of the battle at Neerwinden in the Low Countries in March 1793 where Austrian forces had exposed the inadequacy of the French General Dumouriez's ill-trained army, fearing, as Robertson wrote, the 'utter ruin' of France. At home, and with Spring upon them, planting started in the college garden, but with no potatoes left from the previous season, the family boiled three of Lord Glencairn's crop 'of a superior quality', planted it was said, to Brydone's direction. Giving his blessings to his daughter, Brydone and the children, the Principal closed his letter.[20] He was to die of jaundice, probably suggesting liver failure, at Grange House on 11 June 1793.

Another death that year had been young Frederick's father, Lord North, for whose funeral he had returned home in August 1792. Leaving politics in 1785, and inheriting property worth well over £100,000 a year when his father died in 1790, the second Earl Guilford did not, however, long enjoy his retirement and wealth. Only two years later, undeniable symptoms of dropsy appeared and he died quietly at home in Grosvenor Square, London on 5 August, being buried later that month at All Saints' Church, Wroxton. His son Frederick, now in his late twenties, and having spent some time in Madrid, had been touring the Ionian Islands and Greece, living among the inhabitants of Ithaca. On the mainland he helped fund a school at Preveza before going on to Cyprus, Alexandria, Jerusalem and Constantinople. Fast becoming a philhellene, it was about this time that Frederick became a member of the Greek Orthodox Church, spending Lent in a monastery on the island of Levkas. It was from there that he returned to England, arriving in London hours after his father's death. Vacating Lord North's parliamentary seat at Banbury without much regret, he was to become Comptroller of Customs in the port of London in 1794, a post he held till 1812. The following year, Sir Gilbert Elliot, later the first earl Minto, took him to Corsica as his secretary, and recommended him for a promotion which led to his being appointed governor and vice-admiral of Ceylon.[21]

Writing to his wife at Lennel from St Andrew's Street, Edinburgh in May 1795, Brydone told her that he, his brother Matthew and a servant John, had not only had a pleasant journey but had arrived in the capital 'before it was quite half past eight' and, having done his business with a Mr B Gordon during the morning, had dined with him. He also settled the sale of a small property he owned, and sent the money he received to Child & Co, his bankers in London, with instructions to 'buy into the three percents', Bank of England consols of the day. Patrick had, however, not been able to meet William Scott, Edinburgh's eminent procurator-fiscal, owing to his being busy in court, but he did hope to dine the next day with John Home. Reassuring his wife that he would soon be home, Brydone said he had just sent his servant to secure a seat for himself in the Berwick coach on Saturday morning 'so I shall expect to find Archie ready to set off with Matthew and me by ten o'clock on Sunday. John (the servant), I think, may go by the chariot (the smallest of the carriages) either Saturday or Sunday'.

The undisputed queen of Drury Lane, the Welsh actress, Sarah Siddons, was on an acting tour of Scotland and the North of England. In Edinburgh, she was 'acting away at a great rate and making everybody cry but herself'. She was due to act in Thomas Southerne's *Isabella* but, as Brydone's eyes 'did not agree with being pickled at present', he did not intend going near her. She was due to play Lady Randolph one day the following week in Berwick in John Home's *Douglas*, a blank verse tragedy first performed at Edinburgh in 1756. This Brydone thought well worth seeing, telling Mary she 'must get ready, and we shall insist on your mother being of the party. John Home would take it as the greatest compliment that ever was paid in all his life. I do not think him very well, and she is really an object!' Drawing his letter to a close, and anxious to be back home, Brydone asked his wife to 'kiss our sweet lambs' and give them his blessing, 'as good as the Pope's, at least'.[22]

Some time later Patrick went to Berwick to see his brother Matthew and friends in the neighbourhood. Riding from Lennel where he left Mary with the children, he arrived to find 'the mutton was not spoilt, and we ate it with a good appetite'. The next day he went to see his wife's mother, old Mrs Robertson, who was 'vastly well', whilst Brydone's sister-in-law, Eleanor, who had married into the family of John Russell, the Edinburgh solicitor, had 'a little sore throat, but not bad'.[23] Their children and father were all as well as Brydone had ever seen them. Soon afterwards, John Home, who was then in his late seventies but in good spirits, called on them unannounced as they were about to sit down to dinner. Explaining that he had been 'perfectly well', with 'no remains of (his) complaint, Brydone described 'Jock' Home of Bassendean who had also been at the dinner, as 'looking indifferent, though they say much better than he did'.

Writing to his wife at Lennel, Brydone reported that Sandy Anderson was married and going to settle at St Andrews. Lady Betty Cunningham, they said, was to honour James Watson of Saughton, a house and estate near Edinburgh 'with her fat hand', whilst William Fullarton, the tutor's erstwhile charge, was said to be 'quite well (and living) at Minchinhampton' in Gloucestershire. Telling Mary, that he had not tasted water since leaving home, Brydone said that everybody thought he had 'brought drinking sherry into fashion'. A servant in his brother's household said he had cured her of all her stomach complaints, and John Home was convinced that 'the sherry merchants of Leith ought to make me a present of a butt at least'. Hoping to be with her on Sunday, and to hear from her before then, Brydone asked her to kiss their girls 'all three for me, twenty times'.[24]

In February 1798, a spirited Frederick North was being given passage aboard HMS *Brunswick*, a seventy-four-gun third rate ship of the line, when he wrote to Brydone. En route to Ceylon, he had been appointed the island's first British governor following its capture from the Dutch two years earlier. There he soon became an active reformer, improving the island's civil administration, reorganising the judiciary, tackling corruption and fraud, as well as enforcing the abolition of slavery. 'You know too well the situation of a man on shipboard with a high wind', he told Brydone, 'to be astonished at the brevity with which I thank you for the very kind letter Colonel Fullarton (then still MP for Ayr but without office) has just sent me from you'. Frederick North had 'the greatest desire' to make the acquaintance of Brydone's brothers-in-law, William, the lawyer and later Lord Robertson, and two soldiers, James, who subsequently became General, and David, a Lt-Colonel who married Margaret, the heiress of Kinloch-Moidart. Explaining this, Frederick added that 'you may be sure that their being such near relations of yours will not diminish the claims which their merit will have already have given them in the eyes of their Principal, at least … one of them, for I believe the other is at Madras' – probably a reference to David serving there.[25]

For Patrick and Mary, the new century marked fifteen years of happy marriage, but war in Europe and elsewhere was to be the continuous background to their lives till 1815. Napoleon Bonaparte had staged a *coup d'état* at the end of 1799, installing himself as First Consul in the Tuileries. Pitt found the means to form a new coalition against French and in June 1800 they were driven out of Italy at the battle of Marengo, while another Austrian army defeated them in Germany, pushing them back to the Rhine. Unfortunately for Pitt, he faced a second year of harvest failures at home, for which he could find 'no adequate remedy'.[26] However, the prime minister's belief that Ireland's political, if not all her religious problems, would only be solved if she was united with Great Britain, a view not shared by George III, the Act of Union was passed in 1800.[27]

The couple spent their life together largely in the country, with occasional regular excursions to the academic and social world of Edinburgh then coming to the end of its age of Enlightenment. Brydone's discovery, late in life, of the pleasures children gave was a special delight. Distance and the hazards of rural travel did little to restrict their visits to friends and family. Children had been born and died with a frequency only slightly less than that suffered by the poor, neither infant nor maternal mortality rates being respecters of class. A privileged gentry was not exempt from the dangers of life and death. A letter written to Hugh Scott, the sixth Baron Polwarth and the son of Walter Scott of Harden near Hawick, in

January 1800 from Bath, expressed the Brydone family's genuine affection and concern.[28] 'Sincerely happy ... we most cordially congratulate Mrs Scott and yourself on the safe arrival of your little stranger though somewhat sooner than you expected him', Henry Francis, the couple's eldest son, had been born on 1 January 1800. The sympathy that followed was occasioned by the fact that the couple had obviously been affected by the 'distress and suffering of a sweet little innocent' who could not speak about his pains. 'What a happiness it was', Brydone wrote 'that you found Dr Blair ... the situation at that period must have been dreadful'. He hoped it would be 'an auspicious omen' for the rest of young Henry's life, and so it proved.[29] Brydone also mentioned the premature delivery suffered a few days before by Lady Guilford, Susan Coutts, whom George North had married after his first wife's death in 1794, a member of the Coutts banking family who unlike his first wife had no difficulty in producing a dowry of £150,000. The birth had apparently been brought about by the fright of one of 'her little girls' falling down the stairs, albeit without harm. Reminding his correspondent what objects of anxiety and danger children were to their poor mothers, yet, as he said, 'strange to tell, no objects are prayed for with such ardour and devotion, and happy the mother who possesses the greatest number'.

Accepting that he had become a *babillard*, or a babbler, Brydone spoke of his head being 'either much better or worse than it was'. The giddiness and spasms he had experienced were greatly abated but not yet gone. He now had hopes of 'getting perfectly sound again'. His wife and daughters were well although Mrs Brydone too had had an accident on the first day of the month which had 'nearly confined her ever since'. Explaining further, Brydone told Hugh that while staying in the city they 'had gone to the great concert at the New (Upper) Rooms where all the splendour of Bath was assembled, and a more brilliant company I never beheld'. On breaking up afterwards and going home, Brydone's party found there was not a chaise in sight and everything was silent, dark and gloomy round the building. No chairmen were plying for hire and seven or eight hundred elegantly dressed ladies were obliged to walk home, on one of the most dreadful nights Brydone had ever experienced. There had been a violent storm of sleet and a high wind when they went in and two hours later the ground was completely frozen over, so that at first it appeared not only impossible to walk but even to find John, their servant. Describing him as 'the most careful of all servants' Brydone then told of how he had provided snow shoes and sticks for them all but no snow shoes could prevent the danger. John took care of Mary and brought her safely home although she was 'totally confused'. Mrs Brydone took hold of her husband's arm and they went off but in the Circus 'both her feet flew out and she fell on her back'. Fortunately he held on to her arm, a move that broke the fall. Brydone was convinced that 'had there been a little bairn in the case ... it would have gone at least'.

Writing from a house in Bristol two days later, Brydone continued the story, telling his friend how his wife had insisted that they move to Clifton so that he could 'get a little sleep', he having had 'little rest at Bath'. There he had dined with the Hamiltons 'who rejoiced with me at the happy increase of your family. They have built a house and seem to live very pleasantly here'.[30] However, much on Brydone's mind was an incident that happened just before they left Bath, when a tall, lean man in a rusty black coat that had not been brushed for a twelvemonth called on them. One of his shoes was 'tied with a bit of black rag and the tags of the other were flapping against his ankles at every step'. It was a few minutes before the stranger was identified as someone better known to the Scotts than the Brydones but this did not stop him from soon strongly recommending the reading of the Bible, and asking that the same advice be passed on to Mr and Mrs Scott. Quickly grasping the visitor's incongruity, little Williamina, the youngest of Brydone's daughters said when he had gone, 'that man has a shoe and a slipper', prompting Brydone to recall how children 'twine themselves round one's heart'.[31]

Sadly, in April 1802, the family heard of George North's death from an injury he had incurred earlier in life when he fell from a horse. He had died while in London at Stratton Street off Piccadilly, and been buried at Wroxton. In May, there was another illustration of life at Lennel when Brydone's daughter Mary wrote to Elizabeth Bell, one of two sisters living in Coldingham whom Sir Walter Scott praised for her 'gift of personification', as revealed later in *Tibbie*

*Flint's History*, a series of fictional sketches describing amusing events in the life of 'Tibbie Flint'. Elizabeth's sister Margaret had called the previous day and was to stay the night at Lennel, adding very much as Williamina said, 'to the happiness of the day'.[32]

The occasional visit to his office on the Embankment, alone for the most part, enabled Brydone to keep in touch with his London friends, and, with Napoleon still a threat, the value to the Chancellor of the Exchequer of the sums collected by the Stamp Office in the battle to fund the war was enormous. As comptroller-general, Brydone's declarations of receipts for the years 1804 and 1805, amounting to £7,249,000 and £7,604,000 respectively, must have given much satisfaction. About this time Patrick and Mary would have begun to consider who might make a possible husband for their eldest daughter. It would have influenced much of their social life, especially without the help of Mary's deceased father. Although advice and help would have been enlisted from a wide circle, few could have anticipated the eventual outcome.

Early in June 1806, friends of the family began expressing their great pleasure and happiness, not only at the forthcoming marriage of Brydone's daughter, but also on account of the fact that she would be marrying into the aristocracy. Mary's husband was to be the Rt.Hon. Gilbert Elliot, heir to the earldom of Minto. One of the first to mention the prospect was James Anderson, a well-travelled military man who wrote from Wilton Lodge, near Hawick, an estate he purchased in 1805 from Lord Napier. He and his wife Catherine and her sister Anne, had 'heard many rumours about it which were always accompanied with a wish that it might prove true'.[33] Anderson knew of 'no match that seems to have met with so universal approbation, and I have a very high opinion of Mr Elliot … setting aside all considerations of birth and fortune, I think him far superior to most men of his age. In short, and it is impossible to say more, I think him a young man worthy of Miss Brydon'. Mrs Anderson proposed to write to Mrs Brydone by that day's post. It was a 'great additional pleasure' to them to be able to look forward to the agreeable prospect of the young couple being their neighbours.[34]

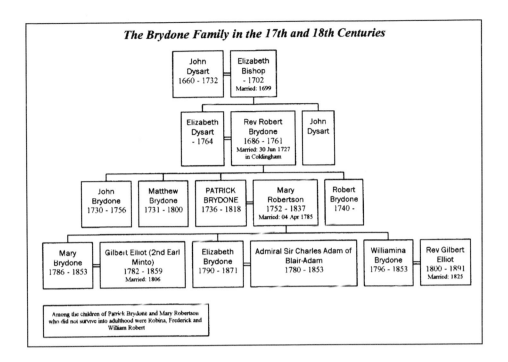

**The Brydone Family in the 17th and 18th Centuries**

John Dysart 1660 - 1732 — Elizabeth Bishop - 1702 (Married: 1699)

Elizabeth Dysart - 1764 — Rev Robert Brydone 1686 - 1761 (Married: 30 Jun 1727 in Coldingham) | John Dysart

John Brydone 1730 - 1756 | Matthew Brydone 1731 - 1800 | PATRICK BRYDONE 1736 - 1818 — Mary Robertson 1752 - 1837 (Married: 04 Apr 1785) | Robert Brydone 1740 -

Mary Brydone 1786 - 1853 — Gilbert Elliot (2nd Earl Minto) 1782 - 1859 (Married: 1806) | Elizabeth Brydone 1790 - 1871 — Admiral Sir Charles Adam of Blair-Adam 1780 - 1853 | Williamina Brydone 1796 - 1853 — Rev Gilbert Elliot 1800 - 1891 (Married: 1825)

Among the children of Patrick Brydone and Mary Robertson who did not survive into adulthood were Robina, Frederick and William Robert

Two weeks after James Anderson's congratulations, it was Frederick North's turn. He had returned from Ceylon the previous summer and had been living at Conduit Street in London. Addressing him as 'my dear friend', Frederick explained to Brydone how he had been told about 'the happy event' by Lord Minto, who had just received news of his own appointment to India. He wished to congratulate Mr Brydone and his wife most sincerely, recalling that he had known Gilbert from his childhood and did not believe that there existed 'a more amiable young man in every respect. There certainly is not a family in the world of which any reasonable person would sooner wish to become a member, and I can assure you from the conversation of the head of it, as well as from the correspondence of all the branches, that they are most truly delighted at the prospect of your daughter becoming one of them. They have the highest opinion of her, and think that she has every chance of a perfect felicity as can be expected by mortal beings'. Frederick asked his old tutor to present his congratulations to Mary, despite his being unknown to her, and as one who was 'interested in your welfare and that of your bairns'.[35] It was a good and caring letter which Brydone must have greatly cherished.

A few days later, Lord Minto himself wrote to Brydone from Arlington Street, London, mentioning that he had penned a few lines to Miss Brydone 'to express some small portion of the joy which her acceptance of my son has given me. I cannot refrain from offering to you and Mrs Brydone, the same assurances. To see the future happiness of one so dear, secured, is no small point and, in the circumstances, which have been confided to you respecting my probable destination, is at this particular moment a great relief and consolation. I shall go with much lighter mind, if that destination is confirmed. I must relieve you and Mrs Brydone, however, from one anxiety. Gilbert in his generosity had I believe thought, and even talked of accompanying me. I am not so selfish as to permit that, and this is a sacrifice of which our minds, and that of Lady Minto, may be confidently discharged. I long to embrace you and Mrs Brydone, to pour out our common joy in the happiness of our children, and to enjoy such share as I may of the pleasure I shall feel in so close and endearing a connection with you and yours, whom I have so long respected and esteemed. I beg Mrs Brydone to accept her share in these sentiments'.[36]

As the month ended, the father of the bride-to-be again heard from William Fullarton who was then living in the south of England at Worton House, near Isleworth. He had heard about the event from his physician friend, Dr Blane, who had called on him the day before. Also born in Ayrshire, Gilbert Blane had sailed with Rodney at the end of the 1770s, becoming surgeon to the West Indies fleet. By using statistics to identify trends he had helped improve sailors' health not only in the tropics but inside prisons and convict ships.[37] Fullarton had been delighted to hear about the intended matrimonial alliance: it gave him, he wrote, 'more satisfaction than any similar event that has occurred for many year', adding that 'the young lady lives not a hundred miles from Lennel House and the young gentleman is heir apparent to a most valuable statesman – who controls all the men and measures of the East'. In a postscript, Fullarton said that he was 'continuing to recover strength'.[38]

A cousin, Matthew Sandilands, heard the good news at the end of June from a friend and asked Brydone to pass on praise for Mary's choice.[39] Writing from Edinburgh, he said 'I had a very particular account of him from an officer in Lord Dalkeith's regiment who spoke very warmly in his favour with regard to good sense, abilities, disposition and manners, in short he considered him as a very superior person in every respect'. From John Marjoribanks, who was to become a baronet in 1815 and Berwickshire's MP three years later, he learned how very fine a couple they were, and how pleased Lord Minto had been with his son's choice – 'Mary is a lovely girl.[40]

Knowledge of the forthcoming marriage spread across the county, and in July, the daughter of the fifth Lord Reay, Marianne (née Mackay), William Fullarton's wife, was congratulating Mary from Worton House, Isleworth, 'with the highest satisfaction'. There was 'the fair prospect of happiness which the whole combining circumstances hold out to your truly amiable daughter'. She struck her as an 'uncommonly clever and equally agreeable' woman. Going on to offer her help with the wedding 'paraphernalia', Marianne hoped Brydone would keep his promise to visit them before long, and that they would all be *en famille* at Worton House. It was a house, 'dry and sheltered, and in every point comfortable and convenient', and seeing each other would mutually refresh Brydone's spirits and those of her spouse.[41] A few days later, David Hume's niece, Catherine, who married Robert Johnston, wrote from Hutton Hall in Berwick.[42] Responding to the notices which had been sent out, she told Mrs Brydone that 'I never in my life wished any person joy with more heartfelt pleasure, and I thank you a thousand times for taking the trouble of writing (to) me of so happy event being soon to take place as that of your daughter's marriage'. 'Dear Mary Brydone' was the style she had always been talked of in this family.

Almost immediately, Mary received the letter which had been promised from Catherine Anderson in Hawick. Her sincere affection for her was obvious, and she had been unable to resist offering not only her own congratulations but also those of her sister Anne. Even an erstwhile playmate, their son Alan, sent his good wishes to both Williamina and Elizabeth if 'Mr Elliot will not be very jealous'.[43] Later that day, John Robertson of Ladybank House, an elderly member of the family, wrote saying 'I have this moment received your very friendly and welcome note. It is quite needless to express the feelings which I have on this event. The opinion I have long ago formed of my young friend proves so strongly in my mind that I cannot help saying that I think the gentleman must have much merit to deserve her. I have always heard him well-spoken of and I have not a shadow of doubt as the connection must be according to your wish in every respect the consequence will be happiness'.[44]

The following day, Elizabeth, the wife of the 10th Earl of Home, wrote from Dalketh House, south east of Edinburgh. Fearing that she might be 'troublesome' by adding to the number of letters received at Lennel, she still could not remain silent. She had to rejoice at anything which was 'so likely to contribute to your happiness, and give you and Mr Brydone satisfaction', adding that 'I trust you will receive no small comfort from having Miss Brydone settled so near you, which will greatly take from you the pain of parting'. Lord Home also desired to send his best wishes.[45] Another pleasing letter addressed to Brydone arrived the next day from Isabella, the second wife of Dr James Gregory, a fellow of the Royal Society of Edinburgh and joint professor in the practice of physic at the University. She begged leave to congratulate the Brydones in a letter sent on 28 August from the manse in Midcalder, saying that both of them had heard of the intended event with very great pleasure and, knowing well the interest which her aunts took in the family at Lennel, Isa, as she was known, had lost no time in forwarding Brydone's news to London.

In what the next correspondent described as this 'season of felicity', the family received a charming letter in a somewhat different vein from William Waite of Castlelaw, a property three miles from Coldstream. 'We hope' he wrote 'that everything that is good and fortunate will attend them. I can safely say that if their happiness and prosperity is equal to the bent of one of the parties at least, it must be very great. The other, we hope in time, to know as well … It gives us particular pleasure to hear that they are to be so soon and so long at Lennel. I have only one favour to ask, which is, if not already anticipated, that the first dinner they eat out of Lennel House may be at Castlelaw. If so disposed, they shall have in the old style, bed and supper into the bargain'.[46]

The quality, variety and age-range of those revelling in the news of the forthcoming wedding spoke for themselves. The day had yet to be fixed but as August arrived the flow of congratulations from those wishing to be associated with the happy event included John Russell of North Frederick Street, the solicitor, and his mother in Edinburgh to whom it was 'an auspicious union'. To Mr and Mrs Brougham then in Edinburgh, it was 'truly delightful', and for Mary Brydone's sister-in-law, Margarita Robertson Macdonald, writing from Appin House, it was 'Mr Elliot's character and disposition' that promised the happiness Mary deserved.[47] She was also glad that young Elizabeth's earlier feelings of repugnance at the idea of Mary marrying were now very different. In September, Lady Charlotte Baillie heard of the marriage 'with infinite pleasure and satisfaction' but belatedly, reading it in the newspapers while visiting her grandmother, Abigail Ramey, in Great Yarmouth.[48] It was 'in every way suitable and desirable' and would 'confer happiness on all the parties'. It must, she said, 'be a delightful thing for affectionate parents to see a daughter so well and happily settled'.[49]

# CHAPTER 13

# Life at Lennel and Minto (1806–1810)

The marriage of Mary, then aged 20, to the Hon. Gilbert Elliot, the eldest son of the first Baron Minto of Minto, was registered for proclamation in Coldstream on 23 August 1806, and the couple were married on the twenty-eighth of the month.[1] Lord Minto (1751–1814) had married Anna Maria, the eldest daughter of Sir George Amyand, in 1777, the same year that he made his maiden speech in the Commons.[2] After visiting the major courts of Eastern Europe in 1781, he broke with the North administration, becoming the first and last viceroy of Corsica in 1794, serving on the island for two years and being made Baron Minto of Minto in 1797. Writing to her husband in London, Lady Minto described Mary Brydone as: 'beautiful, but her beauty is not her principal merit, as she is universally said to have a temper as fair as her face. Her family dote on her and have brought her up with simple tastes, which will not jar with Gilbert's; so that we shall gain a daughter and not lose a son, which might have been the case had she been a London lady, apt to think Scotland a desert'.[3] The twenty-four-year-old groom had left St John's College Cambridge two years previously with a political career in mind. In January 1806, Pitt died and Lord Grenville formed the 'Ministry of all the Talents', which included Fox, Addington and other leading figures. In February, the groom's father, Lord Minto, took office as President of the Board of Control, the body responsible for overseeing the East India Company, employing Gilbert as his pupil companion. With an election likely between the end of October and the beginning of December, the son set out to canvass the Roxburghshire seat, but he had to be content with becoming the member for Ashburton in Devon for a year.

In September, Lord Minto had sent Brydone a deed whereby Mary and her trustees renounced the surety which the marriage contract had given over the lands of Barnhills for her jointure, the provision for a wife after the death of her husband. He explained that it had been renounced in consequence of a deed lately executed by himself and Gilbert, by which Mary would now receive the jointure over the lands of Wester Lochgelly and Eastern Cartmore in Fife – a better proposition than that a few miles west of Jedburgh. The solicitor, Mr Russell, wrote to Brydone about this alteration and Lord Minto therefore assumed that he would not require 'any further explanations'. He did say, however, that 'the lands substituted for Barnhills are at least of equal value ... as appears by a tack of the latter, and a rental of the former'. The reason for the change, he wrote, was that Barnhills was to be entailed in lieu of some entailed lands which he had sold in Fife, and that it was 'necessary for that purpose to discharge Barnhills from all encumbrances'. Adding a postscript, Lord Minto said 'I think it probable that we shall have the pleasure of seeing you at Lennel next Tuesday on our way to London. My kindest wishes to Mrs Brydone and your daughters'.[4]

Back home following an autumn excursion into England which had included a visit to Harrogate, the Brydones were enjoying April-like weather in November. Patrick told Lord Minto that he had seen 'the Minto Hill and Crags tinged with snow, as well as the Cheviot'. He had also been to see the Minto solicitor, and at his request had attested his birth as 6 January 1736.[5] At the beginning of December, the Lennel family heard 'almost every day' from the young couple in London. Both were well and 'just as happy as it is possible to imagine'.[6] 'We enjoy', Brydone said, 'very great pleasure almost every morning in hearing such delightful accounts from St James's and Arlington Street (where they were then staying), and were I to be asked who is the happiest person on earth I should certainly say it was our own dear girl. I hope heaven will grant that she may be deserving of it, and I think almost all our prayers will have been heard'.

Turning to Lord Minto's appointment as governor-general of Bengal, confirmed the previous July, Brydone could easily 'conceive how he must be oppressed with business ... and what a relief it must be when you shall have it in your power to throw it off'.[7] He would, nevertheless, be in the company of other members of the Elliot family. His son George was to command the frigate in which he sailed to India.[8] His youngest son was also a midshipman aboard the vessel, and already there in the service of the East India Company, and about to become Lord Minto's private secretary was John Edmund, his brother. Lady Minto and their daughters were to stay behind, the tropical climate being considered too unhealthy for women.

Writing to Lord Minto on 13 December, Brydone probably flummoxed his Lordship for a moment when he mentioned that there had been 'a strange surmise' in London. Many 'sinecure offices had been condemned', and 'would expire with their present incumbents' and he had 'never been able perfectly to ascertain' whether one or both of his sinecures were of that number. Such an esoteric and personal matter could hardly have been of much interest to a man assuming huge responsibilities halfway across the world. As if suggesting an exchange of favours between them at this relaxed and happy time, Brydone told him that nothing would be more delightful if he could be 'in any way useful to Mr Elliot in his county politics'. Brydone closed with a reference to the weather which had been good, save for 'one or two days' although accounts of it in Edinburgh suggested 'it must have been very bad indeed'. He could only wish that the voyage might be 'most agreeable and prosperous'. It must be 'the ardent prayer of many thousands'.[9]

In February the following year, the family heard about Minto's ship from one in-bound west of Plymouth, after some bad weather two days previously which had 'done more damage than any gale of wind for a long while'. Reaching the Cape in May, he arrived safely at Calcutta two months later. Meanwhile, Mary was being introduced to her husband's life as the Member of Parliament for Ashburton. After explaining to his father that the King had required a written promise from ministers that they would never propose a measure of any sort for the relief of Catholics which, as Gilbert said, of course they refused, he listed the cabinet changes occasioned by the fall of Grenville's ministry, and the appointment of the Duke of Portland as prime minister. Knowing how important it would be, he said 'One thing is certain that their ideas and yours of the system to be pursued in India are very different, and particularly with all the Wellesleys in office, and that they will not view your government with a very partial eye or be very willing to second your endeavours'.[10]

To Mary, her husband explained how he had been 'trying to philosophise' according to her recipe but had 'found it would not do'. The result was that he had 'been groaning over the misfortunes of the country'. He regarded the way ministers had been changed as 'a serious misfortune to the country', and in the case of Europe, he feared 'that it will be impossible any longer to prevent Russia (then at war with France) from treating for peace which, it is said, they were only prevented from doing already by their opinion of the strength and talents of the late government'.[11] His pessimism had disappeared ten days or so later when Gilbert told his father that although ministers were most anxious that he should be recalled, 'the Court would not do it, therefore it can only be by the King, contrary to the wishes of the Court'. Then, almost lost amid Gilbert's on-going political commentary, was the happy family news that his father might expect to find himself a grandfather: when 'you look in the glass sometime in September or October you will find your hair become grey, and that you look more memorable'.[12]

Much on the mind of the family during the summer of 1807 was the possibility that the government might reconsider Lord Minto's appointment to India and decide to recall him. Both Mary and Gilbert wrote long letters on the subject. In June, when they were with the Brydones at Lennel, Gilbert had heard nothing, but he expected that as soon as his father's first dispatches were received in London, ministers would soon find some fault or other 'in order to prepare the country for (his) recall'.[13] By August, however, the entourage had moved to Minto where the couple were 'living so entirely out of the world' that they knew 'very little of what was going on than what one learns from the newspapers'.[14] Gilbert had also been forced to accept that, without the continued support of Grenville for his candidacy at Ashburton, he would be unable to return to Westminster in the forthcoming general election. He did not return to the House of Commons until he sat for Roxburghshire between 1812 and 1814.

Minto House maintained its place in the hearts of all who came to know it. At the suggestion of her mother, young Mary wrote to Lord Minto telling him how speedily the house and garden in Roxburghshire had recovered from the winter, and how pleased she had been that a recent violent thunderstorm and very heavy rain had passed without doing any harm. Both Patrick and his wife were in good spirits, although 'Mama says we intend to kill her as we take her to some new walks every day', adding that she probably would not go home till she was 'quite tired'. Mary confessed that it was impossible 'to live in such a place as this without wishing to know the names of the many plants we find', a comment her father would have approved of. Meanwhile, 'Papa and his white horse' had been exploring the rocks on the estate and was 'looking as well, and is in as good spirits, as I ever saw him'.[15] Brydone was enjoying another phase of an idyllic country life after years of uncertainty, danger and near penury. Even with war still in the background, for those with money and health, life had an attractive mellowness.

With counties in Scotland required to produce a set number of men for service in the war against Napoleon, Gilbert spent three days at the beginning of September in Hawick with the volunteers, and as long in Jedburgh. They were to go into quarters for a fortnight and he was afraid that as soon as the election ballot was over, 'most of them would turn their swords into ploughshares'. Unemployment due to the collapse of the weaving trade meant that recruits were being taken from artisan and even middle-class households. Signing on for life in exchange for a bounty of £23 17s 6d sounded attractive, but much of it was absorbed by the cost of uniforms. A system of limited service involving seven years for infantry, and ten for cavalry and artillery, had been introduced to attract recruits. Writing from Lennel on 9 September, Gilbert told his father about the 'very unsettled state' in Ireland and that peace had been concluded between Russia, Prussia and France. He also reported news of the British pre-emptive attack on Copenhagen, the King having given permission in July for a naval force of twenty or so ships to go into the Kattegat to keep an eye on the Danish navy. He had heard how troops (commanded by Lord Wellesley) had landed on Zealand with very little opposition but nothing about the terms to be agreed by the Danish Crown Prince. Mary's husband had undertaken another three days of training.[16]

Three days into October, the Elliots' first child was born at Minto and christened Gilbert, and unleashed a flood of delight and congratulations across the family. With Patrick's heart 'full of joy … on the birth of the loveliest boy (he) ever beheld', he spoke of the boy's mother already going about as if nothing had happened. He was sure that there was 'not so happier a house in the land', going on to say that the mother 'played on the pianoforte two hours last night, and I verily believe could have danced a reel with as much spirit as ever she did in her life … Mr Elliot seems the happiest man on earth'.[17] Two days later, a message to India spoke of the child's father being 'not a little looked up to and envied as being decidedly his (child's) favourite when he is not hungry. He has not yet begun to eat pudding but you shall hear as soon as that great event takes place'.[18] A warm letter written from Barrackpore arrived from Gilbert's father towards the end of November but he was then still awaiting news of the child's safe arrival.

Gilbert had given Lady Minto, his mother, 'notice' of the prospect of her becoming a grandmother, news which had been received with very great joy at her home in Edinburgh 'as it will be at Lennel'. She was only angry that Mary 'did not allow Lord Minto to have had the pleasant intelligence before he set sail, as it would have added to the many pleasures he seems to be likely to enjoy in his baggage. If she did not like to make it public so soon, there should have been a letter, like sealed orders to be opened in a certain latitude'. Gilbert's mother, then in her mid-fifties and fifteen years younger than Brydone, looked forward to seeing the family when they found it convenient, but she knew 'Mr Brydone's aversion to an east wind, and we never had it more severe for some days past. I hope it will soon change and that he will be able to mount his favourite hills when he comes, without suffering, but I am not sure he should venture from home whilst it prevails – therefore I leave it to you to manage'.[19]

When Mary herself eventually wrote to India, recognising that she could not let another ship leave without telling Lord Minto a little about his grandson, she described him as 'really quite a little love'. The couple, and baby Gilbert, were still at Minto in the New Year, and planning to remain there 'till the little boy has had the cowpox and then we are to go to Lennel'. Family news was scant, except for an alarming episode reported by young Gilbert's father, when the estate factor, Robert Selby, was missing for several weeks after leaving for a visit to Lochgelly in Fife.[20] He arrived safely, but his wife became concerned when he had not returned after a month, at first thinking that he might have fallen overboard from one of the ferries or broken his neck in a tumble. When it emerged that he had fallen into an old pit shaft at some stage and required assistance, Lady Minto was only 'too happy to get him out', organising this from Edinburgh. Gilbert went on to tell his father that he suspected from the beginning that much of what had been said about Selby, his drinking and having 'so many families to maintain' was 'impossible that he should do it all out of his pay ... especially as he was to receive £1,900'. All were relieved when 'the bustle ended very much to Selby's credit, as in our alarm we enquired into the truth of the stories about his families and his drinking and found them to be entirely false'.[21]

Ten days later, a number of events were coming to a head about which Brydone would have been particularly concerned and personally saddened. In 1802, William Fullarton, his wealthy Ayrshire gentleman friend, had no sooner been appointed by Henry Addington, the prime minister, as a commissioner for the government of Trinidad and left the country, than Henry Dundas, who always saw him as a threat to his position as Scottish secretary, had him unseated for holding an office of profit. A clash of personalities in meetings of the colony's governing council followed; the soldier resigned, believing himself 'degraded in the eyes of the world'. Returning to London in December 1803, he was arrested by order of the Privy Council for causing 'picketing' (torture) to be unlawfully inflicted while extracting a confession from a young mulatto girl.[22] The horror and consternation which the crime caused in Britain had been fuelled by pictures and pamphlets, including *Fullarton's Statement, Letters and Documents respecting the affairs of Trinidad – including a reply to Colonel Picton's address to the Council of that Island*, a more than 200-page submission published in 1804. Col. Thomas Picton, who had been in charge of the island's military regime was found guilty, but the affair dragged on and before a second trial could start, at which he was to be acquitted, Fullarton had died from a lung infection on 13 February 1808 while staying at Gordon's Hotel in London, and been buried at Isleworth.

Brydone wrote to his near neighbour Hugh Scott from Minto in March 1808 thanking him for his letter and 'the happy news it announced', that of the birth of Anne, who was to be the last of the Scotts' family. He expressed the hope that by this time, and 'according to her laudable custom', Mrs Scott was quite well again: 'without any weeds (mourning clothes) or other annoyances that distress the best of woman'. Describing little Gilbert as a very fine fellow who promised to be 'a true strapping Borderer', Brydone said that despite some 'foolish alarms about measles and whooping cough', Mary and he were pleased that nothing serious had occurred. Apparently, the previous day, the couple should have dined with Admiral John Elliot, a bachelor then in his seventy-sixth year, but they learned by express in the forenoon that one of his servants who had been in Edinburgh with him had taken ill from the measles.[23]

The Brydone family had been reading Walter Scott's 'wonderful poem', *Marmion; a Tale of Flodden Field* which had been published in February that year. Bess, as her father called Elizabeth, had learned a great deal of it by heart as was her custom and he had watched her on the gravel path at Minto 'mumbling it to herself'. Knowing how much Hugh Scott would have been interested in his opinion of the work, Brydone commented on it at length. It had 'great faults but greater beauties and will require both pruning and polishing, and if that be done judiciously I think it will come out one of the greatest productions in our language'. Many of the characters,

Brydone said, were 'truly Homeric and supported throughout with such propriety and dignity'. The introductions were very beautiful but he advised everybody 'to read the poem first, the thread of which should not be broken in upon, and although I like Mr Skene (a legal friend of Scott) and Mr Erskine (a writer and antiquarian) very well, I do not like their breaking in upon me so abruptly when I am so deeply engaged with better company. There are many times which I think must make a deep impression on every person of taste or feeling, and must put them in mind of similar passages in the Iliad. Marmion's quarrel with Bell, the cat, is nearly equal though not quite so long as that of Achilles and Agamemnon'. In closing, Brydone told his friend that Mary's Gilbert was expected, and that he might like 'to see the fox break cover from the Rocks', at Minto.[24]

Although life both at Minto and Lennel followed a settled tempo, Gilbert, Mary and her parents began to think that a ship must have been lost on its way home. The nephew of a Mr Cobb at India House had been 'very attentive and civil' by letting the family know the dates of sailings, and had 'taken charge of forwarding a good number of newspapers and parcels', but there had been a gap in letters from Bengal. Meanwhile, at the end of March, Brydone took the opportunity of recalling his earlier life and the way his interest in astronomy had burgeoned, in a letter to Lord Minto, almost as if he was celebrating having reached three score years and ten, and his own claim to fame. Patrick had no doubt that the comet which had passed the earth in the autumn and winter had no small influence on the atmosphere. He said: 'the thin transparent vapour which surrounded it extended to many millions of miles and was directed to our earth. For sometime we had no instruments to find its parallax, but I have no doubt that it had a very considerable one as in some parts of its orbit it moved upwards of two degrees in a day'. One thing he observed which surprised him not a little, was his barometer which he had had for thirty years, and which he never saw higher than 31 inches, twice went above that level after the comet disappeared. This seemed to indicate that the atmosphere had become heavier than it was. Then thanking his Lordship profusely for the gift of a cask of Malmsey sent from Madeira to Edinburgh via London, Brydone could only hope that Minto's astronomers in India had been more fortunate than those in Britain.[25]

The summer saw the family's continued concern for anything pertaining to India. It appeared that a commission might be sent out 'to enquire into the conduct of business in the different public departments' of the East India Company as the result of its 'pecuniary embarrassments'. Mary's husband came to the conclusion that since the commissioners were to correspond with the government, and not the directors, the affair looked 'a little like the first steps towards transferring the direction of Indian affairs from the company to the crown', an event which would not happen finally till 1858.[26]

By July, however, domestic affairs and a steady process whereby the couple learned what they could from other landowners, and planned improvements to the Minto estate, had begun. A visit to the Duke of Atholl's estate at Blair, where they heard about his importing insect-repellent seed from Archangel for the hard and softwood forests he had been planting, was followed by others to Dunkeld, Callender and Loch Katrine. The duke planted 'principally larch, at about 9 feet distance in bad land and 18 in good, and fills up a little with hard wood'. The gardener who had been their guide at Blair Castle greatly impressed Mary whilst Gilbert worried that some recent emigration to Prince Edward Island in Canada, and the encouragement Lord Selkirk had given to it, might be tempting poorer tenants away from the land. Mary said 'he was a fine eager Highlander and his affection seemed to be pretty equally divided between the trees, the deer, and the duke.[27]

Mary, the children, and what her husband referred to as their anticipated 'brother or sister' were at Lennel at the end of August. Gilbert hoped to be able to leave the River Tweed once he had 'got rid of our volunteer business' as it would probably be their last visit for some time, adding that 'Mr Brydone intends to pass the winter in Bath. He is quite well, though he would be very angry if he heard me say so'. Minto had become Gilbert's headquarters for army volunteers from the area. Men were being called to the colours to fight in the Peninsula War. Telling his father that 'the Spanish news continues to improve every day' he thought that Britain really had 'a very fair chance of success, at least unless Bonaparte is prepared to enter Spain at the head of a great army'. He felt that Napoleon probably had enough on his hands, it being 'pretty generally understood that Austria (was) preparing for another struggle'. Reports in the newspapers, and the militarist activity around him, would have brought back Brydone's memories as a young officer fighting France and Spain nearly fifty years before, whilst half a world away in India, it was much the same story. Lord Minto had been busy sending missions to Persia, Afghanistan and Sind to drive out French influence there.[28] So far as his own plans were concerned, Gilbert planned to go shooting at Minto with Elliot of Wells near Jedburgh, a distant kinsman who had taken out a licence and was the 'deal keener' of the two.[29]

In September, after watching the arrival and departure of visitors one morning from the sitting room at Lennel, including old Admiral John who was going to Eyemouth to 'try the sea air ... and warm sea-bathing', Brydone would enjoy reading the mail if he was not going out riding. With Lord Minto's 'delightful letters' in front of him, Brydone said 'it was impossible to resist the desire of telling (him) how happy they have made us'. Telling the governor-general that the party at Lennel had been studying astronomy 'with assiduity for some time', he said there had been numerous eclipses of Jupiter and its satellites. Four new heavenly bodies, totally different from anything ever seen before, had been observed, which Brydone said 'some sage philosophers suppose to be a new creation'. They had been given the name of asteroids 'for want of a better' one, but no one had 'been able to get a glimpse of any of them' and possibly never would. The elderly Brydone thought it 'very unsatisfactory' that what had been written on the subject, 'will be found in one of the last volumes of the Philosophical Transactions', presumably because the news had not been carried in the newspapers. Recalling some of the work which had been done at Madras, little more than a thousand miles to the south-west of the governor-general's seat in Calcutta, he suggested that his Lordship 'may be much better acquainted with all this than we are, for we have been told that there are some very good astronomers in India, and they have the advantage of us in a clear sky'. Appointed in 1802, John

Goldingham became the first official astronomer of the Madras observatory, formulating Madras time that year as 5 hours and 30 minutes ahead of Greenwich. Read to the Royal Society of London in 1808, and published in their *Philosophical Transactions* as Brydone expected, Goldingham's paper on *Eclipses of the Satellites of Jupiter* showed his detailed observations had been between January 1794 and December 1802.[30]

Meanwhile, the family was waiting to see whether the seeds which Lord Minto had sent home would flower. The young plants had been moved into the conservatory along with a cinnamon tree. Brydone recommended a literary germination to his Lordship, namely *Marmion*, which had 'already spread over a great part of the continent'. It had been a remarkably good growing season, whether or not it had anything to do with atmospheric movements or stars. Overall, however, Brydone concluded that, 'Our crops … are all fine except the wheat which will be cruelly defective. Many of the richest farms (are) not worth cutting'.[31]

With Elliot of Wells leaving the family to attend the Christmas assembly in his Peterborough constituency, Gilbert decided to take the advantage of attending Edinburgh University for a few months. Telling his father he was an inconsistent 'flirt among books', attending university lectures was an attempt to break himself 'of a habit of idleness and unsteadiness in reading'. Mary expected to be confined about the end of February and humorously promised Lord Minto 'a black granddaughter this time'.[32] Arriving in Bath on 18 December, Patrick and Mary looked forward to spending the winter and resuming their acquaintance with the Regency world that had started at the turn of the century. Gilbert's expectant wife described how 'everything as yet seems to be going on well'. More important was Papa's health which was 'continuing so good, and his eyes which were beginning to fail him sadly are rather better, though I fear he is not yet able to read which is a cruel blow to him. However, at Bath he will probably meet with many agreeable people and old friends, and he will also enjoy Lennel when he comes back much more than if he had spent the winter there'.[33]

As 1808 came to an end, Brydone's son-in-law told Lord Minto about Admiral John Elliot's estate.[34] Unmarried, he had died at

Mount Teviot in September, and having commanded frigates during wartime, part of his fortune derived from bounties and prize money awarded for enemy captures. On 10 February the following year, a much-relieved Gilbert was able to speak of Mary having given birth to twin boys in Edinburgh. Everything was as well as possible. She was 'sitting up in bed suckling her litter' and saying that she was just as strong as she was before they were born, and would get up and be upon the sofa this afternoon. Little Gilbert took charge of his brothers, William and George, believing they were his children 'which, by their size, they might be'. For twins, they were not similar, though their father had certainly never seen such 'miniatures of children'. Sadly, none of this group were to reach maturity, including Frederick born in 1812. Writing from the ordinariness of village life at Lennel, the earl's son was anxious to tell his father that 'we meet with nothing but grateful faces here, and everybody we see desires us to thank you for something or other'. Earlier echoes of the royal plural had been in Gilbert's political update when he wrote 'it is the fashion at present to be gloomy about politics' but he could not see 'anything particularly threatening' and 'many people suffered themselves to be led away by false hopes in the beginning of the Spanish business and expected ... we should conquer Bonaparte'.[35]

Some worrying skulduggery at the Stamp Office would have been drawn to Brydone's attention around this time. In a debate in the Commons, Samuel Whitbread, a whig on the opposition benches, and a frequent and powerful speaker, raised the question of the incidental expenses of staff at both the London and Edinburgh offices. He pointed out that there were 'a number of trifling articles paid by the commissioners on their own authority' which he thought required investigation, such as servant's wages to the housekeeper, and other sums amounting to between £300 and £400. There was also the considerable sum of £2,700 yearly charged as allowances to stampers for extra hours at 6d per hour. In Scotland the sums were larger. Whitbread concluded by asking for an account to be given of the management in both offices, whereupon, William Huskisson, who had been joint secretary to the Treasury but was then in the wilderness, agreed that 'premiums for procuring good bills for the purpose of transmitting duties from Scotland to England, were an unnecessary expense'. Having asked that George Harrison, Assistant Secretary to the Treasury, should explain the matter to the House, the relevant motions were put and agreed to. Reformist trends were in the air.[36]

Towards the end of March Gilbert reported that Lady Minto's household in Edinburgh had 'had a most unhappy time of it for some time past'. Fortunately, Mary's health and temper had been proof against the anxiety and fatigue of watching the children day and night, in the hope of preserving one of them. She had also made 'a very good nurse'. George, probably the weaker of the twins, had died soon after childbirth, and William had been so weak that the family thought he could not live till the morning. Gilbert told his father that 'when Mr Sandford came to christen him, a nurse called Ailsie did not feel sure that he was alive; indeed, he had ceased to breathe several times and she only revived him by blowing into his mouth. Nothing could exceed the care and activity of all in the house, both 'high and low'.[37] A week later, he reported seeing him twice on the point of death, only to find him 'as strong as most children of his age and gaining every day'. However, he again became seriously ill and died after 'a most heartbreaking day and night'. As Gilbert told Lord Minto, 'a few weeks ago we had three thriving boys, and now Gilbert is the only one left. Ever since little George's death, Mary had devoted herself day and night to his brother and his thriving had only just begun to console her for her first loss when this second blow came upon us'.[38]

With 'so melancholy a conclusion' still on his mind, Gilbert reported that Edinburgh was 'thinning very fast', with lawyers having 'taken their flight' and 'all the balls, over'. Lack of employment as an MP in London left him with time on his hands, and Mr Stewart's lectures on political economy and moral philosophy, some of which he had heard, had ended. Apparently Professor Dugald Stewart's lectures, meetings of the 'Brown Toast Club' (founded by Lady Minto and Lady Carnegie), and soirées at which Madame Catalani, a member of the Théâtre-Italien de Paris, sang, had been part of the scene.[39] No immediate career beckoned Gilbert and he was already twenty seven years old. Returning from Bath 'sooner than they intended' the family's concern about Patrick's blindness increased. The prognosis was good, however, on account of his cataract being 'of a very favourable sort, and likely to be removed without any risk or difficulty as soon as it is far enough advanced for the operation'.[40]

In April, the Elliot family determined to leave Edinburgh and settle back at Minto where Gilbert's mother had agreed to meet Archibald Elliot, the architect, in order to think seriously about building a new kitchen there during the summer. This was to be the start of something a little more complicated. In May, when the family was enjoying 'an almost Indian climate', initial plans for the kitchen appeared and there was evidence of Gilbert having taken up the reins of managing the estate. Mary's parents had been left at Lennel and, as Gilbert reported, Patrick was 'looking fresher and is in much better spirits than last year notwithstanding his blindness which has increased very much of late. He expects that his eyes may be in a fit state for the operation about the autumn and he desires me to say that one of the first uses he will make of them shall be writing to you as his letter to you was the last that he has been able to write'.[41] In August, Gilbert and Mary paid a short visit to Lennel where his son-in-law found Brydone 'better than I have seen him for some time ... his spirits which were a good deal depressed with the thoughts of losing his sight are now as good as ever, and he is as cheerful and happy as he ever was'. In addition to estate matters, and the dispatch of his regular political commentary to India in which he reported 'we should have a regency if the King could not form a government', Gilbert had also been busy winding up the Admiral's estate, certifying his legacies before the provost at Jedburgh and visiting the Elliot family's landholdings at Barnhills, Mary's initial dowry from his father, and Langhope, south of Selkirk.[42]

The running of the Kelso races in 1809 had been 'inferior', and the usual requests from those known to both families for introductions to the governor-general, representing as he did the King in India, included one from the Turnbull family that their son serving on the sub-continent, might be honoured with 'a royal smile'.[43] By December, however, John Edmund Elliot in India had married twenty-one year old Amelia, daughter of James

Henry Casamaijor, against a scene on the sub-continent where the governor-general was temporarily and reluctantly based in Madras. Cuts in the pay of European officers in the East India Company's army had led to some disaffection and deaths. Looking back on the year, Gilbert thought his father had suffered 'a year of calamity and disgrace'.

Fortunately HMS *Ganges* arrived in England in January 1810 with news from India, and the anxiety the Elliots had 'lived in for some time past' disappeared. Writing from Lennel, Gilbert said 'Brydone's blindness, I think, a good deal increased since our last visit, however he still continues to ride alone tho' he cannot see the road, or if he can distinguish it at all, it is as much as he can do, yet he persists in not allowing anybody to go with him. His rides are, however, very much shorten'd and I am sorry to say that I think him very much broken of late; his health is good but he is evidently much weaker and older'.[44]

Regaining something of the momentum that had been lost during the first two years or so of his marriage, Gilbert accepted the duty placed on him of visiting the estate's tenants regularly in the absence of his father. Families that had sons serving in India wanted to talk about service pay and promotion (or the lack of it) and be helped to understand such matters. Brydone's friend, James Anderson, pleaded for his nephew, just down from Oxford and about to sail for Bengal to receive some recognition as a writer at the Elliot court in Calcutta. By the end of March 1810, plans for the proposed alterations at Minto, now no longer restricted to the kitchen, had been sent to India with a gentle reminder that the last addition to Minto had been made in 1745. 'Both my mother and I', Gilbert wrote 'would have wished to defer our operations but that would have been attended with so much inconvenience that we have determined to begin without it'. There was an early admission that 'the appearance of the house certainly will not be very regular, nor what you would choose were you at liberty to invent a new plan ... but it is quite simple and without any pretence to beauty or ornament'. Although the focus was on the inside of the house, to 'make up for all of the defects in its architecture', Gilbert also reported that considerable re-shaping of trees and the gardens near the house was called for.[45] A visit by Mr Elliot, the architect, was expected a month later.

Writing from Lennel to Lady Minto who was living at 63 George Street, Edinburgh, Gilbert agreed with her that the capital's builders might well carry out neat work at Minto but he foresaw difficulties arising from the distance, inspection of the quarry, drawings and estimates, which they might 'not choose to do upon the mere chance of the job'. He also warned that 'we shall have a fight to keep the common jobs about the place from standing still whilst the building is going on … as they dwindle sadly in importance before the great work'. As this matter was being sorted out, there was the first reference to young Gilbert being called 'Gilly' who had 'a good deal of fever and was flushed hot, though he slept quietly'. Once awake, he had been given two grains of Dr Robert James's fever powder, a ubiquitous patented medicine made up of antimony and calcium phosphate and which had been known about since 1746. It produced hardly any effect save for his face being covered in 'the most gentle perspiration'. Thinking another dose would probably do him more harm than good, they allowed him to sleep. In the morning, his pulse was still 'a little bit quick' but the doctor thought they had been 'too tender-hearted and should have given him more James's powder' and that if he had any fever again, the remedy would be a dose of antimony powder and calomel, if his bowels were not open. It was fortunate that they were within reach of medicines at the apothecary's shop in Coldstream.[46]

A week later, Mrs Brydone was still bearing an unknown 'affliction with great fortitude and resignation'. Young 'Gilly', on the other hand, had suffered the return of his fever but after taking two more grains of Dr James's powder, and a dose of calomel, he slept quite soundly. He also took some senna before getting up, and his father, who supposed his runny eyes might be due to teething problems, accepted that they would have to be 'very attentive to his bowels for some days'. Mary expected 'to receive her degree … from the College of Physicians and Apothecaries of Minto for her enterprise and skill upon this occasion'.[47]

It was a greatly relieved Gilbert who wrote to Lady Minto from Lennel in the middle of April. 'Mary and I' he said, were 'highly flattered by your commendations of our medical proceedings. The James's powder you will see succeeded perfectly the second time and must have been quite good as they come straight from Newbery', Dr James's manufacturing and marketing partner. Continuing, Gilbert said 'Gilly is quite himself today ... considering the fever and discipline he has gone through'. He suggested that his teeth had been the cause of his illness 'as two of them [were] just about to push through the gum which ... swelled'.[48] Three days later, however, Gilbert told his mother that he had heard of a child with similar symptoms who had also received the smallpox vaccine, revealing the extent to which Edward Jenner's research in 1798 had become common knowledge, to say nothing of the £30,000 paid to him by the government in recognition of his work by 1807. However, although the family conceived that the child had the smallpox, instead of smallpox matter they found that it contained only the clear watery liquid of the vaccine. The inoculation for one disease produced another. One doctor, Gilbert reported, 'had frequently seen instances of a second inoculation in persons who had had the smallpox in which a regular small pock pustule was formed, attended by fever at the proper times, and that having once pricked himself in taking some matter for inoculation from a child in the smallpox, he had all the symptoms slightly, except the eruption which never returns in these last cases'.[49]

Consultation with his father about work at the house was being made difficult by the non-arrival of letters from India, and could not be held up indefinitely. Nevertheless, writing to Lord Minto, Gilbert had the surprising news that it was 'extremely likely that a railroad may be carried from Berwick to Ancrum Bridge, and ultimately to Hawick'. Two years before, powers had been granted by parliament for a nine-mile tram road between Kilmarnock and Troon. Hugh Scott, had long been occupied with the project and Gilbert felt it would be a feather in his cap if he could pull it off. Personally, he had never entertained any hope of sufficient funds being raised but 'the line has been surveyed and the report of the engineer circulated'. He also passed on a rumour that the King intended to be couched, or operated on for a cataract, and although he doubted the report, he recalled that Phipps (Henry Phipps, first Earl Mulgrave) had once told Mr Brydone that 'the King's eyes were not nearly ready for the operation, and if it is tried and fails, it is impossible not to fear that the confinement and disappointment together might drive him mad again, which would be a most serious calamity'. Adding that Mary had sent a gift of some Scottish pebbles for Amelia, John Edmund Elliot's wife, Gilbert feared that they would 'cut but a poor figure' among Lord Minto's other 'eastern treasures'.[50]

In May, correspondence between the Treasury and the Board of Stamps regarding the management of the Stamp Office in Edinburgh would perhaps have caused Brydone to raise an eyebrow. An account was required of all appointments made in that office since the beginning of 1809, and most significantly, 'all fees, prerequisites, emoluments or salaries, increased or decreased, or abolished within the same period' came under scrutiny. On behalf of the Commissioners of Stamps at the Treasury in Whitehall, George Harrison wrote to say that he referred to a duplicate copy of the accounts for 1807 and 1808 where a charge had been made of £1,161 15s 5d for premium-paid remittances. The Lords Commissioners of the Treasury determined that this was 'an expense altogether unnecessary' and not incurred in the remittances of other branches of the Revenue from Scotland. He was ordered to discover the grounds on which the charge had been made. The head collector in Edinburgh at the time, Mr Robert Hepburne, and his staff, were in trouble. No corresponding allowances appeared to have been given to any officers of the department in England.[51]

Those at Minto were 'up to their ears in mortar' by mid-June, and the first storey was 'actually up in some places' in spite of Gilbert's stomach being 'less amiable than usual'. With the result, he and Mary decided to stay at Gilsland Spa, a hotel 18 miles east of Carlisle, famous for its sulphurous spring, and close to Hadrian's Wall. The Kelso physician, Dr Wilson, thought that ten days there would help restore his digestion 'to its natural contempt for toasted cheese or mushrooms before it had time to contract any habits of fastidiousness'.[52] It turned out 'uncommonly well', so much so that when at Gilbert's request Mary gave his father a report, it was one about everyone except her husband. Young Gilbert, the 'little upstart', had been left at Lennel, and Patrick's blindness now meant that he was read to by the family, and enjoying it all the more. Brydone nevertheless clearly gave his wife and sisters a great deal to do by contriving ways of never being left alone. Despite the Lennel ensemble being obviously uncomfortable anywhere but in the immediate area of Coldstream, Mary hoped to be able to persuade her sister Elizabeth to spend a few quiet days at Minto. Williamina was 'so completely altered' that she thought Lord Minto 'would hardly know her', but there was hope that she would 'turn out very pretty; she is extremely like Mama'. It was also clear that Mrs Brydone had suffered a great deal that year from the illness of Uncle James (Colonel Robertson) who had a dreadful paralytic stroke some months ago. His recovery had been 'very wonderful and quite unexpected'.[53]

Three days later there was general approval from India for the redevelopment of Minto. Mr Elliot, the architect, had happened to be visiting and Gilbert had been able to discuss his Lordship's

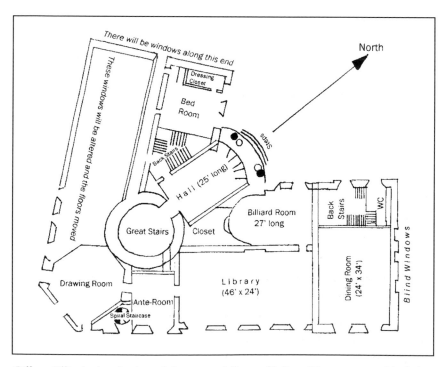

Gilbert Elliot's sketch plan of the ground floor of Minto House sent to his father in India, re-drawn and showing some of the alterations completed and others promised.

most serious objection, the plan for the south front. He wanted the projection widened to make it correspond with the dining room without 'omitting the little stair to the terrace'. It was soon clear that Lord Minto had much yet to appreciate as Gilbert described a great number of major works affecting room heights, new floors, window sizes and 'the round tower for the great staircase' in his long letter. Additionally, a rough sketch of the 'principal storey of the house' was sent to India so that he could digest the changes that had been made from the original. The builders were 'laying the joists on the bedroom storey of the east wing'.[54]

At the end of November, Elizabeth, Brydone's second daughter, wrote a charming letter to Lord Minto thanking him for the 'beautiful presents' he had sent to her and Williamina. She thought herself 'very importunate for venturing to plague (him) with a letter' when he had 'so much to do, and so much to think of, but it is better that you should think me a little importunate than that you should think both Williamina and I ungrateful'. Valuable as the gifts were to two 'very, very vain' young ladies, they showed, she added: 'that we are not forgot by you, which is enough to make us a great deal too proud'. Apparently, a week before, when Gilbert's sister Harriet was staying with them at Lennel, Elizabeth had mentioned how much she wished to write to his Lordship, and have her 'laugh me out of all my foolish fears, as she called them'. Accepting he had 'many better accounts' of little Gilbert, she told Lord Minto that Brydone thought him 'more delightful, and more perfect' than any of them did. At Lennel, Gilbert was always 'Papa's companion', with Brydone telling him everything that went on.

In his seventy-fifth year, Brydone was well, and 'in spite of the state his eyes are in, he is as cheerful and in great spirits as ever he was. He desires me', Elizabeth continued, 'to tell your Lordship that the last letter he ever wrote was to you, and although he cannot now write to tell you so that he looks forward with delight to hearing again, this is not now a very likely prospect'. Happily, despite his reduced sight and some deafness, the rural idyll at Lennel House continued.[55]

# CHAPTER 14

# Brydone, the Elliots and the return of Lord Minto (1811–1814)

The health of George III was much on everyone's mind at the beginning of 1811. The previous year his Majesty had again been overcome by his porphyria, and periods of mental confusion following the death of his youngest daughter, and it was feared he might never resume his duties or even survive an illness. Gilbert told his father that 'the happiest thing for the country certainly would be that the poor old King should die, as during the remainder of his reign we cannot hope for a strong government'.

Brydone's son-in-law, still not yet thirty, was not in London but in daily expectation of Mary's next confinement, and 'as soon as I see that job safely over, I am off. Whether we have a new reign or a regency I conclude that a dissolution of Parliament will take place'.[1] With an election in the offing, it was obvious that if he was to get back into the Commons it was now or never. If a seat in Roxburghshire proved impossible he would seek one elsewhere. Fortunately, a week later, Gilbert heard that John Rutherford had told the Duke of Roxburghe that he would not stand again as the member for the county. Furthermore, a canvass had already begun, and although it was by no means certain that Parliament would be dissolved, Gilbert was 'very confident of success'. The duke's candidate, Sir Alexander Don, had 'not the least chance of winning', and fully aware of how important an opening it could be, Gilbert would 'spare no exertions to make the most of it'. To attach as many of Rutherford's personal friends to him as he could, he had already written 'a kind and handsome letter' to the sitting member, ridden forty miles and nearly as many letters.[2]

Mary could do little to help her husband who, in addition to his political affairs, was wondering what effect his father's successful expedition against Mauritius might have, but a joyful week started on 14 February when Mary gave birth to a little girl at Minto. The first with the name Mary Elizabeth for several generations of the Elliot family, she would become, like her mother, the wife of a diplomat. Gilbert told his father about the arrival of 'a very fat thriving child ... and pretty', and promptly dispatched a servant to Lennel to give Brydone news of the birth. He was overwhelmed, and feeling for something with which to tip him, said, 'Oh ... here, give him this directly, and emptied his purse into Elizabeth's hand'. On her way downstairs, however, she happened to look at what he had given her. Unfolding the bit of paper Brydone had mistaken for a bank note, she found that it contained two pills given him some time before by Lady Minto. A not dissimilar event was to follow in India where there was news that John Elliot's wife, Amelia, would soon be 'brought to bed', inspiring one of the midwives at Minto to swear an oath that she would teach her 'to perform the operation without the assistance of a doctor' if she came back to Scotland and 'got her into her clutches'.[3]

Generally, Brydone was 'in good spirits, and delighted with the prospect of much gaiety, particularly with the thought of another flirtation with Lady Minto'. He had been quite charmed with her kindness in coming to visit him when he could not travel. As doyen of the family, the old traveller always enjoyed having others draw on his knowledge and experience, to say nothing of the occasional weather eye he kept on his son-in-law. Gilbert felt the absence of his father greatly, and was subject to bouts of uncertainty and indecisiveness.[4] Elizabeth had just returned from a three week stay at Spring Gardens in Edinburgh with Lady Minto who, as Mary said, had succeeded in persuading Brydone that Elizabeth was longing for the opportunity to go to more balls and plays, rather than being constantly at Lennel, something which had not entered his head as being at all possible. With her father delighted to find he could make her happier by agreeing to this, Williamina was permitted to visit Minto which she enjoyed as much as Elizabeth did her Edinburgh trip.

Soon afterwards, Harriet Elliot, Gilbert's sister, wrote to him from Minto. He was staying at the Royal Hotel in Pall Mall, described as an extensive establishment for the reception and accommodation of gentlemen of distinction. Harriet reported that Brydone was much better than she had seen him for a long time. He had said he could see 'full as well as he did last spring' and she thought that unless his blindness worsened 'it would be a pity to put it (the idea of an operation) into his head again', adding that she might 'safely lay the case before Mrs Brydone'. Harriet, and probably her mother, had apparently brought Williamina back to Minto for a break and there was news that Elizabeth had obtained another fortnight's leave of absence. Patrick's Mary had recovered from some after-effects of her confinement and was 'able to bear the light of day like other people', having had 'a most wretched time of it' when she could 'do nothing but sit in a dark room and blow her nose'.[5]

Giving Lord Minto the news that both parents had initially thought the new baby girl resembled Lady Minto, Mary later confessed that the very strong likeness was to her grandfather. Mama said she was 'very pretty' though 'the brownest child she ever saw' and Papa said 'he always preferred a brunette to a fair beauty, that everybody of sense does, and with such eyes as hers she will get a great deal of attention in the world'. About Brydone, Mary was delighted to say how she 'never saw him in better health, nor more able to enjoy the society of his friends than he is at present and though his eyes have failed, it has not rendered him incapable of relishing the company of his favourites'. His blindness was, she explained 'an excellent excuse for (him) keeping out of the reach of everybody he does not care about. It is wonderful to see how amazingly good and equal his spirits are, and how easily he can part with Mama and my sisters for a short time'.[6] Brydone had in effect decided he would rather remain as he was than run the risk of taking a long journey which would have been infinitely more formidable to him than any operation he might have had for blindness.

At the end of April, Gilbert returned to Minto from London in order to help the family put a stop to some of the architect's wilder ideas for the house, and to undertake a fortnight's soldiering in Jedburgh where he spent the greater part of his time with Dr William Somerville, a military surgeon.[7] Inundated with letters of gratitude from all the Marjoribanks clan about his father's kindness to them in India, he also told him that the family did not intend to 'meddle with the west wing' that year. Furthermore, if the two wings were to be the same length, something that he admitted would improve the appearance of the house, he would leave such 'extravagance' to his father to insist on. Gilbert was beginning to 'lose all patience' with those 'living quietly and comfortably at home' when his father was 'broiling at the opposite side of the globe' and he could not resist recalling that his father had been 'almost five years out of England'. He felt the family might fairly claim him back towards the end of the sixth year. In the meantime Gilbert told his father about his intention to take another spell at Gilsland, on Dr Wilson's advice, and by way of 'clinching last year's cure'. This time it was to be in the company of Lord John Webb Seymour, a member of the Council of the Royal Society that year, whom Gilbert described as 'certainly one of the very best men in the world'.[8] As an 'irregular and improvident' person himself, he trembled at the thought of being linked with Seymour's 'systematic regularity' for three weeks but his was 'a true Gilsland case' and the spa would help improve his health. It would also be a break from the daily occupation of begging favours 'to the right and left' from all his acquaintances.[9]

The following month, swallowing what Gilbert called her false pride, Mary asked for such assistance as her father-in-law could give him in what had become 'a troublesome affair'. Two brothers of her 'greatest friends', Elizabeth and Margaret Bell, then serving in India, had been helped in their careers but there was more that could be done if his Lordship was so minded. Charles was in the artillery and John an ensign in a native regiment of the East India Company 'which was in January last at Barrackpore'.[10] Confessing that she was far from being blind to her children's faults, Mary updated her father-in-law about young Mary Elizabeth's progress, and hoped her daughter would 'turn out a beauty … if she goes on improving as she has hitherto done'. Her parents and sisters had grown 'quite frisky that summer', she added, and 'had been visiting all Berwickshire and Northumberland'. Furthermore, her father had been feeling so much better that Mary had hopes of getting him to come to Minto for a few days.[11]

Gilbert again attended the Kelso races when he returned to Minto in July. Writing to his father on the eleventh he hoped that something would happen to prevent him from going to Batavia as he intended. In terrier-like mood, he was, however, soon agreeing that there could be no thought of his recall 'after the extraordinary success of your government'. He suggested that the unsettled state of the government at home 'must have made (the Board of Control) abandon for the present, any intentions which they may have entertained in favour of any other person'. An honour for his father, a 'distinguished recompense for all that he had done' was much on his mind, but he would not be surprised to find resistance to any such a proposition.

Elliot of Wells and Gilbert agreed that it would be 'very desirable' for his Lordship to express his desire to resign at least a year and a half before the time he might fix for his departure from India. This would allow time for his letter to arrive in England and for his successor to make the voyage outward. Yawning enough to dislocate his jaws, on account of being up till past five that summer morning, after a French play in Kelso and the journey back to Minto, Gilbert read what he had written, and admitted it was 'a pretty unintelligible jumble'. Anticipating that his father would laugh at all his fears, he wished most heartily that it was he who was safely seated in the armchair in which he was writing – 'instead of being a mark for all your enemies and your friends to fire at'.[12]

Early on an evening in August 1811 a fisherman from New Coldstream, was drowned while bathing in the River Tweed, opposite Lennel House. According to the *Caledonian Mercury*, John, the son of Richard Henderson, had been extracted by 'a person diving for the body after having been about twenty minutes under water, and notice had been sent to … Lennel House'. The newspaper added that Brydone sent off for every assistance with a 'promptitude which has always distinguished that worthy gentleman in cases of distress, issued the directions given by the Humane Society for the recovery of apparently drowned persons, and summoned medical aid from Coldstream'. Unfortunately, 'all their efforts to restore animation proved fruitless'.[13] The society, then called 'the Society for the Recovery of Persons Apparently Drowned' had held its first meeting in 1774 at the Chapter Coffee House in St Paul's Churchyard. It had five key aims – to publish information on how to save people from drowning; to pay two guineas to anyone attempting a rescue in the Westminster area of London; to pay four guineas to anyone successfully bringing someone back to life; to pay one guinea to anyone, often a public house owner, allowing a body to be treated in his house, and to provide volunteer medical assistants with some basic life-saving equipment.[14]

While Mary, Gilbert and Elliot of Wells were alone at Minto, Mrs Brydone, Harriet and Anna Maria (two of Lady Minto's three daughters) amused themselves with a little sketching at Lochgelly. Gilbert told his father that John Drinkwater, who had served with him in Corsica, had lost the appointment he had hoped for, the job going to the prime minister's secretary, but it soon became apparent that he had been offered the post of controller of military accounts instead. His daughter, Georgina, was to become Mary's companion twenty years later. Progress continued on the building work at Minto but any lengthening of the west wing would be left to his father to undertake 'out of the spoils of Java', or such funds as the family thought he would realise from his governor-generalship.[15] Having lessened some of the family's alarms about the climate in Java, a 'pleasant expedition' against the Dutch East Indian island was anticipated by Lord Minto's administration, and 'sea breezes' were to replace the shade of his laurels at Barrackpore in India. The attack on Java had been prepared in consultation with the governor's agent in the Malay States, Stamford Raffles, and, quite extraordinarily, he planned to accompany the expedition himself in his son George's frigate. There was, however, a good deal of concern in London that the unsuccessful Walcheren expedition to the Netherlands two years before might be repeated.[16]

In October, the architect, spent several days at Minto talking over future operations, about which Lady Minto thought her husband would be satisfied, at a cost of around £3,000. Bookcases for the library were to be of waxed American oak and would be made during the winter and erected in the Spring. The upper shelf would be about eight feet six inches from the floor.[17] Gilbert was with Brydone at Lennel in the middle of December when a 'glorious packet' of his letters arrived, invoking the congratulations 'of half the town' for his Lordship's 'splendid achievement' in Java. He did not want to think 'too ill' of his father's masters, and he reported that there was a general expectation that he would receive 'some very signal reward' and that elevation to the peerage was considered certain. Speaking personally, he said he was persuaded that nothing was less likely, and that every attempt would probably be made 'to keep out of sight the share which (he) had in the undertaking'. For their own sake, Gilbert thought, the government would speak highly of the value of the acquisition and they could not pass over the services of the army, but they would 'take the whole conduct of the expedition to themselves'.

One or two members of the family had just returned from a visit to Melgund, part of the estate in Angus, where all the old tenants had, it seemed, consented to manage their farms 'according to the modern system of husbandry'. This was of 'great consequence', wrote Brydone's son-in-law, 'as all their farms will be out of lease in the course of a few years, and they will now be gradually improving, instead of getting out of condition as they must have done under the terms of the old leases'. A great deal of Gilbert's time was, however, being taken up with political canvassing and two days after Christmas, Gilbert wrote to his father from Edinburgh, saying that he was packing up his 'dirty clothes' so that he could 'get away early … and breakfast at midday on his way home', admitting that he was 'almost asleep already', and then more significantly, that Mary had 'another grandchild preparing' for him.[18] It was the evening of 29 December when he arrived back at Minto.

Excavation of the foundations at Minto was expected to start at the end of January 1812, and the estate's factor, Robert Selby, had promised to have all ready for the masons by the first of March. Gilbert had begun copying the roll of voting freeholders in the county to send to India but with 'benumbed' fingers, he handed the job over to Mary who said she would try to make it legible. Those whose support Gilbert would need included David Haliburton, Baillie Turnbull, Kerr of Chatto, Gilbert Bethune, the Riddells, Peter Brown, Captain Ormiston and George Wauchope. Among those against him were Walter Scott, Charles Erskine and Scott of Gala, whilst those who were undeclared included Ramsay of Maxtoun.[19] A day or so later, a list of fifty of those who would likely support Alexander Don, and a list of sixty one predicted to vote for Elliot, was put in the bag for India.

The following spring Mary and Gilbert came to London, amid 'the bustle of this vile town', listening to several debates in Parliament. Surprisingly, they were invited to Blackheath where Princess Caroline, the Prince Regent's wife 'was as gracious as possible and asked and talked a great deal' about Lord Minto. She had 'very much improved in her looks'.[20] Battles in both Houses on the Catholic question were scheduled for the 10 and 14 April, and it was expected that members of the Regent's household would vote for the Catholics, whilst the opposition had taken up with the Princess of Wales, merely 'as affording a good subject of attack'. Gilbert told his father that she was going to Kensington Palace for a few weeks 'just to show herself and give a few great dinners' to prove that she was not banished to Blackheath.[21]

Writing again to Lord Minto towards the end of April Gilbert told him that the Lennel household had been full of invalids. Williamina, still very weak, could only just walk after suffering an intermittent fever but her looks had improved and there was hope of her 'turning out a beauty after all'. The children were perfect, and little Mary 'who did not speak at all when (her parents had) left her now chatters'. The family had, nevertheless, moved into the new wing of the house at Minto by the second week of May, where they received the sad news of Sir William Eliot of Stob's death from a stroke. Gilbert could tell his father little about the funeral arrangements as a consequence of another death three days before, that of the prime minister, Spencer Perceval's assassination, an event which 'naturally excited the utmost horror on all sides'.[22]

Two thirds of the way through May, Mary picked up her pen determined to tell Lord Minto 'the truth, the whole truth, and nothing but the truth' about the children. She perceived 'from all the letters from India lately' that members of the family had said things about Gilbert which were not true, and which she hoped his Lordship would not believe. Reminding him that young Mary was a good example of someone who could twist members of the family round her smallest finger: 'she is not pretty and never will be – remember, you must believe me, nobody does'. Although her eyes were large, black and brilliant, her mouth and nose were nondescript and 'her chin as beautiful as her Papa's ... (and) her colour outdoing Aunt Harriet's', she herself would never be a beauty. Mary feared that little Gilbert had the advantage of his sister and, in her opinion, he was not a handsome boy. Although she knew that 'Lady Minto would kill me' if she knew what she had written, Mary simply wanted everyone to accept that he was a handsome and 'merry, healthy-looking boy', which satisfied her 'most perfectly'.

'A coach load of Brydones' arrived at Minto on 18 May. Entry into the new house had not been easy, the only way in being at a window, then through the north anteroom, the library, the small anteroom, and so into the round hall and the drawing room. The intention was that the family would 'still inhabit some of the rooms in the west wing', but everything was as warm and comfortable as possible and although the bare walls made it look 'like a new item, the rooms are excellent, and the view beautiful'. It was a great treat for them to see the bridge and the pond again. The previous day they had encountered no small difficulty 'in finding a safe way' for Brydone to get around. As Mary explained, 'though he still sees enough to be able to walk about on smooth ground, it would never do for him to go down stairs without banisters, and walk over stones and planks as we do every day, without fear or dread'. Young Gilbert had taken to running about in 'all sorts of dangerous looking places to the great annoyance of all strangers' but he and his mother had no fear so long as he paid attention to those which were strictly forbidden. Hopes were high that the fine Minto air would benefit the whole family but both elderly Mrs Brydone and Williamina found the conditions somewhat harsh when compared to Lennel. So far as Patrick was concerned, he was undoubtedly in good spirits and enjoying the change of scene amazingly, and 'really wild about little Mary', who was as fond of him as he of her, she entertaining her Papa in the nursery 'with a great many extraordinary words and gestures'.[23]

While moving items around at Minto House at the beginning of July, the family began to find 'little comforts' about them in the new wing. Banisters were on the stairs, but 'water closets and a few more such luxuries' were still lacking. Gilbert had examined 'bags of old letters' which had been put in the library closet to await burning 'as they were rather at a loss for room for such things'. A great number of them were from his grandfather to the Justice's clerk, 'full of all the politics and party history of the day', along with 'a great many other very interesting family letters' which, as he told Lord Minto, 'I intend to sort and try if I can (to) get them stitched into a book as they are too brittle and too much torn already to be tied up in bundles, or to bear much handling'. With the fleet for India about to sail, Gilbert closed a long letter to his father with the news that Mary expected to be confined any day, the 'howdie', a midwife, was expected in two days time, and her charge had promised 'not to keep her waiting long'.[24]

In the autumn, Gilbert learned that the government proposed to dissolve parliament 'as soon as the state of the harvest' admitted it. He would soon not have a moment to talk or write to anybody but 'the worthy freeholders of the county of Roxburgh'. On top of other duties, he had been appointed to 'the command of the new establishment of the local militia of the county'. While an election could have taken place under more favourable circumstances, Gilbert accepted the timing could also have been worse. He had more 'absolute promises' and, even supposing the King's death made another dissolution possible, the candidate thought circumstances were in his favour. Not all Gilbert's support could be relied upon, as he soon discovered, and promises began to be reneged upon. Voting intentions altered once electors found that promised appointments in India had been made.

Electioneering meant that Minto was a hive of activity for several weeks, a contrast to the quiet ease of the couple's regular sojourns at Lennel with the Brydones. Visitors included the lawyer and political maverick, Sir Samuel and his wife, Lady Romilly, who were on their way 'to canvass the 7,000 voters of Bristol'.[25] Others were George Wilson (possibly the Edinburgh doctor of that name), Francis Horner, a local politician, and Thomson and Murray – about whom nothing is known. Gilbert accepted that they were at least 'some relief from my 133 friends to whom I have been devoted for some weeks'.

Parliament was dissolved at the end of the month, with voting taking place across the country between 5 October and 10 November. Gilbert won his seat at Roxburgh on the second day of November but the Tory party under Lord Liverpool held on to power. He had a majority over Don of seven votes, large enough to discourage his opponent from petitioning against him for vote rigging, as he had threatened in the early part of the day. The Duke was already talking of bringing more of his friends on to the roll, with the result that Gilbert did not think it would be very long before the battle would have to be fought again. Unexpectedly, Rutherford had taken 'a more active part' against him, losing him several seats towards the end of the canvass, whereas Captain Ormiston, who was on the point of death, had attended the election, being carried into an adjacent room, saying he was determined to vote for Gilbert 'though it should kill him'.

The result of the election nearly coincided with reports about Lord Minto's recall and the appointment of Lord Moira in his stead. Gilbert told his father that he could hardly suppose that they would 'act so ungraciously ... as to recall you so near the time they know you to have fixed for your resignation'. In July that year, Lord Moira, an Irish army officer and politician who had always been expected to become Irish viceroy, had supported Wellesley's narrowly defeated motion in favour of Catholic relief. Financial problems put paid to promotion in Ireland and in October the idea of sending him to India, instigated by the Prince Regent with whom he had long enjoyed a strange but sincere relationship, emerged.[26] Gilbert accepted that Lord Moira's 'desperate circumstances' made India 'a great object to him'.[27]

Writing from Minto, Gilbert's Mary wrote a long letter to her father-in-law in November. Referring initially to her husband's own accomplishments, she was soon referring to the prospect of seeing him, although anxious that he might feel disappointed at seeing his 'Scotch grandchildren'. Mary wanted to prepare him for the one thing she knew he disliked 'excessively', that both Gilbert and Mary spoke 'very broad Scotch' but knowing also that a year's residence in England would cure it entirely. Mary regretted behaving contrary to his wishes in having kept a Scotch nurse but 'it would have been madness in me to have parted with such a treasure as Alice'. The language of the Elliot's young Mary was, she wrote, the most extraordinary thing she ever heard; 'she talks for ever, repeats every word she hears ... but nobody ... can understand a word. It is more like broken German than anything else ... She knows the art of winning gentlemen's hearts already as she is the decided favourite both of Papa and Grandpapa'. As for Gilbert, he was 'as nice a fellow as ever was seen' but she warned Lord Minto to 'beware of expecting to see a handsome boy'. When Frederick, the 'beauty and wonder of the family' arrived, his mother said, 'He really is a magnificent animal, and is not at present very handsome; I am the more proud of him as he is all my own, he never yet having had a spoon in his mouth', being breastfed, and 'he will probably be like any other nice child of a year old'.

With the 'Lennelites' all well, and Papa 'really wonderfully so, and his spirits excellent', the prospect of his being able to see Lord Minto again was a happiness which, as Mary said, 'he says he never durst look forward to and which he now allows himself to indulge in'. Telling his Lordship that her 'headquarters' would be at Lennel while Gilbert was in London, Mary included a 150-word letter written by their five-year-old son to his grandfather, under the eye of Mr Scott, his tutor. It spoke of him being sent to Lennel during his father's election as there was no room for the children at Minto. A history lesson had necessitated a map of Europe on the wall, which was being used for ancient history, being replaced by one of Asia. Telling 'dear Grandpapa' that he didn't know who he liked like best in Roman history, he said it was 'because I have not read it all'.[28]

Rumours in London suggested that Lord Moira would sail for India in early February and Gilbert planned to be in town at the end of January 1813. Writing to Calcutta on 19 January, he admitted that he was 'more in love' with the conduct of ministers and felt that the family had, at last, been compensated by the step up in the peerage from baron to Viscount Melgund and Earl Minto, announced eventually on 24 February, enabling Gilbert and later eldest sons to be given the courtesy title of Lord Melgund. Even so, there was a hitch when Lady Loudoun, Moira's wife, miscarried and the new governor's departure had to be put back to April. With 'glorious news from the continent', and every week producing great events, Gilbert hoped somewhat mysteriously that his brother Captain George was 'filling his pockets with American prizes' during the war of 1812 when he was more likely to have been aboard HMS *Hussar* in the East Indies.[29]

The following month, Gilbert was still in London, Mary with the children at Lennel, and Lady Minto continued to await an opportunity to leave Edinburgh for Minto. Writing to Lord Melville at the Admiralty, Gilbert requested that HMS *Hussar* be sent to Calcutta to bring his father home, only to discover to his chagrin that the gazetting of Lord Minto's earldom was going to cost upwards of a thousand pounds in fees and stamp duty. He consulted Mr Coutts Trotter about the transport of his father's 'savings', and the banker recommended he should bring them back in the form of bullion. Despite the insurance to be paid, there would be 'great gain by doing so'. He 'would know best whether there was any impropriety in it'.[30]

Gilbert, now Viscount Melgund, told Earl Minto that he had listened to two late sessions in the House of Lords in March 1813. Mary, who 'had been as provident as Mrs Gilpin', William Cowper's frugal and careful soul, had packed him off with six large boxes of pills with strict instructions to Robert, his servant, to see that he took them. In London, Gilbert had lived in the houses of the Lansdownes and the Hollands, the great Whig families, also the Carnegies of Gloucester Place, but they had taken a house in Cheltenham for a year. 'They will be' he wrote 'a sad loss to me as their house was a sort of home to me during my widowhood here'. Reporting his experience in parliament, he informed his father that he had 'stood the long nights and bad air of the House of Commons much better than (he) expected' and certainly had very little reason to hope that either his head or his stomach would allow him to sit out a debate of four nights as he had done on Grattan's motion for Catholic relief.[31]

In the event, the early part of 1814 proved especially cold and very snowy. Parts of the Solway Firth were frozen solid by mid-January and the Thames gradually froze such that by the first of February some hardy souls were venturing out on to the ice. As the numbers increased, drinks stalls, printing presses selling souvenir cards marked *Printed on the Thames* had appeared. Swings, merry-go-rounds and donkey rides followed, with one stall building a fire on which a sheep was roasted. The 'Frost Fair' lasted till a thaw was apparent five or six days later. In March, Mary gave birth to William Hugh Elliot who was to become a politician and social reformer. Separated from her husband for seven long weeks, Mary told Lord Minto that it had given her 'very great satisfaction' to have been so long at Lennel since 'I really feel that I have been of use, and every moment spent in Papa's company now is valuable, his health and spirits are excellent but I dare not trust myself to think of the change that you will otherwise perceive in him'. Her mother was 'remarkably well', and young Gilbert's studies though 'not very profound yet', occupied 'a good deal' of Mary's time. Both Frederick and Gilbert were well and 'a double amusement' to Papa, with the older child growing like him in his manners 'and sometimes even in looks'.[32]

The family found it unusually difficult to establish when Lord Minto and his party would reach home waters but at last in April news came that they were off Southern Ireland aboard HMS *Hussar*, Lord Melville having agreed to its deployment. Eleanor Elliot (Nina), his great niece and William's wife, was to describe at the end of the nineteenth century what happened. Good news about the war was passed to Captain George's vessel by a passing frigate which signalled the words '*Peace with France, the old kingdom (of the Bourbons) restored*' and an Irish vessel then told them '*the Emperor of the West is sent to Elba – relegates ad insulas*'. The Allies had entered Paris in March, and with the abdication of Napoleon the following month and his exile, Britain hoped for an end to this long period of war. Eleven days later, Lord Minto was in London writing to his wife, telling her how it was one of the happiest days of his life and that there was 'one happier still in store, when I shall have you once more in my arms'. He reckoned the longest he was likely to remain in the south was a fortnight.[33]

Ironically, Lady Minto had written to her husband at almost the same time, saying how she had begun to think that 'she did a very wrong thing to stay at home'. After such a long separation, she could easily have travelled to London to meet him but she had chosen to leave the arrangements in someone else's hands. As Nina was to say, Lady Minto 'shivered' in Scotland in sympathy with some Malay boys who had been among the first detachment of the returning party. With 'their ship's clothing' exchanged for that made of flannel, one of the children at Minto asked 'are they my cousins?' and on being told not, said 'I am glad of that, as I should rather not have black cousins, but they are very nice'. Black boys and white then 'went off to the hills together, which the little darkies climbed on all fours, chattering most excitedly in their native lingo'.[34] In London, such of the family as were there assembled to receive the returning governor, and he received 'a very cordial reception from everybody of all descriptions', the chairman of the East India Company inviting him to one of the company's court dinners.

Nevertheless on 27 May, Lord Minto playfully warned his wife in Edinburgh that 'young and beautiful as I am, I feel I am not equal to the fatigues, either mental or bodily, of public business in England. My legs improve a little, and I hope to make them younger at Minto, but really young they can never be, of course, and I am not only content to toddle on with you through the rest of my journey, but shall think and find it the best part of our lives'.[35] Apparently the third of June had been fixed for Lord Minto's departure from London to Scotland, but the day after his letter to Edinburgh an event occurred which altered his plan. As Nina wrote: it was 'big with fate'. Explaining more, she said that Lord Auckland, the husband of Lord Minto's sister Eleanor, had gone to rest in perfect health, but 'was found dead in his bed by his daughters when they went to summon him to breakfast'. In order to be with his sister in her overwhelming grief, and to follow his brother-in-law to the grave, Lord Minto at once postponed his departure. Unhappily, the funeral was arranged to take place at night in Beckenham (in Kent), the parish in which Eden Farm, the home of the bereaved family, was situated. The 'sad procession by road from London to Beckenham and the subsequent funeral service occupied five hours – from half past seven till half past twelve, in a cold drizzling rain'.

Four days later, she said, they sensed the coming tragedy when 'a cold which Lord Minto had complained of before had been greatly increased by the exposure of that fatal night. He was ordered to stay indoors'. On 13 June he confessed himself so low in strength and spirit that he could not attempt a letter. In proportion to his bodily weakness was the increase of his passionate longing to reach Minto; and his family, having no apprehension of any impending danger, were equally anxious to get him out of town and in the safe keeping of his home. With the affectionate kindness which never flagged, he resolved to visit Lady Malmesbury at Park Place (in the village of Remenham, near Henley-on-Thames) although this added at least another day to the length of his journey. 'There' Nina continued, 'he made the greatest exertion to conceal his weakness, and his conversation was cheerful and gay; but by this time his eldest son, his constant companion and now tender nurse, was greatly, though still insufficiently, alarmed. A medical man was sent for to attend them on their journey, and from him it was for the first time ascertained that Lord Minto was suffering from an attack of a most alarming disease, which, under the treatment of those days, too frequently proved fatal'.[36] His longing to push on was, however, too strong to be opposed; he had 'but one wish, to see the person on whom his thoughts are ever fixed; one anxiety – to reach home'. The rest, Nina wrote, could be guessed: 'Stevenage in Hertfordshire on the northern road was reached by short stages, but in a state of prostration which left no room for hope; there his Lordship quietly sank early in the night on 21 June', and died.[37] He was buried in Westminster Abbey on 29 June 1814.

In her concluding remarks, Nina made use of 'a few affecting lines' written by Gilbert many years later, and found by his children, obviously intended to find a place in the opening chapter of a biography of his father. After referring to his 'laborious and absorbing duties in India, and his gratifying reception in London', Gilbert turned to his death, writing: 'Thus at once were dashed those hopes in the moment of their accomplishment, which had been the solace of seven years of painful separation ... the first object of our reverence was lost'. Ending her account of the period from 1807 to 1814, Nina said that 'the last year's letters from Minto in India – so full of hope and joy – were found tied together with a black string, and inscribed 'Poor Fools'. With these was a note with unbroken seal, the last written by Lady Minto to her husband'.[38]

Without doubt, Brydone had eagerly awaited the return of Lord Minto from his 'imprisonment' in India, and had been as frustrated as other members of the family by frequently delayed or lost correspondence, which made separation even harder to bear. In particular, the old tutor was to be deprived of any opportunity of meeting to discuss matters of the day with someone he greatly admired. For Mary and her children, Gilbert's father was to remain an important public figure with a warm heart and much love of his family, but someone nonetheless who remained a shadowy influence in their lives. Fortunately for the reader, Mary's use of plain and forthright words without being over-forward in much of her correspondence often revealed what others omitted. To the feminine and motherly point of view was added her father's persistent curiosity. Although there is some doubt whether the Brydones and Lord Minto met, Mary anticipated the event and was constantly probing the outcome, 'when we meet'. She shared a keenly felt disappointment with her father that Lord Minto would never have seen his 'Scotch grandchildren', nor heard the children speak their 'very broad Scotch'. A dislike of sentimentality, and the easy expression she showed in her letters to her aristocratic father-in-law demonstrated an almost unconscious classlessness.

# CHAPTER 15

# The Final Years
# (1815–1818)

Napoleon escaped from Elba at the end of February 1815 and an incident between his 'Hundred Day' rule which ended in June with the Battle of Waterloo, and October when he was began his exile on the mid-Atlantic island of St Helena, would have brought back memories for Brydone. Reaching Rochefort, a port on France's west coast from which he had hoped to cross to America, Napoleon surrendered aboard HMS *Bellerophon* off Rochefort, just south of where Brydone's first encounter with the French had taken place well over fifty years previously. However, with several hundred wounded British officers and men still remaining in Brussels, the effects of war were still being felt.

As we look at the last four years of the ex-soldier, traveller and polymath's life through the eyes of his wife, daughters and son-in-law, his quiet retirement was regularly enlivened by all manner of family activity. After heavy snow at Minto in January 1815, February was marked by several days above freezing point, with Mary recording temperatures between 33 and 35 degrees in her journal. On the eighth, Lord Minto, Captain George and John Elliot, the MP, went to Lauder in order to hunt the following day which turned out to be 'a beautiful morning' and a 'most delightful day'. Five days later, Mary's journal noted the fourth birthday of Mary Elizabeth. As her daily temperature measurements rose into the forties, the first Lord Minto's youngest daughter, Catherine, left them on 20 February, Mary's sister Elizabeth arrived to stay some ten days, and Gilbert and John Elliot hunted at Crailing, a village in Teviotdale. Two days later there was 'drizzly rain' and the two men left Mary to visit Mellerstain House, the home of the Baillie family on their way to Edinburgh. At the end of the month, on a sunny day and in a temperature of 42 degrees, sailor George and his wife Eliza whom he had married in 1810, set off for the capital, while two of Lord Minto's daughters, Harriet and Anna Maria, went to Bothwell, a town to the south-east of Glasgow. It was late at night on 5 March when Gilbert arrived from London and on the twelfth, with wind and 'amid showers of sleet', he went on from Minto to Lennel.[1]

Despite some loss of sight which restricted his movements, Brydone had as normal an old age as many of his contemporaries, with memories playing a disproportionate part. The two family homes, and occasional excursions to Edinburgh provided no mean stimulus. In his own later life, Sir Walter Scott was to say that old Brydone was 'still as good a companion as any he could recommend'. His family usually read a little for his amusement of an evening, and on one occasion he was asked if he would like to hear some of his travels to Sicily. He assented, and seemed to listen with much pleasure for some time but, unable to concentrate for long and starting up from a doze, he exclaimed: 'That's really a very amusing book, and it contains many curious anecdotes. I wonder if they are all true'.[2]

Loss of concentration would have frustrated much of his discourse, but his directness remained. He was always mildly archaic both in language and tradition, and happiest when crossing boundaries, both mentally and geographically. Rarely showing any schadenfreude or delight at another's misfortune, he never acted in a curmudgeonly manner. Money, including gifts or loans to friends, was regularly on his mind and also when he made his will in 1812, appointing his three daughters as his executors. Generous as always, among loans he made at this time were two to members of the Marjoribanks family and bonds of two or three thousand pounds in 1793, 1816 and 1817 to other acquaintances, along with Matthew Sandilands, his solicitor cousin.

Looking back, Brydone would have had no doubt about how significant had been the watershed when Lord North invited him to take his sons George and Francis under his tutorial wing. He would have recalled the greater educative purpose in his work at this time, unlike the brash social climbing motivation exhibited by some of his previous clients, if not their offspring. The North family had a strong sense of honesty and honour which could not have differed more greatly from the situation in corruption-ridden Russia. He also found himself afforded opportunities to learn more about art and the natural world, occasionally finding that his charges had as much concern for him as he did for them. The accolade given him by the boys' grandfather, in respect of the 'rational entertainments' he had provided, was unusual, if not unique. Furthermore, Brydone's subsequent appointment to the Stamp Office had given him the wherewithal to move into Lennel House, the 'snug ... pleasant spot' he had long wished for. His subsequent care of Frederick, the family's youngest son, in Nice further cemented his relationship with the North family.

In many ways, the whole-length portrait of Brydone painted in 1817 by Andrew Geddes and bequeathed to the British Museum in 1902, sums up his life at Lennel House at this time. Born in Edinburgh, Geddes had been five years in the Excise Office there, his father being a deputy auditor. The mezzotint, showed Brydone wearing a coat with a velvet collar, white waistcoat, knee breeches and boots, two sticks are placed at the end of the sofa, with 'chemical apparatus' on the table behind. The evident homeliness is set in time by the reminder of his early life, provided not only by the map of Sicily on the wall but the potted arum lily on the floor symbolising his botanic interests.[3]

Visitors to Lennel from outside the family during these last years were rare. Nevertheless, Robert Burns describes Brydone and Mary, his wife, in the notes he made after taking tea with them at Coldstream where he also spent the night during his journey through the Borders in May 1787. Evoking some of the socialist views which the poet later inspired, Brydone had, Burns said, 'a most excellent heart, kind, joyous and benevolent' despite possessing 'a good deal of the French indiscriminate compliance' (a reference to the French Revolution) on account of 'his situation past and present' and his being 'an admirer of everything that bears a splendid title, or that possesses a large estate'.[4]

Eighty-year-old Brydone, born and married into the manse, had strong views about religion and would have heard of Richard Watson, the Bishop of Llandaff's *Reply to Canon Recupero and others, who suppose that the appearances in the vicinity of Etna and Vesuvius are opposed to the Mosaic account of the Creation* which appeared in 1815. Also that year, Dr Adam Clarke, a liberal Wesleyan minister and scholar, entered the debate. After travelling widely in Europe, and being no stranger to theological controversy, he took issue with Brydone in his commentary on Genesis, asserting that the Mosaic account of creation was 'the most ancient, and the most likely to be true', and that the tutor's views were simply based on 'the evidence of different eruptions of Mount Etna' provided by Canon Recupero, the volcano's expert. It was 'a sneer against revelation, the bishops, and orthodoxy'. He thought that Recupero would be 'exceedingly embarrassed' to know that the eruption to which Brydone referred, formed the lowest of seven distinct lavas which 'must have flowed from the mountain at least fourteen thousand years ago!'. Clarke's description of the tutor's argument as one 'in insidious dress', would certainly not have pleased Brydone.[5]

Gilbert, Brydone's son-in-law, formally took his seat in the House of Lords in March 1816, but his interest in politics had serious competition from his family responsibilities and the efforts being made to rebuild Minto House. Although he attended the Upper House a dozen or so times two years later, and voted assiduously during debates in 1825 about Catholic Relief, it was 1832 before he became a Whig diplomat and minister. Mary and Gilbert had had their first child, Gilbert/Gilly in 1807 but they were to have their lives, and those of their grandparents torn apart like so many others at that time by the early death of children. With few remedies for childhood illnesses, beyond a nourishing diet and keeping the patient warm, it was not surprising that as many as 25 per cent of children died before their fifth birthday. Fortunately for the Elliots, their first girl, Mary Elizabeth, who was born in 1811, was to live for sixty-three years, but Frederick, born in 1812 had died three years later. Other children born by 1818 who had full lives were William (1814), Frances/Fanny (1815), Henry (1817) and Charles

(1818). Two more boys and three more girls were born between 1822 and 1827.

With peace at last in Europe, it would seem that during the winter of 1815/16, several Elliot parents with offspring in or around their teens, or who could be taken with them, met to discuss plans for a visit together to Italy. Those involved were Lady Minto, the first earl's widow with three nearly grown-up daughters, Captain George and his wife Eliza who were just starting their family, along with Gilbert and Mary. The project had been fully explained to Mary's sisters who were not averse to taking full responsibility for their aged parents, and it was ascertained that the family as a whole probably had sufficient financial resources to pay for an extended, if still economical visit. With more children in prospect, and the cost of their upbringing and marriage likely to rise steeply in future years, it seemed a very appropriate time. The traveller Brydone could only be pleased that his eldest daughter and family would be retracing many of the paths he had followed fifty years before.

An unusual traveller and writer, Dr Samuel Heinrich Spiker, a member of the Royal Society and librarian in the Berlin library of King Frederick William III of Prussia, almost passed Brydone's front door at Coldstream in July 1816.[6] Departing from London in the middle of June where he had been warmly welcomed, Dr Spiker visited Oxford, Birmingham, Sheffield, Manchester and Durham, en route for Scotland and later Wales, the Isle of Wight and southern England, returning to Cuxhaven from Harwich. Not unlike our ex-traveller, he wanted to see how the process of industrialisation in Britain was proceeding, and who the people were behind it. His road to Newcastle took him past Ravensworth Castle, the home of Sir Henry Liddell, whose daughter would become the second wife of Gilbert and Mary's son, Admiral Charles Elliot. Reaching Berwick, and its fifteen-arched bridge over the river Tweed, where its chief trade was the salmon fishery, the librarian affirmed from experience 'that the flavour of this fish is fully deserving of the high character it has obtained'. Between Berwick and Press, 'not properly a village but merely a solitary inn for changing horses' as the librarian explained, they 'saw the ocean in all its majesty' but only a few small fishing boats were visible at a considerable distance, with 'their white sails skimming like seagulls along the surface'.[7]

Servants, the post and newspapers, let alone those at Lennel, would have heard about Dr Spiker's progress towards Edinburgh where he was to reside till 26 July. Before reaching Haddington on their way to the capital, and passing over 'a handsome bridge', the rails of which were of 'cast iron, and very light and elegant', the German and his party had been greatly impressed by Amisfield, the country seat of the Earl of Wemys, built in the rich style of the eighteenth century.[8] A month after Brydone's death, *The Scots Magazine*'s 'Monthly List of New Publications' gave news that Dr Spiker's *Travels* had been published in Berlin and that an English translation was in preparation.

So far as Mary and the children were concerned they set out on what was to be their Grand Tour in March 1816 and by the end of the month they were 'near the far end' of England, at Sittingbourne in Kent after an easy and smooth journey. There they were joined by Gilbert and his mother, Lady Minto, and the 'whole train' of her daughters. Mary told her mother that she was 'completely bewildered' by the number of people around her, including some who were only there to wish them *bon voyage*.[9] However, the crossing to France presented no difficulties, and once in Paris Mary was able to acknowledge both the 'delightful account' of her father's progress she had received from Elizabeth, and how there was nothing she liked 'half so well as driving about this beautiful city'. Using a style of writing not dissimilar to that adopted by Brydone, she was soon referring to the 'stiffness in the dialogue' at the theatre, which meant she understood less than she had expected, and noting that the day temperature in Paris was 62 degrees. She also told her father that 'his little Fanny', Frances, was 'the delight of everyone' who saw her; she talked and laughed all the time. William had grown into 'quite a pretty little boy' and was much thinner than when Brydone had last seen him.[10]

Ten days into May found the party in Geneva after a journey marked, as Lord Minto told Mrs Brydone, by 'fine sights, dirty beds, wonderful adventures, lofty mountains (and) jackboots'. The weather across France had been as hot as in Lennel with the trees all in leaf but the pear trees had lost their blossom. Gilbert said that two days of climbing brought them 'to the top of the world' where they shared the snow with cattle, within sight of the lake.[11] In August, after several months in and around Geneva they went on to Chamonix from where they could see Mont Blanc, visiting St Martin where they left their carriage and took a charabanc and two horses. A short stay at Chambéry in the Savoy region of France followed. After a night on the Simplon Pass, the party reached Milan where Captain George, who was staying with Eliza in 'beautiful surroundings' nearby, prior to going to Venice, arranged an evening for the family at *Teatro alla Scala*. Subsequently, Mary and Gilbert were able to leave the children in Milan and explore the Italian Lakes for two days where they were captivated by Belgerate on the banks of Lake Maggiore.

The couple were at Genoa in October, a place which was to play a major role in the latter part of Mary's life. She stayed nearby at Nervi for lengthy periods on medical advice, and was visited there by several of her children before her death. Lady Minto, the Dowager Countess of Minto, and her daughters arrived separately. The sea and ships in the bay caught the eye, along with streets which were both very narrow and very broad. The large house where they were living had ceilings 'all covered with pictures'. The bells of Genoa's many churches were remarked upon, Mary telling those at Lennel that two large and one small bell were 'close to Mr Menzies's room (presumably her husband's valet), and Gilbert threw a stick against the roof of the church one day'. Fanny was beginning 'to talk like a parrot' and sang 'Bow, wow, wow', while William was beginning to say his alphabet.

Halfway through November when shade was still at a premium, and the children were able to play in the garden of their house in Genoa, George and Eliza arrived. Mary wrote that she sincerely pitied them 'for all the discomfort' she anticipated them experiencing. George, she said, was always very much against the Genoa plan and if it had not been for Eliza's confinement she was sure 'he never would have come'. Mary wondered whether she would ever again be able to accept their 'old arrangement' after enjoying a house 'quite to themselves'. It seemed 'so extraordinary to have the children playing in the evening exactly in the way (she had) so long wished them to do'. Both her parents would have been reminded of their own daughters' childhood at Lennel.[12]

When lodgings became a problem in Genoa, opinion about the city altered and Mary was soon calling it 'that vile odorous town'. Negotiations about alternative accommodation followed and by 11 November Mary was writing from the Casa Masson, an apartment near Genoa. The town was a 'trap' and with the possible exception of the opera, social life was tiresome and prosaic, especially the card playing. The dull *conversazione* at Government House showed that the princesses in the palace knew little of such matters, elated as they were 'with their own magnificence'. She had, however, received a 'quite delightful' letter about Brydone from her mother which also said how 'quite right and proper' it was that Elizabeth and Williamina who had visited Edinburgh should 'keep up all the acquaintances they already have and make as many more as possible'. She knew how much 'those little spurts of gaiety' needed to be repeated frequently.[13]

As 1816 came to a close, Mary replied to another supportive letter from old Mrs Brydone, explaining she had been in the kitchen 'weighing beef, mutton and veal, feeling chickens and throwing out bits of butter, legs of ham and dressed meat'. Examining the state of the larder every day, and never allowing the cook to order anything except vegetables and poultry, was routine, but, as she told her mother, he still managed to cheat them and although they were going to part with him, the chances were that they would find 'another just as bad'. She found it 'so abominable … to be surrounded with rogues', and Robert, their servant, 'notwithstanding his many merits', was perfectly useless in a case of this sort, being 'the most extravagant person himself'. Care with money and budgeting in a foreign land was not easy, and Lord Minto was becoming belatedly concerned about economies.

The English community in Genoa was small, some three or four aristocratic families and a few more from among the gentry spending the winter there. It was not long before the daughters of Mrs Locke and those of the Dowager Countess Minto, Anna Maria and Harriet (probably in their early twenties) and Catherine (in her late teens), repeatedly met up at Miss Berry's and other balls. Finding society dull, Mary was thankful that they were living in a country where 'there were always things to interest one'. Furthermore, as she continued telling her mother: 'I have always plenty to occupy and interest me sufficiently at home, and I am so perfectly happy in the enjoyment of my own liberty, that tho' I see all the disadvantages of (Genoa), and even feel some of them, I cannot bear the prospect of quitting it'. She nevertheless realised that financial constraints on the family were such that they would now not be able 'to accomplish as much as (they) expected', and that their stay in Northern Italy would have to end soon if they were to also enjoy the sights of Rome and Naples. Reassuring her mother that the children had 'the highest good looks' Mary told her that William had become a 'noisy fellow' and 'the brats' had struck up a friendship with George, a son of the eponymous captain, and Foley whom 'they meet every five days in the Doria garden'. Young Mary and Georgiana were also great friends and Eliza and 'her very nice baby' were thriving.[14]

Lord Minto also wrote to Mrs Brydone at Lennel at the beginning of January 1817, warning her not to believe a word of what Mary said about Genoa as she was 'unaccountably prejudiced against it'. In his view, it was 'in every respect the most desirable situation in which we could have settled for the winter' and a detailed account of its virtues followed. Knowing full well that one of his three carers would read what he wrote to his father-in-law, Gilbert carefully touched on some of the port's advantages and disadvantages when compared with cities like Paris and London, Genoa's being largely due to its hillside location near the sea. He threatened to write about the environs of the city and send 'a most curious and interesting chapter on society, manners and morals, all of which are equally attractive and novel to persons who have been bred in the barbarous North'.[15]

Soon afterwards, the family set off on their journey southward, passing through Rome and arriving in Naples probably at the end of February. There, the bay captivated their hearts, particularly in the moonlight. The house where they were staying was only a hundred yards or so from that of Sir William Hamilton, with its 'long projection over the sea' which Brydone visited in 1770. Writing to her father on 5 March, Mary expressed her 'surprise and wonder' at Vesuvius, 'that extraordinary mountain'. It was so much more than what she remembered him saying about streams of lava, showers of ash, and craters. Her notions of such matters had been 'extremely imperfect', and a little relieved to learn that a book by a Mr Playfair showed that he too found the mountain very different from what he had imagined.[16] The journey up to the cone of the volcano, Mary said, was 'as easy as it would be to ride in an armchair on the back of the fair Rosebud (a family horse) to Coldstream'. She would not have thought twice about putting her mother on a donkey and having their servant, Antonio, guide them 'in perfect safety'. Closing her letter, she said how delighted she had been to hear that Brydone was determined to have his picture painted with him lying on his couch, doing what he pleased.[17]

Two days later, what Mary had to tell her mother was not all good news. The couple had seen more of Eliza and her children than ever before, but her ménage was more 'wretched and comfortless' than she expected and the tidiness previously in the nursery had disappeared. 'Dreadful mismanagement' had allowed the youngest child to 'become a poor, yellow, lean, non-thriven thing covered from head to foot with a violent rash' which made Lord Minto and her quite wretched'.[18] Happily a day or so later, and with 'the top of Vesuvius white with snow', Mary's mood changed, and to please her mother, she told her that all the children were 'very much admired, and often spoken to', in public. The weather had been rather hazy for some time, with a strong Sirocco blowing and many people complaining about how difficult it was to walk, but she was as 'happy as a princess'. After a visit to Monte Nuovo, Mary told her mother, 'in a short time we shall be off for Paestum', a place, she said, that had enchanted Lady Lansdowne (Louisa Fox-Strangeways).[19]

Three weeks later, Gilbert wrote to Brydone at Lennel, waxing lyrical about the superb view they had enjoyed of Capri and the islands from the Hermitage during a second ascent of Vesuvius. With the help of their guides, Mr Menzies and Uncle George found pieces of soft lava in the ashes. Recalling their visit to Paestum, an important Graeco-Roman city founded in the seventh century, some fifty miles south of Naples, Gilbert said that they dined at Salerno, on the way before reaching Eboli with its olive woods. Seven o'clock the next morning, the party set off for Paestum where they saw a large palace of the King in the wood and three temples. After one dedicated to Neptune, another called 'the Basilica', they went to the temple of Ceres, each with thirteen or fourteen pillars each side and six at the end. Then, 'dining out of doors', they returned to Salerno to sleep. Next day at Pompeii, people were 'very hard at work carrying away ... rubbish'. Almost all 'the fine temples have the floors paved and the walls lined with red marble, and a great deal of mosaic is made of red marble'. Mary and Fanny were well, and William could feed himself.[20]

Leaving its most southerly destination towards the end of April, the party turned northward bound for Rome. Travelling by what Gilbert told Mrs Brydone was called a *voiturino*, a hired coach, proved to have its hazards. Crossing the Pontine Marshes on a bad road to Rome, the first post house changed two of their horses for two that were far worse. 'On the second day', he said, 'one of our horses fell in going down a hill and looked as if he was dead; the postillion beat him on the head as they always do with ... his whip'. At Nitri, everyone was very poor and all the men *banditti*, while the robbers at Fondi were almost as bad. They were apparently nearly stopped on account of some mistake in their passports, and had there been accommodation in the town, 'we should have been obliged to stay there all night', wrote Gilbert, 'knowing that all the inhabitants were *banditti*'. Once in Rome, however, they were greatly impressed by the size of St Peter's and the Vatican, Nero's Palace, the beauty of the statues, and the view from the top of the Coliseum. Days of exploration followed, but the threat of an outbreak of scarlet fever, and after seeing only half of what they had intended, the party brought forward their departure to Florence.

The journey to the capital of Tuscany, a distance of little under 200 miles, was accomplished speedily on account of the party travelling post, and with a courier who spoke English, French and Italian. He went ahead of them, taking the best rooms, one of which often had a fireplace. 'We always had a very good breakfast, dinner and supper', Gilbert explained, 'which was not the case in our other journeys as we always had the worst rooms, the worst meat, and very little of it'. Only in Perugia, 'the largest town except Rome in the Pope's dominions, the posting (was) very bad and we got the worst horses'. With the six-day journey to Florence behind them, they took a room in an inn with a balcony and made much use of the *Barboli* and the *Cascine* gardens for the children. Pictures were painted of the house they rented, with Fanny looking at a coloured picture book, and William running around on a hobby horse called 'Macaroni'. He was 'such a nice fellow', and Mary 'such a thoroughly good and amiable, steady person, and so exactly what an elder sister ought to be'. Understandably, young Gilbert, his heir, was the apple of his father's eye, and he always looked on the boy's faults 'in a far more serious light than those of the rest'. He found him 'exceedingly improved in everything' although he had few friends other than the brother of Mlle. Panchaud, whose family lived nearby. However, it was Gilbert's turn to turn against a city where they were staying, and he was glad it would not be long before they were elsewhere. After a few days, and with excellent weather, he told Mrs Brydone: 'we are going in a *felucca* from Lerici to Genoa which I think I shall like very much'.[21] From there the party returned to Chambéry towards the end of June, staying till early August.

On a decidedly 'rainy Sunday' at the end of the third week in June, Mary updated her mother about the children. Gilbert was 'gleefully engaged reading', Mary and William were 'busily employed painting houses with their aunts' and Fanny was 'looking at a little box of coloured pictures, and talking as fast as … her tongue could go'. The prospect of seeing her father and mother at Lennel was 'no small ingredient' in her happiness, but Mary also wanted to explain the cause of a family squabble that had broken out at Chambéry involving the Dowager Lady Minto. 'Our great difficulty all along', she wrote, had been 'how to dispose of Lady Minto and the girls', to smooth their relationship with each other, and to ensure that they were always within 'the reach of the authority and protection of Lord Minto (Gilbert) and George'. Mary especially wanted to assure her mother (and Brydone himself) that Lady Minto's behaviour had been 'wrong, harsh and violent'. What could be more horrible, she wrote, 'than to hear a mother declare that no consideration whatever would make her consent to live six months alone with her three daughters', adding that although she was 'by no means an easy person to live with', kindness and confidence went a great way with her.

One cause of the clash between the families became clear when Gilbert and George agreed 'to give the choice of a residence next winter to the girls'. Various lengths of stay in Paris and London had been alternatives, but they 'unanimously chose to go to Minto for the winter'. It was at this point, Mary explained to her mother, when Gilbert had written to Selby, the Minto factor, about the arrangements which needed to be made for the family's reception, that Lady Minto discovered that her daughter, Anna Maria, 'considered herself as having made a great sacrifice for the good of the family'. Totally at a loss about how to proceed, Gilbert tried to 'get a direct answer from her', and found it impossible. Referring to the original debate they had had about where they were to stay that winter, she had said 'if Harriet and Catherine choose Minto, she was content, but as Mary said, 'it is quite clear that she is reserving a ground of complaint for herself, and whatever plan is adopted that she (would have) nothing to do with it'. These were signs of mental instability.

A few moments after writing to Brydone's mother at the end of July, having been surprised to learn from a friend that his father-in-law had had 'a slight illness', Gilbert drove his heavily pregnant wife in a buggy to the Rhône where they walked together by the side of the river. Soon afterwards her labour started, and at four o'clock in the morning, Mary gave birth to Henry, 'a great boy ... fully as large as William, and not ugly'. He was to become envoy-extraordinary and minister plenipotentiary to Italy between 1863 and 1867. During the course of the previous fortnight, she 'had contrived to tumble down the stairs once, and to fall flat on her face in the courtyard a second time but neither of these feats of activity had done her the least harm'. Mrs Watson, a midwife from Geneva, had been in the house for ten days. He anticipated that the news he was sending her by the Bern post would probably be overtaken by a letter from Mary herself, using the Paris post which was quicker. He had in the meantime given instructions for the news of the birth to be put in the *Kelso Mail*.[22]

A delighted Mary wrote to her mother on 2 July, also passing on thanks to Elizabeth for her letter, and Brydone for his to Gilbert; they had been 'real cordials' to her and a reward to Papa for getting well so quickly. The other children were 'wild with joy', and Mary happy, if missing her mother coming into her room 'with a wise, mysterious-looking face, and then crouching so comfortably by my bedside'. Such was the love and affection in which both Mary's parents were held, although the family spat meant that any plan about where they would spend the winter was still unconfirmed.[23]

With the midwife gone, and Mary advised to 'live on rich soups, pigeons and generous wines for a few days, and above all things abstain from castor oil', Gilbert told the family at Lennel that 'as soon as Mary and the child are moveable we shall transfer ourselves to Interlaken; if Elizabeth has a mind to join us there we will bring her back to you in November but she has no curiosity about Switzerland and is unworthy of fine scenery, so that I hardly expect her tho' if she had any spirit, she would make one of her Edinburgh *beaux* escort her here'.[24] After four weeks of rest and recuperation, it was early August that the couple started preparing for their departure from Savoy in earnest. Agreeing with her mother that 'a little useless French lassie' was quite unfit to be brought to England with them, and thinking of her offer 'to board and lodge' them all at Lennel, Mary felt she had to remind her mother about 'the noise and racket that the creatures made'. In the meantime, it seems that Gilbert's mother had not altered her intention of wintering in Paris.[25]

On the day in August that the family left for Interlaken, a letter arrived from Mrs Brydone containing what could only be described as a 'generous offer': allowing them to remain abroad two or three months longer. Replying, Mary outlined how their eventual accommodation at Lennel could best be used. 'I positively insist', she wrote, 'that Betsey shall sleep in the house, and in this I will (have) no denial. I know that I shall be supported in my demand by Elizabeth and Williamina and therefore I feel sure that you will consent to it and the whole difference it makes in your arrangement is that Mary and Betsey sleep in the little room, and that Gilbert sleeps in my room'. Her mother was welcome to borrow as much bedding from Minto as she needed but Mary thought one of the children's beds would be in her way at Lennel where space was not very abundant.

Mary told her mother how Lady Minto had always considered a visit by the couple to Interlaken as 'a sort of wild notion', nobody could live there. She had submitted to the idea rather than consented to it. Mary explained that they had given her 'every possible account of the place', both from their own observation and from what others had told them, 'not one word of which she believed'. In the event, Lady Minto's arrival clashed with everything. She and her party came a day sooner than expected and nothing was ready. Mary immediately set about arranging a room for them in their 'wee house', they never having shared a house with Lady Minto since they left England, while Lord Minto set off to find accommodation at inns for her entourage. It was ten that night before Mary could say that 'we got them all housed and next morning … the Jungfrau was sparkling in all her splendour, and the whole valley of Interlaken looked so rich, so gay, so inhabitable that Lady Minto was quite enchanted with it'.

The house Mary and Gilbert hoped to move into was presently occupied by Sir Walter James from Berkshire, but he would soon be leaving. George's house, one of three houses the families occupied, was so near that they could walk down to it. William enjoyed it and could walk to it without being carried a step.[26] Ever practical, Mary thought it time to prepare for winter, telling her mother she was already busy making new flannel petticoats for the girls and drawers for Gilbert. William was to be put into trousers later. Convinced that her mother could have no idea how 'noxious' and noisy the bairns were, she said 'Gilbert, Mary, and William were given to high spirits whenever they had an opportunity. Fanny 'did her little best to make as much noise as they did', and when Henry squalled, he could do it to some purpose. 'This is no joke' she declared.[27]

Halfway through September there was increasing concern about the deteriorating health of young Gilbert. Mary immediately wrote to her sisters and parents at Lennel whilst Gilbert asked Benjamin Constant, the writer, to send them a physician. Unfortunately he thought it was Lord Minto who was ill and not an urgent matter.[28] Dr Peschier from Geneva, who had been attentive beyond any physician Mary ever experienced, concluded that he had 'a bowel fever' which would work itself out. 'Nature was', he thought, 'resuming her functions much more confidently than he could have guessed'. A similar diagnosis had been given by the old doctor at Minto, and all agreed that the patient should not be given medicine of any sort. The nurse whom they hired, and who was 'a real treasure', slept in Gilbert's room, and Mary and her baby Henry in another. It had, Mary wrote, 'a most happy effect upon us both, as we sleep like two tops'. Young Gilbert was growing 'fatter and nicer and rosier than ever' but death was not far away.

The actual date of young Gilbert's death is unclear but towards the end of September, Harriet had written to the family at Lennel,

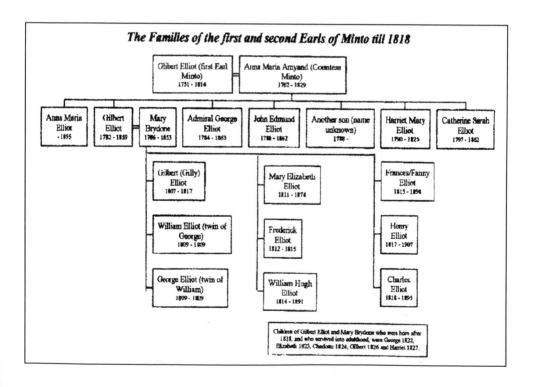

saying that a 'fatal change' had taken place in all their hopes. On 21 September, Mary told her mother that 'Gilbert is all but gone, not one ray of hope remains to cheer our dreary prospect'. Her only object in writing was, she said, 'to assure you upon my honour that nothing has been concealed from you'. Lord Minto was 'perfectly well, and not worn out, and so am I', adding bravely that she prayed 'for all their sakes that they would be able to bear this hard blow with fortitude'. Five days later, Mary again tried to comfort her mother, reminding herself, if not Mrs Brydone, of the effect the heir's death had on his father, and the four remaining children. Such high hopes had been held out for the European tour, and only two days before the crisis broke, even Interlaken had inspired panegyrics about the village's geography, architecture and vegetation. Not surprisingly, the family decided 'to leave this place'.[29]

Arriving from Interlaken for a stay of seven or eight nights, the travellers found themselves 'crammed into the very smallest house' in Bern, with one drawing room being the size of the Lennel closet. A few short, rather purposeless excursions made to Zürich and Rheinfallen convinced them that going 'straight home' might be the best course of action. The general gloom, a night of agony for Mary with the toothache, and a change in the weather reminding the party that winter was 'near at hand and Lennel far off', reinforced the argument. Mary said she 'would not be sorry to get away', but could not give her mother an address beyond Basel, from where they would be going to Paris. Lady Minto, travelling 'very slowly', and George's family with 'his own horses', set off on 4 October, leaving Harriet to be a companion for Mary.[30]

Mary and Gilbert arrived in Paris towards the end of October. It seems that no sooner had he seen the family settled than his Lordship left for England, leaving Mary to deal with several of the family's bankers, one of which was a Monsieur Perigueux. If the French rather than the English capital was to be a satisfactory and economical temporary home, and Minto House was to be readied in all respects for occupation in the late Spring of 1818, there was much to be done, and the couple's separation endured. Certainly by 5 November Gilbert was in London, with Mary writing to him at Coutts & Co, his bank in the Strand, and towards the end of the month at Lennel. Meanwhile in Paris, Mary resolved to make both full use of her mother's dispensation and the best she could of life among the aristocracy of Louis XVIII's France.

As Mary told Gilbert, after 'a great many doubts', her sister Elizabeth had decided not to go to Paris as she 'long ago proposed'. Having given her own affairs 'due deliberation', Mary's first decision she said was to sell her old French carriage for Frs 800 instead of having it repaired, causing her coachman to foresee the possibility of himself being 'packed into a *boitiere de perte*', or being without a job. Not long afterwards, George and Eliza's young son, Foley, died most unexpectedly.[31] Two doctors were baffled by the 'melancholy event', languor being the only symptom of illness they had. Mary could not but 'feel sorry that George didn't have the body opened', despite the opinion expressed by the physicians that nothing would have been discovered. Both George and Eliza were as well as could be expected, very quiet and composed, but Mary could not help wondering whether the death would affect the date of their departure for Scotland, and whether Harriet would go with them. Among English travellers passing through Paris at that time were Lord and Lady Bentinck who had been recalled from India, and Lord North's youngest son, the fifth earl of Guilford whom Mary said 'had repaired himself well', and who was going to Italy, Moscow and St Petersburg 'if he had time'.[32]

The cold and damp of Parisian life produced its own inconveniences, the Dowager Countess found that her drawing room had no chimney, hence no fire. She looked 'pale and thin', cautiously saying nothing, as Mary told her husband. In her 'little apartment which everybody admires', but which was 'awkward', and at Frs.600 a month, 'very dear', Mary looked back over the six months the family had spent in Paris. She admitted going to 'some balls', but the 'hours were absurdly late' for such events. To Mary's relief, Harriet seemed quite happy that she was her temporary 'step' mother. A rumour that George and Eliza might leave for Scotland at the end of December could not be verified, she told Gilbert, as there was no one at home when she called on them. Going on to report the sale of his horse for Frs 160, she explained that nobody had bid for the animal till she suggested it might be shot. Knowing how much Gilbert wanted a French cook for Minto she also told him that her host at a dinner the previous day only paid his cook £35 a year. With political debates causing 'a good deal of commotion' in Paris, Mary duly sent him some French newspapers with her letter.[33]

In early January, as Gilbert was starting to oversee the work at Minto needed to make the house's extensive new accommodation on three floors habitable, to say nothing of the estate, Mary told her husband that George's family had left Paris the previous morning. They would be at Cambrai for a couple of days, followed by three or four more in London. Once at Minto 'it was likely that they would remain there for a fortnight or three weeks'. For her part, Mary felt very forlorn without him, 'having had so much of his society, and having nothing to make up for the loss'.[34] Mary's problem was that she did not want to return to Scotland to be with her parents and sisters till she knew that Gilbert, the dowager, George and Eliza and the Minto household were properly settled in. With no one other than Gilbert at Minto, and the house being virtually unoccupied for more than two years, there was much to be arranged and servants to be found and trained. Gilbert had the keys of plate chests and other items, but 'the trusty persons' he had left in charge could not remember which was which.[35]

Mary's daily walks in the garden of the Tuileries with the four children became a habit. Meeting members of the English and Scottish aristocracy living in Paris on the fringe of the court helped Mary develop a sense of European politics, a far cry from the hustings at home where Gilbert gave her news of friends, and developments in Lennel where cottages had either been demolished or gardens improved. Knowing how concerned her husband would have been about rising land prices across Europe, Mary mentioned encountering the Duke of Buccleuch who seemed as 'hard as his father was indulgent'. She considered 'the whole of the inhabitants of Paris as one and the same thing with no one object but selfishness, or no one virtue, public or private, except the poor Duc de Richelieu', the prime minister.

In the February cold, and without her husband to guide her, Mary was anxious to demonstrate that without her husband she could still keep a keen eye on the budget and economise where possible. She left the door of her drawing room open so that it could benefit from the heat of a small stove in the kitchen. Letting Gilbert know what monies had been drawn from his account, and 'what we shall require before we meet', Mary said that all her expenses, 'independent of the children', had come to about £30 a month, rather what she had expected. The French capital was 'clearly less costly' than London. She had paid the servants to the 'amount of fifty or sixty pounds', and she 'reckoned upon going on … at that rate'. The girls had received about two hundred pounds.[36]

At the end of the month, and contrary to expectation, Mary reported the arrival in France of her sister Elizabeth after a passage of three and a half hours from Dover. She was 'fatter than ever' but 'remarkably well' and, with the *bal contunué* given to please the Duchesse de Berri and others now popular, a ball for her to attend became an immediate consideration.[37] However, ten days later Mary was forced to turn her attention back to matters affecting the dowager Lady Minto's daughter, Anna Maria. She had written saying that she would soon be retuning to Paris from Cambrai; the British army of occupation's headquarters and the location of an important bishopric. Mary and Elizabeth immediately determined 'not to say one word on religious subjects to her' unless she invited it. The Brydone sisters had learned from the dowager and others that she had 'tormented herself' about religion for two years and had 'often been found crying about it'.[38] Unfortunately, two weeks later Mary had to report that she had been 'very unwell, even since her return'. The spirit and the flesh were willing but she was in 'a pitiable state … a lost sheep'.

Thinking she would 'allow herself a good month' to reach Minto from Paris, Mary planned to leave the French capital by the first of May, if Gilbert was 'sure of being settled there by the beginning of June'. Were one of her best friends, Lady Carnegie, to decide to buy her chaise, Mary said, 'I shall let her have it'. Furniture, books and stores bought in France were to go by sea from Dover to London by the hoy, a small sloop-rigged coastal vessel which went to the same wharf as the Leith smacks, vessels operated by the London and Edinburgh Shipping Company.[39]

Meanwhile, about this time an effort was being made at Lennel to have Brydone seen by a London physician. Mary and Gilbert, however, feared that there was every likelihood that he might catch cold during the journey south. Writing to Mrs Brydone from Minto on 23 March, Gilbert said 'we all know that the distance between London and Edinburgh is subject to great variation', and contacting his daughters when Brydone might be somewhere en route might be another problem. On top of this, there was some feeling among the girls that they too could use the occasion to visit the capital but it would be 'impossible for the girls to go about as much as they might have done' and the 'usual fatigue and dissipation of a London life might injure their health'. Apparently, Mrs Brydone had originally 'approved very highly' of the plan, but Gilbert was convinced 'it never appeared to be practical'.[40]

In Paris, those English families who had wintered there were departing. Lord and Lady George Seymour had left, Lord and Lady Pembroke were to cross the Channel towards the end of April, whilst Admiral Sir Thomas Foley, one of Nelson's 'band of brothers', was still awaiting the arrival of one of his wife's sisters. In London, Gilbert was temporarily at 17 Duke Street off Manchester Square but now unlikely to be back at Minto until 10 June. Mary had, however, sent the stores being sent home to Calais, having 'taken every possible precaution to have them admirably packed', to make it difficult for 'the people at the Custom House at Dover to take them out'.[41] Two hogsheads of the wine Gilbert wanted was also to be dispatched.

April passed with few developments in Paris. Mary thanked Gilbert for his offer of a lady's maid, thinking that such a 'damsel' might be better than the one she shared with Catherine. Two days later she told him about the cook she had chosen. He had asked to have his linen washed for him free of expense, such a practice being 'always done in England for either man or woman cooks'. He said he was nine and thirty, and Mary thought him a little like her nephew Robert Elliot. Telling other servants about his appointment, the new employee said 'he was going to that barbarous part of the world called Scotland' where Phillips, another manservant, assured him he would not 'die of the climate'.[42]

On 17 May, in 'the agony of the last day' of her seven-month sojourn in Paris without Gilbert, Mary wished he could see all the luggage that had gone before them to Calais and which was 'still to be piled into the carriages'. If she was lucky enough, she told Gilbert, 'we shall get there at the full moon', and hopefully a good journey 'should the wind be fair next morning'. In the event, after one night on the road at Chantilly, Mary's party sailed from Calais and were soon comfortably enough lodged at London's Thomas's Hotel which Gilbert had arranged before he left for Lennel and Minto, thinking it might have to suffice for quite a time. Horrified by the 'nasty stink and smoky air of this vile town', Mary was, nevertheless, 'quite giddy' at the kindness and generous hospitality extended to her in London. She wrote to ask a family friend in Westmoreland whether they would be able to stay with her on their way North, telling Gilbert she did not plan to set out before the third of June.

Proposing that Mrs Good, the family's housekeeper should take the stage coach to Carlisle, from where she would go on to Hawick in the mail coach, Mary anticipated that the cook would travel 'on the outside, whilst the lady rides within'. She admitted not having the heart to send him by sea, adding that if she was successful in hiring a suitable kitchen maid, 'she may go too'.[43] Three days later, and with her 'last audience with Mrs Good' completed, Mary saw her off along with the cook, the latter being named for the first time as Monsieur Ribbet. Mary was feeling 'young again' but still awaiting news from Westmoreland and wanting to 'get out of the bubble of the elections', a reference to the General Election that year.[44]

Exactly when the celebratory mood of the family's return was extinguished, and whether or not Mary and Gilbert were at Lennel House on 19 June 1818 when the eighty-two-year-old Brydone died quietly, is not known. Prayers would undoubtedly have been offered that his wife and daughters would have been by him at his death, if not also his son-in-law and grandchildren. Brydone was buried inside the south wall of the now dilapidated Lennel Kirk, where a memorial tablet simply states: 'Patrick Brydone Esq., FRS, born 1736 died 1818'. Although *The Scots Magazine* carried a mention in an early August edition, few newspapers reported the event. Fortunately, the obituary writer for the *Annual Biography* in 1820 published the memoirs of twenty 'celebrated men' who had died in the preceding two years.[45] The twenty-seven page account of Brydone's life, based largely on the traveller's account of his *Tour through Sicily* and his scientific papers given to the Royal Society, was warm and fulsome.[46]

It fell to Brydone's second daughter, Elizabeth, to testify at Edinburgh in August 1818 in the presence of William McFarlane, a Justice of the Peace of the county, that her father had died on the date given, and that the Rt Hon. Mary Countess of Minto and Williamina Brydone not only had an interest in the possessions of the deceased but were also executors appointed by their father at the end of July 1812. Elizabeth then affirmed that she did not know of any settlement or article of the deceased person's estate other than those exhibited. Each page of a full and complete inventory of Brydone's personal estate and effects was signed, so confirming that the items 'to her knowledge belonged to him or were due to him beneficially at the time of his death'. The value of the estate in Scotland was at least £10,000, and under the value of £12,000 sterling – all of which, being 'the truth as she should answer to God', and signed by Elizabeth and witnessed by William McFarlane.

Andrew Bennet, an 'appraiser' from Coldstream, had meanwhile valued the household furniture, bed and table linen, and plate at Lennel as £679, and the stock, crop and farming utensils on the farm at £545. Just after his marriage, Brydone had arranged that these assets would pass to Mary his wife in the event that he died first. Among other effects belonging to Brydone were several substantial annuities and stocks together with monies due to him from the Stamp Office, including compensation 'for an office in the Bristol Custom House'. The balance of his bank account with Child & Co. in London had steadily increased and he had settled £10,000 on his eldest daughter when she married Gilbert Elliot. The eventual value of his estate in England (£40,976), added to that in Scotland (£10,548), produced a total of £51,524.

In November 1818, Brydone's widow then in her late sixties, wrote to Gilbert in London from Edinburgh, giving a backward glance to the family as it adjusted to yet another death that year. William Elliot of Wells MP had died at Minto the month before after an attack of asthma, and her husband was staying at William's Burlington Street home while attending to his affairs. She explained that she had come to Edinburgh to sit for Henry Raeburn, the artist who had become a member of the Royal Scottish Academy in 1815. Telling her husband that everyone already thought the picture a striking likeness, she was convinced 'it will be at least in that respect most satisfactory to all that wish to preserve my wrinkles in their memory. It is as near as possible the over view of my Old Phiz (old face) as Sir Joshua took', a reference to an earlier portrait of her painted by Sir Joshua Reynolds. She hoped that 'two more sittings may suffice', and that would conclude her 'residence in this dirty hole'.

The previous day, Mary had dined with Brydone's seventy-eight year old brother, Robert, together with the Dowager Countess and one of her daughters who was 'still much handsomer than her daughter'. Their conversation provided her with 'a very happy opportunity of just saying that Mr Elliot (Gilbert) had mentioned the way in which he had entailed his estate many years ago', following the example of her husband, the first Lord Minto. So far as the development of New Town, the capital's elegant one-family residences were concerned, she said 'I am much pleased with some of the new works ... but not at all with parts of them'. Her short stay in Edinburgh, which may well have been at Dumbreck's Hotel in St Andrew's Square, had only allowed her time to call on a few friends and acquaintances, and she was soon 'even more ... out of humour with great towns in this island'. The 'stink of fog and smoke', the constant noise from an adjacent building, and the smell of rubbish and other detritus 'made us quite sick'. Hoping to get away the following day, Mary added, 'if Raeburn requires another sitting it will be submitted to'. She proposed to sleep at Newbattle, the abbey home of William Kerr, the sixth Marquess of Lothian, and be at home two days later.[47]

The marriage of Brydone's eldest daughter to a member of a family whose forebears could be traced to the fifteen century, and who himself was a second generation member of the Scottish aristocracy, brought new life to the Elliot line, despite so many deaths in early childhood and the especially painful loss of the ten-year-old heir to the title. Although Gilbert was often pompous and could be trapped into over-examination of detail, he became envoy-extraordinary and minister plenipotentiary to Prussia in Berlin in the early 1830s, and envoy in Rome and Revolutionary Sicily between 1847 and 1852, after exemplary attendance in the House of Lords.

As time went by, enjoyable family events greatly outnumbered the more sombre. In 1822, Brydone's second daughter, Elizabeth, married Captain Charles Adam RN at Minto House. Among their children was William Patrick Adam. Serving under Admiral Lord Keith, and later becoming an admiral himself, Charles eventually became a naval lord of the Admiralty between 1835 and 1841, working closely with Gilbert who was by then the First Lord. The son born to Gilbert and Mary in 1818, who also became an admiral, was not only given the full name of Charles Gilbert John Brydone Elliot, but he called his home at Bitterne near Southampton, 'Brydone'. The couple's third and fourth daughters, Elizabeth Amelia (Lizzy) and Charlotte Mary (Bob'm) were born in 1823 and 1825 respectively, one marrying happily, the other coming to be the target of her husband's bullying behaviour. Also in 1825, Brydone's youngest daughter, Williamina, married Gilbert Elliot, the second son of Hugh Elliot, the first Earl Minto's diplomat brother, at St Peter's Church, Halesworth, Surrey where he was the vicar, and later Dean of Bristol. They had three daughters and two sons, the younger of whom, also called Gilbert, apparently became an officer in the Royal Navy but died, lost at sea.

Brydone's wife Mary outlived him by nearly twenty years, dying in 1837 when eighty-five years old. A year later, the Elliot's eldest daughter, Mary Elizabeth, married Ralph Abercromby, the son of the speaker of the House of Commons, who fell in love with her when he was secretary of legation in Berlin. A much-loved husband, and later second Baron Dunfermline, he died aged sixty-five. Fanny (Frances), her sister and a great correspondent of Mary Abercromby, married Lord John Russell in 1841, not long before he became prime minister. Additional dates which complete the chronology include the marriage in 1844 of the Elliots' eldest son, William, to Emma Hislop, who became the third earl Minto on the death of Gilbert in 1859. He proved himself an effective MP with a strong social conscience. His mother Mary, the second Countess Minto, who had stayed several times at the Abercromby's much-loved home at Nervi, near Genoa, partly to alleviate what might have been an arthritic condition, died there in 1853 aged sixty-seven.[48]

Brydone had been a man at the right place, and the right time. Rather than a struggling pioneer expected to make his mark eventually, or someone having repeatedly to pick himself up, Brydone enjoyed a life which progressed steadily. Not only did he achieve most of his aims but often exceeded them. The even tenor and satisfaction of his life had its roots in Brydone's patient temperament and kaleidoscopic interests. Not unlike an Elliot, and certainly others of his generation, Brydone had a keen sense of history to which he added a special flair for conceptualising, or giving a subject an appropriate setting, that greatly enhanced its appreciation and made him different. Artistically, he drew on a full pallet, using all manner of shades and tones. As a scientist, he was for ever exploring, aided by his welcoming personality and a treasury of reminiscences which always made him good company. *A quite remarkable man*, he was very rarely bored wherever he was. Moreover, his late marriage in his fifty-first year and the affection he showed for his three daughters, along with the five Elliot grandchildren that had been born by the end of 1818, greatly added to his delight.

# Notes and References

## The following abbreviations have been used:

| | |
|---|---|
| BM | Blairadam Muniments |
| BL | British Library |
| Chapman | R.Chapman, US publisher |
| HRO | Hampshire Record Office |
| NA | National Archives, Kew |
| NLS | National Library of Scotland |
| NRS | National Records of Scotland |
| NY | Evert Duyckinck, US publisher |
| YBL | Yale University Beinecke Rare Book and Manuscript Library |

## Preface

1. *A Tour through Sicily and Malta* by Patrick Brydone, Letter V.
2. *The Annual Biography and Obituary for the year 1820*, Vol. IV, p.111 published in London.
3. BL Dictionary of National Biography for 1886, pp.166–167.

## Chapter 1 Early Years and the Context of History (1736–1758)

1. Elizabeth Dysart died 20 May 1764, Community Trees Project
2. Paul Fussell Jnr, in *Literature as a Mode of Travel*, and his essay about Patrick Brydone on p.55.

3. From pages 205–6 of Evert Duyckinck's 1813 edition of *A Tour through Sicily and Malta in a series of letters to William Beckford of Somerly, Suffolk* by Patrick Brydone, published in New York .

4. Franklin returned to Philadelphia in November 1762 becoming speaker of the Pennsylvania house of representatives. His 1764–1775 mission to Britain saw him opposing the Stamp Act and being elected a member of the Royal Society's council in 1766, 1767 and 1772.

5. Hauksbee used a glass globe rapidly rotated by a geared handle and rubbed, and a primitive electroscope, a semicircle of wire from which dangled woollen threads. Placed round the globe, the threads straightened as if they were attracted to the centre of the globe, suggesting that electricity was a centripetal force like gravity, but caused by the emission of effluvia (an odour or a secretion). Placed inside the globe, threads were repelled from the centre. Such highly visual experiments changed Newton's theory of forces from one action at a distance to one of 'subtle effluvia' modelled on electricity. (See Stephen Pumfrey's Oxford DNB essay).

6. The Royal Society of Edinburgh was not established till 1783.

7. Sir John Pringle (1707–1782) was born of Magdalen Eliott of Stobs at Stitchel House, in the village of Stichill, two miles from Kelso. After graduating in Leyden and practising medicine in Edinburgh, he was appointed a professor of metaphysics and moral philosophy at Edinburgh University. Somewhat fortuitously in 1742, he became physician to the commander of the British army during the War of the Austrian Succession and in June 1743 he helped bring about an agreement with the French that military hospitals on both sides would be regarded as neutral territory where the sick and wounded would be protected, and each side would care for each other's casualties. The following year he was promoted to the position of physician-general to the forces in the Low Countries, whereupon he resigned his professorship. He returned to Scotland, however, in time to be present at

the Battle of Culloden, and surrendered his post as physician-general in 1748. The following year he settled in Pall Mall and became physician to the Duke of Cumberland, three years later marrying Charlotte, the daughter of Dr William Oliver – of Bath Oliver biscuits fame. He was president of the Royal Society between 1772 and 1778 and a close friend of Benjamin Franklin. Pringle died in 1782 aged 74 and a monument was erected in his memory in Westminster Abbey.

8.  BL Add.4439, p.316.
9.  BL Add.4439, pp.314–315.
10. BL Add.4439, p.308.
11. BL Add 4440, p.20
12. BL Add 4440, p.30
13. BL Add.4440, pp.31–32.

# Chapter 2 Brydone goes to War (1759–1763)

1. The belligerents were the Allies, made up of Great Britain, Prussia, Hanover, Brunswick-Wolfenbüttel, Hesse-Kassel, Schaumburg Lippe and Portugal, against France, Austria, Russia, Spain, Sweden and Saxony.
2. The regiment's total establishment in the early 1740s was one colonel, a lieutenant-colonel, a first major, a second major and captain, along with 13 more captains, 30 first lieutenants and 12 second lieutenants, a chaplain, 2 adjutants, a quartermaster, a surgeon, 56 sergeants and a similar number of corporals, 4 fifers and 1400 men.
3. BM Brydone Papers 4/300/6, Brydone to his mother, 14 February 1760.
4. BM Brydone Papers 4/300/15, Brydone to his mother, 9 August 1760.
5. BM Brydone Papers 4/306/11 and 12, Brydone to his mother, 8 October 1760 and 28 October 1762.
6. Troopships then at Plymouth included the *Prince Ferdinand*, *Industry*, the *Adventure* and the *Princess Amelia* which had run aground but was 'got off without much damage'.
7. Brydone listed 257 killed, of whom 13 were officers and 9

sergeants along with some 259 other ranks. The estimate of those wounded was 435 of whom 21 were officers and 27 sergeants. His overall total for all those who were killed or wounded was a little over 1200.

8. BM Brydone Papers 4/435/1/3-51, Journal No.1, Belle-Isle, March to June 1761.

9. The Treaty of Paris in 1763 returned the island of Minorca to Britain in exchange for the French West Indies and Belle-Isle. General Craufurd was appointed governor of Minorca and died there in August 1764.

10. BM Brydone Papers 4/302/12, includes a letter from Brydone to his mother, 7 June 1762.

11. John Burgoyne (1723–1792) purchased a captain's commission in the 11th Dragoons in 1756 and, distinguishing himself in a landing near St Malo, Pitt named him lieutenant-colonel to recruit a new regiment, the 16th Light Dragoons. The local rank of brigadier followed during the campaign in Portugal and after a period as an MP for Midhurst, Burgoyne became a supporter of Lord North's administration and the repression of the American colonies. He was to command the troops at the battle of Bunker Hill, but he was most widely known for his defeat at Saratoga where he surrendered with 5000 men in October 1777.

12. BM Brydone Papers 4/435/2/1-17, Journal No.2, October to November 1762, Portugal. See also *The 85th King's Light Infantry* pp. 8–21, edited by C.R.B. Barrett, London, 1913.

13. Matthew Dysart (1705–1773) obtained a Master of Arts from Glasgow University in 1724 and seems to have married before 1731, having eight children, three of whom were boys. He assumed the name Sandilands in lieu of Dysart on succeeding to the estate of Couston from his mother. He became the minister at the Church of Scotland at Eccles in 1729, a village near Kelso in the Scottish Borders, remaining its incumbent for forty three years.

14. BM Brydone Papers 4/302/6, Brydone to his mother, 31 January 1763.

# Chapter 3 Becomes a travelling tutor on the continent (1764–1770)

1. From Brydone's *Tour through Sicily and Malta* ... Evert Duyckinck's edition p.166.
2. See *The Annual Biography and Obituary for the year 1820,* Vol. IV, published in London 1820.
3. Saussure's manuscripts had been seen by Voltaire but he recast his experiences of England in the form of letters to an anonymous friend. In 1738 he joined a Freemason lodge in Lausanne only for it to be closed down by the Bernese rulers in 1745. His latter years were spent compiling histories of France and Switzerland and he died in 1783 an ardent protestant believer in Lausanne.
4. In 1758, James Stuart Mackenzie (1719–1800) had been envoy extraordinary to the King of Sardinia, living well in Turin and popular with all.
5. Gavin Rylands de Beer – Annals of the Jean-Jacques Rousseau Society, *Rousseau et Les Anglais en Suisse*, pp.268–270.
6. Styled Lord Glenorchy (1696–1782), John Campbell was the son of the second Earl Breadalbane. He served as envoy-extraordinary and minister-plenipotentiary to the Court of Denmark between 1720 and 1729 and married Arabella Pershall in 1730, his first wife having died while they were in Denmark. They had two sons, George (who died in infancy) and John. A parliamentary career followed his election at Saltash and later at Orford. Succeeding his father as Earl of Breadalbane in 1752 he sat in the Lords, becoming keeper of the seal of Scotland between 1765–6. He died at Holyroodhouse in January 1782.
7. BM Brydone Papers 4/305/30, 25 July, and 4/305/17, 4 September 1766.
8. BM Brydone Papers 4/305/28, undated but probably 1766–67
9. Not to be confused with William Beckford (1709–1770) who married Maria Hamilton, or William Thomas Beckford (1760–1844) whose wife was Lady Margaret Gordon. (See the Family Tree of Peter Beckford's Descendents.)
10. After a change in war plans, Fullarton and Seaforth found

themselves posted to India and involved in operations to defeat Hyder Ali, the ruler of Mysore but his friend was to be mortally wounded in a naval encounter off Bombay. Following the battle of Porto Novo, and the peace which followed, Fullarton had command of some 14,000 men. He came back to Scotland in 1785, and two years later published letters which described the campaign. He married the daughter of the fifth Lord Reay, by whom he had one daughter, and then living on his Ayrshire estates, he resumed his parliamentary career, first as the member for the Haddington Burghs. It was during Addington's premiership that Fullarton was appointed the senior commissioner of Trinidad's governing council, along with Commodore Samuel Hood and the previous governor, Brigadier-General Thomas Picton.

11. Scrawled at the top of the first page of Brydone's third Journal were the words 'To Wilbraham', possibly a reference to either Roger or Randle Wilbraham, both members of the eminent Cheshire family. Brydone, and sometimes a secretary, seem to have only belatedly incorporated such letters into his Journals.

12. BM Brydone Papers 4/435/3, April 1767.

13. *A Tour through Sicily and Malta in a series of letters to William Beckford Esq. of Somerly in Suffolk* (Letter No 35).

14. BM Brydone Papers 4/435/3, May and August 1768.

15. More accurately, Robert Dodsley's piece, written in 1737 and performed at Drury Lane that year, was called *King and the Miller of Mansfield*, a dramatic tale of King Henry II. Music was not involved.

16. Count Wenzel Anton Kaunitz (1711–1794) the Austrian statesman and diplomat initially became ambassador in Turin between 1742–44. He was a lifelong enemy of Prussia.

17. Sir Paul Methuen (*c.*1672–1757) bought Corsham Court in Wiltshire to house his cousin's collection of picture and furniture collection, a Paul Methuen (1723–1779).

18. Hamilton wrote to Dr Matthew Marty, Secretary to the Royal Society, in October 1769. See also '*Observations on Mount Vesuvius, Mount Etna and Other Volcanos*'.

19.Sir William Hamilton (1731–1803) entered parliament as MP for Midhurst in 1761 and although appointed equerry to George III he chose a diplomatic career. Naples was his first posting where he arrived with his wife Catherine who shared her husband's great interest in music. He became a collector of art and antiquities, acquiring some 350 paintings during his lifetime. He became a knight of the Bath in 1772. His service in Naples encouraged an interest in vulcanology and after the death of his wife and remarriage, more travels in Italy followed, till his death in 1803.

20.BM Brydone Papers 4/435/3, November 1769 to February 1770.

21.The Hanbury referred to may have been Osgood Hanbury (1731–1784), a merchant and later banker.

22.BM Brydone Papers 4/435/3, March 1770.

23.Page references from Evert Duyckinck's 1813 New York edition of the *Tour* are shown, for example, as 'NY p.1' etc., and those from R. Chapman's 1813 Glasgow edition of the *Tour* (reprinted electronically by General Books USA) are shown, for example as 'Chapman p. 43'.

24.NY pp.1–7; Chapman pp.4–5.

25.Dr Fussell's *Literature as a Mode of Travel*, 1963, p.59.

26.NY pp. 91–93 and p.117.

27.NY pp.7–20; Chapman pp.6–14.

28.NY pp.21–28; Chapman pp.14–19.

29.NY pp.29–38; Chapman pp.19–25.

# Chapter 4 In Eastern Sicily and Malta (May 1770)

1. NY pp.38–43; Chapman pp.25–28.
2. NY pp.41–42, Chapman p.27.
3. Don Ferdinando Francesco Gravina (1722–1789).
4. NY pp.43–52; Chapman pp.28–34.
5. NY pp.52–55; Chapman pp.34–36.
6. NY pp.55–63; Chapman pp.36–37.
7. R Chapman's 1817 Glasgow edition, p.128.
8. In Act I Sc.III, Othello speaks of 'antres vast and deserts idle'

(not 'wild' as Brydone recalls) in an oration which defines him as 'an erring barbarian'. Antres is, however, one of the rarest of rare words. Shakespeare coined it just for the occasion from the Latin antrum, a cave.

9. NY pp.63–85; Chapman pp.41–56.

10. NY pp.85–104; Chapman pp.56–68.

11. NY pp.105–124; Chapman pp.68–81.

12. NY pp.125–134; Chapman pp.81–89.

13. NY pp.134–138; Chapman pp.89–92.

14. Soon afterwards, Canon Spoto was to show further generosity. In an account of his *Travels through Germany, Switzerland, Italy and Sicily* written a year or so later and before he became a German poet of some repute, Graf Friedrich von Stolberg (1746–1824) also mentions the Canon. He overwhelmed the Count 'with civilities of every kind, supplied us with his own furniture at our inn, and covered our table with his hospitable presents' – to say nothing of writing letters of recommendation. Thomas Holcroft was to translate Stolberg's *Travels* into English in 1797, the work having been reviewed in the *Monthly Review* in 1795.

15. NY pp.138–150; Chapman pp.92–99.

# Chapter 5 The travellers arrive in Palermo (June 1770)

1. NY pp.150–174; Chapman pp.99–114.

2. NY pp.174–195; Chapman pp.114–126.

3. William II of Sicily, who was on the throne between 1166 and 1189, lacked any military enterprise and seldom emerged from palace life in Palermo. From there, however, William championed the papacy and through a league with the cities of Lombardy, he defied Frederick Barbarossa, the Holy Roman Emperor and King of Germany. In 1177, he married Joan, the daughter of Henry II of England and Eleanor of Aquitaine.

4. Brydone was to tell Beckford more about the artists performing at the opera house in Palermo at the end of his correspondence. Not only did he think it would not be long

before his friend would be hearing them in London but that Gabrielli was already 'the greatest singer in the world'. Her 'wonderful execution and volubility of voice' helped greatly. In the case of Pacchierotti, who was very young and an entire stranger in the musical world', Brydone was convinced he 'gave more expression to his *cantabile* airs' than other singers. (NY pp.261–2; Chapman pp.168–9).

5. NY pp.206–233; Chapman pp.132–157.

6. St Bassus of Lucera (on the Italian mainland) was born about 45 AD and matyred by Trajan in 118 AD.

7. Brydone also described some production of cameos made by the people of Trepani, perfect imitations of ancient ones engraved on onyx. They were 'done on a kind of hard shell from pastes of the best antiques … set in gold (and) generally worn as bracclets'. He went on to say that 'Mrs Hamilton procured a pair of them last year and carried them to Naples'.

8. NY pp.234–253; Chapman pp.158–163.

## Chapter 6 Brydone becomes a successful writer (1771–1773)

1. NY pp.274–275; Chapman p.176–177.

2. After three years in Rome, George Robertson (1748–1788) returned to London in 1771 via Germany and Holland, and went out to the West Indies the following year where he drew several views, including those of the *Fort William Estate at Westmoreland* and *The Bridge Crossing the Rio Cobre.*

3. Pringle resigned in 1778 and returned for a while to Scotland, only to die on a visit to London four years later.

4. Brydone's *Tour through Sicily and Malta … NY* Edition p.93; Chapman reprint p.60.

5. BL Letter from Brydone to Sir John Pringle in November 1772, subsequently read to the Royal Society in February 1773 and published in Volume 63 of the Society's 'Philosophical Transactions' in 1774.

6. *Letters of David Hume to William Strahan,* editor, G Birkbeck

Hill, Letter LXVIII (3 June 1772 and footnotes 1 and 2 on pp.249–250,Clarendon Press, 1888.

7.  Leonard W Labaree (Editor), *Papers of Benjamin Franklin,* Volume for 1772.

8.  Originally in George III's King's Library at Windsor, these two volumes are now in the British Library (UIN: BLL01000511297).

9.  NY Edition p.iii; Chapman pp.1–2.

10.Strahan subsequently became master of the Stationers' Company in 1774 and MP for two constituencies. After handing the business over to his son Andrew, he died in 1785.

11.Thomas Cadell, the elder (1742–1802) also published works by Frances Brooke, Fanny Burney, Catherine Macaulay and Hannah More. He was delegated by a group of booksellers to encourage Dr Johnson to give them the biographical prefaces to *The Works of the English Poets,* and in 1785 Cadell published *Prayers and Meditations.* Two years later, he began publishing the poetry of Robert Burns. Cadell became a governor of the Foundling Hospital in 1795, remaining active in retirement and being elected an alderman for the Walbrook ward in the City of London in 1798. He died at his home in Bloomsbury Place four years later.

12.*The Early Diary of Frances Burney 1768–1778, Vol.1.* George Bell, London (1907).

13.See p.268, Volume 1 of *The Letters and Prose Writings of William Cowper*, edited by King and Ryskamp, Clarendon Press 1979.

14.1809 Edinburgh edition of the *Tour*, printed by Abernethy & Walker, pp. 70–71.

15.Boswell, *Life of Johnson*, by Hill and Powell.

16.Friedrich Adolph, Baron von Riedesel (1738–1800) was born into a family of minor German nobility, and after studying at Marburg he was tricked into joining the army, much to his father's displeasure. In 1759 he and his regiment returned from a short posting in London to fight with Britain during the Seven Years' War. By 1761 he was the colonel of two Brunswick regiments but, wounded the next year, he was sent to Minden to recover. Marriage followed and the couple settled in Wolffenbüttel where they lived quietly with their children for a few years. It was during this period that the Baron would appear to have visited Etna. During the American War of Independence, and by then a Major-General, the Baron and his regiment helped expel the French from Canada.

17. BL Volume 49 of the *Monthly Journal*, July 1773, pp.22–33; August 1773, pp.115–121

18. Donaldson's decisive victory in a legal case before the House of Lords followed, and confirmed limited and statutory copyright.

19. Professor Paul Fussell Jr. (1924–2012), Rutgers University and University of Pennsylvania, author of *Patrick Brydone – the Eighteenth-Century Traveller as Representative Man* 1963.

# Chapter 7 Travels to Vienna and thence to Berlin (1775–1776)

1. BM *List of Brydone's Journals,* Journal No 8, 1774.

2. BM *List of Brydone's Journals,* Journal No 9, 1775.

3. Notes and Queries Magazine Vol.193 p.168, Oxford University Press

4. William Morton Pitt's father, John Pitt (1704–1787) of Encombe was MP for Wareham and Dorchester. Appointed Lord of Trade (1744–55) and of Admiralty in 1756, he became Surveyor-General of woods and forests between 1756–68 and 1768–86. At the time his son was being tutored by Brydone he was in his seventies. He died in February 1787.

5. See pp.15–16 of *A Memoir of the Right Honourable Hugh Elliot* by Emma (Nina) Hislop Elliot, published in 1868 in an edition reprinted by Lightening Source UK Ltd. Milton Keynes.

6. William Morton Pitt (1754–1836) failed to induce Pitt the Elder to appoint him to the Board of Trade in 1787 and in 1790 he succeeded his cousin as the County MP for Dorset, a constituency he served for 30 years. He married Margaret Gambier in 1782 and after her death in 1818, Grace Seymer the following year.

7. Hugh Elliot (1752–1830), diplomat and adventurer, joined the Russian army and distinguished himself in the Russo-

Turkish War of 1768–1774. He became envoy-extraordinary in Berlin and later served in Denmark, Paris and Naples, becoming governor of the Leeward Islands and Madras after which he retired.

8. From *A Memoir of the Right Honourable Hugh Elliot* by Emma (Nina) Hislop Elliot, published in 1868. See pp 9, 11 and 14 of an edition reprinted by Lightening Source UK Ltd. Milton Keynes.

9. *The Pembroke Papers (1734–1780),* Letters and Diaries of Henry, Tenth Earl of Pembroke and his Circle (edited by Lord Herbert), Jonathan Cape 1939.

10. His father, Robert Keith (1697–1774) had been appointed British minister at Vienna in August 1748 in succession to Sir Thomas Robinson and conducted negotiations about the alliances which preceded the Seven Years' War with success. At the end of 1753 he was promoted to the rank of minister-plenipotentiary but in 1757 he was transferred to St Petersburg. In retirement he lived at The Hermitage, a property near Edinburgh and died at St Andrews Square, Edinburgh.

11. Brought up in a strict religious household, Count Hieronymus von Colorado (1732–1812) studied philosophy at the University of Vienna and theology in Rome, becoming Prince-Archbishop in 1772. He was to flee Salzburg when Napoleon drew near to occupying the city and he resigned his position as head of state, one which had allowed him to be the patron and employer of Wolfgang Mozart. He continued as the ecclesiastical head of the diocese although not in residence. He died in 1812.

12. BM Brydone Papers 4/437/4/1–44, Journal No 16, Lausanne to Munich and Vienna where they arrive in January 1775.

13. Joseph II (1741–1790), Holy Roman Emperor and ruler of the Hapsburg lands, was greatly influenced by the Enlightenment. He refused to take the Hungarian coronation oath so as not to be constrained by its restrictions, and issued an Edict of Tolerance which gave Protestants and Orthodox Christians full civil rights – and Jews, freedom of worship. He decreed that German should replace latin as the empire's official language

and granted peasants the freedom to leave their holdings, to marry, and place their children in trades. He was to be succeeded by Leopold II who ruled between 1790 and 1792.

14. Baha Banya is probably today's Nova Baoa, a village not far from both Nitra and Trnava

15. BM Brydone Papers 4/438/1/1-40, Journal 17, the tour from Prague to Vienna in April 1776

16. See p.16 of *A Memoir of the Right Honourable Hugh Elliot* by Emma (Nina) Hislop Elliot, published in 1868 in an edition reprinted by Lightening Source UK Ltd. Milton Keynes.

17. Philip Stanhope, 5th Earl of Chesterfield (1755–1815) became a fellow of the Royal Society in December 1776. He served with the 85th Foot becoming a captain in 1779. After holding the office of Lord Lieutenant of Buckinghamshire he became ambassador to Spain between 1784 and 1787, although he never went to Madrid. He held the office of Joint Postmaster-General between 1790 and 1798 and was invested as a Knight, Order of the Garter in January 1805

18. Elector Frederick Augustus III (1750–1827) became King of Saxony in 1806

19. The last Duke of Courland and Semigallia, Peter von Biron (1724–1800) had been born at Jelgava in Latvia and in 1775 he founded the Academia Petrina there, hoping that it would grow into a university. He ceded the government of the Duchy, and then its territory to the Russian Empire in 1795, dying five years later.

20. Christian Clodius (1737–1784) also became professor of logic at Leipzig in 1778 and that of poetry four years later. He was also the permanent secretary of the Jablonski Society, the oldest learned society in existence to promote German-Polish scientific and cultural relations. He probably read the English version of the *Tour through Sicily* given that the German edition was not published in Leipzig till 1777.

21. This may have been Johann Georg Zollikoffer who published a short work of his own in 1770.

22. James Harris (1740–1820), later first Earl of Malmesbury, won the praise of the Prussian court and the esteem of the

king who asked for him to be reappointed but diplomatic relations between the two nations remained cool. In 1777, when he returned to England, he married Harriet, the youngest daughter of Sir George Amyand (1720–1766) MP. His subsequent rise, and postings to St Petersburg and The Hague, followed by missions linked the search for peace with France in 1796–7, led to him being regarded by many as the leading British diplomat of the last quarter of the eighteenth century. A man of intrigue who used all manner of legal and illegal methods to achieve his ends and establish the motivation of others, he was nevertheless, as popular everywhere he served. He became lord lieutenant of Hampshire in 1807 and died at Hill Street, Mayfair in 1820.

23. Sir John Stepney (1743–1811) acknowledged the help of Sir Robert Murray Keith when he wrote to him in Vienna in September 1776. Accepting that the posting somewhat baffled him, he wrote 'that perhaps the fault is in myself and the humour I arrived here in'. He was later transferred to Berlin in 1782 where he served till 1784.

24. Born near Göttingen, Johann Quantz (1697–1773) first studied composition followed by the piano and oboe, becoming the most noted flautist of his day and a composer.

25. Duke Karl of Mecklenburg-Strelitz, heir presumptive till 1794 when he became Karl II, was the brother of Charlotte, King George III's consort, whom he had married in 1761 and who bore him 13 children. Karl served as a young officer at Hannover until 1758 when he spent a year studying in Geneva, and with his elder brother had accompanied Charlotte to England a month before the wedding. He married Princess Friederike of Hesse-Darmstadt seven years later and five of their ten children (four girls and one boy) survived into adulthood.

26. BM Brydone Papers 4/438/1/41-94, Journal 18, the tour to Berlin and Potsdam in April–June 1776.

# Chapter 8 In Poland and the Russian Empire (June to November 1776)

1. BM Brydone Papers 4/438/1/99-111, Journal 18, Berlin to Gross Glogau.

2. *Liberty's Folly*, The Polish-Lithuanian Commonwealth in the eighteenth century 1697–1795, by Jerzy Lukowski, pp 206–7, Routledge.

3. BM Brydone Papers 4/438/1/112-140, Journal 18, Warsaw in June and July 1776.

4. See Dimitry Fedosov's, *The Caledonian Connection, Scotland-Russia Ties (Middle Ages to early Twentieth Century)*, Aberdeen University 1996, and *Scoto-Russian Contacts in the reign of Catherine the Great (1762–1796): Scots in Russia* by Paul Dukes, Professor Cross and others, pp.24–75.

5. The interests of Dr Matthew Guthrie included, botany, zoology, ethnology, history, geography, mineralogy and literature. He was a member of Russia's first musical society in St Petersburg and a founder member of the Royal Society of Edinburgh.

6. Mrs Mariana Starke describes the best inns as *La Ville de Londres, La Ville de Grodno, La Ville de Paris* and *L'Hôtel de Madrid*.

7. Andrey Ivanovich Osterman (1686–1747) came to Russia from Germany in 1703 and was appointed by Peter the Great as an interpreter in the Russian foreign office, being made a secretary in 1710. He was made a baron for the work he did to achieve the Treaty of Nystad (1721) and became Minister of Foreign Affairs. His son, Count Ivan Andreyevich Osterman (1725–1811) had no children of his own, and the name and title passed to a nephew, one Leo Tolstoy.

8. See Herbert H Kaplan's *Russian Overseas Commerce with Great Britain during the reign of Catherine II*, American Philosophical Society.

9. Formerly a Swedish chancellor's estate, Peter the Great built a temporary wooden palace at Strelna in 1718 and it was not until 1741 that his daughter Elizabeth, and the architect

Bartolomeo Rastrelli expanded the original design prepared by Nicholo Michetti. After what Brydone referred to as its 'abandonment', it was not until the end of the century and despite a great fire in 1803 that the present Constantine Pace (named after the second son of Paul I) was completed.

10. Sir Robert Gunning's replacement was James Harris, first Earl of Malmesbury, who had been serving in Berlin. He arrived in St Petersburg in the autumn of 1777.
11. In her journal, Katherine Harris describes her brother playing tennis with his secretary, Richard Oakes.
12. HRO Malmesbury Collection, Letters from William Morton Pitt to Sir James Harris on 20/31 May and 11 June 1778.
13. BM Brydone Papers 4/438/1/145-230, Journal 18, the tour to and from Riga and St Petersburg in August and September 1776.
14. Having lost both parents in 1751, Leopold III (1740–1817), Duke of Anhalt-Dessau, joined the army, fighting at the battle of Kolin in Bohemia during the Seven Years' War.
15. The Polish king was at the head of the Diet. Many members served only two years. Its Permanent Council had five departments – those of foreign affairs, police, war, justice and the treasury.
16. John Sackville, third Duke of Dorset (1745–1799) joined Hambledon Cricket Club in Hampshire, the leading club of its day, and became an elegant and unrivalled cricket, tennis and billiards player,despite the cost of maintaining a cricket team and the serious expense of betting associated with the sport. In 1784 he became ambassador to France and two years later *The Times* reported that the French 'could not imitate us in such vigorous exertions of the body', and His Grace was 'as usual the most distinguished for skill and activity'. He died at Knole House, Sevenoaks in 1799.
17. BM Brydone Papers 4/438/1/231-327, Journal 18, the tour in September–November 1776 from Riga to Berlin, and onward to Calais.

# Chapter 9 Becomes tutor to the Prime Minister's sons (1777–1778)

1. BM Brydone Papers 4/306/5, Letter from Brydone to his brother, Matthew, 18 April 1777.
2. Married three times, Francis North, the first Earl of Guilford (1704–1790), had been at Eton and matriculated from Trinity College, Oxford in 1721. Returned to the House of Commons for Banbury in 1727, he held the seat till he succeeded his father two years later. After service to George II he became an intimate personal friend of George III and Queen Charlotte, sympathising with the crown's dislike of the Fox-North coalition in 1783. He died at his London residence in Henrietta Street, Marylebone and was buried at Wroxton.
3. See volume 1, p.459 of *Lord North* by Alan Valentine, University of Oklahoma Press, 1967.
4. Francis North is several times referred to in Brydone's journals as 'the captain' suggesting that he had not only been promoted sometime in 1778–9 but permitted to continue his travels.
5. See p.5 of Peter D G Thomas's *Lord North*, Allen Lane.
6. In the 17th century, the physician of Dudley North (1581–1666), 3rd Baron North, claimed that the waters in Kent could cure the colic, melancholy and the vapours.
7. BM Brydone Papers, Journal No.10, 19 July to 16 August 1777.
8. BM Brydone Papers 4/301/17, Letter from Lord North to Brydone, 22 August 1777.
9. Monsieur Porta who dealt with Brydone's financial transactions may have been a relative of Minister Chavannes-Porta.
10. BM Brydone Papers 4/302/2, Letter from Lord Guilford to Brydone, 1 December 1777.
11. BM Brydone Papers 4/301/9, Letter from Lord Guilford to Brydone, 23 March 1778.
12. 'Rustic Socrates' was a series of sketches of a Swiss peasant named 'Kleinjogg' and had been dedicated to *l'ami des hommes* in 1762. It dispensed farming advice, endorsed obedience to the dictates of nature, and offered a blueprint for a revitalized peasant economy.
13. Jakob (1694–1758), Johannes (1707–1771) and Hans Ulrich

Grubenmann started as village carpenters in Teufen, becoming famous Swiss civil engineers, along with Hans Ulrich who was responsible for the bridge at Schaffhausen in 1757.

14. BM Brydone Papers, Journal No11, 20 June to 27 July 1778.
15. BM Brydone Papers 4/301/3, Letter from Lord Guilford to Brydone, 19 August 1778.
16. BM Brydone Papers 4/301/4, Letter from Lord Guilford to Brydone, 24 September 1778.
17. Horace-Bénédict de Saussure (1740–1799) was to undertake numerous Alpine climbs. He saw them as the key to unlocking the history of the earth, and in 1783 he published an *Essai sur l'hygromètrie*. He also invented the first successful solar oven. His son, Nicolas-Théodore de Saussure became a specialist in organic chemistry whilst his daughter, Albertine, was a supporter of women's education.
18. John Campbell (1696–1782), the third Earl of Breadalbane, was a retired politician and diplomat. His son by his second wife married Willielma Maxwell (1743–1786) but he died aged 33 without surviving issue. The peerage and estates passed to the Campbells of Carwhin.
19. NRS GD 112/74/2/7-8, Letters from John and Colin Campbell to their mother, November–December 1778.

# Chapter 10 A Third Tour with George and Francis North (May–October 1779)

1. Possibly Thomas Bruce (1766–1841), the seventh Earl of Elgin, despite his youth. He was at Westminster School from 1778.
2. BM Brydone Papers 4/301/6, Letter from Lord Guilford to Brydone, 20 May 1779.
3. *The Pembroke Papers (1734–1780)*, Letters and Diaries of Henry, tenth Earl of Pembroke and his circle (edited by Lord Herbert), Jonathan Cape, 1939 pp.180–181.
4. BM Brydone Papers 4/301/6, Letter from Lord Guilford to Brydone, 20 May 1779.
5. Salt production at Salins-les-Bains and Arc-en-Senans was based on tapping sources of salt deep underground, the use

of fire to evaporate the brine, and a 15 mile pipeline to carry the brine between the two sites.

6. Born in Germany, Hans Holbein (*c*.1497–1543) moved to Basle and between 1523 and 1536 developed the 'Dance of Death'.

7. John Bird (1709–1776), who was born in Co. Durham, constructed a similar brass instrument for the Greenwich Royal Observatory In 1749–50. Orders for a similar instrument followed from St Petersburg, Stockholm and Cadiz.

8. BM Brydone Papers, Journal No.12, 30 May–30 June 1779.

9. At the beginning of 1778, Charles Theodore, Elector of Bavaria (1724–1799) signed an agreement with Emperor Joseph II whereby Southern Bavaria would be exchanged for part of the Austrian Netherlands. The plan was strongly opposed by the next heir of the Palatinate, and given the support of Frederick II of Prussia. The War of the Bavarian Succession lasted only 12 months, and had no battles and was referred to by soldiers who died through cold and starvation as the 'Potato War', It ended in May 1779 with the Peace of Teschen, only a month or so before Brydone and Lord North's sons arrived in Munich.

10. Joseph Adam, Prince of Schwarzen (1722–1782) married MarieTheresa von Liechtenstein (1721–1753) in 1741, and later gained the title of Duke of Krumlov.

11. BM Brydone Papers, Journal No.20, July 1779.

12. Probably Sir William Jerningham (1726–1809) who married the Hon. Frances Dillon.

13. Lewis de Visme arrived in April 1770, residing there for two or three weeks before living most of the time at Munich. He was recalled in 1774, being replaced by Hugh Elliot who also resided in Munich before moving post to Berlin in 1777. Morton Eden (later Baron Henley) arrived in Ratisbon at the beginning of 1777 but left before 1778 and did not return, being re-posted in 1780.

14. BM Brydone Papers, Journal No.20, August–September 1779.

15. The first part of Journal No.21 is addressed to 'Dear Sir' with no date but on the outside is the word 'North' alongside

'Holland'. Below is a list of towns visited i.e. Brussels, Antwerp, Bergen-op-zoom, Rotterdam, Leyden, Utrecht and Amsterdam. Thereafter, the usual format returns.

16. BM Brydone Papers, Journal No.21, October 1779.
17. BL Add.61874 North Sheffield Park Papers ff.63–64, Letter from Brydone to Lord North, 12 July 1779.
18. BM Brydone Papers 4/301/8, Letter from Lord Guilford to Brydone, 2 August 1779.
19. BM Brydone Papers 4/301/5, Letter from Lord Guilford to Brydone, 20 September 1779.
20. BL Add.61874 North Sheffield Park Papers ff.65–69, Letter from Brydone to Lord North, 19 November 1779.

# Chapter 11 Accepts employment with the Stamp Office (1780–1784)

1. BM Brydone Papers 4/300/2 Letter from Francis, Prince of Anhalt to Brydone 24 February 1780.
2. BL Add.35518, f.212–213, Brydone to Sir Robert Murray Keith, 7 April 1780.
3. BL Add.35518, f.23–25, Brydone to Sir Robert Murray Keith, 9 June 1780.
4. Horace Walpole's *Correspondence,* edited by W S Lewis, Yale (1941) pp.232–3.
5. The Somerset House Trust suggests that the Stamp Office formally moved into the new Somerset House in 1789 whilst the London Stamp Office opened premises in Lombard Street in 1795 to deal specifically with insurance policies.
6. *The Universal Gazetteer,* 1822.
7. Louis Dutens (1730–1812), a French writer who lived much of his life in Britain, came to London as a youth to live with his uncle. He obtained a post as tutor in a private family which enabled him to study Greek and mathematics, not unlike Brydone. After taking orders, he became chaplain and secretary to the English minister at the court of Turin in 1758. In the 1760s, he was *chargé d'affaires* at Turin for two periods, during which time he published a complete

edition of the works of Leibnitz. Returning to England in 1763, the Duke of Northumberland obtained the living of Elsdon for him, and appointed him overseer and senior travel companion, in effect tutor to his younger son during his Grand Tour. Writing in his *Memoirs of a Traveller, now in Retirement,* which was published in 1808, Dutens said: 'I was not considered in the capacity of Lord Algernon's tutor, but he had been commanded to conduct himself according to my advice, and to pay the same deference to me that he would to his father himself'.

8. John Byng (1733–1814) became the fifth Viscount Torrington on the death of his brother George in 1812. His travels on horseback across England and Wales during the summers of twelve years between 1781 and 1794, his antiquarian's outlook, his studies of gravestones and ruins, fine sketches but less-successful watercolours, and his love of architecture, were to lead eventually to the successful publication of fifteen or so diaries

9. NA The *Royal Kalendar* for 1782 and 1784

10. Dagnall's *Creating a Good Impression*, p.100.

11. Dagnall's *Creating a Good Impression*, p. 95.

12. Stebbing. *The Victorian Taxpayer and the Law – a study in Constitutional Conflict.*

13. NA AO1/2202/244, General Account of Stamps, 1802

14. NA AO1/2199/232 and AO1/2202/244, General Account of Stamps, 1791 and 1802.

15. NLS MS 11087–88, Brydone to Gilbert Elliot, 1 December 1806

16. *Bristol Presentments 1770–1917,* W E Minchinton, University of Exeter 1986.

17. The second Earl Grosvenor (1767–1845) succeeded his father in 1802, having been a commissioner of the Board of Control (for managing the affairs of India) between 1791 and 1803. One of the wealthiest men in England, he started the development of Belgravia with William Cubitt in the late 1820s.

18. NLS MS 11087–88, Brydone to Gilbert Elliot, 13 December 1806.

19. Published in *Lloyd's Evening Post* (16–19 March 1781

edition).

20. Brydone's requests included the pocket edition of Armstrong's abridged map of Northumberland, and a work on gardening by the Revd William Hanbury, born in 1725, who became Rector of Church Langton in Leicestershire. (Yale University, Beinecke Rare Book and Manuscript Library, Osborn Files. Letter dated 18 June 1782).

21. BM Brydone Papers 4/301/16 Letter to Brydone from George North, 25 September (year not shown).

22. BL Add 61874, North, Sheffield Park Papers, ff.72–73, Frederick to Lord North, before October 1782

23. BL Add.61874, North, Sheffield Park Papers, ff.80–81, Brydone to Lord North, 2 June 1783.

24. BL Add 61874, North, Sheffield Park Papers, ff.92–93, George to Lord North, 21 December 1783.

25. BL Add.61874, North, Sheffield Park Papers, ff.84–86, Brydone to Lord North, 26 December 1783.

26. BM Brydone Papers 4/301/11, Lord North to Brydone, 5 February 1784.

27. BL Add 61874, North, Sheffield Park Papers, ff.90–91, Accounts from Brydone to Lord North, (undated).

28. BM Brydone Papers 4/301/14, Lord North to Brydone, 3 June 1784.

29. Sheila Szatkowski, *Capital Caricatures, p.36*

30. BM Brydone Papers 4/301/13, Letter from Lord North to Brydone 26 December 1785.

# Chapter 12 Brydone marries at last (1785–1805)

1. Thomas Binning, seventh Earl of Haddington (1720–1795) had been educated at Oxford and the University of Geneva, but he played no part in public affairs. James Grimston succeeded his father in 1773, becoming Baron Verulam in 1790. He died in 1808.

2. Mary's younger siblings were William (1753–1835) who became a judge; Eleanor (1755–1837) who married John Russell, a writer to the signet; Janet (1756–1789); James (1762–1845), an army officer; and David (1764–1845) who

became a lieutenant-colonel.

3. It seems that Jenny, as Janet was known in the family, died in December 1789.

4. BM Brydone Papers 4/306/22, Letter from William Robertson to Brydone, 14 April 1785.

5. *The Poetical Works of Sir Walter Scott*, Volume II, p.252, Edinburgh 1857.

6. BM Brydone Papers 4/300/11, Letter from Brydone to his wife, 20 December 1785.

7. BM Brydone Papers 4/301/12, Letter from Lord North to Brydone, 29 December 1785.

8. BL Add.61874, North, Sheffield Park Papers, Brydone to Lord North, 16 January 1786.

9. Leonard S et al, *The Grange: A Case for Conservation*, pp.12–13. A map of the Grange estate around that time shows a road leading from the house towards the West Kirk or St Cuthbert's. A nearby farm and cottages probably belonged to labourers or servants at the house. A map of 1817 suggests other large houses in the grounds, one of which became the home of Lord Cockburn.

10. Charles Stanhope (1753–1816) was a politician and inventor, who as Lord Mahon unsuccessfully contested a seat at Westminster in 1773. He married the sister of William Pitt, the Younger, the following year and in 1780 came into parliament for the pocket borough of Chipping Wycombe. After attending Eton he studied mathematics at the University of Geneva, becoming an accomplished scientist. He was elected a fellow of the Royal Society in 1772, going on to invent a printing press, two calculating machines and the lens that bears his name. He published a volume in 1779 entitled *Principles of Electricity* which contained the beginning of a theory about the electrical power of lightning. Between 1790 and 1807 he registered numerous patents for steamships and worked with the Admiralty and the engineers Boulton and Paul.

11. NLS *Remarks on Mr Brydone's Account* ... by Charles, Earl Stanhope, London, 15 February 1787.

12. George Kearsley (c.1739–1790) was a London bookseller

who enjoyed some initial success, producing sixty or so imprints a year, but who was soon the subject of expensive court cases and made bankrupt on several occasions. Formally discharged in 1765, he re-established his business only to run foul of the authorities again on account of the anomalies in the laws relating to authorship. Nevertheless, in 1785, he came out with a biography of Johnson shortly after his death, and in later years with the firm now profitable, its ownership passed initially to his widow and his son George who ran the business till 1813.

13. NLS *The Present State of Sicily and Malta extracted from Mr Brydone, Mt Swinburne and other modern travellers*, printed for G. Kearsley in 1788.

14. BM Brydone Papers 4/300/19, Letter from William Robertson to Brydone, 4 November 1789.

15. The Jamaica Historical Review 1964, article by Richard B Sheridan about the career of William Beckford 1744–1799.

16. In 1785, William Beckford attended the baptism of one of his Jamaican servants, the 40 year-old Sigismunda Beckford and became one of a number of Suffolk landowners who had retired from plantations both in the West Indies and the southern American states. The names of their male and female servants brought to England to serve in their masters' houses, appear in numerous parish registers.

17. NRS WRH TD 77/142, Letter from William Robertson to Brydone, 29 September 1790.

18. NRS WRH TD 77/142, Letter from Wiilliam Robertson to Brydone, 13 October 1792.

19. NLS MS 3944/131, Letter from Brydone to William Robertson, 1 April 1793.

20. NRS 1454/4/306 Letter from William Robertson to Brydone, 10 April 1793.

21. After asking to be relieved on health grounds, Frederick was sent home in 1805 but he soon resumed his travels, visiting a host of countries from Spain to Russia before settling in Italy. Outliving his elder brothers, he became the fifth Earl Guilford at the beginning of 1817, and three years later was

made director of education for the Ionian Islandswith the help of his cousin, Lord Bathurst. Already president of the Philomousos Society of Athens which had been formed to promote education among Greeks, the earl became chancellor (or *archōn)* of the University of Corfu in 1819 and was created GCMG the same year. He sat in on lectures, provided student bursaries, gave financial support for professorial costs, along with much of his own books and manuscripts in Greek. Again he was forced through ill-health to return to England and he died at the home of his sister Anne, the dowager countess of Sheffield, in Portland Place in October 1827.

22. BM Brydone Papers 4/300/24 Letter from Brydone to his wife, 23 May 1795.

23. John Russell W.S. (1753–1792) married Eleanor Robertson 1755–1837); their son John Russell W.S. (1780–1862) was to marry Cecilia Murray and give birth to another John who also became a Writer to the Signet.

24. BM Brydone Papers 4/300/26 Letter from Brydone to his wife, No Date.

25. BM Brydone Papers 4/301/15 Letter to Brydone from Frederick North, 17 February 1798.

26. See Vol 3, p.249 of the *Life of the Rt Hon William Pitt* by Lord Stanhope (1862).

27. Pitt was exhausted, with his management of the war at its lowest level, and little, if any, strategic vision left, he would resign early in 1801 for a period till his second ministry in 1804.

28. Born at Mertoun in Berwickshire, Hugh Scott (1758–1841) married Harriet de Brühl, the daughter of the Saxon minister to London, becoming MP for Berwickshire in 1780. A consistent supporter of the North administration, he voted against Shelburne's peace preliminaries in 1782 as well as Fox's East India bill in 1783. He was twenty-six when he returned to the life of a country gentleman. He had a lively interest in music and the arts.

29. Henry Francis Scott, seventh Lord Polwarth, married Lady Georgina Baillie in 1835. They had two sons and a daughter. He died in 1867 aged sixty-seven.

30. It seems possible that Brydone dined with Edward Hamilton of Sion Hill, Clifton. The 1814 Bristol Directory lists a Colonel Edward Hamilton of 7 Sion Hill, Clifton and a Miss Elizabeth Hamilton of 11 York Place, Clifton, as living in buildings constructed 'circa 1800' and early 19th century', respectively. However, the church rate for the parish of Clifton for 1798 and 1804, only shows Edward Hamilton of Sion Hill, Clifton in January 1800.

31. NRS GD 157/2338/1 Letter from Brydone to Hugh Scott 24–26 January 1800

32. NLS MS 12981 ff.195–6, Mary Brydone to Elizabeth Bell, May 1802.

33. James Anderson's only surviving child, Mary, came into her inheritance in 1856.

34. NLS MS 12951, ff.1–2, James Anderson to Brydone, 4 June 1806.

35. NLS MS 12951, ff.3–4, Frederick North to Brydone, 15 June 1806.

36. NLS MS 12951, ff.8–9, Lord Minto to Brydone, 23 June 1806.

37. Sir Gilbert Blane (1749–1834) received a degree in medicine from Glasgow University in 1778. He became personal physician to Rodney, with whom he sailed to the West Indies during the American War of Independence. Writing on healthcare followed and he became physician-extraordinary to the Prince of Wales in 1785. He played a significant part in improving surgical procedures and care for the sick and wounded at sea, introducing an issue of lemon juice. He resigned from the navy in 1802 and received a baronetcy in 1812. He became a member of the two Royal Societies and the Imperial Academy of Sciences at St Petersburg.

38. NLS MS 12951, ff.10–11, William Fullarton to Brydone, 30 June 1806.

39. Probably the son of his namesake, minister at Eccles till his death in 1773.

40. NLS MS 12951, ff.12–13, Matthew Sandilands to Brydone, 30 June 1806.

41. NLS MS 12951, ff.40–41, Marianne Fullarton to Mrs

Brydone, 2 July 1806.

42. The Scottish pastel artist, Archibald Skirving (1749–1819) started his career with an exuberant portrait of Catherine Hume of Ninewells, her father being John Hume.

43. NLS MS 12951, ff.42–43, Catherine Anderson to Mrs Brydone, 4 July 1806.

44. NLS MS 12951, ff.44–45, John Robertson to Mrs Brydone, 3 July 1806.

45. NLS MS 12951, ff.46–47, Lady Home to Mrs Brydone, 5 July 1806.

46. NLS MS 12951, ff.14–15, William Waite to Brydone, 28 August 1806.

47. Margarita Macdonald (1773–1844) married Lt.Col David Robertson Macdonald, the son of the Rev William Robertson in 1799. They had a son William who became the 9th of Kinlochmoidart.

48. Abigail Ramey married Reverend Alexander Home, the ninth earl of Home who died in 1786.

49. NLS MS 12951, ff.62–63, Lady Charlotte Baillie to Mrs Brydone, 12 September 1806.

# Chapter 13 Life at Lennel and Minto (1806–1810)

1. Coldstream OPR Marriages; 733.

2. Sir Gilbert (1st Earl Minto) and Anna Maria Amyand had three daughters. Harriet Mary Frances Elliot was born on 5 June 1790, and died at Brougham Hall in Westmoreland in July 1825. Anna-Maria Elliot died in 1855 and Catherine Sarah Elliot, born circa 1798, died in June 1862.

3. Eleanor Elizabeth Elliot (ed.), *Life and Letters of Gilbert Elliot, First Earl of Minto from 1751 to 1806*, vol 3, pp.400–401.

4. NLS MS 12951, ff.18–19, Lord Minto to Brydone, 20 September 1806.

5. NLS MS 11087, Brydone to Lord Minto, 21 November 1806.

6. NLS MS 11087, Brydone to Lord Minto, 1 December 1806.

7. NLS MS 11087, Brydone to Lord Minto, 13 December 1806.

8. George Elliot (1784–1863) went into the navy when he

was 10 and in 1803 he was serving with Nelson in the Mediterranean. Later that year he posted him to the frigate *Maidstone*. Subsequently he became an MP and in 1835 a Lord Commissioner at the Admiralty. After a period as commander-in-chief at the Cape he was sent to China and in 1862, when by then an admiral, he was made a KCB. John Edmund Elliot (1788–1862) sat as the MP for Roxburgh in 1837 and between 1847 and 1859, and became joint secretary to the Board of Control subsequently. He married Amelia Casamaijor in 1809.

9.  NLS MS 11087, Brydone to Lord Minto, a second letter on 13 December 1806.
10. NLS MS 12951, ff.20–23, Gilbert Elliot to Mary, 24 March 1807.
11. NLS MS 11087, Gilbert Elliot to Lord Minto, 28 March 1807.
12. NLS MS 11087, Gilbert Elliot to Lord Minto, 11 April 1807.
13. NLS MS 11087, Gilbert Elliot to Lord Minto, 13 June 1807.
14. NLS MS 11087, Gilbert Elliot to Lord Minto, 1 August 1807.
15. NLS MS 11087, Mary Elliot to Lord Minto, 1 August 1807.
16. NLS MS 11087, Gilbert Elliot to Lord Minto, 9 September 1807.
17. NLS MS 11087, Brydone to Lord Minto, 13 October 1807.
18. NLS MS 11087, Gilbert Elliot to Lord Minto, 15 October 1807.
19. NLS MS 12951, ff.74–75, Lady Minto to Mrs Brydone, 1807.
20. For more information about Robert and the Selby family see *The Victorian Elliots in peace and war, Lord and Lady Minto, their family and household between 1816 and 1901* by the author, published by Amberley Books in 2012.
21. NLS MS 11087, Gilbert Elliot to Lord Minto, 8 February 1808.
22. 'Picketing' was a version of British military punishment, and consisted in principle of compelling the tied-up suspect to stand on one toe, on a flat-headed peg, for one hour on several separate occasions.
23. Born the fourth son of Sir Gilbert Elliot, second baronet, John Elliot (1732–1808) went to sea in 1740, passing his lieutenant's examination in 1752 and after obtaining a commission four years later he was appointed to command

HMS *Hussar*. Service in the English Channel between Quiberon Bay and Ireland followed, and both Westminster and the Irish Houses of Parliament thanked him capturing and killing François Thurot, the French privateer. In 1777 he carried the commissioners appointed to negotiate with the colonists to America, and in November 1781, he commanded HMS *Edgar*, moving to HMS *Romney* the following year, but peace left him unemployed and he was appointed governor of Newfoundland. Retiring from the navy as an admiral of the white in 1795, Elliot retired to his seat at Mount Teviot in Roxburghshire where he lived out his last years. He had been MP for Cockermouth between 1786 and 1788. Never married his estates were left to his nethew, Gilbert Elliot, the first earl of Minto.

24. NRS GD 157/2338/2, Brydone to Hugh Scott 10 March 1808.
25. NLS MS 11087, Brydone to Lord Minto, 31 March 1808.
26. NLS MS 11087, Gilbert Elliot to Lord Minto, 4 June 1808.
27. NLS MS 11976 ff.3–4, Gilbert Elliot's Notebook.
28. NLS MS 11087, Gilbert Elliot to Lord Minto, 21 August 1808.
29. William Elliot (1766–1818) was descended from a branch of the same family as Elliot of Stobs and Minto. Gilbert encountered him as a law student in 1786, describing him as a Whig in politics and 'very sensible, modest and agreeable'. He was MP for Portarlington between 1801and 1802, and Peterborough between 1802 and 1818, living at Wells near Jedburgh and Reigate in England. He became Chief Secretary for Ireland in the Ministry of all the Talents and was made a Privy Counsellor in 1806. Elliot was to be much affected by the death in 1810 of William Windham who had been secretary at war between 1794 and 1801.
30. John Goldingham (1767–1849) used achromatic telescopes designed by Dolland, of three and half feet focal length and a magnifying power of between 70 and 80.
31. NLS MS 11087, Brydone to Lord Minto, September 1808.
32. NLS MS 11087, Gilbert Elliot to Lord Minto, 17 December 1808.
33. NLS MS 11087, Mary to Lord Minto, 18 December 1808.

34. John Elliot (1732–1818), the fourth son of Sir Gilbert Elliot, the lord chief justice of Scotland, entered the navy in 1740, becoming a lord of the Admiralty sixteen years later. On active service as a captain between 1757 and 1786, he served in various ships of the Channel Fleet, being appointed governor and commander-in-chief of Newfoundland in 1786–8. After hoisting his flag as rear and vice-admiral in 1787 and 1790 respectively, his last ship being the Barfleur. He finally became an admiral in 1795 and retired to Mount Teviot, his seat, soon after. He never married. In addition to a bequest of £10,000 to Lady Carnegie, the eldest daughter of the earl of Northesk, and '£500 for a house this year', other beneficiaries were Lord Cathcart, £7,000; Lord Auckland, Hugh and Robert Elliot, £3,000 a piece, Mr Bethune and John received £1,000 each, and in addition to the continuation of her annuity, Miss Marianne received £2,000. Lord Minto was named as his executor, for which he received £2,000.

35. NLS MS 11087, Gilbert Elliot to Lord Minto, 11/12 February 1809.

36. Hansard 1803–2005, House of Commons debate 3 May 1809, volume 14 cc340–1.

37. NLS MS 11087, Gilbert Elliot to Lord Minto, 24 March 1809.

38. NLS MS 11087, Gilbert Elliot to Lord Minto, 28 March 1809.

39. See Chapter X of *Lord Minto in India – Life and Letters of Gilbert Elliot, First Earl of Minto from 1807 to 1814*, edited by Eleanor Elizabeth (Nina) Elliot, third Countess of Minto, Longmans, Green & Co., 1880.

40. NLS MS 11087, Gilbert Elliot to Lord Minto, 31 March 1809.

41. NLS MS 11087, Gilbert Elliot to Lord Minto, 21 and 22 May 1809.

42. NLS MS 11087, Gilbert Elliot to Lord Minto, 21 December 1808.

43. NLS MS 11087, Gilbert Elliot to Lord Minto, 19 October 1809.

44. NLS MS 11087, Gilbert Elliot to Lord Minto, 27 January 1810.

45. NLS MS 11087, Gilbert Elliot to Lord Minto, 25 March 1810.

46. NLS MS 11087, Gilbert Elliot to Lord Minto, 16 April 1810.

47. NLS MS 11087, Gilbert Elliot to Lord Minto, 17 April 1810.

48. NLS MS 11087, Gilbert Elliot to Lady Minto, 18 April 1810.

49. NLS MS 11087, Gilbert Elliot to Lady Minto, 20 April 1810.

50. NLS MS 11087, Gilbert Elliot to Lord Minto, 27 May 1810.

51. House of Commons Papers, 'Incidental Charges for Stamps in Scotland in the years 1807 and 1808, ordered to be printed by the House of Commons 20 June 1810'.

52. NLS MS 11087, Gilbert Elliot to Lord Minto, 13 and 23 June 1810.

53. NLS MS 11087, Mary to Lord Minto, 18 July 1810.

54. NLS MS 11087, Gilbert Elliot to Lord Minto, 21 July 1810.

55. NLS MS 11087, Elizabeth Brydone to Lord Minto, 29 November 1810.

# Chapter 14 Brydone, the Elliots and the return of Lord Minto (1811–1814)

1. NLS MS 11088, Gilbert Elliot to Lord Minto, 5 January 1811.

2. NLS MS 11088, Gilbert Elliot to Lord Minto. 12 January 1811.

3. NLS MS 11088, Gilbert Elliot to Lord Minto, 18 February 1811.

4. Gilbert Elliot wrote some 40 to 50 usually long and often tortuous letters to his father Lord Minto in India between 1806 and 1814. He felt overshadowed and somewhat bewildered by his pre-eminence.

5. NLS MS 11088, Harriet Mary Elliot to Gilbert Elliot, 30 March 1811.

6. NLS MS 11088, Mary to Lord Minto, 7 April 1811.

7. William Somerville (1771–1860) was born at Minto and became a military surgeon, serving in South Africa and later in the Mediterranean on operations against Napoleon. After duty as inspector-general of hospitals in Canada he returned home, working as head of the army medical department in Scotland between 1813 and 1816 when he moved to London. He married Mary Fairfax (1780–1872), a cousin, one of the first two women to be admitted to the Royal Astronomical Society, and who had Somerville College, Oxford named after her.

8. Lord John Webb Seymour (1777–1819) was the youngest son

of the tenth Duke of Somerset who died in 1793. He became a Fellow of the Royal Society and remained unmarried.

9. NLS MS 11088, Gilbert Elliot to Lord Minto, 23 May 1811.

10. The two brothers in India from a family of nine children were John Bell, later major in the EIC forces, and Charles Hamilton Bell.

11. NLS MS 11088, Mary to Lord Minto, 28 May and 4 June 1811.

12. NLS MS 11088, Gilbert Elliot to Lord Minto, 17 July 1811.

13. BL Newspaper Collection

14. A Londoner, William Hawes (1736–1818), philanthropist and physician, attracted attention in 1773 through his interest in resuscitating victims of apparent drowning and other causes of asphyxia. He was instrumental in establishing an institution, after Amsterdam's example, which became the Humane Society in 1776 and acquired the prefix 'Royal' some ten years later. His principal work, which Brydone may have consulted, was *The Transactions of the Royal Humane Society* (1795) which contained much information about resuscitative practice. He received the degree of MD from Aberdeen University in 1779 and began practising as a doctor. At the turn of the century he was still living in the Spital Square area of East London where he had helped save some 1200 families from destitution.

15. NLS MS 11088, Gilbert Elliot to Lord Minto, 30 August 1811.

16. NLS MS 11088, Gilbert Elliot to Lord Minto, 2 September 1811.

17. NLS MS 11088, Gilbert Elliot to Lord Minto, 22 October 1811.

18. NLS MS 11088, Gilbert Elliot to Lord Minto, 25 December 1811.

19. NLS MS 11088, Gilbert Elliot to Lord Minto, 4 January 1812.

20. NLS MS 11088, Gilbert Elliot to Lord Minto, 29 February and 2 March 1812.

21. NLS MS 11088, Gilbert Elliot to Lord Minto, 2 and 4 April 1812.

22. NLS MS 11088, Gilbert Elliot to Lord Minto, 25 April 1812.

23. NLS MS 11088, Mary to Lord Minto, 19 and 20 May 1812.

24. NLS MS 11088, Gilbert Elliot to Lord Minto, 28 June to 1 July 1812.
25. Samuel Romilly (1757–1818) who married Anne Garbett in 1798, became MP for Queenborough (1806), (Wareham (1808) and Arundel (1812). They had one daughter and six sons, the youngest of whom, Frederick, went on to marry Gilbert and Mary Brydone's daughter Elizabeth Amelia Jane Elliot (1823–1892). During the summer of 1818 Sir Samuel suffered considerable mental strain, and when his 'dear Anne' died at the end of October after an illness of several months, he took his own life by cutting his throat a few days later at his house in Russell Square.
26. Once in India, as Roland Thorne writes in his Oxford DNB essay on Francis Rawdon Hastings, first Marquess of Hastings and second Earl of Moira (1754–1826), he restored etiquette in the vice regal household to something like that at Dublin Castle, replacing Lord Minto's informalities. Gilbert Elliot had anticipated that 'Lord Moira will require all the splendour with which he intends to surround himself to conceal the disgrace which he has incurred'. (Gilbert to Lord Minto 29 March 1813).
27. NLS MS 11088, Gilbert Elliot to Lord Minto, 4 November 1812.
28. NLS MS 11088, Mary to Lord Minto, 17 November 1812.
29. NLS MS 11088, Gilbert Elliot to Lord Minto, 19 January 1813.
30. NLS MS 11088, Gilbert Elliot to Lord Minto, 22 February 1813.
31. NLS MS 11088, Gilbert Elliot to Lord Minto, 8 March 1813.
32. NLS MS 11088, Mary to Lord Minto, 27 March 1813.
33. From *Lord Minto in India, Life and Letters of Gilbert Elliot, First Earl of Minto from 1807 to 1811,* edited by his great-niece, the Countess of Minto, Longmans, Green and Co., London, 1880, pp.384–385, Lord Minto to Lady Minto, 19 May 1814.
34. Ibid p.389, Lady Minto to Lord Minto, 19 and 21 May 1814.
35. Ibid p.390, Lord Minto to Lady Minto, 27 May 1814.
36. Michael Duffy, in his Oxford DNB essay, suggests that the

disease suffered by Lord Minto was a 'stranguary' or a urinary disease of some longstanding.

37. From *Lord Minto in India etc.,* pp.390–392, 27 May 1814.
38. Ibid pp.392–394.

## Chapter 15 The Final Years (1815–1818)

1. NLS MS12009, ff.20–23, Mary Elliot's Journal (scribbled notes only) from 1 January to 16 March 1815.
2. Lockhart's *Life of Scott,* ed.1839, Chap. X, page 109.
3. Published by William Ward in 1818 by Colnaghi & Co. of 23 Cockspur Street, London.
4. The diary of Robert Burns, Monday 7 May 1787. See Chapter 12 for Burns's description of Brydone's wife Mary.
5. Adam Clarke's *Bible Commentary,* Notes on Genesis, Chapter 1.
6. Dr Samuel Heinrich Spiker (1786–1858) had been born in Berlin and studied at Halle University where he was awarded a PhD. He came to Britain in September 1815 partly to buy books for the royal library, returning in November 1816 to prepare for his travels through England, Wales and Scotland. Dr Spiker also translated some works of Shakespeare and Sir Walter Scott into German and in 1827, while working in the Royal Library, he became the editor-in-chief of the *Spenersche Zeitung* in Berlin. He also published several songs and met Beethoven who presented him with a handwritten copy of his ninth symphony.
7. Dr Spiker's *Travels through England, Wales & Scotland in the year 1816* Vol 1, pp.136–150.
8. Amisfield House, a Palladian mansion designed by Isaac Ware for Francis Charteris, the seventh Earl of Wemyss, in and around the 1750s. Now demolished it was used between 1881 and the First World War as accommodation for the Lothian and Border Horse regiment.
9. NLS MS 11892, ff.43–44, Mary to Mrs Brydone, 25 March 1816.
10. NLS MS 11892, ff.45–46, Mary to Mrs Brydone, 17April 1816.
11. NLS MS 11892, ff.47–48, Gilbert to Mrs Brydone, 10 May

1816.

12. NLS MS 11892, ff.62–63, Mary to Mrs Brydone, 30 October and 15 November 1816.

13. NLS MS 11892, ff.64–65, Mary to Mrs Brydone, 11 November 1816.

14. NLS MS 11892, ff.66–68, Mary to Mrs Brydone, 21 December 1816.

15. NLS MS 11892, ff.69–70, Gilbert to Mrs Brydone, 3 January 1817.

16. The member of the eminent Edinburgh Playfair family referred to may have been James (1736–1819) who published his *System of Geography, Ancient and Modern* in 1810 and *General Atlas Ancient and Modern* in 1814, or John (1748–1819), another mathematician and geologist.

17. NLS MS 11892, ff.72–73, Mary to Patrick Brydone, 5 March 1817.

18. For the record, Eliza Elliot was to marry the fourth Marquess of Northampton in 1844, have eight children and live till the end of 1877.

19. NLS MS 11892, ff.74–76, Mary to Mrs Brydone, 7 March 1817.

20. NLS MS 11892, ff.77–79, Gilbert to Patrick Brydone, 30 March and 3 April 1817.

21. NLS MS 11892, ff.80–83, Gilbert to Mrs Brydone, 1 May 1817.

22. NLS MS 11892, ff.88–90, Mary and Gilbert to Mrs Brydone, 29–30 June 1817.

23. NLS MS 11892, f.91, Mary to Mrs Brydone, 2 July 1817.

24. NLS MS 11892, ff.92–93, Gilbert to Mrs Brydone, 2 July 1817.

25. NLS MS 11892, ff.98–99, Mary to Mrs Brydone, 6 August 1817.

26. In addition to George and Eliza's daughters, the first of their sons, George, was born in September 1813.

27. NLS MS 12951, ff.85–87, Mary to Mrs Brydone, 20 and 22 August 1817.

28. Benjamin Constant de Rebecque, a Swiss-born French politician and author, had published his psychological novel *Adolphe* in Geneva the previous year.

29. NLS MS 11892, ff.100–103, Mary to Mrs Brydone, 21 and 26 September 1817.
30. NLS MS 11892, ff.105–107, Mary to Mrs Brydone, 3 and 5 October 1817.
31. The name 'Foley' was not to be used again by George and Eliza till the birth of Lt.Horatio Foley Elliot in 1820. This son was to die aged 25.
32. NLS MS 11892, ff.30–35, Mary to Gilbert, 13, 20 and 29 November 1817.
33. NLS MS 11892, ff.41–42, Mary to Gilbert, 11 December 1817.
34. NLS MS 11892, ff.62–63, Mary to Gilbert, 8 January 1818.
35. NLS MS 11892, ff.64–65, Mary to Gilbert, 11 January 1818.
36. NLS MS 11892, ff.78–82, Mary to Gilbert, 2 and 5 February 1818.
37. NLS MS 11892, ff.94–95, Mary to Gilbert, 26 February 1818.
38. NLS MS 11892, ff.106–107, Mary to Gilbert, 19 March 1818.
39. NLS MS 11892, ff.108–111, Mary to Gilbert, 23 and 26 March 1818.
40. NLS MS 12951, ff.88–89, Gilbert to Mrs Brydone, 23 March 1818.
41. NLS MS 11892, f.127, Mary to Gilbert, 26 April 1818.
42. NLS MS 11892, ff.132–135, Mary to Gilbert, 11 and 13 May 1818.
43. NLS MS 11892 f.136, Mary to Gilbert, 25 May 1818.
44. NLS MS 11892 ff.140–141, Mary to Gilbert, 27 May 1818.
45. *Annual Biography and Obituary for the year 1820*, Vol.4, pp.85–112, printed for Longman et al of Paternoster Row by Strahan and Spottiswood, London.
46. BL Dictionary of National Biography 1886, Volume 7, pp.166–167.
47. NLS MS 11892, ff.144–145, Mary to Gilbert, 6 November 1818.
48. See *The Victorian Elliots in peace and war, Lord and Lady Minto, their family and household between 1816 and 1901* by the author, Chapters 2–4, 8 and 10.

# Sources and Bibliography

**Manuscripts**

**(BM) Blairadam Muniments**

BM Brydone Papers 4/300/6, Brydone to his mother, 14 February 1760.

BM Brydone Papers 4/300/15, Brydone to his mother, 9 August 1760.

BM Brydone Papers 4/302/12, Bryone to his mother, 2 May 1760.

BM Brydone Papers 4/302/12, Brydone to his mother, 7 and 12 June 1760.

BM Brydone Papers 4/435/1, Journal No.1, Belle-Isle, March to June 1761.

BM Brydone Papers 4/435/2, Journal No.2, Portugal, October to November 1762.

BM Brydone Papers 4/302/6, January 1763.

BM Brydone Papers 4/305/17 and 20, undated.

BM Brydone Papers 4/305/28, undated.

BM Brydone Papers 4/305/30, 25 July, and 4/305/17, 4 September 1766.

BM Brydone Papers 4/435/3, Journal No.3, Italy, April 1767.

BM Brydone Papers 4/435/3, Journal No.3, Ireland and return to Italy, May and August 1768.

BM Brydone Papers Journal No.8, Switzerland 1774.

BM Brydone Papers Journal No.9, Switzerland 1775.

BM Brydone Papers 4/437/4/1-44, Journal No.16, Lausanne to Munich and Vienna where they arrive in January 1775.

BM Brydone Papers 4/438/1/1-40, Journal No.17, Prague to Vienna, April 1776.

BM Brydone Papers 4/438/1/41-94, Journal No.18, Vienna to Berlin, April to June 1776.

BM Brydone Papers 4/438/1/99-144, Journal No.18, the tour to Warsaw in June and July 1776.

BM Brydone Papers 4/438/1/145-230, Journal No.18, the tour to St Petersburg from and to Riga in August and September 1776.

BM Brydone Papers 4/438/1/231-327, Journal No.18, the tour from Riga to Berlin, and onward to Calais in September–November 1776.

BM Brydone Papers, Journal No.10, 19 July to 16 August 1777.

BM Brydone Papers 4/301/17, Letter from Lord North to Brydone, 22 August 1777.

BM Brydone Papers 4.306/5, Letter from Brydone to Matthew, 18 April 1777.

BM Brydone Papers 4/302/2, Letter from Lord Guilford to Brydone, 1 December 1777.

BM Brydone Papers 4/301/9, Letter from Lord Guilford to Brydone, 23 March 1778.

BM Brydone Papers, Journal No.11, 20 June to 27 July 1778.

BM Brydone Papers 4/301/3, Letter from Lord Guilford to Brydone, 19 August 1778.

BM Brydone Papers 4/301/4, Letter from Lord Guilford to Brydone, 24 September 1778.

BM Brydone Papers 4/301/6, Letter from Lord Guilford to Brydone, 20 May 1779.

BM Brydone Papers 4/301/8, Letter from Lord Guilford to Brydone, 2 August 1779.

BM Brydone Papers 4/301/5, Letter from Lord Guilford to Brydone, 20 September 1779.

BM Brydone Papers 4/300/2, Letter from Francis, Prince of Anhalt to Brydone, 24 February 1780.

BM Brydone Papers 4/306/22, Letter from William Robertson to Brydone, 14 April 1785.

BM Brydone Papers 4/301/11, Letter from Brydone to Lord North, 5 February 1784.

BM Brydone Papers 4/301/14, Letter from Lord North to Brydone, 3 June 1784.

BM Brydone Papers 4/301/12, Letter from Lord North to Brydone, 29 December 1785.

BM Brydone Papers 4/300/19, Letter from William Robertson to Brydone, 4 November 1789.

BM Brydone Papers 4/300/24 Letter from Brydone to his wife, 23 May 1795.


**(BL) British Library**

Letter from Brydone to Sir John Pringle in November 1772, subsequently read to the Royal Society in February 1773 and published in Volume 63 of the society's 'Philosophical Transactions' in 1774.

Volume 49 of the *Monthly Review*, pp.22–33 from the July 1773 edition, and pp.115–121 from the August 1773 edition.

Dictionary of National Biography 1886, Volume 7, pp.166–167.


Add.35518, f.212–213 and f.23–25, Brydone letters to Sir Robert Murray Keith 1780.

Add.4439, ff.308–309 and 314–316, Account of a cure by electricity 1757.

Add.4440, ff.30–32, Brydone letter to R. Whytt 1758.

Add.61874 North Sheffield Park Papers ff.63–64, Letter from Brydone to Lord North, 12 July 1779.

Add.61874 North Sheffield Park Papers ff.65–69, Letter from Brydone to Lord North, 19 November 1779.

Add.61874 North Sheffield Park Papers ff.72–73, Letter from Frederick North to his father, Lord North, October 1782.

Add.61874 North Sheffield Park Papers ff.80–81, Letter from Brydone to Lord North, 2 June 1783.

Add. 61874 North Sheffield Park Papers ff.82–83, Letter from Brownlow North to Lord North, 19 November 1783.

Add. 61874 North Sheffield Park Papers ff.92–93, Letter from George North to Lord North, 21 December 1783.

Add.61874 North Sheffield Park Papers ff.84–85, Letter from Brydone to Lord North, 26 December 1783.

Add.61874 North Sheffield Park Papers ff.90–91, Accounts from Brydone to Lord North, (undated).

ADD.61874 North Sheffield Park Papers ff.92–93, Letter from George North to his father, 21 December 1785.

Add.61874 North Sheffield Park Papers ff.95–96, Letter from Brydone to Lord North, 16 January 1786

Chapman, R, publisher
*A Tour through Sicily and Malta* by P Brydone, London edition of 1817.
Duyckinck, Sr, Evert, New York publisher
*A Tour through Sicily and Malta* by P Brydone, New York edition of 1813.

## (HRO) Hampshire Record Office

Malmesbury Collection, Letter from William Morton Pitt to Sir James Harris, 20/31 May 1778.

Malmesbury Collection, Letter from William Morton Pitt to Sir James Harris, 11 June 1778.

## (NA) National Archives, Kew

T1/431/100, Brydone to Solicitor of Scotland, 30 October 1764.
AO 1/2199/231 General Account of Stamps 1790.
AO 1/2199/232 General Account of Stamps 1791.
AO 1/2202/244 General Account of Stamps 1802.
AO 1/2229/384/ General Account of Stamps 1780.
The *Royal Kalendar* for 1782 and 1784.

## (NLS) National Library of Scotland
## Reference Division

*Remarks on Mr Brydone's account of a remarkable thunder-storm in Scotland* by Earl Stanhope and read to the Royal Society in 1787.

*The Present State of Sicily and Malta extracted from Mr Brydone, Mt Swinburne and other modern travellers*, printed for G. Kearsley in 1788.

## Manuscript Collections

MS 3944/131, Letter from Brydone to William Robertson, 1 April 1793.
MS 11087-88, Letters from Brydone to Lord and Lady Minto between 1806 and 1813.

MS 11746, Letters from Anna Maria, wife of the firsl Earl Minto to Gilbert, 1815–1817.

MS 11892, ff.43–146, Mary Elliot to her parents, 1816–1818.

MS 11976, ff.3–4, Gilbert Elliot's Notebook.

MS 12009, ff.20–23, Mary Elliot's Journal 1815.

MS 12951, ff.1–77, 82–89, 195–6 and 214–5, Correspondence within the Brydone family, 1802 to 1818.


**(NRS) National Records of Scotland (National Archives of Scotland)**

NRS GD 157/2338/1, Letter from Brydone to Hugh Scott 24–26 January 1800.

NRS GD 112/39/318/4, Letter from Brydone to Mrs Campbell 1778.

NRS GD 112/74/2/7 and 8, Letters from John and Colin Campbell to their mother.

NRS WRH TD 77/142, Letter from William Robertson to Brydone, 29 September 1790.

NRS WRH TD 77/142, Letter from William Robertson to Brydone, 13 October 1792.

NRS WRH TD 77/142, Letter from William Robertson to Brydone, 10 April 1793.


**(YBL) Yale University Beinecke Rare Book and Manuscript Library**
Osborn Files


**Books and other Published Material**

Alexander, Boyd, *England's Wealthiest Son, a study of William Beckford*, Centaur Press Ltd, 1962.

*Annual Biography and Obituary for the year 1820 (The)*, Vol. IV (London, 1820)

Barrett, C. R. B., (Editor), *The 85th King's Light Infantry*, (Spottiswoode & Co. Ltd: London, 1913)

De Beer, Gavin, Annals of the Jean-Jacques Rousseau Society, *Rousseau et Les Anglais en* Suisse.

Brydone, Dr James Marr, OBE, *Mungo Park and the Brydones of Selkirk* (London, September 1963)

Campbell, Neil and R. Martin S. Smellie, *The Royal Society of Edinburgh (1783–1983), The First Two Hundred Years* (Edinburgh, 1883)

Cross, Anthony (editor), *St Petersburgh, 1703–1825* (Palgrave Macmillian, 2003)

Cundall, F., 'William Beckford', *Jamaica Worthies* (The Journal of the Institute of Jamaica, 1893)

Cundall, F., 'Historic Jamaica', *The Institute of Jamaica* (London, 1915)

Dagnall, H., *Creating a Good Impression – Three Hundred Years of the Stamp Office and Stamp Duties* (HMSO, 1994)

Dowell, Stephen, *A History and Explanation of the Stamp Duties and Stamp Laws* (Longmans, Green & Co.: London, 1873)

Elliot, Eleanor Elizabeth (ed.), *Life and Letter of Gilbert Elliot, First Earl of Monto from 1807 to 1814* (Longmans, Green & Co.: London, 1874)

Elliot, Eleanor Elizabeth, *A Memoir of the Right Honourable Hugh Elliot* (Edmondson & Douglas: Edinburgh, 1868)

Ellis, Annie Raine (ed.), *The Early Diary of Frances Burney 1768–1778*, two volumes (George Bell & Sons: London, 1907)

Fedosov, Dimitry, *The Caledonian Connection, Scotland-Russia Ties (Middle Ages to early Twentieth Century)* (Aberdeen University, 1996)

Fussell, Dr Paul, *Patrick Brydone – the Eighteenth-Century Traveller as Representative Man* (1963)

Guddey, Ernest, *L'Angleterre dans la vie intellectualle de la Suisse Romande au XVIIIe siècle* (Lausanne, 1974)

Hamilton, Sir William, *Observations on Mount Vesuvius, Mount Etna and other volcanos* (T. Cadell, 1772)

Harlan, Robert Dale, *William Strahan: Eighteenth Century London Printer and Publisher* (PhD Thesis, University of Michigan, 1960)

Herbert, Lord (ed.), *The Pembroke Papers (1734–80), Letters and Diaries of Henry, 10th Earl of Pembroke and his circle* (Jonathon Cape, 1939)

Hill, G. B. (ed.), *Boswell's Life of Johnson; together with Journal of a tour to the Hebrides and Johnson's Diary of a Journey into North Wales*, 6 vols (1934–50)

Horn, D. B., *A Short History of the University of Edinburgh (1556–1889)* (Edinburgh University Press, 1967)

Hume, David, *Letters of David Hume to William Strahan in G. Birkbeck Hill* (ed.) (Clarendon Press, 1888)

Ison, Walter, *The Georgian Buildings of Bath* (Faber & Faber, 1948)

Kearsley, George (ed.), *The Present State of Sicily and Malta, extracted from Mr Brydone, Mr Swinburne, and other modern travellers* (London, 1788)

King, James and Charles Ryskamp (eds), *The Letters and prose Writings of William Cowper*, vol. 1 (Clarendon Press: Oxford, 1979)

Kirby, Paul Franklin, *The Grand Tour in Italy (1700–1800)*, S. F. Vanni (Ragusa) (New York, 1952)

Lukowski, Jerzy, *Liberty's Folly, The Polish-Lithuanian Commonwealth in the eighteenth century 1697–1795* (Routledge)

Malmesbury, Third Earl (ed.), *Diaries and Correspondence of James Harris, First Earl of Malmesbury*, vol.1 (Richard Bentley: London, 1844)

Melville, Lewis, *The Life and Letters of William Beckford, of Fonthill* (William Heinemann: London, 1910)

Minchinton, W. E., *Bristol Presentments 1770–1917* (University of Exeter, 1986)

Pope, W. B. (ed), *The Diary of Benjamin Robert Haydon*, 5 vols.

Robinson, Howard, *The British Post Office: A History* (Princeton University Press, 1948)

Sheridan, Richard B., 'Planter and Historian; The Career of Richard Beckford of Jamaica and England, 1744–1799', *The Jamaican Historical Review*, 4 (1964), pp.36–58.

Spiker, Dr S. H., *Travels through England, Wales & Scotland in the year 1816*, two volumes, translated from the German (London, 1820)

Starke, Mrs Mariana, Information and Directions for Travellers on the Continent (A. & W. Galignani: Paris, 1824)

Stebbing, Chantal, *The Victorian Taxpayer and the Law – a study in Constitutional Conflict* (Cambridge University Press, 2009)

Szatkowski, Sheila, *Captial Caricatures, a selection of etchings by John Kay* (Birlinn, 2007)

Thomas, Peter D. G., *Lord North* (Allen Lane)

Valentine, Alan, *Lord North* (Univeristy of Oklahoma Press, 1967)

Whiteley, Peter, *Lord North – The Prime Minister who lost America* (The Hambledon Press: London, 1996)

Zamoyski, Adam, *The Last King of Poland* (Jonathon Cape: London, 1992)

# Index

Gregory, Dr James (1753–1821), physician, married Isabella Macleod (*c.* 1772–1847) 258

Greig, Samuel (1735–1788), naval officer 163

Grenville, William Wyndham, Baron (1759–1834), politician 261, 264, 265

Grétry, André (1741–1813), Belgian composer 136

Griffiths, Ralph (*c.* 1720–1803), journal editor and bookseller 125, 126, 127

Grimston, James Bucknall (d. 1808), Baron Verulam, friend of Brydone 237, 348

Grosvenor, Richard (1767–1845), second earl Grosvenor, politician and developr 230, 347

Grosvenor Square, No. 41, the home of Lord North 234, 235, 248

Grua, Carlo (1700–1773), composer 202

Grubenmann Hans Ulrich (1709–1783), Swiss engineer 191, 344

Gunning, Sir Robert (1731–1816), diplomat 173, 342

Guthrie, Dr Matthew (1743–1807), physician and natural philosopher 167, 342

Guilford, *see* North

Hadley, John (1731–1764), chemist 29

Haliburton, David, a county freeholder 290

Hamilton, Edward of Clifton 253, 352

Hamilton, Sir William (1731–1803), diplomat and antiquarian 70, 71, 74, 96, 245, 309, 332, 333

Harris, Sir James (1746–1820), diplomat 149, 150, 173, 339, 340

Harrison, George, later Sir, (1767–1841), civil servant 274, 279

Hastings, Francis Rawdon (1754–1826), second earl of Moira, Army officer and politician 293, 294, 295, 359

Hauksbee, Francis (1660–1713), scientist 30, 31, 328

Hawick 23, 241, 251, 254, 257, 260, 278, 322

Haydn, Joseph (1732–1809), composer 211

Heidegger, Hans Konrad, bürgermeister of Zürich 189

Henderson, John and Richard, fishermen 287

Hepburne, Robert, head collector at the Edinburgh Stamp Office 279

Herbert, George Augustus (1759–1827), eleventh earl of Pembroke 165

Herbert, Henry (1734–1794), tenth earl of Pembroke 134, 165, 198, 233, 321, 338

Hillsborough, Trevor Hill (1693–1742), first Viscount Hillsborough 67

Hirzel, Dr Hans Caspar (1725–1803), Swiss physician and writer 189

Hislop, (Nina) Emma Eleanor Elizabeth (d. 1882), wife of William Elliot 132, 141, 296, 297, 298, 299, 325, 326, 337, 338

Hobart, Miss Maria (d. 1794), daughter of George Hobart MP 232

Hodgson, Major-General Studholm (1708–1798), later Field Marshall 41, 48